HUMAN RIGHTS ACT 1998
A PRACTICAL GUIDE

HUMAN RIGHTS ACT 1998
A PRACTICAL GUIDE

General Editor

Rambert de Mello, MA, BCL

Contributors

Yinka Adedeji, MA(Hons), LLB
Shereener Brown, LLB(Hons)Lond
Helen Clarke, BA(Hons)(Oxon), Diplaw
Alev Giz, LLB(Hons)
Satvinder Juss, BA, PhD(Cantab)
Brendan Halligan, BA(Hons), LLB
Shahram Taghavi, LLB(Hons)
Lorna Tagliavini, BA(Hons), LLM, Diplaw

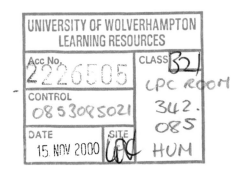

JORDANS
2000

Published by
Jordan Publishing Limited
21 St Thomas Street
Bristol BS1 6JS

British Library Cataloguing-in-Publication Data
A catalogue record for this book is available from the British Library.

ISBN 0 85308 502 1

Typeset by Mendip Communications Ltd, Frome, Somerset
Printed by MPG Books Ltd, Bodmin, Cornwall

PREFACE

The 2nd of October 2000 marks a major step in the progress of English jurisprudence. From that date, the Human Rights Act 1998 incorporates into English law significant provisions of the European Convention on Human Rights. The implications of this step will depend partly upon the readiness of practitioners to recognise and pursue infringements of a party's rights under the Convention.

Many lawyers in the United Kingdom are already familiar with the concepts, jurisprudence and practices, under the Convention, but the majority are not. This book has been written for those who require both an introduction to the Convention and an explanation of the effects that its introduction is likely to have on the various aspects of legal practice. Given the prospective nature of the legislation, no work can seek to be comprehensive in its scope or detail, nor can it be truly certain in its forecast of the application of such legislation. That is so in this case, indeed especially so, because few statutes have sought to achieve such a pervasive influence on the conduct of citizenship. However, it is hoped that this book will provide helpful guidance both to the Act and Convention, and to its impact on discrete areas of law.

This book has been a collaborative effort of contributors all practising from 6 King's Bench Walk. I am grateful to them for all their help.

RAMBERT DE MELLO
August 2000

STRUCTURE OF THE BOOK

This book has been structured to enable the reader not only to understand the Human Rights Act itself but also its impact on different areas of legal practice. Its organisation should ensure that it is possible to access information from a variety of starting points.

Part 1 provides an introduction to the Act itself and to the principles and procedures which underpin it. In Part 2, each of the Articles of the Convention is analysed in turn. Part 3 examines in alphabetical order those fields of practice which are most likely to be affected by the Act. Part 4 comprises a case study demonstrating how a human rights challenge might arise in the context of an employment dispute. The Act, fully annotated, is reproduced in Part 5. Part 6 sets out other useful source materials including the full text of the Convention.

The book has been comprehensively indexed so that a reader can, for example, refer to the wording of the Act itself and to the commentary on an individual Article of the Convention or its impact upon a specific area of law.

CONTENTS

TABLE OF CASES

References are to paragraph numbers. *Italic* references are to Appendix page numbers.

TABLE OF STATUTES

References are to paragraph numbers. *Italic* references are to Appendix page numbers.

TABLE OF STATUTORY INSTRUMENTS

References are to paragraph numbers. *Italic* **references are to Appendix page numbers.**

TABLE OF INTERNATIONAL LEGISLATION

References are to paragraph numbers. *Italic* references are to Appendix page numbers.

TABLE OF ABBREVIATIONS

ABWOR	Advice By Way of Representation
the 1998 Act or the Act	Human Rights Act 1998
the Commission	European Commission of Human Rights
the Committee or the Committee of Ministers	Committee of Ministers of the Council of Europe
the Convention	Convention for the Protection of Human Rights and Fundamental Freedoms
CPIA 1996	Criminal Procedure and Investigations Act 1996
DLP	discretionary life prisoners
DPP	Director of Public Prosecutions
EAT	Employment Appeal Tribunal
EC	European Community
ECJ	European Court of Justice
EC Treaty or EEC Treaty	Treaty of Rome 1957
ERA 1996	Employment Rights Act 1996
EU	European Union
the European Court	European Court of Human Rights
HCP	High Contracting Party
ICA 1985	Interception of Communications Act 1985
ILO	International Labour Organisation
LGA 1988	Local Government Act 1988
MHRT	Mental Health Review Tribunal
PACE 1984	Police and Criminal Evidence Act 1984
PVS	permanent vegetative state
RPA 1983	Representation of the People Act 1983
SSATs	Social Security Appeal Tribunals
TEU	Treaty on European Union 1992 (the Maastricht Treaty)

PART 1

INTRODUCTION

INTRODUCTION TO THE HUMAN RIGHTS ACT 1998

BACKGROUND

Judicial control of abuses of an individual's human rights

1.1 The rule of law implies that an interference by the executive authorities with an individual's rights should be subject to an effective control which should normally be assured by the judiciary, at least in the last resort, judicial control offering the best guarantees of independence, impartiality and a proper procedure.[1]

The basic principle which is fundamental to human rights and which underlies the various specific rights spelled out in the Convention for the Protection of Human Rights and Fundamental Freedoms (the Convention) is respect for human dignity and human freedom. Human dignity and human freedom imply that a person should be free to shape himself and his fate in the way that he or she deems best fits his or her personality.[2,3]

The Human Rights Act 1998 (the Act) seeks to give further effect to rights and freedoms guaranteed under the Convention; to make provision with respect to holders of certain judicial offices who become judges of the Convention; and for connected purposes.[4]

Subsidiarity

1.2 One of the foremost principles of the Convention is the principle of subsidiarity which is that the European Court of Human Rights (the European Court) will not normally entertain a complaint against a State for alleged violations of human rights abuses unless the alleged victim has first brought a complaint before a domestic court. If such a complaint with reference to the Act has not been brought before a UK court then it is highly unlikely that the European Court or the European Commission of Human Rights (the Commission) will entertain a complaint from the victim. It is, however, sufficient for the victim to lay the substance of the complaint on the basis of the national legislation corresponding to the Convention (without invoking the Human Rights Act 1998 directly) before the domestic courts in order to be able to apply to the Commission with reference to Article 26 of the Convention. Article 26 provides that applicants must exhaust domestic remedies before they go to the European Court with their claim under the Convention. Thus, as long as the substance of the matter is raised before the competent domestic courts, a victim can thereafter pursue his complaint before the European Court.[5] If

---

1   *Klass and Others v FRG* (1978) Series A No 28, EHRR 214 at 355 (abuse against telephone tapping).
2   *Cossey v UK* (1990) Series A No 184, 13 EHRR 622 at 648.
3   Hereon, for brevity, the male pronoun shall include the female.
4   Preamble to the Convention.
5   *Austria v Italy* Application No 788/61, (1961) 4 YB 117.

there is no possibility of relying on other domestic legislation to show that there is a breach of some Convention right, a victim may rely on s 7 of the Act to bring a case on a Convention ground alone.

Human rights issues in the national court

1.3 Although it has been omitted from the Act, Article 13 provides that everyone whose Convention rights have been violated shall have an effective remedy before a national court. It is the view of the authors that Article 13 may still be relied upon by an individual in certain circumstances notwithstanding its absence from the Act.

The Lord Chancellor has stated though that the courts may not act as legislators and grant new remedies for infringement of Convention rights unless the common law itself enables them to develop new rights or remedies. The court is not obliged to remedy the failure by legislating via the common law either where a Convention right is infringed by incompatible legislation or because of the absence of legislation.[1]

Article 13 has been interpreted in the following way by the European Court:

(1) where an individual has an arguable claim to be the victim of a violation of the rights in the Convention, that individual should have a remedy before a national authority in order both to have his claim decided and, if appropriate, to obtain redress;[2]

(2) the authority referred to in Article 13 may not necessarily be a judicial authority but, if it is not, its powers and the guarantees which it affords are relevant in determining whether the remedy before it is effective;[3]

(3) although no simple remedy may itself entirely satisfy the requirements of Article 13, the aggregate of remedies provided for under domestic law may do so;[4]

(4) neither Article 13 nor the Convention in general lays down any given manner for the Contracting States to ensure[5] that within their own jurisdiction the provisions of the Convention have been implemented effectively, for example, by incorporating the Convention into domestic law;

(5) the application of Article 13 in a given case will depend upon the manner in which the State concerned has chosen to discharge its obligations under Article 1 directly to secure to anyone within its jurisdiction the rights and freedoms set out in Article 1;[6]

(6) judicial review, which assesses the procedural propriety and reasonableness of decisions but does not retry the merits, provides an effective degree of control over the decisions of administrative authorities in asylum cases (but see below the effect of *Chahal*).[7] However, recently the European

---

1   583 HL 783–785 (24 November 1997).
2   *Silver v UK* Series A No 61, (1983) 5 EHRR 347, para 113.
3   *Klass and Others v FRG* (1978) Series A No 28, 2 EHRR 214, para 64.
4   Ibid, para 67.
5   *Swedish Engine Drivers' Union v Sweden* (1976) Series A No 20, 1 EHRR 617, para 50.
6   *Ireland v UK* (1978) Series A No 25, 2 EHRR 25, para 239.
7   *Vilvarajah and Ors v UK* (1991) Series A No 215, 14 EHRR 248, paras 123, 125–126.

Court has stated that the threshhold at which the domestic courts could find the policy of the Ministry of Defence irrational had been placed so high that it effectively excluded any consideration by the domestic courts of the question whether the interference with the applicants' private lives had answered a pressing social need or was proportionate to the national security and public order aims pursued by the Government, principles which lay at the heart of the European Court's analysis under Article 8. The European Court concluded in that case that the applicants did not have an effective remedy in relation to the violation of their right to respect for their private lives;[1]

(7) in a Community law context where an authority is required to make complex assessments, it enjoys a wide measure of discretion, the exercise of which is subject to a limited judicial review and the judicature may not substitute its assessment of the facts for the assessment made by the authority concerned. Thus, in such cases, the Community judicature must restrict itself to examining the accuracy of findings of fact and law and to veryifying that the action taken by that authority is not vitiated by a manisfest error or a misuse of powers and that it did not clearly exceed the bounds of its discretion.[2]

The Government's White Paper on the Act states that Convention points will normally be taken in the context of proceedings instituted against individuals or already open to them. However, if none is available, it will be possible for people to bring cases on Convention grounds alone. In such instances, a victim must bring proceedings under s 7 of the Act (if there are no other proceedings in play such as criminal or judicial review proceedings or where an administrative decision is being enforced through legal proceedings) before he or she can bring a complaint to the European Court. The European Court has stated that, in certain circumstances, it may, none the less, happen that express reliance on the Convention before the national authorities constitutes the sole appropriate manner of raising before those authorities first, as is required by Article 26, an issue intended to be brought subsequently before the European review bodies if need be.[3] Even if the UK courts determine under the Act that a person's rights have not been breached under the Convention, it does not prevent a person from bringing a complaint before the European Court under Article 25 as long as he can show that his fundamental rights are still being breached.[4] It is also clear that a breach of Article 13 of the Convention (which is omitted from the Act) can be subject of a complaint to the European Court under Article 25. The European Court observed in *Chahal*:[5]

'... that Article 13 guarantees the availability at national level of a remedy to enforce the substance of the Convention rights and freedoms in whatever form they happen to be secured in the domestic legal order. The effect of this article is thus to require the provision of a domestic remedy allowing the competent

---

1   *Lustig-Prean and Becket v UK* Application No 314117/96 (1999) *The Times*, 11 October.
2   *Upjohn Ltd v Licensing Authority* [1999] 1 WLR 927 at 937, para 50 and 945, para 34.
3   *Van Oosterwijk* 3 EHRR 557, para 53.
4   *Eckle v FRG* (1982) Series A No 51, 5 EHRR 1.
5   *Chahal v UK* (1996) RJD-V 1831, (1996) 23 EHRR 413.

national authority both to deal with the substance of the relevant convention complaint and to grant appropriate relief.'

The Act has a clear purpose. It is to enable Convention rights to be asserted directly in domestic courts. This view has been repeatedly expressed by the Government. Thus, whilst Article 13 has been omitted from the Act, it is the Government's view that the Act provides sufficient remedial powers at national level to those who have been victims of an unlawful act. Section 8 of the Act (the remedial powers of the UK courts to grant such relief or remedy or make such order, within its jurisdiction as it considers just and appropriate) bears the widest amplitude.[1] Furthermore, s 2 clearly suggests that the court is required to take into account the jurisprudence of the European Court. The jurisprudence provides a variety of remedies including compensation and costs for alleged violations of the Convention rights. This is therefore one route by which Article 13 may be relied upon.

Binding precedent under the Convention

The Convention is a living instrument

1.4   Constitutions are living and developing institutions. They are different from treaties. The Human Rights Act 1998 brings into force the Convention which is to be viewed as a constitution.

One of the main principles of the Convention is that it is a 'living instrument'. In *Cossey v UK*,[2] the European Court stated that it is not bound by its previous judgments; indeed, this is borne out by r 51(1) of the Rules of the Supreme Court. However, it usually follows and applies its own precedents, such a course being in the interests of legal certainty and the orderly development of the Convention case-law. Nevertheless, this would not prevent the European Court from departing from an earlier decision if it was persuaded that there were cogent reasons for doing so. Such a departure might, for example, be warranted in order to ensure that the interpretation of the Convention reflects societal changes and remains in line with present-day conditions.[3] The European Court also stated that since the Convention always has to be interpreted and applied in the light of current circumstances, it is important that the need for appropriate legal measures in this area (ie transsexuals and their rights) should be kept under review. Section 2 of the Act provides that a domestic court or tribunal determining a question which has arisen under this Act in connection with a Convention right must[4] take into account:

(a)   any judgment, decision, declaration or advisory opinion of the European Court;
(b)   any opinion of the Commission given in a report adopted under Article 31 of the Convention;

---

1   See Human Rights Bill Hansard HL Deb col 1261 (19 January 1998).
2   (1990) Series A No 184, 13 EHRR 622, para 35.
3   See also *Inze v Austria* (1987) Series A No 126, 10 EHRR 394.
4   The court or tribunal, it seems, must take into account judgments etc of the European Court without being invited to do so. It has no discretion to ignore such judgments. The Government's White Paper states that these decisions or judgments will not be binding.

(c) any decision of the Commission in connection with Articles 26 or 27(2) of the Convention;

(d) any decisions of the Committee of Ministers taken under Article 46[1] of the Convention.

Section 2, it seems, does not suggest that European Court cases (not involving the UK) are binding on UK courts. The doctrine of *stare decisis* has no application in this context. The courts must have regard to the judgments of the European Court particularly where they involve the UK, because a judgment given by the European Court is binding on the State concerned, although other States will no doubt consider the judgments for guidance in determining whether their own domestic laws are compatible with the Convention.[2] It would be surprising to suggest that UK courts should be bound by the European Court judgments when the European Court is not bound by its own judgments.

The European Court does not consider errors of law made by national courts nor does it substitute its own assessment of facts for that of national courts.[3] There may be cases in UK courts which mirror the facts of a case in the European Court; if so, there might be a good reason to apply the European Court's judgment to the domestic adjudication process, but this will be a rare occurrence. There might also be good reason why UK domestic courts should follow European Court decisions or judgments, but again, where there is a European Court judgment involving the UK court in a similar context, this would be a rare occurrence. A court might be persuaded *not* to follow a particular European Court judgment on the grounds that the margin of appreciation vests in the UK courts in determining the particular issue before it. There might be specific features of the case or issues which cannot be decided without taking into consideration special situations arising in the domestic context. In *Cossey*, Judge Martens (in the dissenting judgment) recognised that the European Court leaves a certain margin of appreciation to the domestic courts of the Member States and that it would find a violation of Convention rights only if it cannot reasonably be doubted that the acts or omissions of the State in question are incompatible with its obligations under the Convention.[4] Therefore, it is the domestic court which must give full effect to the terms and spirit of the Convention in the first instance and this accords with Article 26 of the Convention which exempts States from answering before an international body for their acts before they have had an opportunity to put matters right through their own legal system. But Judge Martens, in a lecture organised by the Judicial Studies Board, took the view that domestic courts

---

1   Article 46 provides that any of the High Contracting Parties (HCPs) may at any time declare that it recognises as compulsory ipso facto and without special agreement the jurisdiction of the European Court in all matters concerning the interpretation and application of the present Convention. The declarations may be made unconditionally or on conditions of reciprocity.

2   *Brogan and Others v UK* (1988) Series A No 145-B, 11 EHRR 117. The Netherlands introduced criminal legislation concerning the time which may elapse between a person's arrest and his production before a court.

3   *Edwards v UK* (1992) Series A No 247-B, 15 EHRR 417, para 34.

4   (1990) Series A No 184, 13 EHRR 622 at 652.

must bear in mind that, in the interests of the uniform application of the Convention, the European Court has given an autonomous interpretation to many of its terms and has consistently held that it must be interpreted and applied in such a way that the safeguards it provides are practicable and effective. In a recent case, the Court of Appeal has expressed the view that domestic courts will give great weight to the judgments, in particular recent judgments, made by the European Court in cases where the facts are similar to the case before the domestic court.[1]

The Lord Chancellor has stated that s 2 gets it right in requiring domestic courts to take into account judgments of the European Court but not making them binding. The Act would permit UK courts to depart from existing European Court decisions and, upon occasion, it might well be appropriate to do so. It is possible for UK courts to depart from European Court decisions where there has been no precise ruling on the matter and a Commission opinion which does so has not taken into account subsequent European Court case-law. Where the decision is relevant, the UK courts would be expected to apply the Convention jurisprudence and its principles.[2]

Equally, a UK court should be prepared to depart from its earlier decision concerning claims based on Convention rights since the Convention is a 'living instrument'. Equally so, it must be recognised that the common law is a living system of law, reacting to new events and new ideas, and so capable of providing the citizens of this country with a system of practical justice relevant to the times in which they live. One must be prepared to look at judicial decisions with open eyes and reinterpret it in the light of the way in which all judges, common law and equity, actually decide cases today.[3] It remains to be seen whether the principle of *stare decisis* should have any or limited application in Convention cases before UK courts. For example, the European Court in the case of *B v France*[4] (concerning the rights of transsexuals under Article 8 of the Convention) held that there was a violation of the applicant's right to family life under Article 8 and was persuaded to reach an opposite conclusion to those in the *Rees* and *Cossey* judgments.[5] The European Court stated that it considers that it is undeniable that attitudes towards transsexuals have changed, science has progressed and increasing importance is attached to the problems of transsexuals. In short, things are in a state of flux, legally, morally and socially. There is therefore much to be said for the proposition that, if the European Court is prepared to interpret the Convention as a living instrument, and UK courts are not bound by the decisions or judgments of the European Court, then UK courts should be prepared to adopt the same flexible approach. Therefore, a UK court should also view the Convention as a living instrument and be

---

1   *Camelot Group Plc v Centaur Communications Ltd* [1998] 2 WLR 379 at 389E.
2   583 HL 514 at 515 (18 November 1997).
3   *Kleinwort Benson Ltd v Lincoln* [1998] 3 WLR 1095 at 1118–1119. And also see *Luistig-Prean and Becket v UK* Application No 314117/96 (1999) *The Times*, 11 October: the Court considered that it could not ignore widespread and consistently developing views or the legal changes in the domestic laws of contracting States in favour of the admission of homosexuals into the armed forces of those States.
4   (1992) Series A No 232-C, 16 EHRR 1.
5   Ibid, para 48.

prepared, when the occasion demands, to depart from its own earlier judgments (including that of a higher court) when for example, 'science has progressed and increasing importance is attached' to particular issues raised before it. Such an approach will not create legal uncertainty as may be feared, but is consistent with the view that 'the Convention remains a living instrument to be interpreted so as to reflect societal changes and to remain in line with present-day conditions'.[1] It remains to be seen whether a (lower) court will, when cogent reasons exist, be prepared to interpret the Convention differently from an earlier judgment of a (higher) court in the context of Convention rights where there are scientific or societal developments since the earlier judgment was given.[2]

Taking into account other international instruments in a human rights context
1.5   The European Court has stated that in its view the principles underlying the Convention cannot be interpreted and applied in a vacuum. Mindful of the Convention's special character as a human rights treaty, it must also take into account any relevant rules of international law when deciding on disputes concerning its jurisdiction pursuant to Article 49 of the Convention.[3] This is a further reason why it may be suggested that the Convention is to be construed flexibly with regard, where relevant, to different international treaties thereby viewing the Convention as a living instrument.

Furthermore, the European Court has on many occasions taken into account other international Conventions when implementing the Convention and accordingly the UK courts must, when implementing Convention rights, be equally aware of other relevant international Conventions, although these may not be incorporated into domestic law.[4]

The Convention must be interpreted in the light of the rules of interpretation set out in the Vienna Convention on the Law of Treaties 1969. Article 31(3)(c) of the Vienna Convention indicates that account is to be taken of any relevant rules of international law applicable in the relations between the parties. The principles underlying the Convention cannot be interpreted and applied in a vacuum and the relevant rules of international law are to be taken into account when determining disputes.[5]

It is generally accepted that incorporated human rights treaties and the protocols to which the UK is a party are not capable of conferring any rights on individuals which the courts were obliged or at liberty to enforce at the suit of

1   See dissenting judgment of Judge Martens in *Cossey v UK* (1990) Series A No 184, 13 EHRR 622 at 652, para 3.6.31.
2   See *Cossey v UK* (1990) Series A No 184, 13 EHRR 622 at 660 where Judge Martens stated that on societal development grounds there was reason to depart from an earlier judgment on a similar issue concerning transsexuals.
3   *Loizidou v Turkey* (1995) Series A No 310, 23 EHRR 513. The Court, for example, considered the Vienna Convention in reaching a decision under the Convention.
4   For example, see *Jersild v Denmark* (1994) 19 EHRR 1 at 32 where the European Court (dissenting Opinion of Judge Golcuklu) took into account the Convention on the Elimination of all Forms of Racial Discrimination.
5   *Loizidou v Turkey* (1996) 23 EHRR 513 at para 43.

the individuals. International conventions do not alter domestic law except to the extent that they are incorporated into domestic law by legislation. Whilst provisions of an unincorporated treaty may give procedural protection, it does not and cannot by itself give substantive protection.[1]

Domestic courts should, however, be prepared to take into account other international instruments, particularly those which concern human rights. For example, the UN Convention on the Rights of the Child 1989, the Universal Declaration of Human Rights and the International Covenant on Civil and Political Rights are some of the few international instruments considered by the European Court on occasions. The domestic courts should be willing to apply and must have regard to these and other relevant human right instruments in the following circumstances:

(1)   where the parallel Convention rights are found in other international instruments;

(2)   where the European Court has taken them into account and it is relevant to the issues;

(3)   where the ECJ has taken them into account and it is relevant to the issues;[2]

(4)   to interpret ambiguous primary or secondary legislation;[3]

(5)   to inform the common law;

(6)   to govern the exercise of judicial discretion;

(7)   to act consistently with other civilised nations which subscribe to such international human rights instruments;

(8)   where the subject-matter under examination is dealt with in an international instrument. For example, the House of Lords has recently held in the *Pinochet (No 3)* case that the systematic use of torture was an international crime for which there could be no immunity under the International Convention against Torture and other Cruel, Inhuman or Degrading Treatment or Punishment 1984 and there has been a universal jurisdiction in all the Convention State parties to either extradite or punish a public official who committed torture. Lord Millet went so far as to state that customary international law is part of the common law and that English courts would have regard to it;[4]

(9)   where there is no prohibition in the domestic legislation to applying the rules of international law;[5]

---

1   *Thomas v Baptiste* [1999] 3 WLR 249 at 260H and 262H and the dissenting judgment of Lord Goff at 268G.

2   For example, Article 26 ICCPP has been relied upon by the ECJ: *Arantzamendi v Procureur de la Republique* Cases 13–28/82, [1982] ECR 3927.

3   There is a presumption, albeit rebuttable, that our municipal law will be consistent with our international obligations: *Post Office v Estrury Radio Let* [1968] 2 QB 740 per Lord Diplock LJ at 757.

4   *R v Bow Street Magistrates, ex parte Pinochet Ugarte (No 3)* [1999] 2 WLR 827 at 912B. For example, when racial discrimination allegations are examined under the Race Relations Act 1976, regard should be taken of the International Convention on the Elimination of all Forms of Racial Discrimination 1966.

5   See Ian Brownlie *Principles of International Law* 6th edn (1998) ch 2: The Relation of Municipal and International Law (p 41: English courts take judicial notice of international law: once a court has ascertained that there are no bars within the internal system of law to applying the rules of international law or provisions of a treaty; and p 49: English courts have regularly taken into account treaty-based standards concerning human rights in order

(10) where the UK is a signatory to the instrument.

The Act should apply extra-territorially

1.6   Although Article 1 sets limits on the reach of the Convention, the concept of 'jurisdiction' under this provision is not restricted to the national territory of the High Contracting Parties (HCPs). For example, a right under the Convention might be engaged in cases involving the extradition and deportation of aliens from the territory of the Member States.[1] In addition, the responsibility of HCPs can be involved because of acts of their authorities, whether performed within or outside national boundaries, which produce effects outside their own territory, whether performed directly through its armed forces or through subordinate local administration.[2]

The Convention should apply vertically and horizontally

1.7   An important question is whether the Convention rights apply between private individuals (horizontally).[3] UK courts should be willing and prepared to apply the Convention 'horizontally' because the Convention is capable of being applied between individuals. The UK courts have a duty to use European Court case-law[4] and to act compatibly with the Convention, not only in cases involving other public authorities, but also in developing the common law in deciding cases between individuals. There is an obligation on the State to afford protection to individuals against breaches of their fundamental rights under the Convention by other individuals even though the State is not directly involved.

This view is proposed for a variety of reasons.

(1)   A court is a public authority as defined in s 6(3) of the Act. Failure by the courts to provide effective protection under the Convention would not only be contrary to the Convention, but also unlawful under s 6(1) of the Act.

(2)   There is no good reason why the Convention should not be applied where fundamental human rights are involved. The European Court has stated that, although the object of Article 8 is essentially that of protecting the individual against arbitrary interference by the public authorities, it does not merely compel the State to abstain from such interference: in addition to this primarily negative undertaking, there may be positive obligations inherent in an effective respect for private or family life. These obligations may involve the adoption of measures designed to secure respect for

---

to resolve issues of common law, including the legality of telephone tapping and freedom of association).

1   For example, a deportee may claim that by sending him back to his country where he faces death or torture may violate Articles 2 or 3.

2   *Loizidou v Turkey* (1995) Series A No 310, 20 EHRR 99, para 62.

3   The Lord Chancellor has said that the Government has not provided for the Convention rights to be directly justiciable in actions between private individuals. The aim of the Act was to protect the human rights of individuals against the abuse of power by the State, broadly defined, rather than to protect them against each other: 3 November 1997, col 1231.

4   Section 2 of the Act.

private life even in the sphere of the relations of individuals between themselves. There are different ways of ensuring 'respect for private life', and the nature of the State's obligation (eg the domestic court's obligation) will depend on the particular aspect of private life that is at issue.[1] Thus, in cases where the rights of freedom of assembly and association are engaged under Article 11, positive measures might be required to be taken even in the sphere of relations between individuals.[2] Therefore, a demonstration may annoy or give offence to persons opposed to the ideas or claims that it is seeking to promote, but the demonstrators must be able to hold the demonstration without fear that they will be subjected to physical violence by their opponents. In other cases, individuals may seek to enforce their Convention rights against other individuals in a domestic court on the grounds that the law fails to protect them from having their fundamental rights violated. In this kind of situation, an individual may complain that the court or tribunal being a public authority should act compatibly with the Convention and not to do so would be unlawful under the Act.[3]

(3) The court is required to take into account European jurisprudence in arriving at its decision. This section does not state that its application is limited to public bodies only.

(4) There is no good reason why an individual cannot rely on the Convention rights if there has been a violation of the Convention by a public body or a private individual in like circumstances. Thus, a complainant may claim that a neighbouring public body residing next to his home has created a nuisance thereby affecting his rights under Article 8 of the Convention and Article 1 of the First Protocol. It seems absurd to exclude reliance on these Convention rights by the same complainant where the same or similar breach is committed by a neighbouring private individual. It is thought that a complainant may rely on Article 13 combined with the provisions of s 6 of the Act (the court being a public body has to apply the Convention in determining the issues of the case before it).[4]

The Lord Chancellor, in the debate of the Bill, has stated that it is right as a matter of principle for the courts to have the duty of acting compatibly with the Convention not only in cases involving other public authorities but also in developing the common law in deciding cases between individuals. In preparing the Bill, the Government preferred not to exclude the application of Convention principles altogether from cases between individuals which would have to be justified. They did not think it would be justifiable; nor did they think it would be practicable. A good example as to how the Convention rights may be used horizontally in a case is where, for example, an employer dismisses an

---

1   *X and Y v The Netherlands* (1985) Series A No 91, 8 EHRR 235, paras 23–24; also see *Airey v Ireland* (1979) Series A No 32, 2 EHRR 305, para 32.

2   *Platform 'Arzte für das Leben' v Austria* (1988) Series A No 139, 13 EHRR 204, para 32.

3   Under s 6 of the Act, it is unlawful for a public authority to act in a way which is incompatible with one or more of the Convention rights.

4   The Lord Chancellor is recorded as saying that the right to privacy is a basic human right. That right can be infringed by a neighbour, an intrusive commercial agency, private investigators, the police and all manner of other people. The individual needs protection against these bodies: HL 24 November 1997, col 786.

employee for breach of confidence and loyalty. UK domestic law fails singularly to protect 'whistle-blowing'. An employee who is also dismissed for whistle-blowing may find that he is without much protection, particularly under the Employment Rights Act 1996. If the employer were to claim that the decision to dismiss the employee for disclosing such confidential information amounts to misconduct and that dismissal falls within the range of reasonable responses, then the employee will face an uphill struggle to make out that the dismissal was indeed unfair.[1]

The employee may well argue before an employment tribunal that the dismissal must be judged with reference to Article 10 of the Convention. The European Court cases indicate that Article 10 applies to public sector employees. But there is no reason why, given the Lord Chancellor's view referred to above, a private sector employee may not advance an argument based on Article 10 and place some reliance on the European Court's jurisprudence in stating that the sanctions imposed on him (including actions short of dismissal) violate his right under Article 10 (free speech). An employee will have to argue, for example, that the dismissal did not pursue a legitimate aim and further was not 'necessary' in a democratic society. A tribunal faced with such an argument would have to consider the European Court's jurisprudence on this topic and determine the matter against the backdrop of Article 10(2).[2] The tribunal will have to determine whether the dismissal of an employee for such a reason was fair or severe with regard to Article 10. It is arguable that the tribunal task in determining unfair dismissal claims involving an alleged breach of the Convention rights will have to undertake the *primary task* of investigating whether a dismissal is fair or not, and **not** simply whether the dismissal was within the range or band of reasonable responses. How far a tribunal will be prepared to do so will be decided in the future once the Act is in force. The traditional test of whether the employer believed, and had reasonable grounds for believing (after adequate investigation) that the employee was guilty of the misconduct[3] may be inappropriate in cases where the employee says that he was dismissed effectively in breach of a Convention reason. One waits with anticipation to see how the case-law will develop in this field.

A SUMMARY OF THE ACT

1.8 Section 1 of the Act specifies those Articles of the Convention and of the First Protocol to the Convention which are given effect. These Articles are set out in Sch 1 to the Act. Section 2 provides that a court or tribunal determining a question in connection with a Convention right must take account of relevant judgments, decisions, declarations, and opinions made or given by the

---

1   *British Steel v Granada Television* [1981] AC 1097; *Iceland Frozen Foods v Jones* [1983] ICR 17.
2   In *Vogt v Germany* (1995) Series A No 323, 21 EHRR 205, the Court found that there was a breach of Article 10 in the case where a teacher was dismissed for being a member of an extremist political party.
3   *British Home Stores Ltd v Burchell* [1978] ECR 303.

European Commission (the Commission) and the European Court and the Committee of Ministers of the Council of Europe.

The Act states that certain Convention rights will apply which guarantee a number of basic human rights. These Convention rights are as follows:

–   the right to life (Article 2);
–   prohibition of torture or inhuman or degrading treatment or punishment (Article 3);[1]
–   prohibition of slavery and forced labour (Article 4);[2]
–   right to liberty and security of person (Article 5);
–   right to a fair trial (Article 6);
–   prohibition of retrospective criminal laws (Article 7);
–   right to respect for private and family life, home and correspondence (Article 8);
–   freedom of thought, conscience, and religion (Article 9);
–   freedom of expression (Article 10);
–   freedom of peaceful assembly, and freedom of association, including the right to join a trade union (Article 11);
–   the right to marry and found a family (Article 12); and
–   prohibition of discrimination of these rights and freedoms (Article 14).

The UK is also a party to the First Protocol to the Convention which guarantees the right to protection of property (Article 1), the right to education (Article 2) and the right to free elections (Article 3): Part II of Sch 1 to the Act.

The Sixth Protocol requires the abolition of the death penalty other than in time of war or imminent threat of war (Articles 1 and 2): Part III of Sch 1 to the Act.

The provisions under Article 18 of the Convention afford specific protection and can be invoked on their own without reference to other Articles of the Convention: Part I of Sch 1 to the Act.[3]

DEROGATIONS

1.9   Article 15 of the Convention permits a State to derogate from certain Articles in time of war or other public emergency threatening the life of the nation. At such times, the State may take measures derogating from its obligations under the Convention to the extent required by the exigencies of the situation. The UK has one derogation in place in respect of Article 5(3) of

---

1   Treatment is not degrading unless the person concerned has undergone in the eyes of others or in his own eyes humiliation or debasement attaining a minimum level of severity: *Campbell and Cosans v UK* (1982) Series A No 48, 4 EHRR 293, paras 28–30.

2   The detention of habitual offenders at the discretion of the Government did not involve a sufficiently serious form of denial of freedom to amount to servitude. The work which the applicant was asked to do in prison was imposed in the ordinary course of detention and was justified under Article 4(3) of the Convention: *Van Droogenbroeck v Belgium* (1982) Series A No 50, 4 EHRR 443, paras 58–59.

3   The restrictions imposed under this Convention to the said rights and freedoms shall not be applied for any purpose other than those for which they have been prescribed: Article 18: *Quinn v France* 21 EHRR 529, para 57.

the Convention as described in Sch 3, Part I to the Act. Article 5(3) which provides that everyone arrested or detained in accordance with the provisions of para 1(c) of Article 5 shall be brought promptly before a judge or other officer authorised by law to exercise judicial power and shall be entitled to trial within a reasonable time or to release pending trial. Release may be conditioned by guarantees to appear for trial. Article 5(3) does not have effect, by reason of the derogation, in the prevention of terrorism legislation but will continue to have effect in domestic law. The Government has stated that it would not want this derogation to remain in place indefinitely without good reasons. Thus Article 5(3) will have time-limited effect and, if it is not withdrawn earlier, it will expire five years after the Act comes into force unless both Houses of Parliament agree that it should be renewed: s 16(3) of the Act.

Emergency situations may arise so as to justify derogations under Article 15. There is considerable scope to argue that such derogations are justiciable irrespective of the fact that the State is acting in good faith. When such an issue arises for consideration, it is for the European Court to determine in the first instance whether the facts and circumstances fall within Article 15 of the Convention.[1] A court may be prepared to find that the conditions which justify the derogations do exist if there is a public emergency threatening the life of a nation.[2] This view accords with the approach taken by the courts in judicial review cases involving national security matters.[3] In a non-emergency situation, a court may be prepared to find that the conditions do not exist which justify the derogations in question. In such instances, this does not mean that the court's supervision is limited to ascertaining whether a respondent State exercised its discretion reasonably, carefully, and in good faith. Even a Contracting State so acting remains subject to the court's control as regards the compatibility of its conduct with the engagements it has undertaken under the Convention. The State must establish that its decisions and actions are grounded on an acceptable assessment of the relevant facts and that any interference with the Convention rights is no more than is reasonably necessary to achieve the legitimate aim pursued.[4] This suggested approach is different from the usual *Wednesbury* approach adopted by UK courts and practitioners must be fully aware of this jurisprudence. Furthermore, it is suggested that where non-derogable rights are in issue (Articles 2, 3, 4 and 7) then the courts must be prepared to exert control and supervision on the State purporting to rely on Article 15.[5] Practitioners must also be aware of limitations on derogations in other international instruments, such as the Geneva Convention, which do not allow derogations from due process safeguards in times of emergency or war. It is suggested that the Act empowers the UK court to protect

---

1   *Lawless v Ireland* (1961) Series A No 3, 1 EHRR 15.
2   For an exhaustive analysis of this subject see the article by Howard Charles Yourow 'The Margin of Appreciation in the Dynamics of European Human Rights Jurisprudence' (Martinus Nijhoff, 1996).
3   *CCSU v Minister for the Civil Service* [1985] AC 374.
4   *Vogt v Germany* (1995) Series A No 323, 21 EHRR 205; *Sunday Times v UK* (1979) Series A No 30, 2 EHRR 245.
5   See *Brogan and Others v UK* (1988) Series A No 145-B, 11 EHRR 117; and *Brannigan and McBride v UK* (1993) Series A No 258-B, 17 EHRR 557.

non-derogable rights and prevent an infringement of such rights during times of war or emergencies.

Article 64 of the Convention allows a State to enter a reservation when a law in force is not in conformity with a Convention provision. Part II of Sch 3 to the Act contains the reservations; in view of certain provisions of the Education Acts the principle affirmed in the second sentence of Article 2 is accepted by the UK only so far as it is compatible with the provision of efficient instruction and training, and the avoidance of unreasonable public expenditure (the second sentence of Article 2(2) provides that in exercising any functions in relation to education and teaching, the State shall respect the right of parents and to ensure that such education and teaching is in conformity with their own religious and philosophical convictions). This reservation in relation to Article 2 of the First Protocol does not seem incompatible with the European Court case-law.[1] The UK Government has stated that Article 2(2) is in accordance with s 9 of the Education Act 1996, but that a balance must be struck between the convictions of parents and what is educationally sound and affordable. This reservation is not subject to a periodic renewal, but the Secretary of State for Education will be required to review the reservation every five years and to lay a report before Parliament: s 17 of the Act.

The Government has not ratified two out of the four Protocols which contain substantive rights and they are the Fourth Protocol (prohibition on the deprivation of liberty on grounds of a person's inability to fulfil a contractual obligation; a right to liberty of movement; a right to non-expulsion from the Home State),[2] and the Seventh Protocol (prohibition on the expulsion of aliens without a decision in accordance with the law or opportunities for review; a right to a review of conviction or sentence after criminal conviction; a right to compensation following a miscarriage of justice; a prohibition on double jeopardy in criminal cases; and a right to equality between spouses).

The Act makes it unlawful for public authorities to act in a way which is incompatible with the Convention rights. Therefore, a victim of abuse by a public authority in any proceedings may rely on the Act to challenge the particular decision taken by the public body which impinges on his individual rights.[3]

---

1   The obligation to respect religious and philosophical convictions under Article 2 of the First Protocol is not confined to the content of educational instruction of the mode of conveying information and knowledge but includes the organisation and financing of public education, the supervision of the educational system in general and questions of discipline: *Campbell and Cosans v UK* (1982) Series A No 48, 4 EHRR 293, para 35.

2   The ECJ (Luxembourg) jurisprudence requires respect for fundamental rights (eg Case C-260/89 ERT [1991] ECR 1-2925 at 2963-4; and Article F(2) of the Maastricht Treaty (TEU)) and that one such right protected by Article 3(2) of the Fourth Protocol of the Convention requires respect for the right of a national to enter his own country; and that whilst the UK is not party to this Protocol, it is part of the corpus of law to be taken into account by the ECJ (and UK courts) in construing the Treaty (TEU). See *R v Secretary of State for the Home Department, ex parte Kaur* CO/0985/98 (unreported) at p 26 of the transcript. This case concerns the rights of residence in the UK of a British overseas citizen without a right of abode in the UK and whether such a person is a EU national. The case is referred to the ECJ for resolution.

3   Section 6.

PUBLIC AUTHORITIES

1.10   Public authorities includes:

(a)   a court;
(b)   a tribunal which exercises functions in relation to legal proceedings; and
(c)   any person certain of whose functions are functions of a public nature;

but does not include either of the Houses of Parliament or a person exercising functions in connection with proceedings in Parliament.

The present view is that churches may fall under the definition of public authorities. It remains to be seen in what circumstances the civil courts will be prepared to interfere with unlawful actions by a church. The view taken is that civil courts will be prepared to interfere with Convention rights and not with the spiritual government of the church. The civil courts will not interfere with the religious freedoms of the churches as opposed to public functions.[1] The courts will not, it seems, take jurisdiction over spiritual matters or the exercise of jurisdiction by religious courts of any religious denominations.

The suggested approach to be adopted in determining whether a body is a public authority or not will perhaps be based on the same reasoning contained in cases like *R v Disciplinary Committee of the Jockey Club, ex parte Massingberd-Mundy*.[2]

DECLARATION OF INCOMPATIBILITY

1.11   Section 4 of the Act allows for the higher courts to make a declaration of incompatibility. The outcome of such a declaration that this statutory provision is incompatible with the Convention rights will not 'of itself have the effect of changing the law, which will continue to apply, but it will most certainly prompt the Government and Parliament to change the law'.[3] Where there is a clear breach of the Convention, it is highly unlikely that any government will ignore the views of the domestic courts when there is a strong possibility that the European Court will mandate a change to the law. It should be remembered that the Commission cannot consider applicants concerning the implementation or legislation of a European Court judgment or declaration. According to Article 54 of the Convention, the Committee of Ministers supervises the execution of judgments and the Commission can consider whether there has been a new violation of the Convention only following a judgment of the European Court.

---

1   See s 13(1) of the Act.
2   [1993] 2 All ER 207.
3   White Paper: *Rights Brought Home: The Human Rights Bill* 1997 Cm 3782 at para 2.10. The appropriate Minister must then consider whether to make a remedial order and whether it should be retrospective. While the Minister is considering this, one expects the court to grant a stay or injunction and bail if applicable. It is suggested for the reasons given above (with regard to Article 13) that the remedial order is subject to judicial review particularly as a complainant against such a remedial order has a right of access to a court under Article 6(1) of the Convention.

Primary legislation

1.12   Section 4 of the Act provides that specified courts (higher courts) may make a declaration of incompatibility where they are satisfied that a provision of primary legislation is incompatible and the primary legislation under which it was made prevents the removal of that incompatibility. But a declaration would not be binding on the parties concerned and would not of itself create any liability. This position is completely different from a finding under s 6 that a public authority has acted unlawfully by committing a breach of the Convention rights and that the breach is not sanctioned by legislation. It also provides that such a declaration does not affect the validity, continuing operation or enforcement of the provisions in respect of which it is given. Tribunals and lower courts do not have power to make a declaration of incompatibility. In certain cases, it may be appropriate for a victim to bring judicial review proceedings if a declaration of incompatibility is sought before the determination of his rights at a tribunal or lower court. It remains to be seen whether a victim should exhaust his appeal rights before seeking judicial review for a declaration of incompatibility from a higher court.

Section 4, when construed in its entirety, suggests that a court or tribunal may have power and jurisdiction to declare that an administrative decision or an extra-statutory policy is incompatible with a Convention right if this is the case.[1] There is nothing in s 4 which prohibits this reading.

However, in the course of proceedings and after the judgment of the European Court, the States which have incorporated the Convention, as is shown by experience, are better suited to adopt the decisions of the Committee or the judgment of the European Court quickly and alter the relevant legislation to accord with such decisions or judgments as the case may be.[2] The European Court has emphasised that the obligation under Article 53 of the Convention (to abide by its decisions) leaves to each State the choice of the means to be utilised in its domestic legal system because the European Court's judgment is essentially declaratory in character. The European Court does not have the power to change or repeal the domestic legislation found to be in breach of the Convention. Furthermore, the European Court has stated that its judgments do not have retroactive effect.[3]

The Government has reached the conclusion that courts should not have the power to set aside *primary legislation*, past or future, on the ground of incompatibility with the Convention.

Secondary legislation

1.13   National courts will have power to strike down or set aside secondary legislation which is incompatible with the Convention and could have been

---

1   See further at **1.31**.
2   *Bosnisch v Austria* (1985) Series A No 92, 9 EHRR 191; the Austrian Constitutional Court reviewed the framework of the Austrian Constitution a few months after the European Court found that the Austrian authorities acted in breach of Article 6 of the Convention.
3   *Marckx v Belgium* (1979) Series A No 31, 2 EHRR 330, para 38.

framed differently unless the terms of the enabling or parent statute do not render this possible. A court or tribunal confronted with a submission that a particular regulation is incompatible with a Convention right should be persuaded to disapply it because it has a duty to act compatibly with the Convention under s 6. But subordinate legislation insofar as it is incompatible with Convention rights may be corrected by judicial decision or by ministerial order. A declaration of incompatibility will be made only in the case of subordinate legislation if it cannot be amended by reason of the wording of the primary legislation.

Consequent amendment of legislation

1.14 The consequence of the European Court making a declaration that primary legislation is incompatible with the Convention rights will mean that the Government will take serious note of this declaration and it will no doubt have a 'profound impact on the way that legislation is interpreted and applied and it will have the effect of putting the issues squarely to the Government and Parliament for further consideration'.[1]

The Act allows for a fast track procedure for amending the legislation in response either to a declaration of incompatibility by a court under s 4 of the Act, or as a result of a judgment of the European Court that the UK has acted in breach of the Convention. The appropriate Minister will be able to amend the legislation by Order (statutory instrument), under the 90-minute order procedure, so as to make it compatible with the Convention. The Order will be subject to approval by both Houses of Parliament before taking effect, except where the need to amend the legislation is particularly urgent. Then, the Order will take effect immediately, but will expire after a short period if not approved by Parliament. The fast track system allowing for amendment of the primary legislation by an Order is only applicable where the legislation is declared to be incompatible with Convention rights and as such is not available to amend unrelated parts of the Act in which the breach is discovered: ss 10–12 of the Act.

In Scotland, the position with regard to Acts of the Westminster Parliament is the same as in England and in Wales. The position is different, however, in relation to Acts of the Scottish Parliament. The Government has decided that the Scottish Parliament will have no power to legislate in a way which is incompatible with the Convention.

Similarly, the Welsh Assembly does not have the power to make subordinate legislation or take executive action which is incompatible with the Convention.

Acts of the Westminster Parliament will be treated in the same way in Northern Ireland as in the rest of the UK. But Orders in Council will be treated as subordinate legislation.

Armed forces

1.15 The Government's view is that the armed forces fall squarely within the category of an obvious public authority. The European Court case-law treats the

---

1   *Rights Brought Home: The Human Rights Bill* 1977 Cm 3782 at para 2.19.

armed forces in a special way. For example, in the case of *Engel v The Netherlands*,[1] the European Court stated that the confinement to barracks of a member of the armed forces did not involve an infringement of the right to liberty under Article 5 of the Convention (right to liberty), although it would have done so in the case of a civilian.

THE NEW APPROACH PARTICULARLY IN JUDICIAL REVIEW CONTEXTS

1.16   National courts are to apply the Act whenever it is required to do so and this spells the end of the traditional *Wednesbury* test and in its place, it is suggested, the new test of proportionality will be applied where human rights or constitutional rights are involved.[2] The *Wednesbury* test (that is, where a public body fails to take into account relevant matters or takes into account irrelevant matters) is no longer applicable when the Act is applied. The doctrine of proportionality is not an alien doctrine to UK courts and has been applied very successfully in a number of cases where EC law has been applied.[3] This doctrine has also been applied by the European Court. Its application is to ensure that a measure imposes no greater restriction upon a Convention right than is absolutely necessary to achieve its objectives. Closely allied with the doctrine of proportionality is the concept of the margin of appreciation which is considered fully elsewhere in this book.[4] Briefly, the doctrine of margin of appreciation allows national courts a discretion in the application of the requirements of the Convention to the particular situation. But the discretion is not absolute. The reviewing powers of a court under the Convention will have to go further than a *Wednesbury* review (whether the discretion has been exercised reasonably, carefully and in good faith and all relevant matters have been taken into account). The reviewing court will have to go a step further. It has to be satisfied that the decision challenged is based on an acceptable assessment of the facts under scrutiny and that the interference with the fundamental rights is no more than is reasonably necessary to achieve the legitimate aim pursued.

Thus, when a domestic court is faced with a complaint that Article 10(1) is infringed, it appears that it will not approach the matter on a traditional *Wednesbury* basis. It is suggested that the domestic court should adopt the approach taken by the European Court in these situations. Thus, in *Piermont v France*,[5] the European Court was concerned to investigate a violation of Article

---

1   (1976) Series A No 22, 1 EHRR 647; also see *Findlay v Secretary of State for the Home Department* [1985] AC 318 where the Court held that the martial procedure under the Army Act 1955 was in fundamental breach of Article 6 of the Convention.

2   In cases involving human rights, the courts will be anxious to take an interventionist role: *R v Lord Saville of Newdigate and Others* (1999) 22 June, *The Times*; and for example a breach of a defendant's constitutional right to a fair trial must inevitably result in the conviction being quashed: *Mohammed v The State* [1999] 2 WLR 552 at 562G–H.

3   *R v Human Fertilisation and Embryology Authority, ex parte Blood* [1997] 2 WLR 807 at 819G; and *U v W* [1997] 3 WLR 739 at 751E.

4   See further **1.21**.

5   (1995) Series A No 314, 20 EHRR 301.

10(1). Having found such a violation, the European Court stated that freedom of expression constitutes one of the essential foundations of a democratic society; one of the basic conditions for its progress. Subject to para 2 of Article 10, Article 10(1) is applicable not only to information or ideas which are favourably received or regarded as inoffensive or as a matter of indifference, but also to those that offend, shock or disturb. Freedom of political debate is undoubtedly not absolute in nature. A State may make such a right subject to certain restrictions or penalties *but it is for the European Court to give a final ruling on the compatibility* of such measures with the freedom of expression enshrined in Article 10. Thus the court will have to make a primary judgment for itself (and not only a secondary judgment) as to whether there is or is not an infringement of the Convention.

One notable area of change the Act will bring about, for example, are the rights of lesbians and gays. Should the case of *R v Ministry of Defence, ex parte Smith*[1] arise again for any reason for consideration under the Act one would see the courts applying Articles 8 and 14 effectively to determine that the ban on homosexuals serving in the armed forces is indeed unlawful with no justification. In *Dudgeon v UK*,[2] the European Court held that sexual activity between men of any age prohibited by Northern Ireland's legislation contravened Article 8 (respect for private life) and that although some degree of regulation of all forms of sexual conduct by the criminal law can be justified as necessary in a democratic society and this control may properly extend to some consensual acts committed in private, the failure to prosecute homosexual conduct in private between consenting males over the age of 21 makes it impossible to maintain that there is a pressing social need for the prohibition.[3] It remains to be seen how they will apply the Convention in areas where there is judicial discretion to be exercised[4] or where public policy is to be formulated.[5]

STATUTORY INTERPRETATION UNDER THE ACT

1.17 Section 3 of the Act provides that primary and secondary legislation, whenever enacted, must as far as possible be read and given effect in a way which is compatible with the Convention rights. It also provides that the validity operation or enforcement of the incompatible enactment in question will not be affected in any way, if primary legislation prevents the removal of the incompatibility. Lord Irvine of Lairg, in his address at a conference on the Bill of Rights for the UK held at University College London on 4 July 1997, stated that the Government intended to retain its supremacy and that incorporation would be best achieved in a way which does not take away the supremacy of Parliament. It is for the judges to interpret the laws and it is for Parliament to pass the laws. This section creates a new approach and requires all courts to

---

1   [1996] QB 517.
2   (1981) Series A No 45, 4 EHRR 149, paras 49, 60, 61.
3   Thus, the courts will, when applying the Act, effectively reverse such decisions (and legislation) as *Kaye v Robertson* [1991] FSR 62 and *Fitzpatrick v Sterling Housing Association* [1998] 2 WLR 225.
4   *Rantzen v Mirror Group Newspapers* [1994] QB 670; *R v Khan (Sultan)* [1996] 3 WLR 162.
5   *Attorney-General v Guardian Newspaper (No 2)* [1990] 1 AC 109.

interpret legislation consistently with the Convention unless the wording of the Act makes this impossible. It will be the courts' duty to avoid inconsistency by 'reading down' breaches or inconsistent provisions and to 'read in' rights or the necessary Convention safeguards.

It remains to be seen how the courts will apply s 3 of the Act. The following principles should be borne in mind when advancing interpretation techniques.

(1) The words of a statute dealing with the subject matter of the Convention are to be construed as intended to implement the Convention obligations and not to be inconsistent with it if they are reasonably capable of bearing such a meaning.[1] This approach is consistent with Article 13 (which requires States to provide an effective remedy before the national authority for those whose rights are violated).

(2) Furthermore, subject to the principle of Parliament retaining its sovereignty under the Act, s 3 of the Act should not be viewed differently to s 2 of the European Community Act 1972. Therefore, the words of any primary or secondary legislation whether passed before or after the Act should be construed in conformity with the Convention whenever it is possible to do so.[2]

(3) The Lord Chancellor pointed out that the Act will require new judicial techniques of interpretation. The Act will require the courts to read and give effect to the legislation in a way which is compatible with the Convention rights so far as it is possible to do so. It will not be necessary to find an ambiguity. The courts will be required to interpret legislation so as to uphold the Convention rights unless the legislation itself is so clearly incompatible with the Convention that it is impossible to do so. The Ministerial Statement of compatibility (see s 19 of the Act) will inevitably be a strong spur to the courts to find means of construing statutes compatibly with the Convention. This means reading in safeguards to save the statute in accordance with Convention rights and reading down or reading narrowly restrictions upon human rights.

(4) The European Court has preferred the approach of reading a statute so as to conform with the Convention rather than disapplying it. Thus, the European Court has with reference to Article 8 (respect for private life) construed the term 'family life' to apply to 'illegitimate' family in as much it applies to 'legitimate' family.

(5) It is suggested that when a court is applying s 3 in any given case, it should follow the example illustrated in the judgment of Lord Oliver in *Litster v Forth Dry Dock and Engineering Co Ltd*:[3]

'The approach to the construction of primary and subordinate legislation enacted to give effect to the UK's obligations under the EEC Treaty have been subject of recent authority in this House and is not in doubt. If the legislation can reasonably be construed so as to conform with those obligations – which are to be ascertained not only from the wording of the relevant Directives (ie the relevant Convention right) but from the interpretation placed upon it by the European Court of Justice

1   *Garland v British Rail* [1983] 2 AC 751 at 771 per Lord Diplock.

2   For example, see *Marleasing v Alimentacion* [1990] 1 ECR 4135; *Faccini Dori* Case C-91/92 [1994] ECR 1-3325; and see *Pickstone v Freemans Plc* [1989] AC 66.

3   [1990] 1 AC 546 at 559.

at Luxembourg (ie the European Court of Human Rights) – such a purposive construction will be applied even though, perhaps, it may involve some departure from the strict and literal application of the words which the legislature has elected to use.'

(6) In *R v Secretary of State for Transport, ex parte Factortame and Others (No 2)*,[1] the House of Lords stated that, in the event of a conflict between domestic legislation and directly applicable EC law, the courts must first determine whether the statutory provision in question can be interpreted consistently with EC law but, if this is not possible, then the domestic statutory provision is impliedly repealed or treated as invalid and EC law prevails. This position applies irrespective of whether the statutory provision in question was passed before or after the 1972 Act. See also *Equal Opportunities v Secretary of State for Employment*[2] where the House of Lords held that domestic legislation was incompatible with the Equal Treatment Directive and Article 119. Similarly, it is suggested that the courts must first determine whether the statutory provisions in question can be interpreted consistently with the Convention case-law. If not, then the courts should be prepared to make a declaration of incompatibility.

(7) The European Court, in contrast to UK courts, applies teleological rather than historical methods to the interpretation of the Treaties and other EC law. It seeks to give effect to what it conceives to be the *spirit* rather than the letter of the Treaties; sometimes, indeed, to an English judge, it may seem to the exclusion of the letter. It views the communities as living and expanding organisms and the interpretation of the provisions of the Treaties as changing to match their growth.[3]

(8) The approach in EC law should be adopted; therefore, it is necessary to consider in the order of priority:
   (a) the spirit of the Convention;
   (b) the general scheme of the legislation;
   (c) the wording of the particular legislation in light of the fact that the Convention is a living instrument.[4]

(9) The Lord Chancellor has expressed his own view as to technique of construction to be adopted. The court will interpret as consistent with the Convention not only those provisions which are ambiguous in the sense that the language used is capable of two different meanings, but also those provisions where there is no ambiguity in that sense, unless a clear limitation is expressed. In the latter category of case, it will be possible to use the statutory language to read the legislation in a conforming sense because there will be no clear indication that a limitation on the protected rights was intended so as to make it impossible to read it as conforming. The domestic courts will therefore require to apply the same techniques of interpretation and decision making as the European Court.[5]

---

1   [1991] 1 AC 603.
2   [1994] 1 All ER 910.
3   Per Lord Diplock in *Henn and Darby v DPP* [1981] AC 850 at 892.
4   See *N v Algemene Transport-en Expeditie Onderneming Van Gend en Loos v Nederlandse Administratie der Belastingen* [1963] ECR 1.
5   See 'The Development of Human Rights in Britain' Lord Irvine of Lairg [1998] PL 221.

(10) The European Court adopts a teleological approach which is principally concerned with giving the statutory language its presumed legislative intent. The approach is not so much concerned with the literal approach or textual analysis of the statutory language found in our common law heritage.

(11) The Privy Council has on many occasions had the task of interpreting Constitutions of different jurisdictions. It is useful to consider what approach the Privy Council has adopted in interpreting Constitutional rights.[1]

(12) It is to be borne in mind that a constitution is a legal instrument giving rise to individual rights capable of enforcement in a court. Lord Wilberforce stated in one case that respect must be paid to the language which has been used and to the traditions and usages which have given meaning to that language. It is quite consistent with this, and with the recognition that rules of interpretation may apply, to take as a point of departure for the process of interpretation a recognition of the character and origin of the instrument, and to be guided by the principle of giving full recognition and effect to those fundamental rights and freedoms with a statement of which the Constitution commences.

(13) Those statutes (covering such areas as immigration, extradition, health, employment, mental health, criminal trials etc), which affect fundamental human rights in relation to right to life (Article 2), or in relation to degrading treatment of punishment (Article 3) or in relation to forced labour (Article 4) should be interpreted in light of the guidance given by the European Court in these areas. Therefore, the approach to the interpretation of any statute which impinges on these Articles must be guided by the fact that the object and purpose of the Convention as an instrument for the protection of individual human beings requires that the provisions be interpreted and applied so as to make the safeguards practical and effective. Therefore, for example, where national statutory language alludes to such terms as 'an officer may use reasonable force, if necessary, in the exercise of power'[2] and if there is a difference between the national statutory standard and the relevant Convention standard in question, then the standard of justification for the use of force, which results in the violation of the Convention right, ought to be interpreted in light of the Convention jurisprudence. If the Convention standard is stricter than the relevant national standard then the Convention standard ought to prevail having regard to the manner in which the national standard is interpreted and applied. If the difference between the two standards is not sufficiently great then there may be no violation of the Convention right in question.[3]

---

1   *Ministry of Home Affairs v Fisher* [1980] AC 319. Also see *Attorney-General of the Gambia v Momodou Jobe* [1984] AC 689 at 700H. A constitution, and in particular that part of it which protects and entrenches fundamental rights and freedoms to which all persons in the State are entitled, is to be given a generous and purposive construction.

2   For example, see s 117 of the Police and Criminal Evidence Act 1984.

3   *McCann v UK* (1996) Series A No 324, 21 EHRR 97 at 162, paras 154–155. The European Court stated that, in relation to the taking of the life of suspected IRA bombers by British soldiers in Gibraltar, Article 2 of the Gibraltar Constitution is similar to Article 2 of the

(14) The view of the European Court judges is that the norms in the Convention must be interpreted in line with present-day conditions so that looking back at their drafting history does not help.

(15) Furthermore, in a number of cases, the European Court and Commission have had regard to other international instruments in resolving issues.[1]

(16) As far as domestic provisions governing the prevention and detection of serious crime are concerned, it is believed that the Act will allow a greater scope for seeking court intervention than previously was the case. Therefore, for example, the Security Service Act 1996 was passed to give the security service greater powers than ever before for the prevention and detection of serious crime and to give the Secretary of State wide-ranging powers, not subject to control by the courts, to issue warrants allowing the entry into homes or to interfere with property for a variety of purposes including interception of telecommunications.[2] It may well be argued that the 1996 Act is to be construed compatibly with the Convention rights but that if this is not possible in several regards then the court should declare that the 1996 Act is incompatible with the Convention in several aspects. There is scope for arguing that bugging of telephones or entering into private property involves an infringement of Article 8(1) (respect of family and private life). In particular, the wide discretion conferred upon the authorities lacks clarity and defined limits. The law authorising the bugging of telephones or interference with private property for such purposes must be sufficiently clear. It was stated in *Malone v UK*[3] that since the information, in practice, of measures of secret surveillance of communications is not open to scrutiny by the individuals concerned or the public at large, it would be contrary to the rule of law for the legal discretion granted to the executive to be expressed in terms of an unfettered power. In short, it may be said that the powers of the authority to bug telecommunications is not in accordance with the law under Article 8(2) and that such powers do not contain adequate and effective guarantees against abuse and thus are not 'necessary in a democratic society'. It is noted that the 1996 Act does not provide for the person whose telephone has been under surveillance to be notified upon the completion and termination of surveillance. Again, this omission is contrary to Article 8(2). The case of *Klass v FRG*[4] indicates that a person who has been placed under surveillance must be notified of

---

Convention with the exception that the standard of justification for the use of force which results in the deprivation of life is that of 'reasonably justifiable' as opposed to 'absolutely necessary' in Article 2(2) of the Convention. The European Court held that the difference between the two standards is not sufficiently great that a violation of Article 2(1) could be found on this ground alone.

1   In *A v UK* Application No 25599/94, the Commission had regard to the UN Convention on the Rights of the Child in holding that the domestic law failed to provide the applicant with adequate and effective protection against corporal punishment which was degrading within the meaning of Article 3.

2   Sections 1 and 2 of the Security Service Act 1996.

3   (1985) 7 EHRR 14, para 68; *Huvig v France* (1990) 12 EHRR 528; *Kruslin v France* (1990) 12 EHRR 547; *Klass and Others v FRG* (1978) Series A No 28, 2 EHRR 214; *Halford v UK* (1997) 24 EHRR 523.

4   (1978) Series A No 28, 2 EHRR 214, para 58.

this fact soon after the surveillance has been completed and as soon as notification can be made without putting the surveillance under jeopardy. In cases where national security is not an issue, the courts must be prepared to 'read down' the breaches or 'read rights' into the relevant statutory provisions and if this is not possible then to make the necessary declaration of incompatibility.

(17) The rule of construction should also apply to bye-laws, immigration rules, practice directions, Rules of the Supreme Court etc. However, where the enabling power in primary legislation clearly allows for the relevant provision then it will have to be argued, no doubt, that the enabling provision must be construed in a manner which prevents the enactment of subordinate rules (immigration rules, bye-laws, policies based on statutory powers) which are inconsistent with Convention rights and accordingly the rule in question is *ultra vires*.

THE ACT AND ITS INTERACTION WITH EC LAW

1.18   There will no doubt be a role for the Act to apply when EC law is being implemented domestically. In March 1996, the European Court of Justice (ECJ) was asked whether the European Community could accede to the Convention. The ECJ stated that the European Community was not competent to accede to the Convention without there being an amendment to the EC Treaty and that Article 235 of the EC Treaty may not act as a legal basis for the accession to the Convention.[1] In several cases, the ECJ has stated that the Convention forms an 'integral part of the general principles of law the observance of which the Court ensures'.[2] Previously there has never been incorporation of the Convention in EC law. Given that EC law does impinge on fundamental rights, particularly in the areas of social security, freedom of movement of persons, immigration control, anti-discrimination provisions in employment and social advantages (and the European Social Charter), the necessity to consider the Convention as an influence on its construction and application is of considerable importance. The Convention can supply guidelines which should be followed within the framework of EC law.[3] There are also examples where the ECJ has not dealt with a matter in the same way as the European Court would have done.[4] The ECJ and the European Court are sometimes asked, independently, to resolve issues relating to the same

---

1   Opinion 2/94. Article 235 of the EC Treaty provides: 'If action by the Community should provide necessary to attain, in the course of the operation of the common market, one of the objectives of the Community and this Treaty has not provided the necessary powers, the Council shall, acting unanimously on a proposal from the Commission and after consulting the European Parliament, take the appropriate measures'. Now see Article 308 of the Treaty on European Union.

2   *Nold KG v Commission* Case 4/73 [1974] ECR 491.

3   Ibid, para 31; see also *Rutili v Minister for the Interior* [1975] ECR 1219; in this case, the ECJ relied upon various Articles of the Convention as a source of inspiration for the protection of fundamental rights.

4   See *Orkem v Commission* [1989] ECR 3283 at 3337–3338 where Advocate-General Darmon stated that the ECJ may adopt in a particular context a different interpretation from that adopted by the European Court.

fundamental rights and, in doing so, the former has regard to the European Court case-law to enlighten its approach to the particular problem.[1] The Treaty of Amsterdam amends Article L of the Treaty on European Union (the Maastricht Treaty (TEU)) by incorporating Article F2 (which affirms the Convention as principles of EC law) into the main provisions of the TEU. For example, there is an extension of the TEU to include a prohibition of discrimination on grounds of race, sexual orientation, disability and religious discrimination. Article F2 of Title I of the Common Provisions of the TEU now provides that the Union shall respect fundamental rights, as guaranteed by the Convention and as they result from the constitutional traditions common to the Member States, as general principles of EC law. Title 1 and Article F2 do not fall within the jurisdiction of the ECJ.[2] Similarly, the European Court would be reluctant to examine proceedings which are before the ECJ as the European Community is not a party to the Convention. In UK domestic courts, there is no reason why the Convention rights cannot be utilised when Community rights are being enforced. Sometimes the interpretation of an EC Directive may call for a reference to the Convention rights. This will depend on the subject matter. In a transsexual case before the ECJ, the Advocate-General in reaching his decision had regard to all the cases in the Convention jurisprudence relating to transsexuals[3] including *Cossey*;[4] *Rees*;[5] *B v France*.[6] In another case, the ECJ dealing with the Community rights of lesbians considered the jurisprudence of the Convention particularly that stable homosexual relationships do not fall within the scope of the right to respect for family life under Article 8 of the Convention. The European Court reasoned that in the present state of the law within the Community, stable relationships between two persons of the same sex are not regarded as equivalent to marriages or stable relationships outside marriage between persons of the opposite sex. Consequently, an employer is not required by Community law to treat the situation of a person who has a stable relationship with a partner of the same sex as equivalent to that of a person who is married to or has a stable relationship outside marriage with a partner of the opposite sex. The European Court also stressed that although respect for fundamental rights which form an integral part of those general principles of law is a condition of the legality of the acts, those rights cannot themselves have the effect of extending the scope of Treaty provisions beyond

---

1   See, for example, *Society for the Protection of the Unborn Child v Grogan* [1991] ECR 1-4685 (where the ECJ was not prepared to accept that a prohibition in Ireland of the supply of information regarding availability of abortion services in England constituted a restriction of the freedom to provide and receive services within EC law) and contrast this with *Open Door Counselling Ltd and Dublin Well Woman Clinic Ltd v Ireland* (1992) Series A No 246, 15 EHRR 244 (where the European Court stated that a prohibition in Ireland of the supply of information regarding availability of counselling services infringed Article 10 (freedom of expression) and such an interference was not justified).

2   Article L of Title VII (now Title VIII of the TEU) does not include the provisions of Article F2 within its jurisdiction.

3   In *P v S and Cornwall County Council* [1996] IRLR 347 at 350, para 12: the Advocate-General had regard to *Cossey v UK* (1990) Series A No 184, 13 EHRR 622; *Rees v UK* (1986) Series A No 106, 9 EHRR 56; *B v France* (1992) 16 EHRR 1.

4   (1990) Series A No 184, 13 EHRR 622.

5   (1986) Series A No 106, 9 EHRR 56.

6   (1992) 16 EHRR 1.

the competence of the Community (see Article 235 of the EC Treaty above). That being so, the scope of any provision of EC law, is to be determined only by having regard to its wording and purpose, its place in the scheme of the Treaty and its legal context. It concluded that EC law as it stands at present does not cover discrimination based on sexual orientation.[1]

Where domestic legislation is concerned with a situation that does not fall within the scope of EC law, the ECJ cannot, under Article 177, give the interpretative guidance necessary to a domestic court to determine whether that domestic legislation conforms with the fundamental rights observance of which the court ensures, such as rights deriving from the Convention.[2]

The ECJ has held that the right to respect for private life, embodied in Article 8 of the Convention and deriving from the common constitutional positions of the Member States, is one of the fundamental rights protected by the legal order of the Community.[3] These fundamental rights are not absolute and restrictions may be imposed upon them provided that they correspond to objectives of general public interest and do not constitute, with regard to the objectives pursued, a disproportionate and intolerable interference which infringes upon the very substance of the right protected.[4]

The ECJ has used the Convention in the following manner:

(a) as a principle of interpretation in applying Community provisions;[5]
(b) in examining the validity of derogations of domestic law from EC law;[6]
(c) in determining whether domestic law conforms with or exceeds Community law.[7]

The ECJ has, on an number of occasions, taken into consideration international human rights instruments where Community law applies.[8] The ECJ has stated that fundamental human rights are enshrined in the general principles of Community law.[9]

---

1   *Grant v South-West Trains Ltd* Case C-249/96 [1998] IRLR 206, ECJ.

2   *Kremsow v Republik Osterreich* Case C-299/95 (1997) *The Times*, 11 August.

3   *X v Commission of the European Communities* [1995] IRLR 320, ECJ.

4   Ibid, n 72, para 18.

5   *Community v Germany* Case C-62/90 [1992] ECR I-2575, ECJ.

6   *Elleniki R v Dimotiki E P* Case 260/89 [1991] ECR 2925, ECJ.

7   See Bob Watt 'The Legal Protection of HIV-Positive Health Care Workers' [1998] EHRLR p 301.

8   *Elliniki Radiohonioa Tileorani AE v Dimohki Plirofassis* Case C-260/89 at para 42 of the judgment:

> 'As the Court has held *Cinetheque* [1985] ECR 2605 and *Demirel* [1987] ECR 3719, it has no power to examine the compatibility with the ECHR of national rules which do not fall within the scope of community law. On the other hand, where such rules do fall *within* the scope of community law, and reference is made to the Court for a preliminary ruling, it must provide all the criteria of interpretation needed by the national court to determine whether those rules are compatible with the fundamental rights the observance of which the Court ensures and which derive in particular from the ECHR.'

9   *Stauder v City of Ulm, Sozialamt* Case 29/69 [1969] ECR 419 and also see, for example, *Nold KG v Commission* Case 4/73 [1974] ECR 491 at para 13 of the judgment (that international treaties for the protection of human rights on which the Member States have collaborated or of which they are signatories, can supply guidelines which should be followed within the

Leading academic writers have expressed the view that international instruments on human rights are and should be taken into account within a Community context. For example, if Community law is silent on fundamental human rights and if there is a lacuna in the EC Treaty on the issue then the ECJ might fill the gap by reference to human rights instruments.[1]

> 'Recognition of fundamental rights is an essential aspect of the foundational pact between government and the governed and the legal and political value of fundamental rights is also their potentially integrationary and legitimising function in a given legal order ... the construction of a relationship between fundamental rights and Community citizenship could be the means to ensure the steady evolution of an effective and meaningful rights-orientated status of citizenship in the Community'.[2]

Stephen Hall has expressed the view that there is no reason in principle why international agreements such as those of the United Nations could not equally serve guidelines in a Community context. For example, Articles 8 and 9 of the Convention on the Reduction of Statelessness (which was concluded in 1961 and entered into force in 1975), Article 26 of the International Covenant on Civil and Political Rights and the Convention on Racial Discrimination can supply guidelines within the framework of Community law.[3] There is no reason in principle why these international instruments should not be taken into account in a Community context given that all the EU Member States are signatories to these Conventions.

Secondary legislation (EC Directives) are expected to conform with Community human rights principles. The ECJ has repeatedly stated that it will not adjudicate on national measures which are incompatible with fundamental human rights but it will be prepared to ensure the observance of the Community's fundamental human rights in a Community context.[4] Even if national measures fall within the scope of a Community context, the ECJ may not be prepared to rule on its incompatibility with human rights unless the measure complained of has been adopted by Community law.[5] If a national measure does fall within the scope of Community law in the sense of derogating from a Community right on permissible grounds, or it seeks to implement Community law, then it must be consistent with the Community's general

---

framework of Community law) and Case C-260 ERT [1991] ECR 1-2925 (these cases establish that when Member States adopt measures or impose restrictions on EC rights of free movement, then these measures or restrictions should comply with fundamental rights).

1   Stephen Hall *Nationality, Migration Rights and Citizenship of the Union* (Martinus Nijhoff) at p 127 (where the treaties are silent on the protection of individual rights, the ECJ Court has tended, however, to fill the apparent gap by reference to some overriding general principle of Community law rather than by resort to mechanical application of analogous Community legislation).

2   Siofra O'Leary *The Evolving Concept of Community Citizenship from the Free Movement of Persons to Union Citizenship* at pp 311–314.

3   *Nationality, Migration Rights and Citizenship of the Union* (above) at p 86. Article 26 of the International Covenant on Civil and Political Rights was referred to in *Arantzamendi Osa v Procureur de la Republique* Case 13-28/82 [1982] ECR 3927 (all persons are equal before the law).

4   *Nationality, Migration Rights and Citizenship of the Union* (above) at p 92.

5   *R v Kirk* Case 63/83 [1984] ECR 2689.

principles on fundamental rights.[1] Jason Coppel and Aidan O'Neill have remarked that 'only Member States actions which the Court might decline to vet on human rights grounds are … those which occur in an area of exclusive Member State jurisdiction. This concept of Member States jurisdiction may itself be open to future redefinition by the Court'.[2]

Under the Act, the Convention principles might be applicable in the following instances:

(1) Article 15(1) of the Convention (public emergency) may apply in the event of war, alongside Article 297 (ex-Article 224) of the EC Treaty;
(2) Article 8 (respect for family life) of the Convention may apply alongside Directive 64/221/EEC when a decision to expel a citizen of the Union or his spouse who is a national of non-Member State is taken;[3]
(3) if there are no EC secondary regulations in force governing the issue then resort may be made to the Convention principles, eg Article 8 or Article 10 or Article 1 of the First Protocol. If there is a lacuna in the EC Treaty in relation to some issue involving fundamental rights, it is arguable that the ECJ will fill the gap by reference to human rights, ie Articles 8, 10 and Article 1 of the First Protocol;[4]
(4) fundamental human rights should be superior to any implied EC derogations which are applicable. Such national measures (ie Convention principles) cannot be taken to be incompatible with EC law even if they do enter the field of Community law.[5]

RESTRICTIONS UNDER ARTICLE 16 AND EUROPEAN UNION NATIONALS

1.19 A person who is a national of a Member State of the European Union and holds the status of a Member of the European Parliament does not allow Article 16 (restricting the political activities of aliens in relation to Articles 10, 11 and 14) of the Convention to be raised against such a person. Therefore, Article 16 cannot be relied upon to restrict the exercise of the rights by a European national guaranteed under the Convention.[6]

---

1 *Nationality, Migration Rights and Citizenship of the Union* (above) at p 95; see Case C-260 ERT [1991] ECR 1-2925 (where national rules do fall within the scope of Community law, and reference is made to the Court for a preliminary ruling, it must provide all the criteria of interpretation needed by the national court to determine whether those rules are compatible with the fundamental rights the observance of which the Court ensures and which derive in particular from the Convention).

2 Jason Coppel and Aidan O'Neill 'The European Court of Justice: Taking rights seriously' (1992) 12 *Legal Studies* 227 at 236 cited in *Nationality, Migration Rights and Citizenship of the Union* (above) at p 96.

3 *Demirle v Statdt Schwabisch Gmund* Case 12/86 [1987] ECR 3719 (decision to expel a Turkish wife of a Turkish worker from Germany did not contravene the EEC–Turkey Association Agreement) might be distinguished on the ground that the national rule in question (Article 8 of the Convention) does afford the spouse protection in such an event.

4 *Nationality, Migration Rights and Citizenship of the Union* (above) at p 126.

5 For example see *Cinetheque* (above) Joined Cases 60 and 61/84 [1985] ECR 2605.

6 *Piermont v France* (1995) Series A No 314, 20 EHRR 301 at 339, para 64.

THE NEW APPROACH UNDER THE ACT

1.20 The Human Rights Act 1998 is set to reverse many of the cases established by domestic courts in its approach to regulate the interference by the executive of individual rights. The former position was that in some limited circumstances domestic courts were prepared to take the Convention into account in domestic proceedings in the following circumstances:

(1) particularly where legislation was passed to conform with Convention case-law established by the European Court,[1]
(2) where the statutory language is ambiguous, regard may be taken of the Convention to resolve such ambiguity.[2]

As a consequence of the Act, domestic courts will no longer be tied down by the previous views expressed in, for example, *Brind*[3] where the House of Lords decided that the Convention was not part of UK law and that, where an Act confers unambiguously broad statutory discretionary powers on the executive and public bodies, there is no statutory presumption that those powers are to be exercised in accordance with the Convention. In *Brind*, Lord Bridge stated that it would impute to Parliament an intention not only that the executive should exercise the discretion in conformity with the Convention but also that the domestic courts should enforce that conformity by incorporation into domestic law of the text of the Convention and the jurisprudence of the Convention in the interpretation and application of it. In *R v Ministry of Defence, ex parte Smith*,[4] it was held that:

> 'it is not the constitutional role of the court to regulate the condition of service in the armed forces of the Crown, *nor has it the expertise to do so*, but it has the constitutional role and duty of ensuring that the rights of citizens are not abused by the unlawful exercise of executive power. While *the court must properly defer to the expertise of responsible decision-makers*, it must not shrink from its fundamental duty to "do right to all manner of people ..."'

(per Sir Thomas Bingham) (author's emphasis).

The Government in its White Paper *Rights Brought Home: The Human Rights Bill*[5] believes that the previous arrangements as found in limited application of the Convention by the UK are no longer adequate given the importance which it attaches to the maintenance of basic human rights in the UK and that the time has come to 'bring those rights home'. The Act will now reverse the UK courts' traditional approach to these problems (human rights) should it arise for consideration with particular regard to the Convention and its jurisprudence.

---

1 *Norney* [1995] Admin LR 861 at 871: where it is clear that the statutory provision which creates the discretion was passed in order to bring the domestic law into line with the Convention, it is suggested that it would be perverse to hold that, when considering the lawfulness of the exercise of the discretion, the court must ignore the relevant provisions of the Convention.
2 *R v Home Secretary, ex parte Brind* [1991] 1 AC 696.
3 [1991] 1 AC 696.
4 [1996] QB 517 at 556.
5 1997 Cm 3782.

It is unlawful[1] for a public authority[2] to act in a way which is incompatible with one or more of the Convention rights: see s 6(1) of the Act. The UK court in this instance will be required to make primary findings of fact and it is suggested that, whenever s 6(1) is applicable, a court of whatever jurisdiction (including judicial review proceedings) should adopt a primary judicial fact-finding approach with regard to the Convention issues. The court should first ask whether the Convention rights are directly engaged. If yes, it should go on to apply the relevant balancing exercise to adjudicate upon the issue before it. This approach is suggested for the following reasons:

(1) the principle of subsidiarity in the Convention context means that domestic courts have greater powers than the European Court;
(2) the domestic court is free to provide effective and better protection under domestic law particularly where domestic law is seemingly wider than Convention rights: for example, the Race Relations Act 1976;
(3) the Convention does not contain ubiquitous and uniform rules; it merely provides a minimum guidance of behaviour, but it is for domestic courts to implement the spirit of the Convention;
(4) domestic courts are in principle better placed than the European Court to appreciate what is in the public interest and have direct knowledge of their own society's needs and any political, social and economic tensions. The domestic courts, depending on the subject matter, have a wide margin of appreciation where issues of public interest are involved. The margin of appreciation is applied more restrictively where issues of public interest are not a consideration.[3] It varies according to the subject matter of investigation and is wider in relation to property rights (Article 1 of the First Protocol) than, for example, the right to life (Article 2) or freedom of expression (Article 10).

Furthermore, domestic courts will require the decision or decision-maker or public authority responsible for the decision under examination to satisfy the court, according to the gravity of the matter (ie Articles 2 and 3 may require greater scrutiny), that the decision is not inconsistent with the Convention rights (see below). Domestic courts will have to consider the European

---

1   The term 'unlawful' should be construed as widely as possible, having particular regard to the Convention rights.

2   Public authority is to be given a wide meaning and is not to be construed narrowly as is evident from s 6(3). This term includes central government, the police, immigration officers, prisons, court officials, courts and tribunals, privatised utilities, the City Takeover Panel, the BBC, the Church of England, the Advertising Standards Authority but possibly not, for example, the Jockey Club. The actions of Parliament are excluded: s 6(3). It is suggested that the test to ascertain whether a body is a public or private one gains assistance from the dicta in the ECJ jurisprudence: *Foster v British Gas* [1990] IRLR 353 (a body, whatever its legal form, which has been made responsible ... for providing a public service under the control of the State and has for that purpose special powers going beyond those which result from the normal rules applicable in relations between individuals) and *NUT v Governing Body of St Mary's Church of England (Aided) Junior School* [1997] IRLR 242 (Church of England voluntary aided school held to be a public body). A body which falls under the control of the State, directly or indirectly, or which has special statutory or other powers beyond those of a private individual is to be viewed as a public authority: also *Marshall v Southampton and SW Hampshire AHA* [1986] IRLR 140.

3   See *James v UK* (1986) Series A No 98, 8 EHRR 123, para 46.

jurisprudence (s 2 of the Act); they will require the decision-maker to reveal all relevant documents (subject to arguments that the documents are privileged or immunity applies to them) and to demonstrate that the Convention issues have been sufficiently addressed consistently with the Convention jurisprudence.

When the domestic court is faced, under s 6(1) of the Act, with an allegation that a public authority has acted in a way which is incompatible with one or more of the Convention rights then, depending on which rights are said to be violated, the court must, it is submitted, adopt a similar approach to the one adopted by the European Court in resolving the issue. The approach of a domestic court will depend on the subject matter before it with regard to the Convention rights. Some Convention rights are absolute by nature and others contain a degree of discretion. The degree of discretion varies according to the subject matter of the right. The courts, when scrutinising the alleged violations of the Convention rights, will examine the matter against the background of discretion involved (ie margin of appreciation). Judge Martens has perhaps summed up more accurately than most what the margin of appreciation is. States do not enjoy a margin of appreciation as a matter of right, but as a matter of judicial restraint. The European Court finds a violation only if it cannot reasonably be doubted that the acts or omissions of the State in question are incompatible with those engagements.[1] As will be shown below, the margin of appreciation varies according to the subject matter of the Convention engaged. Certain Convention rights allow for a less anxious scrutiny (wider margin of appreciation) whilst other rights allow for greater anxious scrutiny (narrower margin of appreciation). The areas of rights where the courts will subject decisions of public authorities to varying degrees and types of scrutiny are considered very briefly. Those rights which are absolute in nature will call for a greater scrutiny.

THE MARGIN OF APPRECIATION DEPENDS ON THE NATURE OF THE CONVENTION RIGHTS IN ISSUE

Margin of appreciation

1.21   The State's margin of appreciation is found in a number of the Articles in the Convention for example, Articles 2(2), 8(2), 9(2), 10(2), 11(2) and Article 1(2) of the First Protocol (Sch 1, Parts I and II, to the Act).[2] The margin of appreciation is relied upon by the defending authority (or State) when it seeks to justify its actions against an individual under one or more of the provisions set out thereunder where otherwise there would be an interference

---

1   *Cossey v UK* (1990) Series A No 184, 13 EHRR 622 at 652.

2   The English judge could not himself apply or have recourse to the doctrine of the margin of appreciation as implemented by the European Court. He must, however, recognise the impact of that doctrine upon the European Court's analysis of the meaning and implications of the broad terms of the Convention's provisions. Although the margin of appreciation doctrine did not appear to be expressly cited by the European Court in respect of criminal proceedings under Article 6, very similar expressions of policy had formed a part of the European Court's exposition of its role in respect of the rules of criminal procedure of the Member States: *R v Stratford Justices, ex parte Lambert* (1999) *The Times*, 25 February and *Aaidi v France* 17 EHRR 251.

with the person's fundamental rights provided for by the relevant Article. The European Court does not substitute its own judgment for that undertaken by national authorities, but will nevertheless examine, adopting principles formulated in the European Court's jurisprudence, the domestic courts' or authorities' decisions in reaching its own judgment. Depending on the subject matter of complaint the European Court will scrutinise each complaint with varying degrees of attention.[1] The margin of appreciation is a flexible doctrine which sets out, as part of its objective, to achieve a fair balance of justice with regard to the particular merits of each case against the background of the subject matter arising in each State.

ABSOLUTE NATURE OF THE CONVENTION

Articles 2 and 3

1.22   The use of the term 'absolutely necessary' in Article 2(2) indicates that a stricter and more compelling test of necessity must be employed from that normally applicable when determining whether State action is 'necessary in a democratic society' under para 2 of Articles 8 to 11 of the Convention. In particular, the force used must be strictly proportionate to the achievement of the aims set out in sub-paras 2(a), (b) and (c) of Article 2.[2]

Therefore, where an applicant suffering from AIDS claims that his expulsion from the UK constitutes a violation of Article 3 (degrading and inhuman treatment) on the grounds that his removal from the UK would severely reduce his life expectancy because there were no facilities available for the treatment of AIDS in the country to which he is to be removed, then it behoves the European Court to consider the 'absolute nature' of Article 3. In such a case, counter-arguments that immigration control overrides the 'absolute nature' of Article 3 is of little consequence and the European Court must have regard to the principles enshrined in Article 3 when considering the expulsion of such persons.[3] The European Court would be required to have serious regard to those matters existing in the AIDS victim's country before reaching a decision. Similarly, where there is an allegation that there is a violation of Article 2 (right to life) then the European Court would be required to follow the guidelines set out in the Convention jurisprudence: that the object and purpose of the Convention as an instrument for the protection of individual human beings requires that its provisions be interpreted and applied so as to make its safeguards practical and effective.[4] In cases such as these (Articles 2 and 3), the discretion of the domestic court is limited to the principles enshrined in the Convention jurisprudence. For example, where there is a violation of Article 3 the domestic court should interpret this Article as precluding the expulsion of

---

1   Convention rights are not equal. Some might be the subject of derogations: see *R v DPP, ex parte Kebilene and Others* (1999) *The Times*, 31 March and in the House of Lords at [2000] 1 UKHRR 1766.

2   *McCann v UK* (1996) Series A No 324, 21 EHRR 97 at 160, para 149.

3   *D v UK* (1997) 24 EHRR 423.

4   *McCann v UK* (1996) Series A No 324, 21 EHRR 97; *Andreas and Paraskevoula Andronicou and Others v Cyprus* Application No 25052/94.

a person (alien) to another State where that person faces a real risk of torture or inhuman treatment given the irreversible nature of the harm that might occur if the risk of ill-treatment materialised and the importance the European Court attaches to Article 3. In *Chahal*,[1] the European Court stated that prohibition provided by Article 3 against ill-treatment is equally absolute in expulsion cases. Thus, whenever substantial grounds have been shown for believing that an individual would face real risk of being subjected to treatment contrary to Article 3 if removed to another State, the responsibility of the State to safeguard him or her against such treatment is engaged in the event of expulsion. In these circumstances, the activities of the individual in question, however undesirable or dangerous, cannot be a material consideration. The protection afforded by Article 3 is thus wider than that provided under the 1951 Geneva Convention.[2] Article 13 of the Convention requires, in such instances, that there should be an independent scrutiny of the claim that substantial grounds exist for fearing a real risk of treatment contrary to Article 3. This scrutiny must be carried out without regard to what the person may have done to warrant expulsion or to any perceived threat to the national security of the expelling State.[3] The risk of harm an alien might suffer in the country to which he is to be removed is not merely a factor to be weighed in the balance against the public interest of immigration control, but is a prohibition against expulsion. It will not do to say that national security requires such a person to be expelled and the Court must review all the evidence relating to such a claim. As a matter of precedent fact the UK Court must be satisfied that there is no real risk of harm (contrary to Article 3) awaiting the deportee in the country to which he is being returned. If real risk of harm is found to exist then national security considerations cannot override the prohibition on expulsion. Thus, in *Cruz Varas v Sweden*,[4] where the European Court was concerned to examine the effect of deportation and whether there was a real risk of ill-treatment awaiting the aliens in the country to which they were being deported, the European Court's view was that its assessment of this risk must necessarily be a rigorous one but that the risk had to be assessed primarily with reference to the facts which were known or ought to have been known to the State concerned at the time of deportation.

In a private action in the county court or High Court, the courts will have the same obligation to try similar Convention issues with reference to Convention rights. For example, in a civil action against the police for assault or excessive force, the court will have to be satisfied that such force was strictly necessary in response to a detainee's conduct because physical force against a detainee amounts to both inhuman and/or degrading treatment and is in principle an infringement of Article 3.[5]

In cases concerning Article 2(2) of the Convention, the right to life is not violated when deprivation of life results from the use of force, which is no more

---

1   (1996) RJD 1996-V 1831, (1996) 23 EHRR 413, para 80.
2   *Chahal v UK* (1996) RJD 1996-V 1831, (1996) 23 EHRR 413, para 80.
3   Ibid; *Soering v UK* (1989) Series A No 52, 11 EHRR 439; *Vilvarajah v UK* (1991) Series A No 215, 14 EHRR 248.
4   (1991) Series A No 20, 14 EHRR 1.
5   *Ribitsch v Austria* (1996) Series A No 336, 21 EHRR 573.

than absolutely necessary in defence of any person from unlawful violence. When three IRA members were shot dead in Gibraltar by British soldiers who mistakenly, but honestly, believed that it was necessary to shoot them in order to prevent them from detonating a bomb and causing injury to people, the European Court stated that it considers that the use of force by agents of the State in pursuit of one of the aims delineated in Article 2(2) of the Convention may be justified under this provision where it is based on an honest belief, which is perceived for good reasons to be valid at the time, but which subsequently turns out to be mistaken. To hold otherwise would be to impose an unrealistic burden on the State and its law-enforcement personnel in the execution of their duty, perhaps to the detriment of their lives and those of others.[1]

NON-ABSOLUTE RIGHTS (MARGIN OF APPRECIATION)

Article 1 of the First Protocol (protection of property)

1.23   The margin of appreciation varies depending on the nature of the aim of the restriction and the subject matter of the right involved.[2] For example, where the aim of the restriction is to afford protection of public morals, an authority will enjoy a broad margin of appreciation or a broad sense of discretion.[3] When applying the margin of appreciation, the domestic courts will be required (as stated above) to look to Convention jurisprudence on the subject matter. If there is no agreement or consensus on a particular topic or on the substantive issue before it in the law of the other Member States which are signatories to the Convention, then the domestic court or authority will have a wider discretion or margin of appreciation. On the other hand, where there is found to be a consensus on a particular topic or issue amongst the Member States which are signatories to the Convention then a narrow band of discretion or margin of appreciation will apply. If no restrictions are found on a particular matter in other Member States, a court may well conclude that a restriction imposed by an authority is not justified or necessary in a democratic State. Practitioners therefore have to be aware of this utility principle of uniformity.[4] If the domestic court is out of step with the rest of the Member States in its approach to examining the restriction imposed by an authority on a fundamental right, then there would be scope to complain to the European Court that there is a breach of the Convention. Practitioners should be aware of the common ground between the law and practice of the Contracting States in

---

1   *McCann v UK* (1996) Series A No 324, 21 EHRR 97, paras 58–59.
2   *Gillow v UK* (1986) Series A No 109, 11 EHRR 335.
3   *Müller v Switzerland* (1988) Series A No 133, 13 EHRR 212.
4   *Sunday Times v UK* (1979–80) Series A No 30, 2 EHRR 245: the majority of the European Court expressed the view that the domestic law and practice of the Contracting States reveal a fairly substantial measure of common ground in this area which is, in respect of the necessary restrictions on freedom from repression, to protect the authority and impartiality of the judiciary. In *F v Switzerland* (1987) 10 EHRR 411 at 420, the European Court stated that the fact that, at the end of a gradual evolution, a country finds itself in an isolated position as regards one aspect of its legislation does not necessarily imply that that aspect offends the Convention, particularly in a field which is closely bound up with the cultural and historical traditions of that country.

order to determine whether a particular restriction under scrutiny is necessary or unnecessary in a democratic society.[1]

However, where a court is concerned with Article 1 of the First Protocol (peaceful enjoyment of his possessions) the enquiry is more or less similar to a *Wednesbury* test currently applied by the courts (failing to take into account relevant matters, etc; irrationality). Here the margin of appreciation is different to that of Articles 2 and 3. Article 1 of the First Protocol recognises the right of a State to enforce such laws as it deems it necessary to control the use of property with the general interest. Thus, only if the public authority's decision affecting an individual's property rights is 'manifestly without reasonable foundation' will it be unlawful.[2]

Article 3 of the First Protocol (right to free elections)

1.24 The HCPs undertake to hold free elections at reasonable intervals by secret ballot, under conditions which will ensure the free expression of the opinion of the people in the choice of the legislature. Article 3 applies both to domestic and European elections.[3]

The European Community is not an HCP. It is HCPs only to which Article 3 of the First Protocol applies. Thus, the UK is bound by the terms of Article 3 of the First Protocol.

The term 'legislature' in Article 3 of the First Protocol does not include only Parliament. The word is to be interpreted in the light of the constitutional structure of the State or body in question.[4] Regard must be had to the body's role in the overall legislative process.

Article 3 of the First Protocol possesses a characteristic of an effective political democracy and is one of the fundamental tools by which effective democracy is maintained.[5] The choice of electoral systems by which the free expression of the opinion of the people in the choice of legislature was ensured is a matter in which States enjoy a wide margin of appreciation.[6] To deny a person a right to vote to choose the legislature contravenes Article 3 of the First Protocol. The rights set out in Article 3 of the First Protocol are not absolute, but may be subject to limitations. The Contracting States enjoy a wide margin of appreciation in imposing conditions on the right to vote but it is for the domestic court in the last resort to determine whether the requirements of Article 3 of the First Protocol have been complied with. The courts have to be satisfied that:

---

1   In *Dudgeon v UK* (1981) Series A No 45, 4 EHRR 149 at 167 the European Court stated that there is now a better understanding, and in consequence an increased tolerance, of homosexual behaviour.
2   *James v UK* (1986) Series A No 98, 8 EHRR 123.
3   *Mathews v UK* Application No 24833/94, 28 EHRR 361, (1999) *The Times*, 3 March. The UK was held responsible for the lack of elections to the European Parliament in Gibraltar.
4   *Mathieu-Mohin and Clerfayt v Belgium* 2 March 1987, Series A No 113, p 23 at para 53. In *Mathews* (above) the European Court held that the European Parliament had the characteristics of a 'legislature' in Gibraltar.
5   *United Communists Party of Turkey and Others v Turkey* RJD 1998–1, 30 January 1998, pp 22–23 at para 45.
6   *Mathews* (above).

(a) the conditions imposed do not curtail the right to vote to such an extent as
     to impair its very essence and deprive it of its effectiveness;
(b) the restrictions imposed are in pursuit of a legitimate aim;
(c) the means employed are not disproportionate and that it must not
     frustrate the free expression of the people in the choice of the legislature.
     A resident of Gibraltar was therefore held to have been denied an
     opportunity to express her opinion in the choice of the members of the
     European Parliament.[1]

The subjective right to vote and to stand for election are not absolute since they
are not set down in express or defined terms and there was therefore scope for
limiting them. The restrictions imposed on local government officers to
contest seats at elections was justifiable because the regulations in question
were aimed at securing political impartiality and the restrictions operated only
so long as the officers held politically restricted posts. These officers were able
to resign from their posts if they wished to contest the elections and, therefore,
the restriction imposed on their right to stand for elections was legitimate and
did not constitute a violation of Article 3 of the First Protocol.[2]

Article 8 (right to respect for private and family life) and Article 10 (freedom of expression)

1.25 In relation to those provisions of the Convention which permit
interferences which are 'necessary in a democratic society', such as Articles
8(1) or 10 of the Convention, the European Court has utilised a more stringent
approach to the review of decisions taken at national levels. The European
Court has adopted the view that States possess a 'margin of appreciation' in
these contexts.[3] The scope of the margin of appreciation will vary according to
the circumstances, the subject matter and its background.[4] The domestic court
will usually ask itself the following questions:

(1) has there been an identified interference with the Convention right;
(2) if yes, is the interference 'prescribed by law';
(3) does the interference pursue a legitimate aim set out in the Article in
     question;
(4) is the interference identified necessary in a democratic society?

The court's task particularly with reference to breaches of Article 10(1) is best
revealed by having regard to a number of judgments including the judgment in
Observer and Guardian v UK:[5]

---

1   *Mathews* (above).
2   *Ahmed v UK* 5 BHRC 111.
3   Even having regard to the margin of appreciation left to the State, the Family Court
    concluded that Article 8 had not secured to the applicant the 'respect' for their family life
    to which they were entitled and that there was no obligation requiring the law to give
    unmarried fathers exactly the same rights as married fathers. There is a policy basis for
    suggesting that some differentiation between them has an objective and reasonable
    justification with regard to Articles 8 and 14: *In Re W (Minors) (Abduction: Father's Rights)*
    [1998] 3 WLR 1373 at 1393A–C and 1394A–C.
4   *Rasmussen v Denmark* (1984) Series A No 87, 7 EHRR 371, para 15.
5   (1991) Series A No 216, 14 EHRR 153; this judgment states that the exceptions in Article
    10(2) (freedom of expression) must be narrowly interpreted and their necessity
    convincingly established.

'The court's task, in exercising its supervisory jurisdiction, is not to take the place of competent national authorities but rather to review under Article 10 the decisions they delivered pursuant to their power of appreciation. This does not mean that the supervision is limited to ascertaining whether the respondent State exercised its discretion reasonably, carefully and in good faith; what the Court has to do is to look at the interference complained of in the light of the case as a whole and determine whether it was proportionate to the legitimate aim pursued and whether the reasons adduced by the national authorities to justify it are relevant and sufficient.'

In an earlier case, *Markt Intern*,[1] the European Court stated that the domestic court must confine its review to the question whether the measures taken on the national level are justifiable in principle and proportionate, and that the European Court should not substitute its own evaluation for that of the domestic courts in the instant case where those courts on reasonable grounds, had considered the restrictions to be necessary.

Finally, in *Oberschlick v Austria*,[2] the European Court remarked that its task has to be viewed in light of the principle that freedom of expression is one of the essential foundations of a democratic society. Furthermore, what is at stake are the limits of acceptable criticism in the context of public debate on a political question of general interest. In such cases, the European Court has to satisfy itself that the national authorities did apply standards which were in conformity with these principles and, moreover, that in doing so they based themselves on an acceptable assessment of the relevant facts.

The domestic courts may be prepared in some cases where there is a breach of Article 8(1) (respect for private life) not to make an enquiry whether the interference found was necessary in a democratic society. One such instance is where the domestic court makes a finding that, although lawful in domestic law, the interference resulting from the existence of the practice in question was not in accordance with the law under Article 8(1). In *Malone v UK*[3] (a case concerning the interception of telephone calls), the European Court cited with approval the general principles stated in *Silver v UK*[4] and *Sunday Times v UK*[5] and went on to state that a law which confers a discretion must indicate the scope of that discretion, although the detailed procedures and conditions to be observed do not necessarily have to be incorporated in the rules of substantive law. The degree of precision required of the law in this connection will depend upon the particular subject matter. Consequently, the law must indicate the scope of any such discretion conferred on the competent authorities and the manner of its exercise with sufficient clarity, having regard to the legitimate aim of the measure in question, to give the individual adequate protection against arbitrary interference. Undoubtedly, the existence of law granting powers of interception of communications to aid the police in their function of investigating and detecting crime may be necessary in a democratic society for the prevention of disorder or crime within the meaning of Article 8(2).

---

1   (1989) Series A No 1164 at 20, 12 EHRR 161.
2   (1991) Series A No 204, 19 EHRR 389.
3   (1984) 7 EHRR 14.
4   (1983) Series A No 61, 5 EHRR 347, para 85.
5   (1979) Series A No 30, 2 EHRR 245.

However, the exercise of such powers, because of its inherent secrecy, carries with it a danger of abuse of a kind which is potentially easy in individual cases and could have harmful consequences for democratic society as a whole. This being so, the resultant interference can be regarded as 'necessary in a democratic society' only if the particular system of secret surveillance adopted contains adequate guarantees against abuse.

In *Berrehab v The Netherlands*,[1] the European Court was concerned with a complaint whether the expulsion of an alien leading to the separation from his child and inhibiting contact between them amounted to a violation of their right to family life. The European Court stated that in determining whether an interference was 'necessary in a democratic society' the European Court makes allowance for the margin of appreciation that is left to the Contracting States. In this connection, it accepts that the Convention does not in principle prohibit the Contracting States from regulating the entry and length of stay of aliens. According to the established case-law of the European Court, 'necessity' implies that the interferences correspond to a pressing social need and, in particular, that it is proportionate to the legitimate aim pursued.

In *Piermont v France*,[2] the European Court was once more concerned to investigate a violation of Article 10(1). Having found that there was a violation of Article 10(1), the European Court stated that freedom of expression constitutes one of the essential foundations of a democratic society; one of the basic conditions for its progress. Subject to para 2 of Article 10, it is applicable not only to information or ideas which are favourably received or regarded as inoffensive or as a matter of indifference, but also to those which offend, shock or disturb. Freedom of political debate is undoubtedly not absolute in nature. A State may make it subject to certain restrictions or penalties, but it is for the European Court to give a final ruling on the compatibility of such measures with the freedom of expression enshrined in Article 10.

Article 11 (freedom of assembly and association)

1.26   In cases where there is a violation of Article 11, the European Court has applied the same principles as applied to Article 10 in construing the restrictions set out in Article 11(2). Notwithstanding its autonomous role and particular sphere of application, Article 11 must be also considered in the light of Article 10. The term 'restrictions' found in Articles 10(2) and 11(2) are to be interpreted similarly.[3]

Needless to say that, when Convention rights are raised in legal proceedings, it will be a defence for a person to show that he was acting in accordance with the Convention rights or derogations. Thus, if a person alleges that his private rights have been infringed under Article 8, the public authority may argue by way of defence that the act in question was 'necessary' to pursue one of the aims permitted by Article 8(2), which include the rights and freedoms of others, including Convention rights. So, for example, the public authority may say that it acted in accordance with Article 10(1) of the Convention (freedom of

---

1   (1988) Series A No 138, 11 EHRR 322, para 27.
2   (1995) Series A No 314, 20 EHRR 301 at 340, para 76.
3   *Ezelin v France* (1991) Series A No 202, 14 EHRR 362 at 386, paras 37–40.

expression). The UK court may then have to look beyond Article 8, for example, to Articles 9 or 10. In this kind of situation where two Articles are in tension the court will not state that the actions by the public authority are in accordance with Article 10, but it is suggested that the courts will say, after carrying out a balancing exercise between these two Articles, whether there is or is not a breach of Article 8. This approach finds itself commendable to the terms of Article 17 of the Convention which provides that:

> 'Nothing in this Convention may be interpreted as implying for any State, group or person any right to engage in any activity or perform any act aimed at the destruction of any of the rights and freedoms set forth herein or at their limitation to a greater extent than is provided for in the Convention.'

Article 17 (prohibition of abuse of rights)

1.27 Article 17, therefore, points the way forward that the courts should undertake a kind of balancing exercise to adjudicate whether the alleged infringement of a Convention right has or has not occurred. It is not the case of two litigants each asserting that their Convention rights have been breached. It is suggested that the balancing is to be carried out principally in the context on which the claimant bases his claim. Thus, in an Article 8 or Article 10 complaint, the court will determine the issue whether there is or is not an infringement within the context of the issue which has been raised. An example is that, if a claimant asserts that the BBC has televised something about his private rights, the courts, in deciding between the forces of Article 8(1) and Article 10, will resolve the issue by considering whether Article 8 has been infringed by taking into account the derogation contained in Article 8(2). Clearly, there is a need for different balancing exercises to be done by the courts in different claims. Thus, the right of education guaranteed by the first sentence of Article 2 calls for the regulation by the State, but this must not injure the substances of the right or conflict with other rights enshrined in the Convention. Therefore, a condition of access to an education establishment which conflicts with another right under the First Protocol cannot be described as reasonable and falls outside the State's power of regulation.[1]

In respect of Article 11 (freedom of assembly), the European Court has stated that it is the duty of Contracting States to take reasonable and appropriate measures to enable lawful demonstrations to proceed peacefully. They cannot guarantee this absolutely and they have a discretion as to the choice of the means to be used. In this area, the responsibility of States is an obligation as to measures to be taken and not as to the results to be achieved. Hence, there is a wide discretion given to States when imposing restrictions on the exercise of the right of freedom of assembly.[2]

Article 5 (right to liberty and security)

1.28 Article 5(1)(c) contains an element of discretion. This discretion is expressed in language familiar to courts in the UK namely arrests on grounds of 'reasonable suspicion' of having committed an offence or where it is reasonably

---

1   *Campbell and Cosans v UK* (1982) Series A No 48, 4 EHRR 293, para 41.
2   *Platform 'Ärzte für das Leben' v Austria* (1988) Series A No 139, 13 EHRR 204, paras 34–38.

considered necessary to prevent the commission of an offence. These provisions are no different to those found in the Police and Criminal Evidence Act 1984 (PACE 1984). The European Court has emphasised repeatedly that whether detention can be considered 'reasonable' must be assessed in each case according to its special features. Continued detention can be justified in a given case only if there are specific indications of a genuine requirement of public interest which, notwithstanding the presumption of innocence, out-weighs the rule of respect for individual liberty.[1] Furthermore, the European Court has construed the term 'promptly' in Article 5(3) narrowly. Thus, everyone so arrested shall be brought promptly before a judge.[2]

Article 6 (right to a fair trial)

1.29   In cases involving alleged breaches of Article 6, the European Court has rarely invoked the doctrine of margin of appreciation. The European Court has stated in cases before it that it is for the domestic courts to determine for themselves, for example, the procedure adopted in their own domestic courts. What is essential is that parties should be able to participate properly in the proceedings before the 'tribunal'. Moreover, the Convention does not lay down rules of evidence as such. It is for the domestic courts to assess the evidence they have obtained and the relevance of any evidence that a party wishes to have produced. The European Court is more concerned as to whether the proceedings as a whole, including the way in which the evidence was taken, are fair as required by Article 6(1).[3] The requirement of fairness does not necessarily require the same treatment in civil cases as in criminal cases.[4]

Article 2 of the First Protocol (right to education)

1.30   The discretion given to local authorities under Article 2 of the First Protocol is a wide one. The European Court has stated that it is not for it to rule on the expediency of educational methods, and thus the setting and planning of the curricula fall within the competence of the authorities, but the penalty of suspension from school cannot be regarded as an exclusively educational measure and may have some psychological impact on the pupil on whom it is imposed. It appears, therefore, that as far as school discipline is concerned, the domestic court will have a wider margin of appreciation with regard to examining its reasonableness than in relation to examining school curricula.[5]

Although individual interests must on occasions be subordinated to those of a group, democracy does not simply mean that the views of a majority must always

---

1   *Scott v Spain* RJD 1996-VI 2382, (1997) 24 EHRR 391, para 74.
2   *Brogan and Others v UK* (1988) Series A No 145-B, 11 EHRR 117.
3   *Schenk v Switzerland* (1991) Series A No 140, 13 EHRR 242, para 46; *Mantovanelli v France* (1997) 24 EHRR 370, para 34.
4   *Beheer v The Netherlands* (1993) Series A No 274/3; *R v Secretary of State for Trade and Industry, ex parte McCormick* (1998) *The Times*, 10 February, CA.
5   *Valsamis v Greece* RJD 1996-VI 2312, (1996) 24 EHRR 294, para 28; *Campbell and Cosans v UK* (1982) Series A No 48, 4 EHRR 293, paras 33–35.

prevail; a balance must be achieved, which ensures the fair and proper treatment of minorities and avoids any abuse of a dominant position.[1]

REMEDIES

Damages

1.31 A domestic court which grants a declaration that primary legislation is incompatible with the Convention may not be able to award damages or grant a remedy to the individual complainant unless s 8 of the Act is applicable. It is to be hoped, however, that in such circumstances individuals so affected would qualify for ex gratia payments from the relevant Government Minister under the prerogative power and that in criminal cases convictions would be quashed as a consequence of declarations of incompatibility.

Section 8(1) of the Act provides that in relation to any act (or proposed act) of a public authority which the court finds is (or would be) unlawful, it may grant such relief or remedy, or make such order, within its jurisdiction as it considers just and appropriate. According to the Government, this section has the 'widest amplitude' and is wide enough to do the job in that it is capable of providing all the equitable remedies necessary to meet the Convention obligations. The 'courts are rich in remedies and have every freedom under' s 8 of the Act, which gives the court ample scope for implementing justice when unlawful acts are committed.

It is to be remembered that Article 1 of the Convention provides that the HCPs shall secure to everyone within their jurisdiction the rights and freedoms defined in Section I of the Convention. Section I then stipulates the Convention rights including that, under Article 13, everyone whose rights and freedoms set forth in this Convention are violated shall have an effective remedy before a national authority, notwithstanding that the violation has been committed by persons acting in an official capacity.

As previously stated, Article 13 notably has been omitted from the Act. The House of Lords has previously taken into account Article 13 in its judgment and has stated that this Article requires that the law of the UK must provide an effective remedy for any breach of the Convention rights.[2] In *Chahal*, the European Court stated that Article 13 guarantees the availability at a national level of a remedy to enforce the substance of the Convention rights and freedoms in whatever form they happen to be secured in the domestic legal order. The effect of this Article is thus to require the provision of a domestic remedy allowing the competent national authority both to deal with the substance of the relevant Convention complaint and to grant appropriate relief.[3]

---

1   *Young, James and Webster v UK* (1981) Series A No 44, 4 EHRR 38, para 63; and *Valsamis v Greece* RJD 1996-VI 2312, (1996) 24 EHRR 294, para 27.
2   See *R v Khan* [1996] 3 WLR 162 at 165B, HL.
3   *Chahal v UK* (1996) RJD 1996-V 1831, (1996) 23 EHRR 413.

The suggested view is that when s 8 of the Act is in play, the domestic court should and must take into account Article 13. The Government has stated that it has not the slightest idea what remedies the courts might develop outside s 8 if Article 13 was included. Therefore, it is arguable that where a declaration of incompatibility is made concerning, for example, the Convention rights of an alien who is the subject of a deportation order or expulsion order, then that alien may well argue that although the declaration is not binding (s 4(6) of the Act), nevertheless, under Article 13, combined with other Articles if applicable, he should not be removed from the UK until and unless the relevant Minister considers the declaration of incompatibility.

In awarding damages, the court may do so only if it has the power to award damages or to order compensation in civil proceedings. Therefore, s 8 does not extend payment of damages in criminal proceedings. However, it remains to be seen in what circumstances the criminal courts, when exercising their powers to award compensation,[1] will take into account Article 13 and the principles of 'just satisfaction'. No award of damages is to be made unless, taking account of all the circumstances of the case, including any other relief or remedy granted, or order made, in relation to the act in question (by that or any other court), and the consequences of any decision (of that or any other court) in respect of that act and the court is satisfied that the award is necessary to afford *just satisfaction* to the person in whose favour it is made. The Government has made it clear that the aim is for people to receive damages equivalent to what they would have obtained had they taken their case to the European Court.

The European Court has applied previous Article 50 (as replaced by the Eleventh Protocol) to award compensation to successful candidates in the following situations:

(1) damages for pecuniary losses;
(2) non-pecuniary losses.

Previous Article 50 of the Convention provided:

> 'If the Court finds that a decision or a measure taken by a legal authority or any other authority of a High Contracting Party is completely or partially in conflict with the obligations arising from the present Convention, and if the internal law of the said Party allows only partial reparation to be made for the consequences of this decision or measure, the decision of the Court shall, if necessary, afford just satisfaction to the injured party.'

In awarding damages for pecuniary losses, the European Court has usually awarded damages where there is proved a violation of a substantive Convention right.[2] Where there is a breach of some procedural Convention right, the European Court has been reluctant to award damages.[3] In some cases, the European Court has awarded non-pecuniary compensation where there has been extremely serious violation of the Convention and where anxiety and

---

1   For example, see s 35 of the Powers of the Criminal Courts Act 1973.
2   Compensation for damage to real property: *Henritch v France* (1995) 21 EHRR 199; *López Ostra v Spain* (1994) Series A No 303-C, 20 EHRR 277.
3   The European Court refused to award compensation where a fine was imposed by an administrative body exercising a criminal jurisdiction in contravention of Article 6: *Schmautzer v Austria* (1995) Series A No 328-A, 21 EHRR 511.

distress was suffered[1] not only by the victim but by the parents of the victim, for example where the father has continued with the case after his son's (the victim) death.[2]

In cases where the applicants have been convicted of serious criminal offences, the European Court has been reluctant to award damages. Thus, where an applicant sought compensation at a rate of £30,000 per annum for what he considered had been an unnecessary and unjustified period of detention, the European Court did not award damages for this period of detention. The European Court noted that the applicant's extradition was granted on condition that the time spent in prison pending extradition was deducted from the sentence that would eventually be imposed by the English courts. No evidence had been adduced before the European Court to suggest that the UK authorities would not honour that condition. The European Court went on to award legal costs and expenses and the statutory rate of interest in force in the UK.[3] With regard to injury, although the European Court could not speculate on the outcome of a trial where there had been no violation of the Convention, it was not unreasonable to consider that the applicant had suffered a loss of opportunities, for which compensation should be assessed on an equitable basis.[4]

Recently, the High Court in *R v Ministry of Agriculture Fisheries and Food, ex parte Lower Burytown Farms Ltd and the National Farmers Union and Ors*[5] awarded simple interest on sums due in circumstances where the Ministry had delayed in making payments to the applicants. The High Court accepted that sums due amounted to a debt owed under statute and that interest was payable under s 35A(1) of the Supreme Court Act 1981. This approach is no different in principle from that adopted by the European Court where the applicant claimed interest on the late payment of an invalidity pension which had been denied to her contrary to the Convention rights (Article 6, para 1 and Article 14). The European Court awarded her pecuniary damages representing the interest on late payments.[6]

There is clearly scope for claiming damages where breach of the Convention rights is established. The domestic court must take into account the principles applied by the European Court in relation to the award of compensation.[7] It

---

1   Damages were awarded on an 'equitable basis' for non-pecuniary injury because the applicants had for a long time suffered substantial anxiety and distress as a result of the violations of Article 6 and Article 8: *Eriksson v Sweden* (1989) Series A No 156, 12 EHRR 183 at 208, para 97.
2   *Aksoy v Turkey* RJD 1996-VI 2260, (1996) 23 EHRR 553 at 596, para 113. See also: *Papamichalopoulos v Greece* (1995) 21 EHRR 439 where the European Court awarded £1,000 per applicant as compensation for anxiety and distress because of an official's failure to comply with the Convention rights; and see *Hokkanen v Finland* (1994) Series A No 299-A, 19 EHRR 139. For a detailed discussion, see 'The European Court of Human Rights' Approach to Just Satisfaction' Alastair Mowbray [1997] PL 647.
3   *Scott v Spain* RJD 1996-VI 2382, (1996) 24 EHRR 391, paras 86–91; also see *Pelladhoah v The Netherlands* (1994) 19 EHRR 81; *Bunkate v The Netherlands* (1993) EHRR 97.
4   *Delta v France* (1990) 16 EHRR 574.
5   1998, unreported CO/8/95; CO/956/95.
6   *Schuler-Zgraggen v Switzerland* (1995) 21 EHRR 404.
7   Section 8(4) of the Act.

will remain to be seen whether, in judicial review proceedings, damages for violation of Convention rights will be awarded or whether the courts will restrict the award of damages. Under RSC Ord 53, r 7 an applicant for judicial review may claim damages if they are sought in the filed statement and if damages could have been awarded in an action brought for the purposes.[1] Currently, there is no general right to indemnity by reason of damage suffered through invalid administrative action or for breach of rules.[2] Whether the courts will entertain a claim for damages for anxiety and distress brought about by breach of Convention rights is uncertain. Non-pecuniary damages for unlawful detection is available.[3]

A finding of a breach of Article 7 (retroactive criminal penalty) constitutes in itself a sufficient just satisfaction.[4]

There might be scope for arguing that, in the absence of a remedial clause, a claim for damages could be brought against the State for violation of human rights which the State guarantees so far as the actions of the officials of the State are involved. For example, whether a Clerk to the Justices is exempt from liability in the event of an individual suffering damage from official court maladministration may arise for consideration under the Act.[5] Similarly, if a person suffers loss as a consequence of relying on a decision from a Government official whose actions (misfeasance apart) are *ultra vires* then there is no reason why compensation from the State should not be available if such actions violate the person's fundamental rights. After all, the Parliamentary Commissioner for Administration has awarded individuals compensation in a number of such cases.[6] Where fundamental rights are violated as a result of official actions amounting to a breach of statutory duty causing loss to an aggrieved individual, then it may be possible to argue that the breach of statutory duty does create a private right of action for damages. The conventional test adumbrated in domestic law to determine whether breach of statutory duty does give rise to damages may have to be revisited applying principles found in European Court jurisprudence.[7] Thus, Article 1 of the First

---

1   See *Chief Constable of the North Wales Police v Evans* [1982] 1 WLR 1155, at 1175H.
2   See *R v Secretary of State for Transport, ex parte Factortame and Others (No 2)* [1991] 1 AC 603, at 672H; and *R v Deputy Governor of Parkhurst Prison, ex parte Hague* [1992] 1 AC 58.
3   *Quinn v France* 21 EHRR 529, para 64. In *Aydin v Turkey* (1998) 25 EHRR 251, the applicant was awarded a substantial sum (about £25,000) for a violation of Article 3 (raped whilst in police custody).
4   *Jamil v France* (1995) 21 EHRR 65 at 81, paras 38–39.
5   Damages however, may not be awarded in proceedings under this Act in respect of any act of a court: see s 9(3), (4). Quaere: is the administrative act of a court official an 'act of court' and is it immune from civil proceedings under s 9(4)? In a Privy Council case the court held that the State was directly liable for the acts of a judge, not on the basis of vicarious liability: *Maharaj v A-G of Trinidad and Tobago (No 2)* [1979] AC 385. This case was applied in *Simpson v A-G* (Baigent's case) [1994] 3 LRC 202: a claim for compensation could be made against the Government of New Zealand under the New Zealand Bill of Rights even though there was no specific provision for damages in the Bill (the Court stated that 'we would fail in our duty if we did not give an effective remedy to a person whose legitimately affirmed rights have been violated').
6   For an interesting discussion on compensation, see Wade and Forsyth *Administrative Law* 7th edn (Clarendon Press, 1994) at p 376.
7   *X v Bedfordshire CC* [1995] 3 WLR 152.

Protocol (no one shall be deprived of his possessions except in the public interest) allows the State a wide margin of appreciation to justify legislation interfering with property rights.[1] Whether an action based on nuisance in common law against the lawful exercise of statutory powers where a fundamental right has been violated may result in damages on Convention principles will have to arise for consideration.

There may also be scope for arguing that the Government can be sued as being responsible for legislation which contravenes fundamental rights guaranteed by the Convention even if, for example, the Government is not the employer of a complainant[2] or responsible for the direct act which gives rise to the complaint. Under Article 1 of the Convention, each Contracting State 'shall secure to everyone within their jurisdiction the rights and freedoms defined in Section I of this Convention'. Hence, if a violation of one of those rights and freedoms is the result of non-observance of that obligation in the enactment of domestic legislation, the responsibility of the State for that violation is engaged.[3]

It is beyond the aim of this book to deal with the detailed and multifarious claims for damages which may be brought by an individual against the State or public authority when his fundamental rights under the Convention are violated.[4]

The court may also grant declarations that an applicant's Convention rights have been violated where such decisions are based on statutory provisions, or administrative decisions which are based on policies including prerogative policies. The terms of the declaration would clarify the status of the applicant although it would not affect the 'validity, continuing operation or enforcement of the provision in respect of which it is given', and although it is not binding on the parties to the proceedings in which it is made.[5] It is possible to argue that the declaration of incompatibility of an administrative decision (policies) with Convention rights as opposed to statutory provisions being incompatible with a Convention right is binding on parties and alternatively invalid. Such an

---

1   The Government was able to justify the absence of compensation under the Leasehold Reform Act 1967 to those individuals whose property interests were expropriated because Article 1 of the First Protocol allowed the Government sufficiently wide discretion to justify the legislation: *James v UK* (1986) Series A No 98, 8 EHRR 123.
2   Applicants who were dismissed fairly for refusing to join a union on grounds of personal conviction (not on religious grounds which was an exception contained in the legislation) complained that under the old unfair dismissal law their dismissal violated Article 11 (freedom of association). The European Court held that the law as it stood in 1976 violated the applicant's freedom of association guaranteed by Article 11. The Government was responsible for the legislation and could be sued and that it was not necessary to decide if it was also liable as an indirect employer of the applicants: *Young, James and Webster v UK* [1981] IRLR 408, ECHR (merits); [1983] IRLR 35, ECHR (compensation). As a result of this judgment, the Government made provision for a retrospective compensation out of public funds for those applicants who were unfairly dismissed on the grounds of the closed shop agreement between 1974 and 1980.
3   *Young, James and Webster* (above), para 49.
4   See generally *Maharaj v A-G of Trinidad and Tobago* [1997] AC 385.
5   Section 4(6)(a) of the Act.

argument may extend to decisions based on prerogative powers or extra-statutory powers. The usual rule concerning decisions whether the decision-maker has exceeded the margin of appreciation the human rights context is out in *R v Ministry of Defence, ex parte Smith*;[1] the more substantial the interference with human rights, the more the court will require by way of justification before it is satisfied that the decision is reasonable in the sense that it may not interfere with the exercise of an administrative discretion on substantive grounds save where the court is satisfied that the decision is unreasonable (*Wednesbury* reasonableness). However, the courts are no longer, as stated above, confined to this type of examination. Furthermore, it is also arguable that a declaration of incompatibility of an administrative decision gives rise to damages. Consequently, where the prospective loss which may be caused by an order is pecuniary, the applicant may be compensated if necessary.[2] The ordinary rules would apply requiring the applicant to plead and establish his loss.

---

1   [1996] 2 WLR 305, at 336D-E; *R v Secretary of State for the Home Department, ex parte Bentley* [1993] 4 All ER 442.
2   *Hoffman-La Roche v Secretary of State for Trade and Industry* [1975] AC 295, para 395B as per Lord Wilberforce (dissenting).

PART 2

THE ARTICLES OF THE CONVENTION AS CONTAINED IN THE SCHEDULE TO THE HUMAN RIGHTS ACT 1998 ANALYSED

ARTICLE 2 – RIGHT TO LIFE

2.1   *'Article 2*

Right to life

1.   Everyone's right to life shall be protected by law. No one shall be deprived of his life intentionally save in the execution of a sentence of a court following his conviction of a crime for which this penalty is provided by law.

2.   Deprivation of life shall not be regarded as inflicted in contravention of this Article when it results from the use of force which is no more than absolutely necessary:

   (a)   in defence of any person from unlawful violence;

   (b)   in order to effect a lawful arrest or to prevent the escape of a person lawfully detained;

   (c)   in action lawfully taken for the purpose of quelling a riot or insurrection.'

Article 2 enshrines the right which forms the foundation of all other human rights; one which, if left unprotected, would render all other protected rights nugatory.

THE GENERAL OBLIGATIONS OF THE HIGH CONTRACTING PARTIES

2.2   The supremacy of the right is confirmed by the fact that it is non-derogable, even in times of national emergency.[1] The only exceptions to the otherwise absolute protection offered by Article 2 are found in the text of the Article itself.[2]

The first sentence of para 1 imposes a broader obligation on a High Contracting Party (HCP) than that contained in the second sentence. The words 'everyone's right to life shall be protected by law' enjoins an HCP not only to refrain from taking life in a manner contrary to Article 2, but also to take 'appropriate steps to safeguard life'.[3] Therefore, in order to satisfy the first sentence of para 1, an HCP must have in place laws which adequately protect citizens from interference with their right to life so that, for instance, an HCP who does not criminalise murder would be in breach. To adequately protect against the taking of life, legal safeguards must be 'practical and effective'.[4]

In certain circumstances, there can also be a duty on an HCP to take 'positive action' to protect life.[5] That does not mean, however, that an HCP will automatically be in breach of Article 2 merely by reason of the fact that a citizen

---

1   Article 15(2). Although derogation during times of war is also generally prohibited, Article 15(2) limits the prohibition to acts which are not 'lawful acts of war'.

2   See below.

3   *X v UK* Application No 7154/75, (1978) 14 DR 31 at 32; *Naddaf v FRG* Application No 11604/85, (1986) 50 DR 259; *H v Norway* (1992) 73 DR 155 at 167.

4   *Soering v UK* (1989) Series A No 161, 11 EHRR 439; *Loizidou v Turkey* (1995) 20 EHRR 439; *McCann v UK* (1996) Series A No 324, 21 EHRR 97, para 146.

5   *X v FRG* Application No 10565/83, (1985) 7 EHRR 152 at 153.

has been killed; there is no positive obligation on an HCP to exclude *all possible* forms of violence.[1]

Effective investigation of death

2.3 A general legal prohibition of arbitrary killing would, however, be ineffective in practice if there existed no procedure for reviewing the lawfulness of the lethal force used. The obligation under Article 2 to protect life, read in conjunction with an HCP's general duty under Article 1,[2] requires by implication that not only should there be some form of investigation when individuals have been killed, but also that the investigation should be 'effective' and 'official'.[3] Such an investigation should include a mechanism whereby the circumstances of the death may receive 'public and independent scrutiny'.[4] This last requirement cannot be dispensed with, however, merely because of the prevalence of violent armed clashes or high incidence of fatalities in the HCP's territory.[5] Moreover, an HCP's obligation to carry out an effective investigation into a killing is not confined only to those cases where the killing is alleged to have been caused by an agent of the HCP but also extends to cases where there is 'mere knowledge' of a killing on the part of an HCP.[6]

Intent

2.4 The text of Article 2 is of only limited assistance as to whether a recognised breach requires the offender or offenders to have intended death. Although the second sentence of para 1 expressly prohibits the intentional deprivation of life, the remainder of Article 2 does not clarify whether acts resulting in unintentional death can *never* amount to a breach. The European Court[7] and the Commission[8] have, however, confirmed that the sphere of protection afforded by Article 2 goes beyond the intentional deprivation of life. The enumerated exceptions found in Article 2 do not primarily define the situations where it is permitted intentionally to kill an individual, but rather define the situations where it is permissible to use force which may result, as an unintentional outcome, in the deprivation of life.[9] Assistance for this interpretation has been derived from the fact that the three exclusions found in para 2

---

1   *W v UK* Application No 9348/81, (1983) 32 DR 190 at 200.
2   Article 1 requires HCPs to 'secure to everyone within their jurisdiction the rights and freedoms defined in [the] Convention'.
3   *McCann v UK* (1996) Series A No 324, 21 EHRR 97, para 161; *Kaya v Turkey* (1999) 28 EHRR 1 paras 78, 86; *Ergi v Turkey* Application No 2381/94, para 82; *Yasa v Turkey* (1999) 28 EHRR 408, para 96.
4   *McCann v UK* (above), para 193; *Kaya v Turkey* (1999) 28 EHRR 1, para 87.
5   *Kaya v Turkey* (above), para 91.
6   *Ergi v Turkey* Application No 2381/94, para 82.
7   *McCann v UK* (1996) (above), para 148.
8   *X v UK* (1978) 14 DR 31, at 32; *Stewart v UK* Application No 10044/82, (1984) 39 DR 162 at 170, para 15. In *Stewart v UK*, in the course of finding that Article 2 had not been breached, the Commission rejected the defendant State's suggestion that, as the applicant had been killed by a stray (as opposed to a directed) plastic bullet, Article 2 could not be said to have been breached.
9   *Stewart v UK* Application No 10044/82, (1984) 39 DR 162 at 170, para 15.

do not, unlike the single exclusion found in the second sentence of para 1, refer to 'intentionally' taking life.[1]

Planning and execution of operations by the police and security forces

2.5 In assessing whether Article 2 has been breached, bodies will take into account not only the actions of the agents of the HCP who actually administer the force, but also all the surrounding circumstances including such matters as the planning and control of the actions under examination.[2] An HCP can, therefore, be held accountable under Article 2 for deaths which follow a police or military operation which was unsafe or improperly planned.[3] An HCP must ensure that the operation is planned and controlled and that the relevant participants in the operation receive sufficient information and instruction so as to 'minimise, to the greatest extent possible, recourse to lethal force'.[4] 'Feasible precautions' have to be taken by the HCP when choosing the means and methods of a security operation so as to avoid and, in any event, minimise incidental loss of civilian life.[5] A policy of 'shooting to kill' in preference to the inconvenience of resorting to the procedures of criminal justice would, for instance, be a 'flagrant violation' of Article 2.[6]

EXCEPTIONS

2.6 The text of Article 2 provides four exceptions to the otherwise absolute protection it provides for life: the first exception is found in the second sentence of para 1 (execution ordered by a criminal court) and the remaining three exceptions (self-defence or defence of others; arrest and prevention of escape; quelling of riots or insurrection) are enumerated in para 2. These situations, being exceptions to a fundamental human right, are 'exhaustive and must be narrowly interpreted'.[7]

'Absolutely necessary'

2.7 Paragraph (2) of Article 2 permits the use of force for the purposes enumerated in sub-paras (a) to (c) provided the force is 'absolutely necessary'. The use of the term 'absolutely necessary' indicates that a stricter and more compelling test of necessity must be employed than that normally applicable when determining whether an HCP's action is 'necessary in a democratic society' under para 2 of each of Articles 8 to 11 of the Convention.[8] Any force used, however, must be 'strictly proportionate to the achievement of the

---

1   *Stewart v UK* Application No 10044/82, (1984) 39 DR 162 at 170, para 15.
2   *McCann v UK* (1996) Series A No 324, 21 EHRR 97, para 150; *Andronicou and Constantinou v Cyprus* (1998) 25 EHRR 491.
3   See, for example, *Ergi v Turkey* Application No 2381/94.
4   *McCann v UK* (1996) Series A No 324, 21 EHRR 97, paras 194 and 201.
5   *Ergi v Turkey* (above), para 79.
6   *McCann v UK* (above).
7   *Stewart v UK* Application No 10044/82, (1984) 39 DR 162 at 169, para 13; *Kelly v UK* Application No 17579/90, (1993) 74 DR 139 at 145.
8   *McCann v UK* (1996) Series A No 324, 21 EHRR 97, para 149.

permitted purpose'.[1] In assessing whether the force used was 'strictly pro-portionate', regard must be had to all the circumstances surrounding the deprivation of life and, in particular, 'the nature of the aim pursued, the dangers to life and limb inherent in the situation and the degree of risk that the force employed might result in the loss of life'.[2]

The fact, however, that the domestic law of an HCP imposes a test which, at least on its face, seems to be more lenient than the 'absolutely necessary' test (for instance, 'reasonably justifiable') will not automatically result in a finding that the Convention's standard has not been met.[3]

Capital punishment

2.8 Although Article 2 permits the taking of life in execution of a criminal sentence, such a sentence must presumably be proportionate to the particular crime concerned, so that a sentence of death for theft of a motor vehicle would be in breach of Article 2 despite the wording of the Article. However, this exception has to some extent been superseded by the Sixth Protocol to the Convention. Not all HCPs have, however, ratified the Protocol which requires the abolition of the death penalty other than in time of war or imminent threat of war. The death penalty was abolished for all civilian crimes other than treason and piracy. The Crime and Disorder Act 1998 has now abolished this. Furthermore, although a sentence of death may not constitute a breach of Article 2 in cases where the relevant HCP has not ratified the Sixth Protocol, there may nevertheless be a breach of Article 3.[4]

Defence

2.9 By virtue of Article 2(2)(a), an HCP is permitted to use force in order to defend a citizen or its citizens from imminent 'unlawful violence' provided the force used is 'no more than absolutely necessary'. The word 'person' clearly excludes from the ambit of the exception force used to protect property. There is very little case-law relating to para 2(a) and an HCP has not, as of yet, been found to have been in breach of it.[5]

Arrest and escape

2.10 Force can be used to 'lawfully arrest' a person or to 'prevent the escape of a person lawfully detained'.

In deciding whether the force used to effect arrest or escape was absolutely necessary, the Commission and the European Court will take both an objective and, to a limited extent, a subjective approach. The belief of the offender will, therefore, be relevant, particularly if that belief was genuinely and reasonably held.[6]

---

1   *McCann v UK* (1996) Series A No 324, 21 EHRR 97, para 149. *Stewart v UK* Application No 10044/82, (1984) 39 DR 162 at 171, para 19.
2   *Stewart v UK* Application No 10044/82, (1984) 39 DR 162 at 171, para 19.
3   *McCann v UK* (1986) Series A No 324, 21 EHRR 97; *Kelly v UK* Application No 17579/90, (1993) 74 DR 139.
4   See further at **2.33**.
5   See *McCann v UK* (1986) Series A No 324, 21 EHRR 97 and *Woolfgram v FRG* Application No 11257/84, (1986) 49 DR 213.
6   *Kelly v UK* Application No 1759/90, (1993) 74 DR 139.

As yet, there have been no decisions relating to the prevention of escape.

Riot or insurrection

2.11   Article 2(2)(c) permits force to be used to quell a riot or insurrection.

No definition or elucidation of the term 'riot' has been provided so far, save for the finding that an assembly of 150 people throwing missiles at a patrol of soldiers to the point that they risked serious injury constituted, 'by any standard', a riot.[1]

For this exception to apply, the force used must not only have been 'absolutely necessary'[2] but also have been lawfully applied.[3]

RELEVANT FIELDS OF APPLICATION

Prisoners

2.12   As noted above, in addition to a negative duty not to take life, HCPs have a duty to take 'positive action'[4] to safeguard life. An HCP has a particular obligation to take active measures to save life when it has taken a person into its custody.[5] This has raised difficult questions in circumstances where a prisoner has gone on hunger strike. Where a prisoner maintains such a strike and the HCP wishes to force-feed the prisoner in order to keep him alive, a conflict arises between his right to physical integrity and the HCP's obligations under Article 2 of the Convention. The Convention itself has not provided a solution to this conflict. Factors which are relevant in such cases seem to include whether the HCP acted 'solely in the best interests of the applicant' and the length of period during which the prisoner was force-fed.[6] In its attempts to force-feed a prisoner, however, an HCP must not 'subject an applicant to more constraint than necessary' to achieve the goal of securing his health or saving his life.[7]

Abortion and the rights of the unborn child

2.13   It is still not clear whether the termination of an unborn child's life can amount to a breach of Article 2. The words 'everyone' and 'life' in Article 2 have been found, by their very nature, to concern persons already born and cannot therefore be interpreted as providing an 'absolute right of the foetus'.[8] That

---

1   *Stewart v UK* Application No 10044/82, (1984) 39 DR 162 at 172.
2   See *Gulec v Turkey* (1999) 28 EHRR 121, where firing live ammunition at a demonstration, albeit not a peaceful demonstration, was held not to be 'absolutely necessary'.
3   See *X v Belgium* Application No 2758/66, (1969) 12 YB 174 where Article 2(2)(c) was found not to apply because the police officer who had fired live bullets at an innocent bystander did not have authorisation under Belgian law to use his firearm and, consequently, the force had not been applied 'lawfully'.
4   See above (ie *X v UK* Application No 7154/75, (1978) 14 DR 31; *Naddaf v FRG* Application No 11604/85, 50 DR 259; *H v Norway* (1992) 73 DR 155; and *X v FRG* Application No 10565/83, (1985) 7 EHRR 152).
5   *X v FRG* Application No 10565/83, (1985) 7 EHRR 152 at 153.
6   Ibid at 154.
7   Ibid.
8   *X v UK* Application No 8416/79, (1980) 19 DR 244 at 250, paras 8–9.

does not mean, however, that Article 2 can *never* protect the rights of the foetus. It merely means that either Article 2 does not cover the rights of a foetus at all *or* it does recognise a right to life of the foetus with certain limitations.[1] The Commission and the European Court have not, to date, decided which of the two scenarios is the correct one.

What is clear, however, is that HCPs are permitted to have domestic laws in place which allow foetuses to be aborted in order to protect the physical or mental health of a mother,[2] or even to protect a mother from social hardship.[3] It still remains to be seen whether there comes a time when a foetus cannot be aborted without there being a breach of Article 2, particularly when it has already been recognised[4] that, in such a 'delicate area', HCPs must have 'a certain discretion'. However, the discretion in this field, involving as it does the protection of morals, is not unfettered and unreviewable. The discretion merely acknowledges that the national authorities enjoy a wide margin of appreciation in matters of morals, particularly in an area such as abortion which touches on matters of belief concerning the nature of human life.[5]

The protection offered by Article 2 in this area also extends to the provision of counselling for pregnant mothers considering abortion. A law which places a restraint on the provision of information to pregnant women concerning abortion facilities outside the HCP's State, regardless of age or state of health or their reasons for seeking counselling on the termination of pregnancy, is likely to be found to be 'overboard and disproportionate'.[6] Relevant factors are whether the relevant body advocates or encourages abortion, as opposed to only confining themselves to an explanation of the available options,[7] whether a large number of women from the State are, in any event, able to obtain abortions abroad,[8] whether there is evidence that the law creates a risk to women's health because they cannot obtain counselling or medical help after abortion has taken place[9] and whether some women may not have the necessary resourcefulness or have the necessary level of education to have access to alternative sources of information.[10]

A complaint can be brought by a woman who is affected by the relevant law or practice,[11] or by a potential father,[12] whether he is married to the mother or

---

1   *X v UK* Application No 8416/79, (1980) 19 DR 244 at 252, para 17; *H v Norway* Application
     No 17004/90, (1992) 73 DR 155 at 167.
2   *X v UK* Application No 8416/79, (1980) 19 DR 244 (8-week-old child aborted to protect
     mother's health).
3   *H v Norway* Application No 17004/90, (1992) 73 DR 155 (14-week-old foetus).
4   Ibid, at 168.
5   *Open Door Counselling and Dublin Well Women Clinic Ltd v Ireland* (1992) Series A No 246, 15
     EHRR 244, para 68.
6   Ibid, paras 73–74.
7   Ibid, paras 73–75.
8   Ibid, paras 73–76.
9   Ibid, paras 73–77.
10   Ibid.
11   Eg *Brüggeman and Sceuten v FRG* (1977) 10 DR 100.
12   *X v UK* Application No 8416/79, (1980) 19 DR 244.

not.[1] It cannot, however, be brought by a concerned ordinary citizen,[2] or a minister of religion who is opposed to abortion in principle.[3]

Patients in hospital who are refused life-saving treatment because of the high expense may well argue that Article 2 has been violated. It is unlikely that a defence by a hospital authority that its failure to provide the life-saving treatment was on the grounds of expense will succeed. A court will have to examine such a defence in the light of Article 2(1). Similarly, the switching off of the life-support machine of a patient who is in a permanent vegetative state (PVS) may be unlawful. However, a court has to examine all the circumstances surrounding these decisions in the light of the narrow exceptions permitted by Article 2. Such decisions are prima facie unlawful and constitute a breach of the Article. If any justification is permitted then this will be on very narrow grounds (ie the action was absolutely necessary).

Expulsion and asylum

2.14   If the removal of a person[4] in the HCP's territory to a particular country would result in the person being killed as a result of persecution or any other form of harm covered such as, for instance, harsh prison conditions following lawful conviction in the recipient country for a crime, then a valid claim can be made under Article 2 on the grounds that the proposed removal or deportation would be in breach of the deportee's right to life. Unlike Article 1A(2) of the United Nations Convention on the Status of Refugees 1951 and the Protocol of 1967, however, Article 2 of the Convention does not limit its protection to death brought about because of the victim's race, religion, ethnic group or membership of a social group or political opinion. *Any* death caused by persecution, for instance by groups of organised criminals in the recipient State, can fall within the ambit of Article 2.

Similarly, where an HCP, in extradition proceedings, proposes to return a defendant accused of a crime to a country which may impose a sentence of death on conviction, the HCP may be in breach of Article 3.[5]

State protection of particular citizens

2.15   Although it is not clear whether an HCP can be expected to provide a citizen with special protection (such as provision of a 24-hour bodyguard) when he fears imminent serious injury or death, it is clear that such protection cannot be demanded from an HCP for an indefinite period.[6]

---

1   *H v Norway* Application No 17004/90, (1992) 73 DR 155.
2   *X v Austria* Application No 7045/75, (1975) 7 DR 87.
3   *Knudsen v Norway* Application No 11045/84, (1985) 42 DR 247.
4   The person need not be a national of the HCP or any other European country.
5   See further at **2.34**.
6   *X v Ireland* Application No 6040/73, 16 YB 388 at 392.

PART 2
THE ARTICLES

ARTICLE 3 – PROHIBITION OF TORTURE

2.16   *'Article 3*

Prohibition of torture

No one shall be subjected to torture or to inhuman or degrading treatment or punishment.'

GENERAL PRINCIPLES

2.17   In conjunction with Article 2, Article 3 seeks to protect the individual's dignity and physical integrity.[1] It prohibits all forms of serious ill-treatment, whether physical or psychological and makes no provision for exceptions. Derogation from it is not permissible even in time of war or other public emergency threatening the life of the nation.[2] It prohibits in absolute terms torture or inhuman or degrading treatment or punishment, irrespective of the victim's conduct, whether it be terrorism or any other criminal activity.[3] This absolute nature shows that it enshrines one of the fundamental values of democratic societies and is generally recognised as an internationally accepted standard.[4] When dealing with the rights protected by Article 3, the European Court's 'vigilance must be heightened'[5] and examination of the evidence 'rigorous'.[6]

'Negative' obligation of Contracting States

2.18   The terms of Article 3 are extremely clear: a Contracting State must *refrain* from subjecting any individual within its territory (whether a national or non-national) to any form of ill-treatment.

This 'negative' obligation also renders Contracting States strictly liable for the conduct of their subordinates; Contracting States are under a duty to impose their will on their subordinates and cannot shelter behind their inability to ensure that Article 3 is respected.[7] Nor can a Contracting State avoid being held responsible for a violation by claiming that it was unaware of the existence of the ill-treatment.[8]

---

1   *Tyrer v UK* (1978) Series A No 26, 2 EHRR 1, para 33.
2   Article 15(2); *Ireland v UK* (1978) Series A No 25, 2 EHRR 25, para 163; *Soering v UK* (1989) Series A No 161, 11 EHRR 439, para 88.
3   *Tomasi v France* (1992) Series A 241–A, 15 EHRR 1, para 115; *Chahal v UK* RJD 1996-V 1831, (1996) 23 EHRR 413, para 79; *Aksoy v Turkey* (1997) 23 EHRR 553, para 62; *Aydin v Turkey* Application No 23178/94, (1998) 25 EHRR 251, para 81; *Selçuk and Asker v Turkey* Application Nos 23184/94 and 23185/94, (1998) 26 EHRR 477.
4   *Soering v UK* (1989) Series A No 161, 11 EHRR 439, para 88. See also the similar prohibitions in Article 7 of the International Covenant on Human Rights 1969 and Article 5 of the American Constitution on Human Rights 1969.
5   *Ribitsch v Austria* (1996) Series A No 336, 21 EHRR 573, para 32.
6   *Vilvarajah v UK* (1991) Series A No 215, 14 EHRR 248, para 108.
7   *Ireland v UK* (1978) Series A No 25, 2 EHRR 25, para 159.
8   Ibid.

Severity threshold

2.19   The conduct complained of must attain a minimum level of severity if it is to fall within the scope of Article 3.[1] The assessment of this minimum is relative; it depends on all the circumstances of the case, such as the nature and context of the treatment or punishment, the manner and method of its execution, its duration, its physical or mental effects and, in some instances, the sex, age and state of health of the victim.[2] However, provided it is sufficiently real and immediate, a mere threat of conduct prohibited by Article 3 may itself be in conflict with that provision.[3] Thus, to merely threaten an individual with torture might in some circumstances constitute at the least 'inhuman treatment'.

In determining whether substantial grounds have been shown for believing that there has been or will be a serious risk of treatment contrary to Article 3, the European Court will assess the issue in the light of all the material placed before it or, if necessary, material obtained *proprio motu.*[4]

'Positive' obligation of Contracting States

2.20   In addition to their primary obligation under Article 3 to refrain from subjecting individuals to the ill-treatment,[5] Contracting States also have an obligation under Article 1 of the Convention to *secure* to everyone within their jurisdiction the rights and freedoms defined in the Convention. This obligation, taken together with Article 3, requires Contracting States to *take measures* designed to ensure that individuals within their jurisdiction are not subjected to torture or inhuman or degrading treatment or punishment.[6] Furthermore, because the prohibition contained in Article 3 is absolute, such an obligation also applies where the danger emanates from persons or groups of persons who are not public officials.[7] In particular, children and other vulnerable individuals are entitled to State protection in the form of effective deterrence against the serious breaches of personal integrity prohibited by Article 3.[8]

Interpretation of the prohibited forms of ill-treatment

2.21   Article 3 refers to five forms of ill-treatment: 'torture', 'inhuman treatment', 'inhuman punishment', 'degrading treatment' and 'degrading punishment'. In interpreting these terms, regard must be had to the Convention's special character as a treaty for the 'collective enforcement' of

---

1   *Ireland v UK* (1978) Series A No 25, 2 EHRR 25, para 162.
2   Ibid; *Tyrer v UK* (1978) Series A No 26, 2 EHRR 1, para 30; *Soering v UK* (1989) Series A No 161, 11 EHRR 439, para 100; *Selçuk and Asker v Turkey* (above).
3   *Campbell and Cosans v UK* (1982) Series A No 48, 4 EHRR 293, para 26.
4   *Ireland v UK* (1978) Series A No 25, 2 EHRR 25, para 160.
5   See above (ie '"Negative" obligation of Contracting States').
6   *A v UK* Application No 25599/94, para 22.
7   *HLR v France* RJD 1997-III No 36, (1998) 26 EHRR 29, para 40; *A v UK* (above), para 22.
8   See *X and Y v The Netherlands* (1985) Series A No 91, 8 EHRR 235 at 11–13, paras 21–27; *Stubbings and Others v UK* RJD 1996-IV 1487, 23 EHRR 245 at 1505, paras 62–64; *A v UK* (above), para 22.

human rights and fundamental freedoms.[1] Thus, the object and purpose of the Convention as an instrument for the protection of individual human beings requires that Article 3 be interpreted and applied so as to make its safeguards practical and effective.[2] In addition, any interpretation of the rights and freedoms guaranteed by Article 3 has to be consistent with the general spirit of the Convention as 'an instrument designed to maintain and promote the ideals and values of a democratic society'.[3]

Standard of proof

2.22 In determining whether there has been a violation of Article 3 the Convention bodies will examine whether the facts upon which the alleged violation are based have been proved beyond a reasonable doubt.[4] In cases where the complainant complains of an imminent breach of Article 3, such as expulsion cases, the Convention bodies will have to be satisfied that there are 'substantial grounds' for believing that there is a 'real risk' of ill-treatment.[5] The mere possibility of a risk of ill-treatment will not be sufficient.[6]

TORTURE

2.23 In order to determine whether any particular form of ill-treatment qualifies as 'torture', the European Court will have regard to the distinction drawn in Article 3 between this notion and that of 'inhuman or degrading treatment'. The distinction derives principally from a difference in the intensity of the suffering caused[7] and would appear to have been embodied in the Convention in order to attach 'a special stigma to deliberate inhuman treatment causing very serious and cruel suffering'.[8] Similarly, the Commission has noted that 'torture' is often used to describe 'inhuman treatment, which has a purpose, such as the obtaining of information or confessions, or the infliction of punishment'.[9]

---

1   *Ireland v UK* (1978) Series A No 25, 2 EHRR 25, para 239; *Soering v UK* (1989) Series A No 161, 11 EHRR 439, para 87.
2   See, for example, *Artico v Italy* (1980) Series A No 37, 3 EHRR 1, para 33.
3   *Kjeldsen, Busk, Madsen and Pedersen v Denmark* (1976) Series A No 23 at 27, para 53, 1 EHRR 711.
4   *Ireland v UK* (1978) Series A No 25, 2 EHRR 25, para 161; *Aydin v Turkey* Application No 23178/94, (1998) 25 EHRR 251, para 70.
5   *Cruz Varaz v Sweden* (1991) Series A No 210, 14 EHRR 1, paras 75–76; *Vilvarajah v UK* (1991) Series A No 215, 14 EHRR 248, paras 107–108.
6   *Vilvarajah v UK* (1991) Series A No 215, 14 EHRR 248, para 111.
7   *Ireland v UK* (1978) Series A No 25, 2 EHRR 25, para 167; *Soering v UK* (1989) Series A No 161, 11 EHRR 439, para 91; *D v UK* (1997) 24 EHRR 423, para 50; *Chahal v UK* RJD 1996-V 1831, (1996) 23 EHRR 413, para 97.
8   *Ireland v UK* (1978) Series A No 25, 2 EHRR 25, para 167; *Aksoy v Turkey* RJD 1996-VI 2260, (1997) 23 EHRR 553, para 63; *Aydin v Turkey* Application No 23178/94, (1998) 25 EHRR 251, para 82. Article 1 of Resolution 3452 adopted by the General Assembly of the United Nations on 9 December 1975 declares: 'torture constitutes an *aggravated* and deliberate form of cruel, inhuman or degrading treatment or punishment'.
9   *The Greek Case* Application Nos 3321–3/67 and 3344/67, 12 Yearbook 1 at 186.

INHUMAN TREATMENT

2.24 The suffering occasioned must attain a particular level before a punishment can be classified as 'inhuman' within the meaning of Article 3.[1] Treatment is 'inhuman' if it causes, if not actual bodily injury, at least 'intense physical and mental suffering'.[2]

INHUMAN PUNISHMENT

2.25 In order for a particular form of punishment to be 'inhuman', the humiliation or debasement involved must attain a particular level of severity[3] and must, in any event, be more severe than the usual humiliation inherent in any punishment.[4] Indeed, Article 3, by expressly prohibiting 'inhuman' and 'degrading' punishment, implies that there is a distinction between such punishment and punishment in general.[5]

DEGRADING TREATMENT

2.26 Conduct will be 'degrading' when it is 'such as to arouse in [its] victims feelings of fear, anguish and inferiority capable of humiliating and debasing them and possibly breaking their physical or moral resistance'.[6] The requisite 'humiliation' which the person has to undergo can either be in the eyes of others or himself, provided that it attains a minimum level of severity.[7] Nor will conduct be excluded from the category of 'degrading', within the meaning of Article 3, simply because the measure has been in use for a long time or even meets with general approval.[8]

DEGRADING PUNISHMENT

2.27 Judicial punishment *per se* is not 'degrading'. This is due to the fact that judicial punishment, by its very character, involves an almost inevitable element

---

1   *Ireland v UK* (1978) Series A No 25, 2 EHRR 25, para 163; *Tyrer v UK* (1978) Series A No 26, 2 EHRR 1, para 29.
2   *Ireland v UK* (1978) Series A No 25, 2 EHRR 25, para 167. The Commission in *The Greek Case* Application Nos 3321–3/67 and 3344/67, 12 Yearbook 1 at 186 defined inhuman treatment as 'treatment as deliberately causes severe suffering, mental or physical, which in a particular situation, is unjustifiable'.
3   *Ireland v UK* (1978) Series A No 25, 2 EHRR 25, para 162.
4   See *Tyrer v UK* (1978) Series A No 26, 2 EHRR 1, para 30.
5   *Costello-Roberts v UK* (1993) Series A No 247–C, 19 EHRR 112, para 30.
6   *Ireland v UK* (1978) Series A No 25, 2 EHRR 25, para 167. In *The Greek Case* Application Nos 3321–3/67 and 3344/67, 12 Yearbook 1 at 186, the Commission stated that 'treatment or punishment may be said to be degrading if it grossly humiliates him before others or drives him to act against his will or conscience'.
7   *Tyrer v UK* (1978) Series A No 26, 2 EHRR 1, para 32; *Campbell and Cosans v UK* (1982) Series A No 48, 4 EHRR 293, para 28.
8   Ibid, para 31; ibid, para 29.

of humiliation.[1] In order for a punishment to be 'degrading' and in breach of Article 3, the humiliation or debasement involved must not only attain a particular level of severity but must, as with 'inhuman punishment', also go beyond that inevitable element of suffering or humiliation connected with a given form of legitimate punishment.[2]

The assessment is, in the nature of things, relative: it depends on all the circumstances of the case and, in particular, on the nature and context of the punishment itself and the manner and method of its execution.[3] Account is to be taken not only of the physical pain experienced but also, where there is a considerable delay before execution of the punishment, of the 'mental anguish' of anticipating the punishment to be inflicted.[4]

Conduct will, however, neither be excluded from the category of 'degrading' simply because the measure has been continuing for a long time, nor on the grounds that it meets with the general approval of the citizens of the Contracting State.[5] It may well be that one of the reasons why citizens view the penalty as an effective deterrent is precisely because of the element of degradation which it involves. Similarly, a punishment does not lose its degrading character merely because the Contracting State's citizens believe it to be, or because it actually is, an effective deterrent or aid to crime control.[6] However, the European Court cannot but be influenced by the 'developments and commonly accepted standards' in the penal policy of Contracting States.[7]

Similarly, non-custodial punishment which exceeds the level of suffering permitted by Article 3 cannot be justified on the grounds that it is an alternative to a period of detention. The fact that one penalty may be preferable to, or have less adverse effects or be less serious than, another penalty does not of itself mean that the first penalty is not 'degrading'.[8]

Moreover, although publicity can be a relevant factor in assessing whether a punishment is 'degrading' within the meaning of Article 3, the absence of publicity will not necessarily prevent a given punishment from falling into that category.[9]

IMPRISONMENT, REMAND, DETENTION

2.28   Although individuals serving a sentence of imprisonment lose their right to liberty, they continue to be afforded the protection offered by Article 3. In

---

1   *Tyrer v UK* (1978) Series A No 26, 2 EHRR 1, para 30.
2   Ibid; *Costello-Roberts v UK* (1993) Series A No 247–C, 19 EHRR 112, para 30.
3   *Tyrer v UK* (1978) Series A No 26, 2 EHRR 1, para 30.
4   Ibid, para 33; *Soering v UK* (1989) Series A No 161, 11 EHRR 439, para 100.
5   *Tyrer v UK* (1978) Series A No 26, 2 EHRR 1, para 31; *Campbell and Cosans v UK* (1982) Series A No 48, 4 EHRR 293, para 29.
6   *Tyrer v UK* (1978) Series A No 26, 2 EHRR 1, para 31.
7   Ibid.
8   Ibid, para 34.
9   Ibid, para 32.

order for Article 3 to come into play, however, the prisoner has to be exposed to ill-treatment which passes the severity threshold of the Article.[1]

Length of imprisonment

2.29　The length of imprisonment imposed by a Contracting State's courts will not normally justify an application under Article 3. Circumstances may arise, however, where, exceptionally, the term of imprisonment imposed may be incompatible with Article 3.[2] The European Court will undoubtedly be very reluctant to interfere with a Contracting State's discretion in this field and will have to be faced with a wholly disproportionate term of imprisonment before it will declare a violation.

Provision of food and water

2.30　The withholding of an adequate supply of food and drinking water can, not surprisingly, constitute 'inhuman treatment'.

Segregation and sensory isolation

2.31　The segregation of a prisoner from the prison community does not in itself constitute a form of 'inhuman treatment'. Segregation may be necessary to prevent escape, attack or disturbance of the prison community, or even to protect a prisoner from his fellow-prisoners.[3] Certain forms of segregation may, however, fall within the ambit of Article 3. In assessing whether a particular form of isolation violates Article 3, regard must be had to the particular conditions, the stringency of the measure, its duration, the objective pursued and its effects on the person concerned.[4] Complete sensory isolation coupled with complete social isolation can ultimately destroy the personality and thus constitutes a form of 'inhuman treatment' which cannot be justified by the requirements of security.[5] Prolonged solitary confinement should, where possible, be avoided, particularly where the person is detained on remand.[6]

Provision of medical care and general well-being

2.32　Contracting States have an obligation to maintain a continuous review of detention arrangements employed by them with a view to ensuring the health and well-being of all prisoners, having due respect to the ordinary and reasonable requirements of imprisonment.[7] This obligation remains even

PART 2
THE ARTICLES

1　*Ireland v UK* (1978) Series A No 25, 2 EHRR 25, para 162. In *Cyprus v Turkey* Application Nos 6780/74, 6950/75, (1976) 4 EHRR 482, for instance, the Commission held that the requirement to wear a prison uniform is not inherently 'degrading'.
2　*Weeks v UK* (1987) Series A No 114, 10 EHRR 293 at 25, para 47.
3　*Ensslin, Baader and Raspe v FRG* Application Nos 7572/76, 7586/76 and 7587/76, (1979) 14 DR 64 at 109. See also *McFeeley and Others v UK* Application No 8317/78, (1980) 20 DR 44; *Kröcher and Möller v Switzerland* Application No 8463/78, (1983) 34 DR 24; and *X v FRG* Application No 6038/73, (1973) 44 CH 115.
4　*Ensslin, Baader and Raspe v FRG* (above).
5　Ibid.
6　*X v FRG* Application No 6038/73, (1973) 44 CH 115.
7　*Ensslin, Baader and Raspe v FRG* Application Nos 7572/76, 7586/76 and 7587/76, (1979) 14 DR 64 at 111; *Bonnechaux v Switzerland* Application No 8317/78, (1980) 18 DR 100; *McFeeley*

when prison authorities are faced with an unlawful challenge to their authority, such as revolt or non co-operation.[1]

In certain circumstances, 'inhuman treatment' may be found to exist when a person's detention results in a serious deterioration in health. In such cases, relevant factors for consideration will be the form of medical treatment at that person's disposal as well as his willingness to make use of any available services.[2] In exceptional cases of ill-health, the proper administration of criminal justice may require remedies to be taken in the form of humanitarian measures.[3]

Remand prisoners

2.33 The same protection offered by Article 3 to individuals serving a term of imprisonment also applies to those detained while awaiting a trial or, if they have been found guilty following a trial, pending sentence.

Criminal proceedings and detention on remand are in themselves elements likely to seriously disturb the mental well-being of the person concerned. Such unavoidable results have to be accepted,[4] however, as it is in the public interest that the possible authors of criminal offences are prosecuted and punished.[5]

Capital punishment[6]

2.34 Although permitted by Article 2 in certain circumstances, the death sentence can constitute a breach of Article 3 of the Convention. There are a number of reasons, however, why Article 3 cannot be interpreted as generally prohibiting the death penalty.[7] Such a construction would nullify the clear wording of Article 2(1) which expressly permits the death penalty following a conviction for a crime. The subsequent agreement reached by the majority of the Contracting States in Protocol 6 to abolish the death penalty indicates that the Contracting States preferred to amend the text of Article 2 by means of an optional agreement and allow each State to choose the moment when to undertake such an abolition.

That does not mean, however, that the circumstances relating to a death sentence can never give rise to an issue under Article 3. Factors capable of bringing the treatment or punishment received by a condemned person within the proscription under Article 3 include: the manner in which the sentence is imposed or executed, the personal circumstances of the condemned person (in particular his age and mental state at the time of the offence[8]) as well as the

---

      and Others v UK Application No 8317/78, (1980) 20 DR 44, para 44; *X v UK* Application No 8231/78, (1982) 28 DR 5 at 32; *B v FRG* Application No 13047/87, (1988) 55 DR 271.

1   *Ensslin, Baader and Raspe v FRG* (above).

2   *B v FGR* (above).

3   *Chartier v Italy* Application No 9044/80, (1983) 33 DR 41, para 53. The Commission relied upon the fact that, under Italian legislation, even where provisional release was not allowed, provisional release could be granted 'to someone whose state of health is particularly serious and who cannot be given the necessary care while in detention'.

4   Assuming, presumably, that the period of remand is reasonable.

5   *X v FRG* Application No 9610/81, (1984) 6 EHRR 110 at 112.

6   See **2.1–2.15**.

7   *Soering v UK* (1989) Series A No 161, 11 EHRR 439, para 103.

8   Ibid, paras 109 and 111.

conditions of detention while awaiting execution.[1] The present-day attitudes in the Contracting States to capital punishment are also relevant in assessing whether the acceptable threshold of suffering or degradation had been exceeded.[2]

(i) Lapse of time between sentence and execution

2.35 In determining whether a sentence of death constitutes a breach of Article 3, account is to be taken not only of the physical pain experienced but also, where there is a considerable delay before execution of the punishment, of the 'mental anguish' involved in anticipating death or the method of bringing about death.[3]

For any prisoner condemned to death, some element of delay between imposition and execution of the sentence and the experience of severe stress in the conditions necessary for strict incarceration are inevitable. Similarly, a time lapse between sentence and execution is inevitable if appeal safeguards are to be provided to the condemned person. It is, however, part of human nature that a condemned person will cling to life by exploiting any such safeguards to the full.[4] Accordingly, however well-intentioned and even potentially beneficial the provision of complex post-sentence procedures are in a particular country, the consequence can be that the condemned prisoner has to endure a very lengthy period of anguish and mounting tension of living in 'the ever-present shadow of death'.[5]

(ii) Extradition

2.36 If there is a substantial risk that an individual will be sentenced to death in a State requesting extradition, then, irrespective of whether capital punishment is banned in the Contracting State's own territory, the removal of that individual to the requesting country may constitute a failure to secure that individual's rights under Article 3 and consequently amount to a violation of the provision.[6]

POLICE CUSTODY

2.37 Article 3 guards against any ill-treatment caused by the police during arrest and any subsequent period of detention thereafter. Any recourse to physical force while an individual is in police custody, which has not been made 'strictly necessary' by the individual's conduct, will diminish human dignity and is in principle an infringement of Article 3.[7] Similarly, the requirements of an investigation and the undeniable difficulties inherent in the fight against crime

---

1 *Soering v UK* (1989) Series A No 161, 11 EHRR 439, para 104. The European Court held that extradition of the applicant to the USA would constitute a breach of Article 3.
2 See **2.1–2.15**.
3 *Soering v UK* (1989) Series A No 161, 11 EHRR 439, para 100.
4 Ibid, para 106.
5 Ibid.
6 Ibid.
7 *Ribitsch v Austria* (1996) Series A No 336, 21 EHRR 573, para 38.

cannot justify placing limits on the protection to be afforded in respect of the physical integrity of individuals.[1]

Where an individual is taken into police custody in good health but is found to be injured at the time of release, it is incumbent on the State to provide a plausible explanation as to the causing of the injury, failing which a clear issue arises under Article 3 of the Convention.[2]

CORPORAL PUNISHMENT

2.38   Corporal punishment may constitute an assault on a person's dignity and physical integrity as protected under Article 3. However, in order for corporal punishment to be in breach of Article 3, particularly in alleged cases of 'degrading punishment', the humiliation or debasement involved must attain a particular level of severity and must in any event be other than that usual element of humiliation inherent in any punishment.[3] In order to be 'degrading', the person concerned must undergo, either in the eyes of others or in his own eyes, humiliation or debasement attaining a minimum level of severity.[4] Factors such as the nature and context of the punishment, the manner and method of its execution, its duration, its physical and mental effects and, in some instances, the sex, age and state of health of the victim must all be taken into account.[5] Account is to be taken of both the physical pain experienced and, where there is a considerable delay before execution of the punishment, of the mental anguish of anticipating the violence to be inflicted.[6]

Corporal punishment need not, however, occasion severe or long-lasting effects before it can be said to violate Article 3. A punishment that does not occasion such effects may fall within the ambit of Article 3 provided that, in the particular circumstances of the case, it exceeds the required threshold of severity.[7] Furthermore, as already noted above, a mere threat of conduct prohibited by Article 3 may, provided it is sufficiently real and immediate, itself be in conflict with that provision.[8]

---

1   *Tomasi v France* (1992) Series A No 241-A, 15 EHRR 1, para 115; *Ribitsch v Austria* (above).

2   Ibid, paras 108–111; *Ribitsch v Austria* (1996) Series A No 336, 21 EHRR 573, para 34; *Aksoy v Turkey* (1997) 23 EHRR 553, para 61. See also *Aydin v Turkey* (1998) 25 EHRR 251, paras 83–87.

3   See *Tyrer v UK* (1978) Series A No 26, 2 EHRR 1; see further at **2.27** et seq.

4   Ibid, para 32; *Campbell and Cosans v UK* (1992) Series A No 48, 4 EHRR 293, para 28 and further at **2.27** et seq.

5   *Ireland v UK* (1978) Series A No 25, 2 EHRR 24, para 162; *Tyrer v UK* (1978) Series A No 26, 2 EHRR 1, paras 29–30; *Soering v UK* (1989) Series A No 161, para 100; *Costello-Roberts v UK* (1993) Series A No 247-C, 19 EHRR 112, para 30.

6   *Soering v UK* (above), para 100.

7   *Tyrer v UK* (1978) Series A No 26, 2 EHRR 1, para 33; *Costello-Roberts v UK* (1993) Series A No 247-C, 19 EHRR 112, para 32.

8   See *Campbell and Cosans v UK* (1982) Series A No 48, 4 EHRR 293, para 26, and further at **2.27** et seq.

A particular form of corporal punishment will not be excluded from the category of 'degrading', within the meaning of Article 3, simply because the measure has been in use for a long time or even meets with general approval.[1]

EXPULSION AND EXTRADITION

2.39 A decision by a Contracting State to expel a non-national or extradite a fugitive to another country may give rise to an issue under Article 3. Before the responsibility of a Contracting State can be engaged in such circumstances, however, substantial grounds have to be shown for believing that the person concerned, if expelled or extradited, faces a real risk of being subjected to the forms of ill-treatment which are prohibited by Article 3 in the receiving or requesting country.[2] The establishment of such responsibility inevitably involves an assessment of conditions in the receiving or requesting country against the standards of Article 3 of the Convention. There is, however, no question of adjudicating on or establishing the responsibility of the receiving country, whether under general international law, the Convention or otherwise. Insofar as any liability under the Convention is or may be incurred, it is liability incurred by the Contracting State expelling or extraditing the individual by reason of it having taken action which has as a direct consequence on the exposure of an individual to the proscribed form of suffering.[3]

Non-State perpetrators of ill-treatment

2.40 The feared form of ill-treatment need not be brought about by the authorities of the receiving or requesting State. Owing to the absolute character of the right guaranteed, Article 3 may also apply where the danger emanates from persons or groups of persons who are not public officials.[4] In such circumstances, however, it must be shown that the risk is real and that the authorities of the receiving State are not able to obviate the risk by providing appropriate protection.[5]

Assurances of safety provided by receiving or requesting States

2.41 Contracting States, in the course of arriving at a decision to expel or extradite, often rely upon assurances provided by the receiving or requesting State that the individual would be afforded the full protection of their country's law. Although such assurances are relevant, little, if any, weight will be attached to such assurances if the evidence shows that the protection that will be offered would not be effective.[6]

---

1   See *Tyrer v UK* (1978) Series A No 26, 2 EHRR 1, para 31; *Campbell and Cosans v UK* (1982) Series A No 48, 4 EHRR 293, para 29, and further at **2.27** et seq.
2   *Soering v UK* (1989) Series A No 161, 11 EHRR 439, para 91; *Cruz Varaz v Sweden* (1991) Series A No 210, 14 EHRR 1, paras 69–70.
3   *Soering v UK* (1989) Series A No 161, 11 EHRR 439, para 91.
4   *HLR v France* RJD 1997–III 1004, (1998) 26 EHRR 29, para 40.
5   Ibid.
6   *Chahal v UK* RJD 1996-V 1831, (1996) 23 EHRR 413, para 105.

Relevant time at which to assess risk

2.42   Since the Contracting States' responsibility under Article 3 is activated by the act of exposing an individual to the risk of ill-treatment, the existence of the risk must be assessed primarily with reference to those facts which were known, or ought to have been known, to the Contracting State at the time of the expulsion or extradition; the European Court is not precluded, however, from having regard to information which comes to light subsequent to the expulsion or extradition.[1] This may be of value in confirming or refuting the appreciation that has been made by the Contracting Party or the well-foundedness or otherwise of an individual's fears.

Expulsion

2.43   Contracting States have the right, subject to their treaty obligations, including the Convention, to control the entry, residence and expulsion of aliens.[2] The Convention does not, accordingly, provide a non-national with a right to reside in, or not to be expelled from, the Contracting State.[3]

(i) Asylum and the European Convention
2.44   Similarly, there is no right to political asylum contained in either the Convention or its Protocols.[4] This is borne out by several recommendations of the Assembly of the Council of Europe on the right of asylum[5] as well as a subsequent resolution and declaration of the Committee of Ministers.[6]

However, as already noted above, a Contracting State's proposed expulsion[7] or actual expulsion[8] of a non-national (such as, for example, an unsuccessful asylum applicant), can give rise to an issue under Article 3, and hence engage the responsibility of the State under the Convention, if there are substantial grounds for believing that the person concerned would face a real risk of being subjected to treatment prohibited by Article 3. In these circumstances, Article 3 implies the obligation not to remove or deport the person in question to that

---

1   *Cruz Varaz v Sweden* (1991) Series A No 210, 14 EHRR 1, para 76.
2   *Abdulaziz, Cabales and Balkandali v UK* (1985) Series A No 94, 7 EHRR 471, para 67; *Berrehab v Netherlands* (1998) Series A No 138, 11 EHRR 322, paras 28–29; *Moustaquim v Belgium* (1991) Series A No 193, para 43; *Vilvarajah v UK* (1991) Series A No 215, 14 EHRR 248, para 102; *Chahal v UK* above, para 731; *D v UK* (above), para 46.
3   *Agee v UK* Application No 7729/76, (1977) 7 DR 164, para 9.
4   *Vilvarajah v UK* (1991) Series A No 215, 14 EHRR 248, para 102; *Chahal v UK* (above), para 73.
5   See Recommendation 293 (1961), Texts Adopted, 30th Ordinary Session, 21–28 September 1961, and Recommendation 434 (1965), Yearbook of the Convention, Vol 8 at pp 56–57 [1965].
6   See Resolution 67 (14), Yearbook of the Convention, Vol 10 at pp 104–105 [1967], and Declaration on Territorial Asylum, adopted on 18 November 1977, Collected Texts, 1987 edn, at p 202.
7   See, for example, *Chahal v UK* (above). The Commission and the European Court do not normally pronounce on the existence of potential violations of the Convention. However, where a person claims that a decision to remove or extradite him would, if implemented, breach Article 3 by reason of its foreseeable consequences in the receiving or requesting country, the Convention institutions will depart from this principle in order to ensure the effectiveness of the safeguard provided by Article 3.
8   See, for example, *Cruz Varaz v Sweden* (above) and *Vilvarajah v UK* (above).

country[1] and the activities of the individual in question, however undesirable, dangerous or reprehensible, cannot be a material consideration.[2]

In assessing whether removal of an asylum-seeker to a particular country would constitute a breach of Article 3, the courts will adopt a 'rigorous' examination of the evidence.[3] As well as looking at the evidence relating to the individual complainant, the courts will also examine and attach importance to the knowledge and experience of the relevant Contracting State in evaluating and dealing with asylum claims from the feared country.[4]

Thus, although not providing for a right to asylum as such, the protection afforded by Article 3 is, so far as asylum-seekers are concerned, wider than that provided by Articles 32 and 33 of the United Nations Convention on the Status of Refugees 1951 and the Protocol of 1967.[5]

(ii) The Stateless

2.45 The repeated expulsion of an individual who is Stateless, or whose identity was impossible to establish, to a country where his admission is not guaranteed may raise an issue under Article 3.[6]

(iii) Children

2.46 Contracting States have to be particularly cautious when deciding whether to remove a child from their territory. The removal of a child to a country where there would be no one able to take care of him may result in a breach of Article 3.[7]

Similarly, where a child, unlike his parents, has acquired the nationality of the Contracting State, the decision whether to refuse admission to or expel the

---

1   *Soering v UK* (1989) Series A No 161, 11 EHRR 439, para 91; *Cruz Varaz v Sweden* (1991) Series A No 210, 14 EHRR 1, paras 69–70; *Vilvarajah v UK* (1991) Series A No 215, 14 EHRR 248, para 103; *Chahal v UK* RJD 1996–V 1831, (1996) 23 EHRR 413, para 74; *Ahmed v Austria* (1997) 24 EHRR 278, [1997] INLR 65, para 39; *HLR v France* RJD 1997–III 1004, (1998) 26 EHRR 29, para 34. The European Court, in *HLR v France* (above), para 41, also stated that, although it will note the level of violence existing in the country of destination, such a circumstance would not in itself entail, in the event of deportation, a violation of Article 3.

  In *D v UK* (1977) 24 EHRR 423, at para 48, the European Court confirmed that the protection offered by Article 3 extends to all removals and deportations under the Immigration Act 1971. Regardless of whether or not the individual ever entered the UK in the technical sense, he would have been physically present and thus within the jurisdiction of the UK within the meaning of Article 1 of the Convention.

2   *Chahal v UK* RJD 1996–V 1831, (1996) 23 EHRR 413, para 80; *Ahmed v Austria*, (1997) 24 EHRR 278, [1997] INLR 65, para 38; *D v UK* (above), paras 47–48.

3   *Vilvarajah v UK* (1991) Series A No 215, 14 EHRR 248, para 108. See also *Ribitsch v Austria* (1996) Series A No 336, 21 EHRR 573, where the European Court stated (at para 32) that its 'vigilance must be heightened' in cases alleging a violation of Article 3.

4   *Cruz Varaz v Sweden* (1991) Series A No 210, 14 EHRR 1, para 81; *Vilvarajah v UK* (1991) Series A No 215, 14 EHRR 248, para 114.

5   *Chahal v UK* RJD 1996-V 1831, (1996) 23 EHRR 413, para 80.

6   *Giama v Belgium* (1981) 21 DR 73; *Harabi v The Netherlands* Application No 10798/84, (1986) 46 DR 112.

7   *Taspinar v The Netherlands* Application No 11026/84, (1985) 44 DR 262. The application was subsequently withdrawn after the authorities agreed to allow the child to reside in The Netherlands.

parents will require caution. When faced with such a dilemma, the Contracting State has effectively to choose between either allowing the parents to enter or remain in its territory and live with the child, or refuse admission to or expel the parents. If the latter course is taken, a breach of Article 3 may, in exceptional circumstances, occur if the Contracting State's refusal to admit or expel the parents in effect obliges the child to leave the Contracting State's territory and live in the parents' country of birth in circumstances which 'radically' change the child's life-style and where he is faced with extremely poor living conditions.[1]

Availability of medical treatment in the receiving State

2.47   Non-nationals who are subject to expulsion cannot, in principle, claim any entitlement to remain in the territory of a Contracting State in order to continue to benefit from medical, social or other forms of assistance provided by the expelling State during their stay in its territory.[2]

In exceptional circumstances, however, compelling humanitarian considerations may mean that the implementation of the decision to remove a non-national would violate Article 3.[3] Therefore, where an individual has reached a critical stage of a fatal illness, the proposed or actual implementation of a decision by a Contracting State to expel him to a receiving State can amount to 'inhuman treatment' if his expulsion would expose him to a real risk of dying under most distressing circumstances.[4]

Extradition

2.48   As a result of Article 5(1), which permits 'the lawful ... detention of a person against whom action is being taken with a view to ... extradition', no right to not be extradited is as such protected by the Convention. Nevertheless, insofar as a measure of extradition has consequences adversely affecting the enjoyment of a Convention right, it may, assuming that the consequences are not too remote, attract the obligations of a Contracting State under Article 3.[5]

The European Court, in its overall assessment under Article 3, as well as looking at the proportionality of any contested extradition, will search for 'the requisite fair balance of interests' between, on the one hand, the need to ensure that a fugitive criminal does not go unpunished and, on the other, the need to ensure that the risk of intense or protracted suffering is minimised or avoided.[6]

---

1   *Fadele v UK* Application No 13078/87, (1991) 70 DR 159. In this case, the mother had died
    while living with her children in the UK. The father, who lived in Nigeria at the time of the
    mother's death, requested that he be allowed to live with the children in the UK. Following
    the refusal of the father's request, the children moved to Nigeria where they were alleged
    to have suffered great hardship which caused them severe health problems. The case
    subsequently resulted in a friendly settlement: the children returned to the UK and their
    father was allowed to reside in the UK with them.
2   *D v UK* (above), para 54.
3   Ibid.
4   Ibid, para 53.
5   *Soering v UK* (1989) Series A No 161, 11 EHRR 439, para 85.
6   Ibid, para 100. See also *Abdulaziz, Cabales and Balkandali v UK* (1985) Series A No 94, 7
    EHRR 471, paras 59–60.

(i) Prosecution for political offences

2.49 If there are reasons to fear that extradition, although requested exclusively for offences under ordinary law, may be used to prosecute the person concerned for political offences or even simply because of his political opinions, there may be a violation of Article 3.[1] In such circumstances, the Convention bodies will consider whether there is a risk of prosecution for political reasons which could lead to an 'unjustified or disproportionate sentence being passed' on the applicant resulting in 'inhuman treatment'.[2]

(ii) Death penalty[3]

2.50 In cases where a person may be sentenced to death in the receiving State, a further consideration of relevance would be whether the legitimate purpose of extradition could be achieved by another means which would not involve suffering of exceptional intensity or duration.[4]

ADMISSION

2.51 Neither Article 3 nor any other provision of the Convention provides non-nationals with a right to enter the territory of a Contracting State. The Convention bodies, however, attach great importance to any form of discrimination based on colour or race because such discrimination constitutes 'a special form of affront to human dignity'.[5] Accordingly, the Commission has held that domestic legislation or policies which discriminate on the grounds of colour or race against a group of non-nationals seeking to enter the territory of a Contracting State can of itself amount to 'degrading treatment',[6] even if differential treatment on some other ground would not.[7]

PART 2
THE ARTICLES

---

1 Where the prosecution is solely on account of the fugitive's political opinion, there may also be an issue under Article 1A(2) of the United Nations Convention on the Status of Refugees 1951 and the Protocol of 1967.

2 *Altun v FRG* Application No 10308, (1984) 36 DR 209 at 232, para 8.

3 See **2.34**.

4 *Soering v UK* (1989) Series A No 161, 11 EHRR 439, para 111. In *Soering v UK*, the European Court relied upon the fact that the UK could have extradited the applicant to Germany where the death penalty did not exist.

5 *East African Asians v UK* (1994) 78-A DR 5.

6 Ibid.

7 Ibid, para 208.

ARTICLE 4 – PROHIBITION OF SLAVERY AND FORCED LABOUR

2.52   *'Article 4*

Prohibition of slavery and forced labour

1.   No one shall be held in slavery or servitude.
2.   No one shall be required to perform forced or compulsory labour.
3.   For the purpose of this Article the term 'forced or compulsory labour' shall not include:
      (a)   any work required to be done in the ordinary course of detention imposed according to the provisions of Article 5 of this Convention or during conditional release from such detention;
      (b)   any service of a military character or, in case of conscientious objectors, in countries where they are recognised, service exacted instead of compulsory military service;
      (c)   any service exacted in case of an emergency or calamity threatening the life or well-being of the community;
      (d)   any work or service which forms part of normal civic obligations.'

Article 4 protects individuals against 'slavery or servitude' and 'forced or compulsory labour'. The protection offered against the former is absolute, whereas there are express exclusions to the latter.

SLAVERY AND SERVITUDE

2.53   Paragraph 1 of Article 4 prohibits a person being held in 'slavery' or 'servitude'. The prohibition is absolute and therefore non-derogable even in times of national emergency.[1]

'Slavery'

2.54   No definition of 'slavery' is found in the text of the Convention. Nor is there any case-law on its meaning. A definition of the term is found, however, in Article 1 of the Slavery Convention 1926.[2]

'Servitude'

2.55   Although the term 'servitude', like 'slavery', has not been defined by the Convention,[3] some light has been shed on its meaning by case-law. 'Servitude' has been said to be 'an obligation to provide another with certain services' coupled with 'an obligation on the part of the "serf" to live on another's property and the impossibility of changing his condition'.[4]

---

1   Article 15(2).
2   See Slavery Convention 1926, 60 LNTS 253.
3   See, however, the definition of 'servitude' in Article 7 of the Supplementary Convention on the Abolition of Slavery, the Slave Trade, and Institutions and Practices Similar to Slavery 1956.
4   *Van Droogenbroeck v Belgium* (1982) Series A No 50, 4 EHRR 443, para 79.

It should also be noted that as Article 4(1) does not exclude from its ambit services exacted as a result of military service,[1] it is, at least in theory, possible for military service to amount to 'slavery or servitude'.[2] However, the circumstances surrounding the military service would presumably have to be extremely harsh and oppressive to bring about such a result in practice.

'FORCED OR COMPULSORY LABOUR'

2.56 Subject to the exclusions found in Article 4(3), Article 4 lays down a general and absolute prohibition of 'forced or compulsory labour' but does not, however, define the term. It merely defines a number of circumstances which *cannot* amount to forced or compulsory labour. Nor is any guidance on the meaning of the words found in the various Council of Europe documents relating to the preparatory work of the Convention.

It is evident, however, that the authors of the Convention, like the authors of Article 8 of the draft International Covenant on Civil and Political Rights, to a large extent based themselves on two earlier International Labour Organisation (ILO) Conventions (Convention No 29[3] and Convention No 105[4]) which similarly concerned forced or compulsory labour.[5] These ILO Conventions complemented each other in prescribing 'the immediate and complete abolition of forced or compulsory labour' in certain specific circumstances. Article 4, however, has gone further and imposes a general prohibition, subject to a number of identified exceptions.

Article 2(1) of Convention No 29 defines 'forced or compulsory labour' as 'all work or service which is exacted from any person under the menace of any penalty and for which the said person has not offered himself voluntarily'. The European Court has adopted this as 'a starting-point for interpretation of Article 4 of the European Convention', although it has also stated that 'sight should not be lost of [the European Convention's] special features or of the fact that it is a living instrument to be read in the light of the notions currently prevailing in democratic States'.[6]

There may be an overlap as to what in fact amounts to 'servitude' and 'forced compulsory labour'. As, however, Article 4 expressly distinguishes between the two, they should not be treated as equivalent.[7]

---

1   Compare with Article 4(3)(b), which expressly excludes, inter alia, 'service of a military character'.
2   *X, Y, Z, V and W v UK* Application No 3435–38/67, (1968) 11 Yearbook 562 at 596.
3   Adopted on 28 June 1930 and came into force on 1 May 1932.
4   Adopted on 25 June 1957 and came into force on 17 January 1959.
5   There is, for instance, a striking similarity between the wording of Article 4(3) of the European Convention and that of Article 2(2) of Convention No 29.
6   *Van der Mussele v Belgium* (1983) Series A No 70, 6 EHRR 163, para 32.
7   *X, Y, Z, V and W v UK* Application No 3435–38/67, (1968) 11 Yearbook 562 at 596.

'Forced or compulsory'

2.57   The word 'forced' has been said to bring to mind the idea of 'physical or mental restraint', whereas 'compulsory' has been said to be incapable of referring to any form of legal compulsion or obligation.[1] Article 4(2) cannot, therefore, be involved merely because, for instance, one of the parties to a freely entered and enforceable legal contract is obliged to honour his promises under the contract because of the threat of financial sanctions if he breaches any of its terms. The labour has to be exacted under the 'menace of any penalty' and performed against the will of the person concerned, that is, work for which the person has not 'offered himself voluntarily'.[2]

In deciding whether a person had, prior to a complaint to the European Court, 'offered himself voluntarily', decisive weight will not be attached to the prior consent of the person. A person's prior consent, without more, does not warrant the conclusion that the obligations incumbent on him did not constitute compulsory labour for the purposes of Article 4(2) of the Convention.[3] In determining whether any particular service required falls within the prohibition of compulsory labour, regard must be had to all the circumstances of the case whilst bearing in mind the underlying objectives of Article 4.[4]

In the case of a service required in order to gain access to a given profession, the service may not be treated as having been voluntarily accepted beforehand if it is 'so excessive or disproportionate to the advantages attached to the future exercise of that profession'.[5] In such circumstances, relevant factors can include whether the service was for a short period, provided favourable remuneration, did not involve any diversion from the person's chosen professional work, and did not involve any discriminatory, arbitrary or punitive application.[6]

Nor will the fact that the relevant work is remunerated be determinative. Whilst remunerated work may qualify as forced or compulsory labour, the lack of remuneration and of the reimbursement of expenses constitutes a relevant factor when considering what is 'proportionate' or 'in the normal course of affairs'.[7]

Labour

2.58   The European Court has stated that the English word 'labour' is often used in the narrow sense of manual work and has emphasised that the broader meaning found in the equivalent French word of '*travail*' should be adopted.[8]

---

1   *Van der Mussele v Belgium* (1983) Series A No 70, 6 EHRR 163, para 34.
2   Ibid, para 34.
3   Ibid, para 36.
4   Ibid, para 37.
5   Ibid, paras 37–38. An example given by the European Court was that of 'a service unconnected with the profession in question'.
6   *Iversen v Norway* Application No 1468/62, (1963) 6 YB 278, Commission at 328.
7   *Van der Mussele v Belgium* (1983) Series A No 70, 6 EHRR 163, para 40.
8   Ibid, para 33. Corroboration for this view is derived from Article 2(1) of Convention No 29 ('tout travail ou service'), Article 4 of the European Convention ('tout travail ou service')

EXCLUSIONS

2.59   Article 4(3) excludes four particular circumstances from the definition of 'forced or compulsory labour'. It does not in any way limit the ambit of the prohibition against 'slavery or servitude' found in Article 4(1). Notwithstanding their diversity, the four sub-paragraphs of Article 4(3) are 'grounded on the governing ideas of the general interest, social solidarity and what is the normal or ordinary course of affairs'.[1] These exceptions do not, however, limit the exercise of the right guaranteed by Article 4(2), but merely delimit the content of the right protected by it. The exceptions form a whole with Article 4(2) and indicate what the term 'forced or compulsory labour' shall not include. Therefore, Article 4(3), as well as listing a number of exceptions to Article 4(2), also serves as an aid to the interpretation of Article 4(2).[2]

Article 4(3)(a): Work exacted during the ordinary course of detention

2.60   Paragraph 3(a) of Article 4 authorises work ordinarily required of individuals deprived of their liberty. It excludes from the general prohibition of Article 4(2) 'any work required to be done in the ordinary course of detention' or 'during the conditional release from such detention'.

In order for an HCP to be able to rely on the exclusion contained in Article 4(3)(a), the detention should have been imposed in accordance with the terms of Article 5 of the Convention which sets out the circumstances in which an HCP can lawfully restrict a person's right to liberty. A violation of the rights guaranteed by Article 5 will not, however, automatically lead to a violation of Article 4.[3]

In considering whether the duty to work imposed on a detainee has exceeded the 'ordinary' limits, within the meaning of Article 4(3)(a) of the Convention, the European Court will attach weight to whether the work was aimed at rehabilitation of the detainee and whether the work was based on a general standard which finds its equivalent in other Member States of the Council of Europe.[4]

Article 4(3)(b): Military service or service exacted instead of compulsory military service

2.61   Article 4(3)(b) excludes two forms of 'service'. First, it excludes 'any service of a military character'. The exclusion of military service applies irrespective of whether the service was compulsory or voluntary.[5]

---

and the name of the International Labour Organisation ('Organisation internationale du Travail').

1   *Van der Mussele v Belgium* (1983) Series A No 70, 6 EHRR 163, para 38; *Schmidt v FRG* (1994) Series A No 291–B, 18 EHRR 513, para 22.

2   *Van der Mussele v Belgium* (1983) Series A No 70, 6 EHRR 163, para 38.

3   *De Wilde, Ooms and Versyp v Belgium* ('Vagrancy cases') (1971) Series A No 12, 1 EHRR 373, para 89; *Van Droogenbroeck v Belgium* (1982) Series A No 50, 4 EHRR 443, para 59.

4   *De Wilde, Ooms and Versyp* ('Vagrancy cases') (1971) Series A No 12, 1 EHRR 373, para 90.

5   *X, Y, Z, V and W v UK* Application No 3435–38/67, (1968) 11 YB 562 at 594.

The second limb of Article 4(3)(b) excludes, in countries where conscientious objectors are recognised and provided with alternative service, civilian work exacted as a substitute to military service. That does not mean, however, that an HCP is obliged to provide substitute civilian service for conscientious objectors to military service.[1]

Article 4(3)(c): Emergency or calamity

2.62   Article 4(3)(c) excludes 'service exacted in the case of an emergency or calamity threatening the life or well-being of the community'. This permits HCPs to require citizens to assist in particularly difficult times such as natural disasters affecting the community.

The effect of Article 4(3)(c) is similar, although not identical, to that of Article 15. Article 15, inter alia, permits an HCP to derogate from its obligations under the Convention in times of 'public emergency threatening the life of the nation'. Article 4(3)(c), however, is relatively less stringent because it permits services to be exacted not only in times of emergency threatening the life of a community, but also when the '*well-being*' of a community is threatened.

Article 4(3)(d): Civic obligations

2.63   Article 4(3)(d) excludes 'any work or service which forms part of the normal civil obligations'. The exact ambit of this sub-paragraph and the meaning of 'normal civic obligations' is still unclear.[2]

---

1   *Johansen v Norway* Application No 10600/83, (1985) 44 DR 155 at 162.
2   See, however, *Schmidt v FRG* (1994) Series A No 291–B, 18 EHRR 513, para A 291–B; *X v Austria* Application No 5593/72, (1973) 45 CD 113; *S v FRG* Application No 9686/82, (1984) 39 DR 90; *Four Companies v Austria* Application No 7427/76, (1976) 7 DR 148.

ARTICLE 5 – RIGHT TO LIBERTY AND SECURITY

2.64   '*Article 5*

Right to liberty and security

1.   Everyone has the right to liberty and security of person. No one shall be deprived of his liberty save in the following cases and in accordance with a procedure prescribed by law:

   (a)   the lawful detention of a person after conviction by a competent court;

   (b)   the lawful arrest or detention of a person for non-compliance with the lawful order of a court or in order to secure the fulfilment of any obligation prescribed by law;

   (c)   the lawful arrest or detention of a person effected for the purpose of bringing him before the competent legal authority on reasonable suspicion of having committed an offence or when it is reasonably considered necessary to prevent his committing an offence or fleeing after having done so;

   (d)   the detention of a minor by lawful order for the purpose of educational supervision or his lawful detention for the purpose of bringing him before the competent legal authority;

   (e)   the lawful detention of persons for the prevention of the spreading of infectious diseases, of persons of unsound mind, alcoholics or drug addicts or vagrants;

   (f)   the lawful arrest or detention of a person to prevent his effecting an unauthorised entry into the country or of a person against whom action is being taken with a view to deportation or extradition.'

Article 5 is not absolute. In times of war or emergency, it can be derogated from under Article 15. The exceptions set out in Article 5 are to be given a narrow interpretation.[1]

Loss of physical liberty

2.65   The right to liberty contemplates the physical liberty of a person and therefore its loss must involve a certain level of physical restraint.[2] There is no requirement that there should be a total restraint of liberty. It suffices if the liberty is seriously restricted.[3] The difference between deprivation of and restriction upon liberty is merely one of degree or intensity and not one of nature or substance.[4] The aim of the Article is to ensure that no one should be deprived of his liberty in an arbitrary fashion and is not merely a restriction upon liberty of movement. For example, Article 2 of the Fourth Protocol guarantees this liberty only in the case of persons lawfully within the territory of a State.[5] In order to determine whether someone has been deprived of his

---

1   *Winterwerp v The Netherlands* (1979) 2 EHRR 387.
2   *Amuur v France* (1996) 22 EHRR 533, para 44 (Opinion).
3   Ibid at 553 (Opinion).
4   *Guzzardi v Italy* (1980) Series A No 39, 3 EHRR 333, para 92; and *Amuur v France* (1996) 22 EHRR 533, para 43.
5   Confinement of asylum seekers to the international zone of an airport accompanied by suitable safeguards for the persons concerned, is acceptable only in order to enable

liberty within the meaning of Article 5, the starting point must be his concrete situation. The fact that an asylum seeker can escape detention in the country he is seeking protection from by leaving that country is insufficient to say that he is at liberty. The ability to go to a third country to escape detention is illusory, particularly as the Convention right guarantees concrete and effective rights. Therefore, it is necessary to examine whether such an asylum seeker has a real possibility of freeing himself from detention, for example, in an international zone of the airport if it means going to a country which is neither his country of origin nor a country which is likely to hand him over to the authorities from whom he is fleeing.[1] Account must be taken of a whole range of criteria such as the type, duration, effects and implementation of the measure in question.[2]

A period of detention must comply with the conditions of legality and lawfulness. Thus, detention must be in accordance with a procedure prescribed by domestic legislation and the procedure laid down by it and this requires an examination of the quality of the law in question, requiring it to be compatible with the rule of law.[3] Quality in this sense implies that, where the rule of law authorises deprivation of liberty, it must be sufficiently accessible and precise in order to avoid all risk of arbitrariness.[4] A detention failing to conform to its legal purpose is necessarily unlawful and therefore arbitrary and cannot be deemed to comply with the spirit of the Convention.[5] If, for example, the proceedings are not conducted with requisite diligence or, if the detention results from some misuse of authority, it ceases to be justifiable under Article 5(1)(f) (deportation or extradition).[6] Deprivation of liberty under Article 5(1)(f) will be justified only for as long as extradition or deportation proceedings are being conducted. Thus, if such proceedings are not being prosecuted with due diligence, the detention will cease to be justified under Article 5(1)(f).[7] For example, a holding of an asylum seeker should not be prolonged excessively, otherwise there would be a risk of it turning a mere

---

prevention of unlawful immigration while complying with the obligations under the 1951 Geneva Convention and the ECHR Convention. But holding of asylum seekers for excessive periods of time could turn what would otherwise be a mere restriction into a deprivation of liberty: *Amuur v France* (1996) 22 EHRR 533, para 43.

1   *Amuur v France* (1996) 22 EHRR 533, para 48 (Opinion).

2   *Engel and Others v The Netherlands* (1979) 1 EHRR 706, paras 58–59; *Guzzardi v Italy* (1980) Series A No 39, 3 EHRR 333, para 92; and *Amuur v France* (1996) 22 EHRR 533, para 44 (Opinion).

3   *Amuur v France* (1996) 22 EHRR 533, para 50.

4   In *Amuur v France* (1996) 22 EHRR 533, for example the European Court stated that the rules of law in France did not provide for legal, humanitarian and social assistance, nor did they lay down procedure and time-limits for access to such assistance so that asylum seekers could take the necessary steps to pursue their asylum applications and therefore those rules did not sufficiently guarantee their liberty: para 53. See also *Bozano v France* (1986) Series A No 111, 9 EHRR 387, para 55; and *Quinn v France* (1995) Series A No 311, 21 EHRR 529 at 550, para 47.

5   *Winterwerp v The Netherlands* (1979) Series A No 33, 2 EHRR 387, paras 37–39.

6   *Lynas v Switzerland* Application No 7317/75, (1977) 6 DR 141 and 167.

7   *Quinn v France* (1995) Series A No 311, 21 EHRR 529 at 550, para 48. The delays of some three and ten months between stages of extradition proceedings made the total duration of detention excessive.

restriction on liberty into a deprivation of liberty and its prolongation requires speedy review by the courts.[1]

For a deprivation of liberty to be lawful under Article 5(1), it must at any given moment fall within one of the categories of arrest or detention set out in sub-paras (a) to (f) of the Article. These categories constitute an exhaustive list of exceptions to a fundamental right and therefore the exceptions must be narrowly interpreted.[2]

The European Court, the Commission and the UK Government agree that having a reasonable suspicion presupposes the existence of facts or information which would satisfy an objective observer that the person concerned may have committed the offence. What may be regarded as 'reasonable' will, however, depend on all the circumstances. Article 5(1)(c) authorises arrest and detention of persons on reasonable suspicion of having committed an offence.

> 'Certainly Article 5(1)(c) ECHR (the lawful arrest or detention of a person effected for the purpose of bringing him before the competent legal authority on the reasonable suspicion of having committed an offence or when it is reasonably considered necessary to prevent his committing an offence or fleeing after having done so) should not be applied in such a manner as to put disproportionate difficulties in the way of the police authorities of the Contracting States in taking effective measures to counter organised terrorism. It follows that the Contracting States cannot be asked to establish the reasonableness of the suspicion grounding the arrest of a suspected terrorist by disclosing the confidential sources of supporting information or even facts which would be susceptible of indicating such resources or their identity.
>
> Nevertheless the Court must be enabled to ascertain whether the essence of the safeguard afforded by Article 5(1)(c) has been secured. Consequently the respondent Government has to furnish at least some facts or information capable of satisfying the Court that the arrested person was reasonably suspected of having committed the offence.'[3]

A period of detention will, in principle, be lawful if it is carried out pursuant to a court order. A subsequent finding that the court erred, under domestic law, in making the order will not necessarily retrospectively affect the validity of the intervening period of detention. The fact that a conviction resulting in the imposition of a custodial sentence is quashed on appeal does not of itself deprive the detention of its 'lawful' character for the purpose of Article 5(1)(a), (b).[4] It is arguable that whether the detention is to be treated as lawful for the purpose of these sub-paragraphs depends on the grounds on which the conviction is quashed or the order for detention set aside. If, in convicting a person or ordering his detention, the court acted without jurisdiction or exceeded its proper jurisdiction (eg a magistrate tries a defendant for an indictable offence only or imposes a sentence of imprisonment where only a

PART 2
THE ARTICLES

---

1   *Amuur v France* (1996) 22 EHRR 533, para 43.

2   *Winterwerp v The Netherlands* (1979) Series A No 33, 2 EHRR 387, para 37; and *Quinn v France* (1995) Series A No 311, 21 EHRR 529 at 540, para 35 (Opinion) and at 548, para 42: a detention of some 11 hours was unreasonable.

3   See *Fox, Campbell and Hartley v UK* (1991) 13 EHRR 157 at paras 32 and 34 of the judgment.

4   *Kryzychi v FRG* Comm Rep (1978) 13 DR 57 and also see *R v Governor of Wandsworth Prison, ex parte Sorhaindo* (1999) TLR, 5 January.

fine could be imposed) then it is clearly arguable that the detention was without jurisdiction and unlawful ab initio.[1] But it may be that a mere misdirection or misunderstanding of the law or where the court reaches a conclusion to convict which is unsupported by evidence then in principle the detention resulting from the court's order remains lawful, notwithstanding the fact that the order is subsequently quashed on appeal. For example, where:

(i) the magistrates had no jurisdiction to entertain the proceedings at all or to impose the sentence or make the order in question;

(ii) in the course of hearing a case within their jurisdiction the magistrates were guilty of some gross and obvious irregularity of procedure (serious breach of the rules of natural justice);

(iii) the sentence or order was not based on any proper foundation in law because of a failure on the part of the court to fulfil a statutory condition precedent to the imposition of the sentence or the making of the order;

(iv) where the magistrates have acted in bad faith or recklessly or where they neglected the attempt to apply the relevant legislation correctly

then a detention resulting from the conviction which is subsequently quashed on appeal may be said to be unlawful for purposes of Article 5(1).[2]

Detention following a decision of a court concerning release or continued detention is immediately enforceable. Thus, a detained person must be immediately released following a court's decision ordering his release.[3] However, some delay in executing a decision ordering the release of a detainee is understandable.[4]

A delay in an order extending a person's detention cannot be considered as rendering the remainder of the detention illegal or unlawful.[5]

ARTICLE 5(1)(e)

2.66　Article 5 generally safeguards an individual's right to liberty and security. Article 5(1)(e) protects in particular the rights of those who are suffering from a mental illness. It does this by setting out the minimum requirements before a mentally ill person can be lawfully detained.

Winterwerp v The Netherlands[6]

2.67　In *Winterwerp v The Netherlands*, the European Court took the opportunity to state conditions that must be satisfied for detention of mentally ill patients to be lawful. In 1968, Mr Winterwerp came to the attention of the authorities as a result of his arrest for stealing a quantity of documents from the local registry office. He was committed to a psychiatric hospital in accordance

---

1　*Benham v UK* RJD 1996–III 738, (1996) 22 EHRR 293 at 311 (Opinion of Mr N Bratza).

2　Ibid at 312 (Opinion of Mr N Bratza), and paras 43–46.

3　*Quinn v France* (1995) Series A No 311, 21 EHRR 529 at 540, para 44 (Opinion).

4　Ibid, para 42.

5　*Wassink v The Netherlands* (1979) Series A 185-A, paras 23–26.

6　(1979) 2 EHRR 387; and (1982) 4 EHRR 288.

with an emergency procedure. Mr Winterwerp remained in detention pursuant to orders that were renewed annually. These annual orders were made on the basis of psychiatric reports submitted by the doctor in charge of his treatment. The last such renewal before the application to the European Court was made in 1977. During his years of detention, Mr Winterwerp was never notified about the hearings or the orders made. He was never represented at the hearings nor was he afforded the opportunity to challenge the medical evidence submitted at the hearings.

Objective medical evidence must be sought

2.68 The decision to detain must be supported by objective and reliable medical evidence showing the patient to be of 'unsound mind'. The European Court did, however, state that in emergency cases this requirement could be temporarily dispensed with. They expressed that a detention of six weeks would not be so excessive as to render it unlawful.

The nature and degree of the disorder

2.69 The objective medical evidence must show that the disorder is of such a kind and degree as to warrant compulsory confinement. As a result, confinement will follow where the patient's disorder manifests itself in violence toward others. Often a patient will be detained in circumstances when the only danger is to himself (although commonly danger to self and others go hand in hand). It is suggested that in those circumstances detention would not be warranted.

What constitutes a mental disorder?

2.70 The European Court declined to define mental disorder as the categories of disorder are constantly changing with medical knowledge. In those circumstances, a fixed definition would be unduly restrictive upon the Contracting State.

Detention only as long as the disorder persists

2.71 It follows that once the disorder that initially called for detention ceases, then the patient should be released. Furthermore, it is suggested that once the kind and degree of the disorder alters so that the patient can no longer be considered to be a danger to the public, then similarly release should follow.

Periodic review of detention

2.72 The European Court held that continued detention of a patient under the Mental Health Act 1986 must be subject to periodic review by a court-like body. The review should be at reasonable intervals. In addition, the patient should be afforded the opportunity to make representations either in person or through representation. Without these guarantees the legislation would violate Article 5(4).[1]

---

1   Confirmed by *X v UK* (1981) Series A No 46, 4 EHRR 188.

The role of the Mental Health Review Tribunal

2.73 The European Court in *X v UK* also stated that the Mental Health Review Tribunal (MHRT) was capable of satisfying the requirement for review by a court-like body. However, the MHRT's role must not be merely advisory and it should have the power to release the patient if such a course is warranted. Further, with regard to Article 5(4), the MHRT has a positive duty to ensure a patient is represented at a hearing.[1] Legal aid is available for hearings before the MHRT under the Advice By Way Of Representation (ABWOR) Scheme.

Imposing conditions on the release of a patient

2.74 There can be many practical difficulties in releasing a patient, especially after a long period of detention. In many cases, some form of supervised release is necessary. This is commonly achieved by imposing conditions upon release such as residence in an approved hostel. In *Johnson v UK*,[2] it was held that it was not unlawful to impose conditions on the release of those subject to hospital orders. However, where those conditions result in the patient being held for an indefinite period, this amounted to a breach of Article 5(1)(e). The MHRT, in order to comply with Article 5, must also have the power to order such conditions to be in place at a certain date effecting a speedy release after the disorder has ceased.

ARTICLE 5(3)

'3.   Everyone arrested or detained in accordance with the provisions of paragraph 1(c) of this Article shall be brought promptly before a judge or other officer authorised by law to exercise judicial power and shall be entitled to trial within a reasonable time or to release pending trial. Release may be conditioned by guarantees to appear for trial.'

Reasonableness of the length of detention

2.75 The pre-trial detention of an accused person should not exceed a reasonable time.[3] In *Quinn v France*,[4] the European Court did not regard the period of one year and three days as excessive in the absence of any negligence on the part of the authorities who acted with necessary promptness. Article 5(3) refers only to persons charged and detained. There must be special diligence in the conduct of the prosecution of the cases concerning such detained persons. Article 5(3) is an independent provision imposing obligations irrespective of the reasons for arrest or the circumstances which made the preliminary investigation as long as it was. Therefore, even if the duration of the preliminary investigation is not open to criticism, the detention must not exceed a reasonable time.[5] In one case, a defendant was held in custody for four years

---

1   *Megyeri v FRG* (1992) Series A No 237–A, 15 EHRR 584.
2   Case no 119/1996/738/937.
3   *Kemmache v France* 14 EHRR 520, para 45 (see the provisions of PACE 1984, ss 41–46 relating to detention).
4   (1995) Series A No 311, 21 EHRR 529, para 56.
5   *Stogmuller v Austria* (1969) 1 EHRR 155 at 191.

from the time of his arrest to the date of conviction and yet the European Court refused to declare that there had been a violation of Article 5(3) because of the complexity of the case, the nature of the investigation of the offence and consideration of the conduct of the defendant.[1] In a recent case, the Commission was asked to consider whether s 25 of the Criminal Justice and Public Order Act 1994 which provides that a person charged with murder, attempted murder or manslaughter, should not be granted bail, contravened Article 5(3). The refusal of bail precluded the judiciary considering whether the accused should be released and, if so, on what terms. Therefore, the national legislature removed the judicial control envisaged by Article 5(3) regarding the pre-trial detention.[2] A Kurd who was detained for 14 days because it was alleged that he was a terrorist, and whose detention was not subject to judicial control, had his rights under Article 5(3) violated.[3]

Article 5(3) is distinguishable from Article 6. However, Article 6 may apply in other circumstances, such as where an administrative decision has taken a long time to promulgate.[4]

Reasonableness of the length of pre-trial detention

2.76 When an arrest is based on reasonable grounds for suspecting a person of having committed an offence, this condition may justify the initial arrest and detention but after a certain lapse of time it no longer suffices.[5] There must be other relevant grounds for justifying detention. Where there are relevant and sufficient grounds for detaining a person, there must also be special diligence in the conduct of the prosecution of the person charged and detained. An accused person has the right to have his case dealt with expeditiously. Thus, if the trial of a simple case without complexities were to take a long time then this might be a powerful reason why release is to be preferred to detention. Where a person's case is not complex and could have been dealt with more speedily, but forms part of an extremely complicated investigation, the diligence examined is in relation to the entire investigation of the offence.[6]

The danger of absconding because of the nature of the offence cannot be assessed solely on the basis of the severity of the possible sentence. It must be assessed with reference to a number of other relevant factors, such as the character of the person involved, his morals, his domicile, his profession, his

---

1   *W v Switzerland* (1993) 17 EHRR 60. *R v Manchester Crown Court, ex parte McDonald* [1999] 1 WLR 832 at 850F: detention of an accused in custody for a period of 112 days prescribed by the regulations imposes what by international standards is an exacting standard.
    Unconvicted defendants should be held in custody awaiting trial for as short a period as reasonably and practically possible, of obliging prosecutors to prepare for trial with all due expedition and of investing the court with the power to control any necessary extensions.
2   *CC v UK* Application No 32819/96 Commission level. It is justifiable to refuse bail if the accused is likely to abscond (*Stogmuller v Austria* (above); or where the accused is likely to reoffend if given bail (*Toth v Austria* (1991) 14 EHRR 551).
3   *Askoy v Turkey* (1997) 23 EHRR 533.
4   In *Zimmerman and Steiner v Switzerland* (1983) 6 EHRR 17, the Swiss Federal Court took 3½ years to determine a matter. The heavy workload and backlog did not excuse the excessive delay.
5   *Mitap and Muftuoglu* (1996) 22 EHRR 209 at 214, para 56 (Opinion).
6   *Van der Tang v Spain* (1996) 22 EHRR 363, paras 72–75.

assets etc[1] and the state of the evidence cannot in itself justify continued detention on remand particularly as an accused person is presumed innocent until he is found guilty.[2] The existence of a strong suspicion of the involvement of the person concerned in serious offences, while constituting a relevant factor, cannot alone justify a long period of pre-trial detention.[3] Furthermore, the substantial risk of absconding persisting throughout the length of detention constitutes a relevant and sufficient ground for refusing an application for release or bail.[4]

Continued detention may be justified if it is in the public interest which outweighs the rule of respect for individual liberty.[5] Even when an accused person is reasonably detained during periods for reasons of the public interest, there may be a violation of Article 5(3) if, for whatever cause, the proceedings continue for a considerable length of time. The exceptional length of the investigation and complexity of the trial are matters which may justify delay. While an accused in detention is entitled to have his case given priority and conducted with expedition, this must not stand in the way of the efforts of the judges to clarify fully the facts in issue, to give both prosecution and defence all facilities for putting forward their evidence and presenting their cases and to pronounce both judgment after careful deliberation on whether the offences were in fact committed, and on the sentence.[6]

The provisions of Article 5(3) refer only to Article 5(1)(c) and are, therefore, for example, not applicable to detention pending deportation or extradition as provided for by Article 5(1)(f) of the Convention.[7]

ARTICLE 5(4)

> '4.   Everyone who is deprived of his liberty by arrest or detention shall be entitled to take proceedings by which the lawfulness of his detention shall be decided speedily by a court and his release ordered if the detention is not lawful.'

Applicability of Article 5(4)

2.77   Even if there is no violation of Article 5(1), there must still be an examination of whether there has been a violation of Article 5(4). The latter is a separate provision and everyone who is deprived of his liberty, lawfully or not, is entitled to a supervision of lawfulness by a court. A violation can therefore result either from a detention which is incompatible with Article 5(1) or from

---

1   *W v Switzerland* (1993) 17 EHRR 60, para 33; and *Yagci and Sargin v Turkey* (1995) 20 EHRR 505.
2   *Kemmache v France* (1992) 14 EHRR 520; and *Mitap and Muftuoglu* (1996) 22 EHRR 209 at 215, para 65; *Van der Tang v Spain* (1996) 22 EHRR 363.
3   *Van der Tang v Spain* (1996) 22 EHRR 363 at para 63; and *Tomasi v France* (1993) 15 EHRR 1, para 89.
4   *Van der Tang v Spain* (1996) 22 EHRR 363, para 67.
5   Ibid, para 55.
6   *Wemhoff v FRG* (1968) 1 EHRR 55 at 77–78.
7   *Quinn v France* (1995) Series A No 311, 21 EHRR 529, para 53.

the absence of any proceedings which satisfy Article 5(4), or even from both at the same time.[1]

Where the decision depriving a person of his liberty is one taken by an administrative body, then Article 5(4) obliges the authority to make available to the person detained a right of recourse to a court; but there is nothing to indicate that the same applies when the decision is made by a court at the close of judicial proceedings. In the latter case, the supervision required by Article 5(4) is incorporated in the decision; this is so, for example, where a sentence of imprisonment is pronounced after 'conviction by a competent court'.[2]

Article 5(4) does not require the continued detention of a mandatory life prisoner to be subject to review by a court.[3] However, as is the case with any sentence of a court, the common law does require compliance with the principles of fairness or of due process not only before sentence but also after sentence while it is being carried out. The principle of due process does not apply only to the procedure; it can also have effect on the substance of what is happening in carrying out the sentence.[4]

Lawfulness of detention by a competent court or administrative body: recourse to court

2.78 The supervision provided for in Article 5(4) could be incorporated in the decision ordering arrest or detention if this decision was taken by a court which provided the fundamental guarantees of procedure.[5] Where the decision depriving a person of his liberty is one taken by an administrative body (eg immigration officials), there is no doubt that Article 5(4) obliges the government to make available to the person detained a right of recourse to a court. In order for the guarantees laid down in Article 5(4) to be incorporated in the decision depriving a person of his liberty, this decision should be delivered by an authority providing the fundamental guarantees of procedure applied in matters of deprivation of liberty. In other words, the procedure followed should possess a judicial character and gives to the individual concerned the guarantees appropriate to the kind of deprivation of liberty in question[6] but there is nothing to indicate that the same applies when the decision is made by a court at the close of judicial proceedings.

As stated above, Article 5(4) is a separate provision from Article 5(1) and everyone who is deprived of his liberty, lawfully or not, is entitled to a supervision of lawfulness by a court. A violation can therefore result either from a detention which is incompatible with Article 5(1) or from the absence of any proceedings satisfying Article 5(4), or even from both at the same time.[7]

---

1   *De Wilde, Ooms and Versyp v Belgium* (1971) Series A No 12, 1 EHRR 373, para 73.
2   Ibid, para 76.
3   *Synne v UK* (1994) 19 EHRR 333.
4   *R v Home Secretary, ex parte Hindley* [1999] 2 WLR 1253 at 1260B–C (leave to appeal to the House of Lords granted).
5   *De Wilde, Ooms and Versyp v Belgium* (above).
6   Ibid, para 76.
7   Ibid, para 73.

Detention after conviction: whether such detention is immune from subsequent review

2.79   In the latter case, the supervision required by Article 5(4) is incorporated in the decision; this is so, for example, where a sentence of imprisonment is pronounced after conviction by a competent court.[1] Where a person is convicted by a competent court in accordance with Article 5(1)(a), the judicial appeal provided for in Article 5(4) is not applicable, since the supervision required is incorporated in the initial decision.[2] This means that only the initial decision is incorporated and not the ensuing period of detention in which new issues affecting the lawfulness of the detention might subsequently arise.[3] But Article 5(4) sometimes requires the possibility of subsequent review of the lawfulness of detention by a court. This usually applies:

(i)   to the detention of persons of unsound mind within the meaning of Article 5(1)(e), where the reasons initially warranting confinement may cease to exist;[4]

(ii)   the continuing detention of a person sentenced to an 'indeterminate' or 'discretionary' sentence;[5]

(iii)   placing of a recidivist at the government's disposal;[6]

(iv)   detaining for security reasons of a person with an impaired mental capacity.[7]

It is normal that the judicial control should be carried out during the proceedings preceding conviction and that there is a right to subsequent judicial control in respect of imprisonment following a criminal conviction.[8]

Who may bring proceedings under Article 5(4)?

2.80   Despite the broad terms of this Article, it appears only to apply to a particular category of prisoner. It does not apply to mandatory life prisoners[9] nor to the majority of prisoners who receive a determinate sentence proportionate to their offence.[10] Consequentially, these prisoners have no right under the Convention to parole or release before the determinate period. However, this Article does cover discretionary life prisoners and, it is submitted that it should also cover those prisoners who are sentenced to longer terms of imprisonment under s 2(2)(b) of the Criminal Justice Act 1991 (see **2.84**).

---

1   *De Wilde, Ooms and Versyp v Belgium* (1971) Series A No 12, 1 EHRR 373, para 73.
2   *Engel and Others v The Netherlands* (1976) Series A No 22, 1 EHRR 706, para 77.
3   *X v UK* (1981) Series A No 46, 4 EHRR 188, para 51.
4   *Winterwerp v The Netherlands* (1979) Series A No 33, 2 EHRR 387, para 55.
5   *Weeks v UK* (1987) Series A No 114, 10 EHRR 293; *Thynne, Wilson & Gunnel v UK* (1990) Series A No 1990, 13 EHRR 666.
6   *Van Droogenbroeck v Belgium* (1982) Series A No 50, 4 EHRR 443.
7   *Iribarne Perez v France* (1996) 22 EHRR 153, para 30.
8   Ibid, para 39 (Opinion).
9   *Wynne v UK* (1995) Series A No 294–A, 19 EHRR 333.
10   *Van Droogenbroeck v Belgium* (1982) Series A No 50, 4 EHRR 433.

Mandatory life prisoners are not covered by Article 5(4)

2.81 At present, it appears that mandatory life prisoners cannot avail themselves of the protection of Article 5(4). This view was upheld in *X v UK* where it was decided that Parliament had in mind very different considerations with regards to this class of prisoner, their crime being serious enough to warrant a mandatory life sentence.[1] For this class of prisoner the review of their detention is currently not a right protected by the Convention.

Fixing the tariff

2.82 The review of mandatory life sentences is provided for by s 29 of the Crime (Sentences) Act 1997. The Home Secretary fixes a tariff to meet the needs of retribution and deterrence. The trial judge and the Lord Chief Justice are requested to give recommendations on setting the tariff. However, the Home Secretary has a wide discretion in considering the release of such prisoners and he need not follow those recommendations. Further, he can take into consideration public acceptability and public confidence in the criminal justice system. This power has been recently confirmed as lawful in *R v Secretary of State for the Home Department, ex parte Hindley*.[2] It is suggested that considerations such as public acceptability and confidence are irrelevant to the issue of release and are not necessary under Article 5.

The Home Secretary exercising a judicial function in fixing tariffs

2.83 It is recognised that in setting the tariff the Home Secretary is exercising a judicial function as confirmed in *R v Secretary of State for the Home Department, ex parte Pierson*.[3] It is suggested that once a mandatory lifer has served his tariff and is no longer considered to be a danger to the public, he should be released. A court and not the Home Secretary should review any further detention. This would appear to be the correct position given the acceptance that, generally speaking, life does not mean life and therefore this category of prisoner can expect release during their lifetime. Accordingly, it is suggested that European jurisprudence in this area of prison law is misconceived and in need of challenge. Further, the fixing of the tariff should be in accordance with Article 6, given that it is accepted that it is essentially a sentencing exercise. The Home Secretary's current role in fixing the tariff is incompatible with Article 6 principles.

The Criminal Justice Act 1991, s 2(2)(b)

2.84 Under this statutory regime, prisoners who have been convicted of a violent or sexual offence and who are considered to be a danger to the public if released, are given sentences that are longer than the normal punitive sentence. The section is increasingly being used in relation to offenders who are considered to be a danger to the public due to some characteristic peculiar

---

1   See the decision in *Thynne, Wilson & Gunnel v UK* (1990) 13 EHRR 666 at 686, para 81 and also *R v Secretary of State for the Home Department, ex parte Stafford* (1997) *The Times* 28 November, CA.
2   (1997) *The Times*, 19 December.
3   (1997) 3 WLR 492.

to the offender. Commonly there will be psychiatric evidence in support of the degree of danger presented by the offender. The sentencing judge would usually state what sentence the offender would normally expect to receive and then increase it to reflect dangerousness. Although such prisoners may, during the currency of their sentence cease to be dangerous, it seems they have no right to insist upon a periodic review of their continued detention. No doubt this is because technically they receive determinate sentences. It is submitted that where a prisoner ceases to be a danger while serving part of the sentence, then that prisoner should be released.

Discretionary Life Prisoners

2.85   Article 5 does, however, apply to discretionary life prisoners (DLPs). The ethos behind these sentences is different to those receiving a determinate sentence (see below) and so attracts the protection of Article 5.

Article 5(4) calls for periodic review
2.86   In *Thynne, Wilson & Gunnel v UK*,[1] the European Court held that, in order to comply with Article 5(4) of the Convention, it was necessary for the detention of such prisoners to be periodically reviewed once the punitive element of the sentence has been served.

The parole board not a 'court' for the purposes of Article 5(4)
2.87   The parole board does not satisfy the requirement under Article 5(4) to have detention reviewed by a court. The parole board lacked impartiality due to its connection with the executive and could not order release if the detention was found to be unlawful. Discretionary Life Panels have now been created to satisfy this requirement.

Reforms made by the Criminal Justice Act 1991 insufficient?

2.88   Despite the legislative attempts to bring domestic law into line with the Convention, some commentators remain of the view that the statute does not go far enough. In particular, it is argued that once the punitive element of the sentence has been served, it should be incumbent upon the State to justify the need for continued detention.[2]

Application of Article 5(4) to children convicted of murder

2.89   Young offenders convicted of murder were in the past treated the same as adult mandatory life prisoners. It is now clear that such sentences are more comparable to the discretionary life sentence.

The decision in ex parte Venables and Thompson[3]
2.90   In *R v Secretary of State for the Home Department, ex parte Venables and Thompson*, it was held that the correct approach with respect to young offenders

---

1   (1990) Series A No 1990, 13 EHRR 666.
2   See the article entitled 'The Criminal Justice Act 1991: Preventative Detention of the Dangerous Offender' by Edward Fitzgerald QC (1995) *European Human Rights Review* at p 39.
3   [1997] 3 WLR 23.

convicted of murder, was for the Home Secretary to keep the sentence under review in accordance with his duties under s 44(1) of the Children and Young Persons Act 1933. This approach recognises the fact that the imposition of a custodial sentence is not punitive and instead regard should be had to the welfare of the child.

Review by the Home Secretary not a review by a 'court'
2.91   The Home Secretary's review of these sentences does not appear to be in keeping with the principles under Article 5(4), which requires detention to be reviewed by a court. As a member of the executive, the Home Secretary lacks the requisite impartiality necessary for a reviewing body. If detention at Her Majesty's Pleasure is truly analogous to the discretionary life sentence, then review by the Home Secretary is unsustainable and should be replaced by a system of review similar to Discretionary Life Panels.

ARTICLE 5(5)

'5.   Everyone who has been the victim of arrest or detention in contravention of the provisions of this Article shall have an enforceable right to compensation.'

2.92   Article 5(5) guarantees an enforceable right to compensation only to those who have been the victims of arrest or detention in contravention of the provisions of Article 5.[1]

If a violation of Article 5(1) to (4) is established then compensation is due under Article 5(5). Conversely, if there is no violation of Article 5 then no compensation is due and Article 5(5) is not applicable.

Thus, if an imprisonment under domestic law is unlawful, a statutory immunity from liability will not be regarded under the Convention as excusing the failure to provide compensation. The right to compensation under Article 5(5) is unqualified.[2] The Lord Chancellor has stated that, where a complaint is made that Article 5 has been breached as a result of a judicial act or omission, it will be necessary first to establish whether the judicial act complained of was unlawful, then to rule on whether the aggrieved person is entitled to compensation under Article 5(5) and then to determine the amount of compensation. In determining those questions, the court will take into account the European jurisprudence on unlawful detention and on the award of damages.[3]

---

1   *Wassink v The Netherlands* (1990) Series A No 185–A, para 38; and *Benham v UK* (1996) 22 EHRR 293, para 50.
2   *R v Governor of HM Prison Brockhill* (1998) QBCOF 97/0925/4, CA at 18 as per Lord Woolf MR.
3   HL 585 Col 289 (29 January 1998). See *R v SSHD, ex parte Garner and Others* (1999) *The Times*, 3 May, regarding a claim for compensation from a person being wrongly detained.

ARTICLE 6 – RIGHT TO A FAIR TRIAL

'Article 6

Right to a fair trial'

INTRODUCTION

2.93   The Human Rights Act 1998 guarantees the right to a fair hearing under the Convention for the Protection of Human Rights and Fundamental Freedoms[1] to anyone whose civil rights and obligations are affected by official action. When the 1998 Act comes into force, this right under Article 6 of the Convention will provide an object lesson in how a new human rights oriented judicial interpretation of legislation is to be undertaken. The right to a fair hearing already exists under judge-made common law.[2] However, traditionally, the search by the courts has been for the true meaning of legislation when interpreting it. Now the search will be for a possible meaning[3] that would prevent the making of a declaration of incompatibility by the courts when called upon to construe legislation.[4] This means it will no longer be necessary to search for an ambiguity. The courts will simply be required 'to interpret legislation so as to uphold the Convention rights unless the legislation itself is so clearly incompatible with the Convention that it is impossible to do so'.[5] Therefore, contrary to what might have been initially thought, Article 6 is likely to have a major impact on the development of the common law right to a fair hearing by an independent and impartial tribunal. This is because the requirement of a fair hearing in Article 6 is to be given a 'broad and purposive interpretation.'[6]

Yet, it was initially felt that Article 6 may have a limited impact given the existing requirement of the fairness of proceedings under the common law. In the 1998 case of *Witham*[7] the applicant could not pay fees for issuing a writ and

---

1   The right to a fair trial is guaranteed in Article 6 of the Convention and s 1 of the Human Rights Act 1998 states that:
     '(1) In this Act, the "Convention rights" means the rights and fundamental freedoms set out in
     (a) Articles 2 to 12 and 14 of the Convention ...'.
2   The well-known cases in this area comprise *Dr Bentley's Case* (1723) 1 Sta 557; *Ceylon v University of Fernando* [1960] 1 All ER 631; *Breen v AEU* [1971] 2 QB 175; *Cooper v Wandsworth Board of Works* (1863) 14 CB (NS) 180 at 194 (Byles J); *Ridge v Baldwin* [1964] AC 40 at 117 (Lord Morris of Borth-y-Gest) and *R v Barnsley Council, ex parte Hook* [1976] 3 All ER 452.
3   See the Lord Chancellor, Lord Irvine of Lairg, when moving the Second Reading of the Human Rights Bill in the House of Lords on 13 November 1997 (582 PD 1272–1273).
4   Under s 4(2):
     'If the court is satisfied that the provision [ie of primary legislation] is incompatible with a Convention right, it may make a declaration of that incompatibility'.
5   From the Tom Sargant Memorial Lecture given by the Lord Chancellor (quoted in the House of Lords by Lord Lord Lester in 584 PD 1291–1292).
6   See *Moreiva de Azvedo v Portugal* (1990) 13 EHRR 721.
7   See *R v The Lord Chancellor, ex parte Witham* [1998] QB 575.

successfully challenged an order to that effect. Although he based his arguments on Article 6, the court made only a passing reference to the case-law under that provision. Instead, it granted him relief on the basis that a constitutional right of access to the courts was a common law right that could not be infringed by a court order. The court further held that a common law right of access to court provided no lesser protection than the European Court jurisprudence. This Article shows that the initial view of Article 6, as explicated in *Witham,* is misconceived and already out-dated. Even one year after that case, there have already been a flurry of cases, not only in the European Court but in our own domestic courts, that demonstrate that not only is Article 6 broader than existing common-law rights, but that it is a truly foundational provision in the protection and promotion of *due process rights* in the broadest sense. Article 6, so far as relevant, provides as follows:

> '1. In the determination of his civil rights and obligations . . . everyone is entitled to a fair and public hearing within a reasonable time by an independent and impartial tribunal established by law. Judgment shall be pronounced publicly but the press and public may be excluded from all or part of the trial in the interests of morals, public order or national security in a democratic society, where the interests of juveniles or the protection of the private life of the parties so require, or to the extent strictly necessary in the opinion of the court in special circumstances where publicity would prejudice the interests of justice.'

The reference in Article 6 to a 'fair and public hearing' that is undertaken 'within a reasonable time' by an 'independent and impartial tribunal' that is 'established by law' has had an impact in UK law in four major ways:

(1) tribunals have already faced challenges where they are not deemed to be independent and impartial;

(2) where in the determination of a person's 'civil rights and obligations' the requirements of the Article have been ignored;

(3) where the decision in question has had the effect of restricting access to court; and

(4) where a litigant has been hampered by procedural obstacles such as time-limits and immunities.

THE REQUIREMENT OF AN 'INDEPENDENT AND IMPARTIAL TRIBUNAL'

2.94 The common-law cases in this area are generally known to be covered under 'the rule against bias'. They are, however, restricted to two situations, namely:

(1) where a decision-maker has any direct pecuniary interest in the subject-matter of the inquiry;[1] and

(2) where there is a real likelihood of bias in favour of one party on the part of the decision-making body.[2]

---

1   See *Dimes v Grand Junction Canal* (1852) 3 HLC 759.

2   It is unnecessary to find that the decision was in fact biased: see *R v Sussex JJ v ex parte McCarthy* [1924] 1 KB 265.

The modern test, as established by the House of Lords in 1993, is simply whether there was a real likelihood, in the sense of a real possibility, of bias on the part of the decision-maker.[1] This is the same test, in the House of Lords' view, as asking whether there was a 'real danger' that the trial might not have been fair.[2] Expansive as these common-law principles are in their scope and application, European Human Rights law still goes further in concentrating on the entire breadth of interests that a decision-maker may have outside of his judicial function. This is where the difference with common law principles lies. Outside interests, even if they are non-pecuniary, can impact upon a decision-maker's independence. Yet, under domestic administrative law, the court is concerned only to ensure impartiality. It is not concerned to ensure independence as well. However, the Convention requires a tribunal to be both impartial and independent in the determination of a person's civil rights and obligations. The result is that, under the Convention, there could be an administrative decision that amounts to a determination of a person's civil rights and obligations and yet does not satisfy the requirements of the Article.

In *McGonnell v UK*,[3] the Commission decided overwhelmingly, by 25 votes to 5 votes, that the Royal Court of Guernsey was not an independent and impartial tribunal within the meaning of Article 6. This case demonstrates how far the impact of Article 6 will be in the future in the UK. Mr McGonnell wanted to build a dwelling-house on his land. He applied for planning permission which was refused. He appealed to the Royal Court. In the Royal Court, questions of law are determined by the Bailiff of Guernsey. Therefore, his appeal was heard by the Bailiff of Guernsey. However, the Bailiff also has other functions in Guernsey such as being president of the legislature and the head of the island's administration. Consequently, the question of a legitimate doubt of bias could not be excluded on this matter.

This was despite the fact that the Commission found that the Bailiff 'spends most of his time in judicial functions' and that the Bailiff's other functions 'did not directly impinge on his judicial duties in the case' of Mr McGonnell. Nevertheless, the fundamental principle remained that 'it is incompatible with the requisite appearances of independence and impartiality for a judge to have legislative and executive functions as substantial as those' that were being carried out by the Bailiff. The fact was that 'his independence and impartiality are capable of appearing open to doubt'.[4] With this, the Commission declared the UK to be in breach of Article 6. It appears from this that UK lawyers, like their American counterparts, will have to get used to using the language of proceedings being 'tainted' by untoward appearances if they are to succeed in having them set aside.

Today, the potential impact of Article 6 infringements is beginning to make itself felt in ways more fundamental than one could have imagined. In an unprecedented move recently, the House of Lords sent shock waves in the legal world and beyond when it impugned one of its own decisions on the grounds of

1   *R v Gough* [1993] AC 128.
2   *R v Spencer* [1987] AC 128.
3   *McGonnell v UK* Application No 28488/95, 20 October 1998.
4   Ibid.

potential basis. It held that one of its members, Lord Hoffman, should not have participated in the extradition proceedings of General Pinochet of Chile.[1] This was because of his close connections with Amnesty International.[2] As a result of this ruling, judges everywhere have been declaring their interests before hearing a case. The Lord Chancellor's position has been questioned and Lord Lester of Herne Hill has attacked his Constitutional position.[3] The Lord Chancellor combines three top roles. He is a judge when he sits as a member of the appellate committee of the House of Lords. He is a legislator when he presides in the Upper House. He is a member of the Cabinet and therefore of the Executive in Parliament. Yet, his judicial function is increasingly untenable if present arrangements continue. In May 1999, a committee of the law reform group, Justice, and consisting of nine legal peers and a law professor, said that the rule allowing the Lord Chancellor to sit in the House of Lords was 'inherently flawed' as it created an appearance of bias. Reform, said the committee, was 'an urgent practical necessity'. Lord Steyn also warned in May that failure to remedy this anomaly could lead to the Pinochet debâcle taking place again. Yet, in a world-wide conference of common-law judges from Australia, Canada, New Zealand, India, Ireland, Israel, New Zealand, Britain and the United States, in Edinburgh on 5 July 1998, the Lord Chancellor, Lord Irvine, defended his right to sit as a judge. He claimed that his office and his functions were necessary to protect the independence of the judiciary. Further, unless he was head of the judiciary, he could not command 'the same respect and confidence of the judiciary'. For this reason, it was important for the Lord Chancellor to sit as judge.[4]

However, this has not only difficulties in principle of the kind mentioned, but practical difficulties also. The choice of when the Lord Chancellor may sit lies with the Lord Chancellor. The choice of when he may not sit because the case is 'political' is his choice also. His decision in this respect is bound to prove practically difficult in high-profile cases. In addition, there are the inherent difficulties of his office. The existence of the Lord Chancellor's other responsibilities may not, just as in *McGonnell*, directly impinge on his judicial functions. Yet, the judicial function is nevertheless tainted by the failure to observe the principle of the separation of powers in exactly the same sense as it was in *McGonnell*.

Moreover, in matters of public policy, whenever the executive interest is affected or the government has a view, the Lord Chancellor's judicial function is plainly incompatible with the holding of his non-judicial offices just as it was

PART 2
THE ARTICLES

---

1   *R v Bow Street Metropolitan Stipendiary Magistrate, ex parte Pinochet Ugarte (No 2)* [1999] 2 WLR 272. For a countervailing view see, Philip Havers QC and Owain Thomas, 'Bias Post-*Pinochet* and Under the ECHR' [1999] *Judicial Review* at p 111.

2   The case has had far-reaching implications. It has been reported that 'The affair was unprecedented. It put the elite group of 12 men who constitute the highest court in the land under public scrutiny for the first time – making them what one senior judge called "a laughing stock" and yet all of this in a case which as Lord Browne-Wilkinson observed "was a unique, first occasion concerning an interest which was not a financial interest" ': see Frances Gibb 'The Law Lord who took the rap over Pinochet' (1999) *The Times*, 19 October (at p 3, Law Section).

3   See (1999) *The Times*, 23 February.

4   See Claire Dyer 'Irvine defends his right to sit in court' (1999) *The Guardian*, 6 July at p 12.

in *McGonnell.* Of course, the implications of Article 6 do not end there. Already, the Royal Commission, looking into the future of the House of Lords, and headed by Lord Wakeham, is considering whether Law Lords should sit in Parliament. It is well known that a number of Law Lords have spoken and voted on controversial matters of public policy, such as penal reform and refugee policy.[1] For example, Lord Hoffman has had to stand down from another two cases after *Pinochet.* In two cases involving the issue whether the media should have the special protection from libel actions when reporting the activities of politicians, Lord Hoffman's independence was felt to have been compromised by his earlier extra-judicial involvement in the corruption case of the Tory MP, Mr Neil Hamilton. Mr Hamilton wanted to sue *The Guardian* over allegations that he took cash for asking parliamentary questions. Traditionally, the courts have no jurisdiction over what goes on in Parliament. Lord Hoffman moved an amendment in 1996 at the request of the then Lord Chancellor, Lord Mackay, to the Defamation Bill allowing MPs to waive the traditional privilege that prevents courts from inquiring into parliamentary proceedings. Lord Hoffman declared that MPs should have the same right to sue for libel as the general public. The two cases that arose were in July 1999: one a New Zealand case in the Privy Council; the other an English case in the House of Lords. The two linked appeals in the libel actions against *The Sunday Times* were brought by two ex Prime Ministers, New Zealand's David Lange, and Ireland's Albert Reynolds. In the *Lange* case, lawyers on both sides objected to Lord Hoffman because he had expressed views impacting on the limits of press freedom in the debates over the Defamation Bill in the House of Lords. Accordingly, Lord Hoffman was replaced by Lord Hobhouse.[2] Indeed, the practice of challenging judges because of their personal interests is growing. It was reported in September 1999 that some City law firms have started compiling files on High Court and Court of Appeal judges with the aim of having a judge removed from a case if that is in their client's interest and the practice has been giving concern to senior judges.[3]

Nevertheless, public concern about the activities of senior judges extends far and wide. It extends to the less well-known Law Lords' chairmanship of parliamentary committees. The developing jurisprudence of Article 6 means that, increasingly, the fundamental concerns about judicial practice are raised when questions of independence and impartiality of a tribunal fall into question. In all these instances, it is doubtless the case that if the Law Lords or the Lord Chancellor insist on combining judicial with executive and legislative functions, they will risk such decisions being successfully reviewed in the European Court under Article 6. The lessons of *McGonnell* will need, therefore, to be speedily learned.

---

1   Lord Ackner speaking on the Asylum and Immigration Appeals Bill in 1992, for example, famously inveighed against the proposed removal of the right to an oral hearing by declaring that: 'It will cost the Government nothing to be generous' Satvinder Juss, *Immigration, Nationality and Citizenship* (Mansell, 1994) at p 25.
2   See, Claire Dyer 'Pinochet Law Lord replaced again as judge' (1999) *The Guardian,* 8 July at p 12.
3   See Frances Gibb 'Judges fight "conflict ploy"' (1999) *The Times,* 6 September at pp 1–2.

The lessons indeed are already being learnt in domestic law. Recently, in *Smith v Secretary of State for Trade and Industry*,[1] the Employment Appeal Tribunal (EAT; Mr Justice Morrison) when considering an appeal, questioned whether the Employment Tribunal was an 'independent and impartial' tribunal in relation to a determination of a claim brought by the complainant, a director and controlling shareholder of an insolvent company, who was said to be not entitled[2] to recover a redundancy payment from the Secretary of State for Trade and Industry on the grounds that he was not an employee. The EAT accepted that :

> 'The lay members of the employment tribunal were appointed by the Secretary of State and were paid for by him ... Lay members held their appointment through an instrument of appointment the terms of which might be varied by the Secretary of State. Their remuneration was determined by the Secretary of State. Their appointment might be terminated by the Secretary of State. Tribunal chairmen were appointed by the Lord Chancellor but their remuneration was determined by the Secretary of State. The rules of procedure were made by the Secretary of State.'

The EAT submitted that there was a lack of transparent objective independence from the Secretary of State. It accepted that it was something of an anomaly that the employment tribunal should have such close links with 'an executive arm of the Government'. There was a real and troubling question whether employment tribunals should properly and lawfully adjudicate on claims made against the Secretary of State. Accordingly, permission to appeal would be granted to the Court of Appeal even though the 1998 Act was not yet in force because where proceedings yet to be determined were unlikely to be concluded before the implementation date (ie October 2000), the court might intervene.

THE DETERMINATION OF A PERSON'S 'CIVIL RIGHTS AND OBLIGATIONS'

2.95 In recent months, a number of important cases have arisen which epitomise the importance of an individual's 'civil rights and obligations' in the context of the requirements of a fair trial. Where the court is reviewing a decision, which is itself a determination of civil rights or obligations within the meaning of Article 6, but which does not comply with that Article, there will be violation of Article 6. The European Court's jurisprudence has been particularly powerful here because, unlike public law adjudication at common law,

---

1   *Smith v Secretary of State for Trade and Industry* (1999) *The Times*, 15 October, EAT. Also see, *Isha Mohammed* HX/71091/96 where the same argument was used against the Immigration Appeals Tribunal (Chairman, Mr Care) on account of its close connections with the Home Office in a hearing on 19 October 1999.

2   Reliance had been placed on the decision in *Buchan v Secretary of State for Employment* [1997] IRLR 80 that a controlling shareholder could not be an employee, although in *Secretary of State for Trade and Industry v Bottrill* [1999] ICR 592 the Court of Appeal held that a controlling shareholder was not, on its own, determinative of the issue. The appeal tribunal had allowed the appeal on the basis of *Bottrill* without considering the implications of Article 6, at which point, when the matter was referred back to the tribunal, the proper implications of Article 6 of the Human Rights Act 1998 came into focus.

which is concerned with issues of public law, the 'civil' rights and obligations jurisprudence is concerned with essentially private law rights. Many matters which were hitherto regarded as being within the realm of public law will now be justiciable as Article 6 issues in judicial review applications. Thus, this will impact on what we mean by 'determinations' in Article 6. Certainly, where the outcome is 'directly decisive' for the rights and obligations concerned, the civil rights and obligations can be said to have been 'determined' by those proceedings.[1] Already there have been in a number of cases findings of admissibility by the Commission against the UK Government. But the Court of Appeal here has also been remarkably forthright and has determined to apply the principles in the way discussed above.

In *R v DPP, ex parte Kebilene and Others*,[2] the Court of Appeal invoked the fair hearing provisions of the Human Rights Act 1998 more than one year before it came into effect to uphold the presumption of innocence in criminal proceedings. It is a marvellous example of legislation being applied retrospectively and of the conventional rules of constitutional law being turned on their head thereby. The Court of Appeal held that ss 16(A) and (B) of the Prevention of Terrorism (Temporary Provisions) Act 1989 were incompatible with the Human Rights Act 1998. Lord Bingham ruled that the prosecution of four men by the Director of Public Prosecutions (DPP) violated their right to a fair trial under Article 6. He ruled that the sections undermined 'in a blatant and obvious way' the right of a defendant to be presumed innocent until proven guilty because those sections reversed the normal burden of proof by requiring a defendant to establish that he had the suspect items on his person for an innocent purpose. In this case, four Algerians were accused of 'having in their possession chemical containers, radio equipment, manuals, documents, credit cards and sums of money in circumstances which give rise to a reasonable suspicion that the articles were in their possession for a purpose connected with the commission, preparation or instigation of acts of terrorism'. Lord Bingham held that the DPP should consider whether the Prevention of Terrorism Act (Temporary Provisions) 1989 was compatible with the Convention before proceeding any further with the prosecutions. He could, he said, 'conceive of no circumstances' in which, if the court concluded that the trial was unfair, it would not go on to finding a violation of the European Convention'. Other challenges are now likely to follow across the whole investigative process, such as granting bail, police interview techniques, police surveillance and sentencing provisions.

The European Court's decisions show that the fair hearing principle has been invoked most obviously, however, where the hearing in question has not been public. In *Scarth (Norman) v UK*,[3] the defendant in county court proceedings, by way of arbitration, for debt applied for the trial of the issue to be in public with evidence to be given on oath. The application was refused by the district judge. No formal reasons were given. The defendant was convicted in the private arbitration proceedings. A note prepared by the judge in the subsequent

---

1   See *Le Compte, Van Leuven and De Meyer v Belgium* (1982) 4 EHRR 1.
2   *R v DPP, ex parte Kebeline and Others* [2000] 1 UKHRR 176.
3   *Scarth (Norman) v UK* Application No 33745/96, 21 October 1998.

European Court proceedings did not show why the hearing had to be in private. The applicant argued a violation of Article 6 for the denial of a public hearing. The Government argued that private hearings allowed for claims to be dealt with speedily, informally and inexpensively. Moreover, the threat of costs would privilege a wealthy party over a poorer one in public proceedings. The Commission unanimously found there to be a violation of Article 6(1). The public character of court proceedings in the transparent rendering of the administration of justice was strongly emphasised by the Commission. It concluded that the exclusion of the public was right only 'to the extent strictly necessary in the opinion of the court in special circumstances where publicity would prejudice the interests of justice'. The district judge had not applied that test. He had considered that the case was 'no different from the usual "run of the mill" arbitration disputes heard in any county court'. Given that the Court of Appeal had a limited function here, it was prevented from providing the necessary 'full jurisdiction' to cure the defect of the district court in the lower court.

The 'James Bulger' case, however, raised an Article 6 issue before the Commission, partly because a public trial was inappropriate for juvenile defendants. This shows that the crucial question is how the 'civil rights and obligations' of the individual concerned are determined. In *T and V v UK*,[1] the European Commission heard before it allegations under Articles 3, 5, and 6 of the Convention. The applicants were convicted at the age of 11. They were ordered to be detained at her Majesty's pleasure. When they were aged 10, they had abducted the two-year-old boy, James Bulger, from a shopping precinct, battered him to death, and left him on the railway line to be run over. The trial judge recommended a tariff of eight years following conviction for murder. The Lord Chief Justice raised it to 10 years. The Secretary of State set the tariff at 15 years. The trial had taken place in public and in an adult Crown Court. There had been enormous media publicity and crowds greeted the applicants' arrival at Court with open hostility each day. The names of the boy assailants were made public at the end of the trial and their pictures were shown on national television and the press.

The European Commission found there to be a violation of Article 6 (although not of Article 3 in respect of the trial, or of Article 5 in respect of the sentences). It did uphold a violation of Article 5(4) on the grounds that the applicants were denied any opportunity for a review of their detention. The finding of a breach of Article 6 arises from the subjection of the two juvenile defendants to the full rigours of a public trial as if they were adults. This constituted a deprival of the opportunity to participate effectively in the determination of the criminal charges against them. The trial could not be fair, therefore. The involvement of the Home Secretary in the setting of the tariffs was also held to be incompatible with Article 6(1).

Yet other cases before the Commission demonstrate that Article 6 may be linked with breaches of Article 8. One recent case, *Sultan Khan v UK*,[2] involved the inadmissibility of improperly obtained evidence. In this case, Mr B was

---

1　*T and V v UK* Application Nos 24724/94 and 24888/94, 4 December 1998.
2　*Khan (Sultan) v UK* Application No 35394/97, 20 April 1999.

under investigation for dealing in heroin. A tape-recording of a conversation was obtained by the police where the applicant admitted being involved in the importation of drugs. At trial, the applicant argued that the tape-recording was inadmissible as evidence. He argued that it had been improperly obtained. The trial judge ruled that it was admissible and the applicant was convicted and sentenced to three years' imprisonment. Both the Court of Appeal and the House of Lords dismissed his appeals.[1] Before the Commission, the applicant complained of violations of Articles 6, 8, and 13 and the Commission unanimously declared the application to be admissible. In relation to Article 6, the Commission held that the admission of a surveillance tape, recorded without Mr B's knowledge at his home, rendered the proceedings as a whole unfair because that evidence against the applicant was the only evidence and it had been obtained in circumstances without any domestic safeguards in law.[2]

RESTRICTING ACCESS TO COURT

2.96   Access to court considerations are very wide-ranging as the decided cases against the UK government are already beginning to show. They will range from judge-made restrictions on the availability of common-law remedies to governmental attempts to regulate the provision of publicly funded litigation. As regards the former, the immunity in law traditionally given to the police from actions relating to their duty to investigate and suppress crime was found recently by the European Court to be a violation of Article 6(1). In particular, it was a disproportionate restriction on the applicant's right of access to court. In *Osman v UK*,[3] the applicant had attempted to sue the police in negligence for failing to protect him and his father from violent attacks. His claim, however, was struck out in the domestic courts on the basis that well-established authority gave the police an immunity from such claims.[4] The European Court found in the applicant's favour and awarded £10,000 for the loss of the opportunity to bring the claim in the domestic courts. The European Court held that the immunity in negligence offended both Article 6 of the Convention guarantee-ing access to a 'fair hearing' and offended the 'proportionality rule':

> 'The Court would observe that the application of the rule in this manner without further enquiry into the existence of competing public interest considerations only serves to confer a blanket immunity on the police for their acts and omissions during the investigation and suppression of crime and amounts to an unjustifiable restriction on an applicant's right to have determination on the merits to a domestic court to have regards to the presence of other public interest considerations which pull in the opposite direction to the application of the rule. Failing this, there will be no distinction made between degrees of negligence or of harm suffered or any consideration of justice of a particular case.'

---

1   See *R v Khan (Sultan)* (1996) 3 All ER 289, HL.
2   In this respect the case was different from *Schenk v Switzerland* (1990) Series A No 140, 13 EHRR 242.
3   *Osman v UK* Application No 87/1997/871/1083, 28 October 1998.
4   This was based on the House of Lords' decision in *Hill v Chief Constable of West Yorkshire Police* [1989] AC 53.

The European Court was particularly concerned with the idea of a blanket immunity being given to the police. The European Court acknowledged that there were public policy reasons for protecting the police from suit, but stated that there were also important public policy reasons for allowing a person to sue the police, particularly where the negligence of the police and the harm suffered by the person were very serious. The two competing public interests should be balanced depending on the merits of the case.[1] It is likely that in many cases the balancing act of the public interest will still result in no liability being imposed on the police. However, there is no longer an absolute immunity. This means that rather than cases being struck out, each will have to be considered on its merits. The same kind of challenge is likely now to be permitted to other 'immunities' that the police (and other agencies) enjoy, such as misfeasance in public office.

In *Faulkner (Ian) v UK*,[2] the applicant was arrested for theft under an arrest warrant issued in Guernsey. He was arrested by Surrey police who escorted him to Guernsey where the magistrates there released him on bail. The applicant was charged with four charges of theft but was acquitted on all four. A further charge was later dismissed by the magistrates. The applicant was unable to pay his lawyers' fees in these abortive proceedings under the theft laws because of his impecuniosity. He owed outstanding fees as a result of the criminal proceedings. In the circumstances, no lawyer, he argued, would be prepared in Guernsey to represent him in civil proceedings against the Guernsey authorities for false imprisonment, assault and battery. He complained about this to HM Comptroller in Guernsey but he was informed that no legal aid was available to bring civil proceedings in Guernsey. The Commission unanimously found there to be a violation of Article 6(1) but not of Article 13. It was satisfied that the applicant needed legal assistance to have access to a court which would have been competent to hear his action in Guernsey and that his financial position effectively prevented him from paying a lawyer to represent him. There was no possibility of his obtaining legal aid. The Government, moreover, failed to demonstrate that the applicant's proposed action lacked any prospects of success. The applicant, therefore, could not have achieved access to court to determine his civil rights and obligations. The UK member of the Commission, Nicholas Bratza, commented in a concurring opinion that the underlying problem was the lack of any coherent system of civil legal aid in Guernsey.

TIME-LIMITS, IMMUNITIES, AND PRIVILEGES

2.97   The existence of obstacles to the bringing of potential claims will also lead to a violation of Article 6. To date, this has not featured prominently as a concern in the UK. One reason for this is that, for most cases, legal aid is still available. *Locus standi* requirements are relatively generous allowing most

---

1   In *Tinnelly v UK* (1998) *The Times*, 5 November, a 'conclusive' national security was held to be contrary to Article 6 in the absence of effective scrutiny by the court. Presumably, if the scrutiny was effective, it would not be contrary to Article 6. This view is supported by the European Court ruling in *Bryan v UK* (1996) 21 EHRR 342.

2   *Faulkner (Ian) v UK* Application No 30308/96, 1 December 1998.

people to sue.[1] There is, moreover, a power of discretion in the court for the time-limit for applications for permission, and this is unlikely to lead to much hardship. However, an Article 6 issue could arise in relation to the non-extendable time-limit for various statutory appeals and challenges. The difficulty is exemplified by the French case of *De Geouffre de la Pradelle*.[2] Here, a landowner was not informed about the adoption of a decree affecting his land and was therefore unable to challenge it before the period for appeal had expired. It was held that the relevant time-limit provisions were incompatible with Article 6.[3] Nevertheless, there still remain some outstanding questions in relation to permissions. For example, given that it is for the State to justify an interference with a Convention right, it could be argued that all that the applicant need do is to demonstrate at the permission stage a *prima facie* interference with his rights. The respondent could then provide whatever justification for such interference as there is at the substantive stage. On the other hand, it could also be argued that the applicant himself has to demonstrate an arguable absence of justification by the respondent as well. It could be plausibly suggested that if the coming into force of the Human Rights Act 1998 generates an avalanche of claims, some weak and some strong, then the added burden on the applicant to prove absence of justification could be a useful filter to sift through the unmeritorious claims.

The other two obstacles concern immunities and privileges. Both these areas currently need developing and are relatively under-used. Immunities have already been considered at length with regard to the recent decisions on *Scarth* and *Osman* (see **2.95** and **2.69** respectively above). The third aspect of obstacles, namely that of privileges, is yet to be developed but it is to be hoped that the current application by Al Fayed will shed much needed light on the application of parliamentary privilege to potential claims. This may be less useful than it otherwise could have been because the privilege in this case is underpinned by primary legislation under Article 9 of the Bill of Rights.[4]

CONCLUSION

2.98   It is clear that the common-law approach as exemplified in *Witham*[5] will prove insufficient as an analytical tool for human rights cases after October 2000. The courts will have to adopt more sophisticated principles such as proportionality to enable them to meet the full demands of Article 6. This will clearly range from legal aid decisions and alternative methods of promoting access to justice to such questions as the resourcing of the court system so as to prevent unreasonable delay. What is more difficult to predict is that, since many

---

1   This may change under s 7 of the Human Rights Act 1998.
2   *De Geouffre de la Pradelle v France* (1992) Series A No 253-B.
3   A challenge might now, however, be thwarted under the Human Rights Act 1998 because time-limits are usually contained, not in subordinate, but in primary legislation. The challenge would be easier if there existed discretionary powers to enable the problem to be overcome, such as by revoking and reissuing the decision.
4   See *R v Parliamentary Commission for Standards, ex parte Al Fayed* [1998] 1 All ER 93.
5   *R v The Lord Chancellor, ex parte Witham* [1998] QB 575.

matters which were hitherto classified as private will now become public once they are seen as affecting the 'civil rights and obligations' of a party, the dividing line between public law and private law will need re-drawing once again.

SUMMARY OF CASES

Procedural

2.99   Civil rights and obligations under Article 6 include all private law matters such as discovery of documents and admissibility, and disclosure of evidence and documents: *McMichael v UK* (1995) 20 EHRR 205; and prevents unreasonable restrictions on access to evidence: *McGinley and Egan v UK* (1998) 4 EHRC 421. For example, the use of evidence obtained by compulsion in criminal proceedings violates the right against self-incrimination: *Saunders v UK* (1997) 23 EHRR 313; *James v UK* (1986) 8 EHRR 123; *Staines v UK* Application No 41552/98. Article 6 may be relied upon in collateral proceedings: *Airey v Ireland* (1979–80) 2 EHRR 305.

To strike out a claimant's case solely because he had been found to be in contumacious breach of the rules or an order of the court was an improper exercise of the court's power. That was so even where the claimant was guilty of conduct amounting to fraud on the court: *In re Swaptronices Ltd* (1999) *The Times*, 17 August; *Arrow Nominees Inc and Another v Blackledge and Others* (1999) *The Times*, 10 December; *Canada Trust v Stolzemberg* (1998) New Law Digest 14.

Article 6 also applies to all other matters with a financial or economic element although regulated by public law: *Francesco Lombardo v Italy* (1996) 21 EHRR 188.

Public hearings

2.100   Article 6 may be relied upon by an individual in any stage of the proceedings. A person may insist on a right to a public hearing. Such a right may be withheld on limited grounds such as national security, confidentiality or to protect the identity of children or those suffering mental disability: *Scarthy v UK* Application No 33745/96.

Witnesses

2.101   Article 6 confers the right to call and examine witnesses: *Dombo Beheer v The Netherlands* (1994) EHRR 18; and also confers the right to have an expert witness: *Brandsetter v Austria* (1995) 15 EHRR 378; and the right to make oral submissions at the end of the evidence: *Lobo Machado v Portugal* (1997) 23 EHRR 79.

Fair trial

2.102   Article 6 confers rights on defendants ensuring a fair trial free from racial bias in judges and juries: *Sanders v UK* Application No 34129/96; *Remli v*

France (1996) 22 EHRR 253; *Gregory v UK* RJD 1997–I 296, *Pélissier and Sassi v France* Application No 25444/98, *Garcia Ruiz v Spain* Application No 30544/96, 21 January 1999.

The right to be defended was a fundamental right deriving from the constitutional traditions common to the Member States, and the European Court has held that the right of every person charged with a criminal offence to be effectively defended by a lawyer was one of the fundamental elements in a fair trial and that an accused person did not forfeit entitlement to such a right simply because he was not present at the hearing.

Failure to disclose confidential information to the trial judge in criminal proceedings which may assist the defence cannot be cured by an appeal process which does not have the same scrutiny procedures as the first trial judge. The defence must have the opportunity to comment on evidence adduced by the other side: *Rowe and Davis v UK* Application No 28901/95, paras 60–65.

Impartiality and independence

2.103

(i) Article 6 emphasises the right to an impartial and independent judiciary free from ministerial involvement: *Bryan v UK* (1996) 21 EHRR 342; *Van de Hurk v The Netherlands* (1994) 18 EHRR 481. Independence and impartiality are distinct and separate requirements. Impartial connotes absence of bias and independence connotes judicial independence: see, for example, *Quebec Inc v Quebec* [1996] 3 SCR 919. Three main components of judicial independence are security of tenure, financial security and institutional independence: *Valente v The Queen* [1985] 2 SCR 673 at 685.

(ii) In judging whether a tribunal is impartial, both a subjective and objective test must be applied: *Crummock (Scotland) Ltd v HM Advocate* (2000) *The Times*, 9 May (CA). Impartiality was to be determined according to a subjective test on the basis of the personal conviction of a particular judge, and also according to an objective test, by ascertaining whether the judge offered guarantees sufficient to exclude any legitimate doubt in this respect: *Clancy v Caird (Court of Session Inner House)* [2000] 3 UKHRR. Should the tribunal fail either test, it was not to be regarded as impartial: *Persack v Belgium* (1982) Series A No 53, para 30; *Hauschildt v Denmark* (1989) Series A No 154, paras 46–48 and endorsed in *Locabail v Bayfield Properties* [2000] 1 All ER 65. Judges were entitled to criticise developments in the law, whether in the form of legislation or judicial decisions but what they were not entitled to do is to publish criticism or praise in such language as to give rise to a legitimate apprehension that, when called upon in the course of their judicial duties to apply that particular branch of the law, they would not be able to do so impartially: *Hoekstra v HM Advocate* (2000) *The Times*, 14 April.

(iii) As to impartiality and independence of court martials see: *Dupuis v Belgium* Application No 12787/87, *Findlay v UK* (1997) 24 EHRR 221, *Sutter v Switzerland* Application No 8209/78, *Engel v The Netherlands (No 1)* (1976) 1 EHRR 647.

(iv) Cases regarding allegations of lack of independence and impartiality of a judgment by a judge who had played a part in the preparatory stages of a case see: *Belilos v Switzerland* (1998) 10 EHRR 466, *Bulut v Austria* (1997) 24 EHRR 84, *De Cubber v Belgium* (1984) 7 EHRR 236, *Piersack v Belgium* (1982) 5 EHRR 169.

(v) As to impartiality and independence of professional disciplinary bodies etc, see *Le Compte v Belgium* (1981) 4 EHRR 1, *Debled v Belgium* (1994) 19 EHRR 506.

(vi) Temporary judges appointed by the Crown to hold office for three years, where the Crown itself was not involved in the claim might be acceptable to hear cases and could not reasonably be regarded as giving rise to a perception of undue influence by the Crown over the court or lack of independence or impartiality: *Clancy v Caird* [2000] 3 UKHRR.

(vii) An examination of the independence and impartiality of a jury has to proceed on different considerations from the scrutiny of those qualities from a judge. Practical steps, including directions given to them by a judge that they should put to one side their personal feelings to prejudice or dislike, were open to safeguard not only the reality but also the appearance of independence and impartiality under Article 6(1): *Crummock (Scotland) Ltd v HM Advocate* (2000) *The Times*, 9 May (CA).

Waiver of the right to a fair hearing under Art 6

2.104 A party might lose the right to object to a particular tribunal under Article 6(1) if an objection is not raised at the appropriate time: *Oberschlick v Austria* (1991) 19 EHRR 389; *Bulut v Austria* (1997) 24 EHRR 84; *Hakabssib abd Styrrsib v Sweden* (1990) 13 EHRR 1; *Deweer v Belgium* (1980) 2 EHRR 439.

Reasons

2.105 The right to a reasoned judgment or decision is expected under Article 6. Article 6(1) obliges a court to give reasons for its decision, but cannot be understood as requiring a detailed answer to every argument: *Van de Hurk v The Netherlands* (1994) 18 EHRR 481, para 61. In the context of Article 6(1), the duty is seen as an ingredient implied in the requirement for a fair trial in the resolution of a person's civil rights and obligations: *Stefan* [1999] 1 WLR 1293 at 1299E; *Bryan v UK* 21 EHRR 342, para 40 (even where a body does not comply with Article 6(1), no violation of the Convention can be found if the proceedings are subject to subsequent control by a judicial body which has full jurisdiction and does provide the guarantees of Article 6(1)). The extent to which the duty to give reasons applies may vary according to the nature of the decision at issue: *Helle v Finland* (1997) 26 EHRR 159 at 183; *Georgiadis v Greece* 24 EHRR 606 at 620, para 42.

Access to courts

2.106 Prevents blanket immunities denying claimants a right to sue public bodies on policy grounds: *Osman v UK* (1998) 5 BHRC 382; *Barret v Enfield LBC* [1999] 3 WLR 79; imposes limits on security for costs: *Tolstoy-Miloslavsky v UK* (1995) 20 EHRR 442; governs limitation periods: *Stubbings v UK* (1996) 1 BHRC 316; prevents conclusive certificates excluding jurisdiction of courts: *Tunnelly v UK* (1998) 4 BHRC 393.

Speedy trials

2.107

(i)   The right to a fair and prompt trial without delays is ensured: *Matter v Slovakia* Application No 31524/96: *X v France* (1992) 14 EHRR 483; *Robins v UK* (1998) 26 EHRR 527.

(ii)   A speedy trial falls within Article 6: the failure to deal with this response speedily offends Article 6 of the Convention: *R v Manchester Crown Court ex parte McDonald* [1999] 1 WLR 832 at 850F: a number of factors have to be taken into account including the complexity of the case, the parties' conduct, the length of the delay, the fault of the judicial authorities: *Vernillo v France* (1991) 13 EHRR 880, paras 30–38; *Eckle v Federal Republic of Germany* (1982) 5 EHRR 1 at 27; whether the delay was caused by the requirement of a careful investigation into matters of scientific complexity: *Crummock (Scotland) Ltd v HM Advocate* (2000) *The Times*, 9 May (CA). Administrative proceedings fall within the 'civil rights and obligations' and are therefore subject to the same rule that length of the legal proceedings should not be excessive and should meet the reasonable time requirement: *Osteo Deutschland GmBH v Germany* Application No 26988/95, 28 EHRR CD 50.

(iii)   An unexplained delay of three years and nine months between interviewing a suspect about an allegation and subsequently charging him was to be attributed to the Crown, and was unreasonable, and therefore rendered further prosecution a breach of the accused human rights: *Hoekstra v HM Advocate* (2000) *The Times*, 14 April (the Crown was not able to explain why there was a delay in bringing about the charges sooner in this case).

(iv)   Excessive workload and chronic backlog provides no more than a partial excuse for the delay: *Zimmermann and Steiner v Switzerland* (1983) 6 EHRR 17 (three and a half years delay).

(v)   The underlying purpose of the right to trial within a reasonable time was designed to avoid that a person charged should remain too long in a state of uncertainty about his fate: *McNab v HM Advocate* (2000) JC 80 at 84; *Stogmuller v Austria* (1969) 1 EHRR 155; *HM Advocate v Little* (1999) SCCR 625 at 635; *Crummock (Scotland) Ltd v HM Advocate* (2000) *The Times*, 9 May (CA).

Enforcement of judgments

2.108   Proper mechanisms for judgments are to be enforced: *Hornsby v Greece* (1997) 24 EHRR 250. Court procedures are required to be simplified: *De Geouffre de la Pradelle v France* (1993) 14 HRLJ 276.

Silence

2.109

(i)   The right to silence is not absolute. Whether the drawing of inferences from an accused's silence during police interview infringed Article 8 was a matter to be determined in the light of all the circumstances of the case: *Murray v UK* (1996) *The Times*, 6 February. Leaving the question of a defendant's silence to a jury to determine was not incompatible with Article 6. But it might be incompatible with the right to silence to have a conviction solely or mainly on the defendant's silence or on a refusal to answer questions or to give evidence himself. The right to silence could not and should not prevent an accused's silence, in situations which clearly called for an explanation from him, being taken into account in assessing the strength of the prosecution evidence. In *Condron and Another v UK* Application No 35718/97 (2000) *The Times*, 9 May, the European Court stated that, as a matter of fairness, a jury should have been directed that if it was satisfied that the accused's silence at a police interview could not sensibly be attributed to the accused having no answer or none that would stand up to cross-examination, it should not draw an adverse inference.

(ii) A person charged with an offence had a right under Article 6(1) to remain silent and not to contribute to incriminating himself. Thus, if a constable suspected someone of driving whilst drunk and required the person to say whether he had been driving his car then the reply given by that person is subject to the rule of Article 6(1): *Brown v Procurator Fiscal Dunfermline* (2000) *The Times*, 14 February.

(iii) The public interest cannot be invoked to justify the use of answers compulsorily obtained in a non-judicial investigation and to incriminate the accused during the trial proceedings: *Saunders v UK* (1996) 23 EHRR 313 at 340, para 74. A judge at a criminal trial at which an answer to a request is provided in evidence will have to consider whether Article 6(1), as interpreted in *Saunders* (above) requires him to exercise the discretion to exclude the evidence: *R v Hertfordshire CC ex parte Green Industries Ltd* (HL(E)) [2000] 2 WLR 373 at 381C.

(iv) The right to silence is not absolute.

Civil obligations

2.110 Disputes relating to the recruitment, employment and retirement of public servants are as a general rule outside the scope of Article 6(1): *Massa v Italy* (1993) 18 EHRR 266, para 26; *Balfour v UK* Application No 15058/89 (1991) 69 DR 306. But disputes relating to pensions, compensation or economic rights may fall within the scope of Article 6: *Huber v France* (1998) 26 EHRR 457; *Benkessiouer v France* [1998] HRCD 814; *Neigel v France* Application No 18725/91, 17 March 1997.

Disclosure

2.111 Failure to disclose confidential information to the trial judge in criminal proceedings which may assist the defence cannot be cured by an appeal process which does not have the same scrutiny procedures as the first trial judge. The defence must have the opportunity to comment on evidence adduced by the other side: *Rowe and Davis v UK* Application No 28901/95, paras 60–65.

Nature of proceedings

2.112 In considering whether the proceedings involved criminal charges, three factors are relevant: domestic law, which treats the matter as a disciplinary body, the nature of the offence and the nature and severity of the penalty. Deprivation of liberty as a punishment will, in general, belong to the criminal sphere. The imposition of a measure of such gravity, in respect of such serious charges should be accompanied by the guarantees of Article 6: *Campbell and Fell v UK* (1984) 7 EHRR 165, paras 67–73 of the judgment. In *R v Secretary of State for the Home Department ex parte Shaw* (2000) *The Times*, 16 March, the QBD stated that a prisoner was not entitled to make representations about a decision of the prison service not to allow him to take part in a rehabilitation programme which might improve his early release: *Campbell* it appears was not cited.

The European Court's jurisprudence under Article 6(1) is rooted to the fairness of the trial and may not apply to extrajudicial enquiries: *R v Hertfordshire CC ex parte Green Industries Ltd* (HL(E)) [2000] 2 WLR 373 at 381H. Article 6(1) is applicable to an investigation which is essentially investigative in nature and involves a criminal charge. However, Article 6(1) may not apply where a preparatory investigation is conducted by DTI inspectors because the guarantees of such a judicial procedure as set forth in Article 6(1) would hamper the effective regulation in the public interest of complex financial and commercial activities: *Saunders v UK* (1996) 23 EHRR 313 at 337, para 67.

Presumptions of law and fact

2.113
(i)   Article 6 does not prohibit presumptions of law or fact operating in a legal system but such presumptions in criminal law must remain within certain limits which take into account the importance of what is at stake and maintain the right of the defence: *Salabiaku v France* (1989) 13 EHRR 379 at 388, para 28.
(ii)   A fair balance is to be struck between the demands of the general interests of the community and the protection of the fundamental rights of the individual: *Sporrong & Lönnroth v Sweden* (1983) 5 EHRR 35 at 52, para 69; *H v UK* (unreported) 4 April 1990; *Bates v UK* (unreported) 16 January 1996. In considering where the balance lies, the following considerations arise:
       (a)   what does the prosecution have to prove in order to transfer the onus to the defence?;
       (b)   what is the burden on the accused? Is it difficult or possible for him to prove?;
       (c)   what is the nature of the threat faced by a society which the provision is designed to combat?: *R v DPP ex parte Kebilene* (HL(E)) [1999] 3 WLR 972 at 998H.

Publicity of trial

2.114
(i)   Failure to give proper consideration or to make appropriate provision for the welfare of the juvenile in a criminal trial may infringe the juvenile defendant's right to a fair trial under Article 6(1): *R v UK* Application No 2472/94; *V v UK* Application No 24888/94, 4 December 1998.
(ii)   It is arguable that excessive or inappropriate publicity concerning a juvenile defendant, who is subject of a criminal trial in an adult court, may affect the juvenile's welfare and infringe Article 6(1): *R v Manchester Crown Court ex part H(DC)* [2000] 1 WLR 760 at 771A.

ARTICLE 7 – NO PUNISHMENT WITHOUT LAW

2.115   '*Article 7*

No punishment without law

1.   No one shall be held guilty of any criminal offence on account of any act or omission which did not constitute a criminal offence under national or international law at the time when it was committed. Nor shall a heavier penalty be imposed than the one that was applicable at the time the criminal offence was committed.

2.   This Article shall not prejudice the trial and punishment of any person for any act or omission which, at the time when it was committed, was criminal according to the general principles of law recognised by civilised nations.'

CRIMINAL LAW

2.116   Article 7 has been considered by UK courts primarily in criminal cases and has been discussed to a large degree within the criminal jurisdiction. The purpose of Article 7 enables an individual to know what acts and omissions will make him liable to criminal prosecution. The aim of this Article is to secure for the individual adequate protection against arbitrary prosecution and conviction. Therefore, for example, a person who is sentenced to a greater term of imprisonment than that which applied at the time that the offence was committed will have grounds for saying that such greater sentence should not be imposed because this will be contrary to Article 7 of the Convention.[1]

Retroactive law

2.117   Article 7 quite clearly shares a common heritage with the presumption, in English criminal law, against retroactive effect. The UK courts have previously taken the view that if Article 7(1) is part of English law, the qualification in Article 7(2) is not incompatible with the common law approach.[2] Thus, there would be a violation of Article 7(1) if a confiscation order is made under the Drug Trafficking Offences Act 1986 in respect of a

---

1   See *R v Derry* [1977] Crim LR 550 (Northern Ireland): it was held that the imposition of a sentence which was greater than permitted at the time the offence was committed was contrary to law and was reduced to the maximum sentence permitted at the time. Also see *R v Miah* [1979] 1 WLR 683 where Lord Reid referred to Article 7 of the Convention and stated that Parliament could not have intended to ignore circumventing retrospective criminal legislation. Article 7 of the Convention is not dissimilar to Article 15 of the International Covenant on Civil and Political Rights 1966. See also *R v Penwith JJ, ex parte Hay* (1979) 1 Cr App Rep (S) 265; *R v Craig* [1982] Crim LR 132. In *R v Kirk* [1985] 1 All ER 453, Article 7 was cited supporting the principle that penal provisions may not have retrospective effect and that this principle is one which is common to all the legal orders of the Member States of the European Community and takes its place among the general principles of law whose observance is ensured by the ECJ.

2   *R v SW* [1991] 2 All ER 257, CA: the marital exemption from rape case.

related offence committed before the Act came into force[1] and, accordingly, a confiscation order is a penalty.[2] Article 7 does not guarantee the right to have the more favourable criminal law applied in the event that it is amended after the commission of the offence. On the other hand, the principle of the non-retroactivity of a more severe criminal law arising from the principle of the legality of offences and penalties must be ensured.[3] A new law which is more severe in its definition but less severe in its penalty may not offend Article 7.[4] Essentially, Article 7 prohibits the retrospective application of the criminal law where it is to an accused's disadvantage but not if it operates to his advantage.[5] The second sentence of Article 7(1) prohibits the imposition of a heavier penalty than that applicable at the time the criminal offence was committed.

Furthermore, the English criminal law attitude, like the European Court's attitude, to Article 7 is that criminal law should not be retroactively interpreted.[6] No derogation from Article 7 is permissible under Article 15 in time of war or other public emergency.

Article 7(1) guarantees the right to the legality of offences and penalties. The concept of legality of a penalty implies not only that the penalty has a basis in law, but that the law itself satisfies the conditions of accessibility and foreseeability.[7] It should be construed and applied, as follows from its object and purpose, in such a way as to provide effective safeguards against arbitrary prosecution, conviction and punishment.[8] Article 7 is not confined to prohibiting the retrospective application of the criminal law to an accused's disadvantage: it also embodies, more generally, the principle that only the law can define a crime and prescribe a penalty (*nullum crimen, nulla poena sine lege*) and the principle that the criminal law must not be extensively construed to an accused's detriment, for instance by analogy. From these principles, it follows that an offence must be clearly defined in law.[9] This requirement is satisfied where the individual can know from the wording of the relevant provision and, if need be, with the courts' interpretation of it, what acts and omissions will make him criminally liable. This applies both to written and unwritten law and implies qualitative requirements, notably those of accessibility and foreseeability.[10] No matter how clearly drafted a legal provision may be, in any system of law, including criminal law, there is an inevitable element of judicial interpretation. There will always be a need for elucidation of doubtful points

---

1   *Welch v UK* (1995) Series A No 307-A, 20 EHRR 247: the European Court found that there was a violation of Article 7(1) because a confiscation order was made under the Drug Trafficking Offences Act 1986 in respect of an offence committed before this Act came into force. See also *Ronald JM Taylor v UK* Application No 31209/96, where the Commission treated the application as inadmissible.

2   *Welch v UK* (above).

3   *G v France* (1995) 21 EHRR 288 at 296, para 36.

4   Ibid at 297, paras 39–46.

5   Ibid, paras 24–26.

6   *Welch v UK* (above).

7   *G v France* (1995) 21 EHRR 288 at 295, para 32.

8   *SW v UK* (1966) Series A No 335–B, 21 EHRR 363 at 398, paras 34/32.

9   Ibid, paras 35/33; *Kokkinakis v Greece* (1994) 17 EHRR 397, para 52.

10   *Tolstoy Miloslavsky v UK* 20 EHRR 442, para 37.

and for adaptation to changing circumstances.[1] In a common law system, therefore, the courts may exercise their customary role of developing the law through cases, but in doing so may not exceed the bounds of reasonably foreseeable change. Article 7(1) excludes that any act not previously punishable shall be held by the courts to entail criminal liability or that existing offences should be extended to cover facts which previously clearly did not constitute a criminal offence.[2]

DEFINITION OF CRIME (THE FACTORS)

2.118   Although Article 7 does not define the term 'crime', it allows for the gradual clarification of the rules of criminal liability throughout judicial interpretation from case to case, provided that the resultant development is consistent with the essence of the offence and could be reasonably foreseen. Consistent with this view, the English courts were acting within the spirit of the Convention in developing the common law to reflect the view that non-consensual sexual intercourse within marriage constitutes rape.[3] Article 7 will no doubt bring changes to the domestic law in the sense that criminal offences ought to be defined with reasonable precision to permit a person to regulate his or her conduct. Using this yardstick, it is difficult to see how far a court may rely on its residual or inherent power to convict a person for a matter not falling within the criminal law offences such as conspiring to corrupt public morals.[4]

In a society subscribing to the rule of law, there belong to the 'criminal sphere' deprivations of liberty liable to be imposed as a punishment, but not those which by their nature, duration or manner of enforcement cannot be appreciably detrimental.[5]

Interpretation of crime

2.119   In the first place, it is for the national authorities, notably the courts, to interpret and apply national law. The Commission and the European Court have been prepared to review the interpretation and application of municipal law by domestic courts[6] having regard to the qualifications set out in Article 7(2). The Commission has consistently stated that the European Court organs are empowered under Article 7 to verify whether, on the facts of the case, the domestic courts could reasonably have arrived at a conviction under the applicable rule of municipal law. The European Court has to be satisfied that the conviction not only was based on a pre-existing (and sufficiently precisely worded) provision of criminal law but also that it is compatible with the

---

1   *SW v UK* (1966) Series A No 335–B, 21 EHRR 363 at 399, paras 36/34.
2   Ibid, at 395.
3   *CR v UK* (1996) Series A No 335–C and *SW v UK* (above).
4   *Shaw v DPP* [1962] AC 220 is an example where the court used its inherent power to prosecute a citizen for the offence of conspiring to corrupt public morals which was not an offence defined in criminal law.
5   *Engel v The Netherlands* (1976) Series A No 22, 1 EHRR 647, para 82.
6   See Craig Osborne 'Article 7, and the Marital Rape Exemption' [1996] EHRLR 406.

principle of restrictive interpretation of criminal legislation.[1] Furthermore, if the domestic law is sufficiently precise to enable a person to predict that his act might render him liable to criminal prosecution, there might be no violation of Article 7.[2]

Proceedings for disqualification were not criminal proceedings under domestic law, nor was the nature and severity of the penalty such that they would be so classified under the case-law of the European Court.[3]

Disqualification proceedings of a company director under the Companies Act 1985 are not criminal proceedings, nor is the nature and severity of the penalty such that they would be so classified under the case-law of the European Court.[4]

PENALTIES

Is a measure a penalty?

2.120   Punitive measures fall within the scope of Article 7. Confiscation of assets as a preventive measure does not require that a specific offence has been committed and thus does not constitute a penalty within Article 7(1).[5] The wording of the second sentence of Article 7(1) indicates that the starting point in any assessment of the existence of a penalty is whether the measure in question is imposed following conviction for a 'criminal offence'. Other factors that may be taken into account as relevant in this connection are the characterisation of the measure under national law; its nature and purpose; the procedures involved in the making and implementation of the measure; and its severity.[6]

The requirement on a sex offender, convicted of a sexual offence, to inform the police of any names he used, his date of birth, his home address, any change of name or address, his name and address at the date of his conviction and any address he has stayed at for 14 days or longer does not constitute a penalty because these measures were preventative in nature and scope and did not form part of a sentencing scheme. The offender was merely required to register his details and no more and therefore there was no violation of Article 7(1).[7]

---

1   See the dissenting Opinion of Judge Martens in *Kokkinakis v Greece* (1993) Series A No 260–A, 17 EHRR 397 at 434, para 6.

2   A disciplinary penalty imposed on a soldier, acquitted earlier for being in conflict with his superiors, for writing a letter of criticism to his superiors did not violate Article 7 of the Convention because the wording of the Army Criminal Code was sufficiently precise to inform the applicant that if he sent such a letter to his commanding officer he would be liable to criminal prosecution: *Panayiotis v Greece* Application No 24348/94.

3   *R v The Secretary of State for Trade and Industry, ex parte McCormick* (1998) *The Times*, 10 February.

4   Ibid.

5   *M v Italy* Application No 12386/86, (1991) 70 DR 59.

6   *Jamil v France* (1995) 21 EHRR 65 at 80, para 31.

7   *Ibbotson v UK* Application No 40146/98.

Is a prison sentence for non-payment of a fine a penalty?

2.121   Even if a confiscation procedure is severe in effect, but the measure is intended to be reparative and preventive, it is not of a punitive nature. Therefore, if a debtor risks prison if he fails to pay the sum due to the authorities and which is aimed at reparation or which is intended to remove the proceeds of the offence then the prison sentence he may get for non-payment is not a punitive measure.[1] But if imprisonment in default of paying a fine is imposed by a criminal court, particularly following the trial, and is intended to be a deterrent and leads to a punitive deprivation of liberty then such imprisonment is a penalty within Article 7(1).[2]

By causing detention to continue at the end of a sentence for substantially longer than would otherwise have been the case (because of non-payment ordered by a court), the sanction comes close to a deprivation of liberty and is sufficiently severe to be regarded as penal.[3]

How to determine whether criminal convictions or penalties are compatible with Article 7(1)

2.122   In ascertaining whether a conviction for a criminal offence is compatible with the requirements of Article 7, the following factors are relevant in determining this issue.

(1)   Is the criminal provision vague?[4] Does it use very general terms or give the impression of uncertainty which may lead to abuse by the prosecuting authority? For example, can the accused be convicted for acts differing from those described in the criminal provision which is being attacked? (Thus a person who is convicted and punished for an offence in breach of the statutory nature of the offence and penalties may successfully claim that his rights under Article 7 have been violated.) Or, can it be said that the absence of any description of the 'objective substance' of the offence for which the accused is convicted and punished allows for the risk of the offence being extended by the police, prosecuting authorities and the courts? Or, is the definition of the provision in question deliberately left vague because of the need to avoid excessive rigidity and to keep pace with changing circumstances?[5]

---

1   *Jamil v France* (1995) 21 EHRR 65 at 77, para 43.
2   Ibid, para 32.
3   *Campbell and Fell v UK* (1984) Series A No 80, 7 EHRR 165, para 72.
4   Criminal legislation that is restricted to vague incriminations which leave it to the subjective evaluation of the judge to repress or to relax may well violate Article 7. The European Court had shown its concern in *Lingens v Austria* (1986) Series A No 103, 8 EHRR 103; in the context of freedom of expression, the fact that ample discretion was left to the magistrate to determine the concept of truth.
5   *Müller v Switzerland* (1988) Series A No 133, 13 EHRR 212, para 29.

(2) Is the punishable act defined with the clarity[1] required in the criminal sphere, particularly with reference to violence? For example, if the definition of the crime takes the form of a non-exhaustive list of illustrations, it is impossible to define the criminal act with any precision and there might well be a violation of Article 7[2] (the criminal law must not be construed to an accused's detriment, for instance by analogy);[3]

(3) Does the criminal law apply retroactively particularly with regard to the imposition of heavier penalties to the detriment of the accused?

(4) Is the punishable act clearly set out in the legislation? (This requirement is satisfied where it is possible to determine from the relevant statutory provisions what act or omission entails criminal liability, even if such determination may be ascertained from: (a) the case-law (is there a body of settled domestic case-law on the particular issue in question?);[4] or (b) the court's interpretation of the statutory language concerned.)[5]

IS THE CRIME PRESCRIBED BY LAW?

2.123   The term 'prescribed by law' in Article 7 involves a requirement to set the standard of foreseeability to that of reasonable certainty and it must be formulated with sufficient precision to enable the citizen to regulate his conduct as a consequence. The citizen must be able, if need be with appropriate advice, to foresee the consequences which a given action might entail.[6] Even when therefore, the House of Lords changed the law of marital rape, under the Convention it was considered that the debasing feature of rape remained unchanged, so that a conviction for the offence of marital rape, which was a new event in English law, did not violate Article 7.[7]

Margin of appreciation

2.124   The Convention recognises that the domestic courts have a wide margin of appreciation in deciding what is a crime, having particular regard to the present-day conditions in society, including the fact that women possess equal status with men within the confines of marriage and outside it.

---

1   *Handyside v UK* (1974) Yearbook 17, at pp 228.

2   Thus, in *Kokkinakis v Greece* (1993) Series A No 260–A, 17 EHRR 397, the applicant argued that his conviction for improper proselytism was incompatible with the requirements of Article 7 because for example: (i) the imprecision of the provision in question was aggravated by the abstract and vague definition of the punishable act; and (ii) in practice it was impossible to define the type of action or speech which entailed the commission of the offence of 'proselytism' (at 406, para 39). The counter-argument advanced was that the offence of 'proselytism' was precisely defined.

3   Ibid, at 423, para 52.

4   *Hadjianastassiou v Greece* (1992) Series A No 252–A, 16 EHRR 219, para 42.

5   *Kokkinakis v Greece* (1993) Series A No 260-A, 17 EHRR 397 at 410, paras 50–51.

6   *Sunday Times v UK* (1979) Series A No 30, 2 EHRR 229.

7   *SW v UK* (1966) Series A No 335–B, 21 EHRR 363 at 399.

New offence

2.125 The fact that there was no violation of Article 7 of the Convention when the English courts were prepared to treat marital rape as a new offence culminating in a criminal conviction is consistent with the view expressed in the opening chapter of this book that the Convention is a 'living instrument'. It must be interpreted and applied according to present-day societal values and according to the general principles of law recognised by civilised nations. The object and purpose of the Convention as an instrument for the protection of individual human beings from crime requires that its provisions be interpreted and applied so as to make its safeguards practical and effective both for the accused and the victim. Thus, a retrospective prosecution of a particularly debasing crime such as marital rape deserves the condemnation of the Convention and the spirit of the Convention recognises this in Article 7(2). Article 15(2) of the Convention confirms that Article 7 cannot be derogated from in times of war or public emergency.

SUMMARY OF CASES

2.126 Article 7(1) enshrines, inter alia, the principles that only the law can define a crime and penalty and that criminal offences must be clearly defined and not extensively construed to an accused's detriment. These principles were satisfied in the case where the applicant could know from the wording of the relevant provision with the assistance of the court's interpretation of it, what acts and omissions would make him liable.[1]

Article 7 of the Convention allows for the gradual clarification of the rules of criminal liability through judicial interpretation from case to case, provided that the resultant development is consistent with the essence of the offence and could reasonably be foreseen. The common law had evolved to a point that judicial recognition of the absence of a marital exemption from rape had become a reasonably foreseeable development of the law. The UK courts were continuing an evident evolution, which was consistent with the very essence of the occurrence of rape, or the criminal law through judicial interpretation towards treating non-consensual sexual intercourse within marriage as within the scope of the offence. The essentially debasing character of rape was so manifest that the results of the decision in the UK courts were not at variance with the object and purpose of Article 7, namely to ensure that no one could be subjected to arbitrary prosecution, conviction or punishment. Further, the abandonment of the unacceptable idea of a marital exemption from rape conformed with a civilised concept of marriage and with the fundamental objectives of the Convention, the very essence of which is respect for human dignity and human freedom.[2]

An applicant convicted of accepting bribes and of indecent assault as a driving test examiner, complained that there had been retrospective application of the

---

1   *Lozidiou v Turkey* (1995) 20 EHRR 99 at 133, para 71; *Kokkinakis v Greece* (1993) Series A No 260–A, 17 EHRR 399.
2   *CR v UK* (1996) Series A No 335–C; and *SW v UK* (1996) Series A No 335–B, 21 EHRR 363.

criminal law. Article 7(1) embodies the principle that only the law can define a crime and prescribe a penalty. Further, Article 7 prohibits the retrospective application of the criminal law where it is to an accused's disadvantage. But even though the application of the law had been retrospective, there was no breach of Article 7(1) because such retrospectivity operated in the accused's favour.[1]

A Brazilian national, convicted of drug smuggling was sentenced, inter alia, to pay a fine with imprisonment in default. The appeal Court increased the term of imprisonment in default pursuant to a law which was passed after the offence was committed. The word penalty in Article 7(1) is autonomous in scope. The starting point in any assessment of the existence of a penalty is whether the measure in question is imposed following conviction for a criminal offence. Other factors that may be taken into account are the characterisation of the measure under domestic law; its nature and purpose; the procedures involved in the making and implementation of the measure; and its severity. The sanction imposed on the applicant was ordered by a criminal court, was intended to be a deterrent and could have led to a punitive deprivation of liberty. It was therefore a penalty.[2]

1   *G v France* (1995) 21 EHRR 288.
2   *Jamil v France* (1995) 21 EHRR 65.

ARTICLE 8 – RIGHT TO RESPECT FOR PRIVATE AND FAMILY LIFE

2.127   *'Article 8*

Right to respect for private and family life

1. Everyone has the right to respect for his private and family life, his home and his correspondence.
2. There shall be no interference by a public authority with the exercise of this right except such as is in accordance with the law and is necessary in a democratic society in the interests of national security, public safety or the economic well-being of the country, for the prevention of disorder or crime, for the protection of health or morals, or for the protection of the rights and freedoms of others.'

INTRODUCTION AND SCOPE

2.128 Article 8 of the Convention seeks to protect individuals from interference with the right to private and family life, the home and correspondence. The second part of the Article sets out the circumstances in which the State can legitimately interfere with these rights. In decisions of the European Court, this latter part has so far afforded a wide discretion or 'margin of appreciation' to Member States.

There are essentially four rights or interests that are afforded protection by Article 8:

(1) private life;
(2) family life;
(3) home; and
(4) correspondence.

In terms of the duty that is placed on public authorities, there is both a positive and a negative obligation. The rights or interests guaranteed by the Article have to be respected. This can mean not just the negative obligation 'not to interfere', but also the obligation to protect those rights by the taking of positive steps. Such positive steps may involve the enacting of primary or secondary legislation to provide for the effective protection or exercise of Article 8 rights or protection from the acts of others which prevent the proper enjoyment of Article 8 rights. There is considerable overlap between the four rights and quite often an infringement of more than one at a time will be argued. There is also overlap between Article 8 rights and the rights protected in other Articles, most particularly the right to marry and to found a family contained in Article 12.

THE FOUR RIGHTS

(1) Private life

2.129   In decided cases of the Commission and the European Court, this right has been quite widely construed so as to go beyond a mere right to privacy. It has been said to include the right to establish and develop relationships with other human beings.[1] It has further been said that this is particularly important for the development and fulfilment of an individual's personality.[2] The right has been further defined to cover the freedom to associate with others, applicable also to prisoners[3] and also the 'possibility of establishing relationships of various kinds, including sexual, with other persons'.[4] The right to private life also encompasses a person's sexual life and 'the physical and moral integrity of the person'.[5] These areas of life are therefore included alongside the more expected right to privacy of space, information and communication. Indeed, the scope of what constitutes private life seems to be widening and will be ripe for argument under the Human Rights Act 1998. There are some areas of private life where infringement is readily argued and which merit closer attention. ~

Moral or physical integrity

2.130   Generally, compulsory physical treatment of an individual will constitute an interference with his private life and this will be so however slight the level of interference may be. For example, where a specimen of blood or urine is taken by virtue of a statute or order of the court, this will be an interference with private life. Any medical treatment that is forced on, for example, a mental patient will also be such an interference. Where such treatment involves sterilisation, this is an interference with the rights to family life and to marry and found a family under Article 12 and with the right to private life.

A physical assault by one individual on another can constitute an interference with private life.[6] In the context of school discipline, corporal punishment is capable of constituting an interference with private life, but this would seem to depend on the context and degree, it being held that not every measure which has an adverse affect on an individual's moral or physical integrity will constitute an interference with his private life.[7]

---

1   *Niemietz v FRG* (1992) Series A No 251-B, (1993) 16 EHRR 97.
2   *X v UK* (1983) 5 EHRR 260 at 263.
3   *McFeely v UK* Application No 8317/78, (1980) DR 44; and *X v UK* (above).
4   *Application No 10083/82 v UK* (1984) 6 EHRR 50 at 143.
5   *X and Y v The Netherlands* (1985) Series A No 91, 8 EHRR 235.
6   As in *X and Y v The Netherlands* (above) which concerned a sexual assault by a man on a mentally handicapped woman.
7   *Costello-Roberts v UK* (1993) Series A No 247-C, 19 EHRR 112. Here the European Court considered the corporal punishment of a pupil by a school master in a private school and decided that, whilst such punishment could constitute an interference with private life, the particular punishment complained of 'did not entail adverse effects for his physical or moral integrity sufficient to bring it within the scope of the prohibition contained in Article 8'.

Noise nuisance, if it is considerable, has been held to be capable of constituting an interference with private life.[1] The way seems to have been paved for future arguments over environmental issues and whether noise nuisance or even pollution constitutes an interference with private life.

Space

2.131   The right to enjoy physical space free from interference is clearly an aspect of private life and overlaps with the right to respect for one's home. Private space has been held to extend beyond the home to areas which are, even if temporary, for personal use, for example, a hotel room or a prison cell. There is no clear guidance on whether interference with private acts done in public spaces constitutes an interference with private life. It seems that if there is no intrusion into the private space of the individual in some way, a violation of Article 8 is unlikely to be found. A prime example of this reasoning is in *Freidl v Austria*[2] where the applicant complained that he was photographed while taking part in a political demonstration in a public place which led to his being identified by the police. It was said that there had been no intrusion into the applicant's private life and a clear distinction was drawn between the taking of photographs in a public place and the taking of photographs in the applicant's home after entry by the public authorities (which case might have constituted an intrusion and a breach of Article 8).

Most significantly in this area perhaps are the possibilities for secret surveillance, entry and search, security vetting and telephone tapping. In *Malone v UK*,[3] police surveillance by means of telephone tapping and interception of correspondence was held to be an interference with private life. There was considerable argument over whether the interference was justified under Article 8(2) given that the action was lawful under the Post Office Act 1969. The European Court held that there had been a violation of Article 8, based mainly on the lack of rules governing the scope and manner in which the surveillance was carried out by the police, rather than the fact of the surveillance.

Gathering information

2.132   Gathering of information by officials of public authorities without the individual's consent will constitute an interference with that individual's right to private life. The gathering of such information and the building up of a 'file' on an individual without his knowledge has also been said to constitute an interference with private life which may or may not be justified according to the circumstances. Fingerprints or the analysis of any forensic tests should, for example, be destroyed once the individual has been released or is no longer a suspect in an investigation. In this sphere, crime prevention, anti-terrorist

---

1   *Rayner v UK* Application No 9310/81, (1986) 47 DR 5. Here an applicant sought to argue that persistent aircraft noise interfered with his right to private life and respect for his home. The importance of the decision lies in the recognition that noise nuisance can constitute an interference with private life although it was decided that the claim fell outside Article 8.

2   (1995) A 305-B, (1994) Com Rep.

3   (1984) 4 EHRR 330.

activity and national security will no doubt provide the basis for arguing against an Article 8(2) violation.

Identity

2.133 It has generally been recognised that there is a right to determine personal identity which falls within private life. Personal identity will comprise such areas of identity as name, address, mode of dress etc. This has been most pertinent in change of name cases and cases involving transsexuals and the right they have claimed to determine their sexual identity. The European Court cases do not arrive at a conclusion with respect to this area and it would seem that there remains a tension between the individual's right to decide whether to be male or female and the right of the State to make that same decision, proven for example, by the refusal to allow any change of particulars on a birth certificate following gender reassignment.

Sexual relations

2.134 These have been held to fall clearly within the scope of private life. In respect of homosexual relations, there have been challenges to the age of consent where it has been held that the fixing of the age of consent at 21 was an interference in the applicant's private life. The interference has, however, been held to be justified as being necessary in a democratic society for the protection of the rights of others.[1] There has been a challenge to the anti-homosexuality law in Northern Ireland. This was successful, leading to a finding by the European Court that the relevant Irish law interfered with the applicant's private life and that insofar as the private life concerned consensual, private homosexual conduct with persons over 21, there could be no justification for such interference.

There remains some doubt over whether homosexual and transsexual relations come within the scope of family life or private life. This is important in the context of, for example, a threatened deportation where it might be argued that removal would interfere with the right to family life. It has been held that such action disrupting homosexual relations does not violate Article 8 as it does not interfere with the right to private life.[2]

(2) Family life

2.135 What constitutes a family and therefore family life has been a concept under change and development in recent years. The European Court has been keen to keep up with such change and recognise family situations that fall outside the more readily acceptable and conventional family relationships. To bring a case within the ambit of Article 8, there must already be some family life. It is not the right to achieve family life that is protected by the Article, but the maintenance of family life already in existence. It does not, therefore, cover the right to a divorce.[3] Some prospective relationships may, however, be recognised and come within the Article. The relationship between a couple engaged

---

1   *X v UK (Wells v UK)* Application No 7215/75, (1978) 3 EHRR 63.
2   *Application No 12513 v UK* (1989) 11 EHRR 46.
3   *Johnston v Ireland* (1986) Series A No 112, 9 EHRR 203.

to be married may be seen as family life if it is significantly and sufficiently established,[1] for which purpose cohabitation would seem not to be an essential ingredient.

It would appear that the reality of a subsisting relationship is the relevant factor and not merely the fact of blood relations as in the case of a father who has donated sperm to enable a baby to be born within another family unit. It cannot be said that he has a family life with the child born as a result of that arrangement. A blood link will not therefore be sufficient on its own to establish the existence of family life. By the same reasoning, it might be thought that the seeking of information by adopted children which would lead to the identification of their birth parents would fall outside family life and more appropriately within private life. Surprisingly, this is not so and has been held to be an aspect of the family life of the child seeking to inspect his adoption records.

The family relationships falling clearly within family life are the relationships of husband and wife, parent and child, siblings, grandparents and their grand-children, adoptive parent and child, cohabitants (where stable and presumably of some long-standing), parents and an illegitimate child and foster parent and child. The farther removed the family tie may be or the more removed in the sense of infrequency of contact, so much less will the requirement be on the public authority to respect the tie, and it may even lead to an easier justification for interference. The father of a foetus, estranged from the mother, has failed in his attempt to secure an injunction to prevent an abortion despite his argument that his right to family life encompassed a right to consultation prior to an abortion.[2]

Respect for family life includes the right of each member to the consortium of every other member, which also encompasses the right of each member to live in the chosen residence of the family unit. There follows the right not to have the family unit disrupted by the removal of any members by, for example, removal from the country or removal of a child into the care of a public authority.

As stated earlier, it seems that homosexual relations are not recognised as part of family life and are therefore not entitled to protection under this right. The main recourse in such cases will be under the right to private life, which probably would not cover a situation where the family unit of a homosexual couple is disrupted by the removal of one of them.[3]

(3) Home

2.136   Article 8 seeks to protect the right to respect for one's home. There is considerable overlap between the right provided here and the general protection of property provided by Article 1 of the First Protocol. Under this aspect of Article 8, there are a number of protected rights including the right to peaceful occupation, the right to occupy free of noise nuisance or pollution,

---

1   *Alam and Khan v UK* Application No 2991/66 (1967) 10 YB 478.
2   *X v UK* Application No 8416/78, (1980) 19 DR 244.
3   *S v UK* Application No 11716/85, (1986) 47 DR 274.

and free of interference by public authorities conducting a search or seizing belongings. Again, there is overlap with the right to private life. A very clear and obvious violation of the right to respect for one's home is illustrated by *Akdivar v Turkey*[1] where Turkish national security forces were found to have acted in clear violation of Article 8 in burning the homes of Turkish villagers and thereby forcing them to evacuate their village. There had been a violation of the right to respect for the family lives of the villagers, the right to respect for their homes and the right to peaceful enjoyment of their possessions.

As with family life, it is an existing arrangement that the Article seeks to protect so that only a home once established will be protected. The Act provides no right to acquire a home or to any assistance in acquiring it. A home once acquired, even if acquired unlawfully in violation of the national law will still be a home that is entitled to respect under Article 8. This appears clear from *Buckley v UK*,[2] where a gypsy living with her children in a caravan parked on land without permission made a retrospective application for planning permission which was refused by the district council. The council thereafter issued an enforcement notice requiring the removal of the caravan. Article 8 was held to be applicable notwithstanding the fact that the home was set up without any permission and therefore unlawfully. The particular facts of the case, including such matters as the availability of alternative sites for the applicant's home and the detailed consideration of her plight by the council, led to a finding that Article 8, although applicable, had not in fact been violated.

(4) Correspondence

2.137   Article 8 affords the right to respect for one's correspondence. This is in many ways an extension of the right to private life and encompasses the right to uninterrupted and uncensored communications. Precisely what communication will qualify is a developing concept in the light of developing technology and should cover letters, fax transmissions, and even e-mail correspondence. It is clear that telephone calls, whether made from home or business premises, constitute correspondence in Article 8 and would also come more generally within private life.[3]

OBLIGATIONS OF PUBLIC AUTHORITIES UNDER ARTICLE 8

2.138   On the whole, the obligation imposed on public authorities will be a negative one; ie *not* to act in such a way as to interfere with the right of the individual to respect for his private and family life, home and correspondence. As briefly stated above, this may in fact involve a positive obligation from time to time to change law, review and change policy or even to prevent the action of one individual or group where there is a duty to do so, those actions constituting a violation of Article 8. In *Stubbings and Others v UK*,[4] it was held that

---

1   (1996) 23 EHRR 143.
2   RJD 1996-IV 1271, (1996) 23 EHRR 101.
3   See *Halford v UK* RJD 1997-III 1004, (1997) 24 EHRR 523.
4   RJD 1996-IV 1487, (1996) 23 EHRR 213.

the positive obligation did not extend to the provision of limitless civil remedies where clear and effective criminal sanctions were in place. A group of applicants who had suffered childhood sexual abuse sought to bring claims for damages against their alleged abusers. Their claims were time-barred by virtue of the Limitation Act 1980. They claimed that there had been an interference with their private lives contrary to Article 8 and also that they had been denied access to a court contrary to Article 6(1). It was recognised that Article 8 did not merely compel the State to abstain from interference with Article 8 rights and that sometimes there may be positive obligations inherent in the respect for private or family life. In the sphere of child sexual abuse, vulnerable individuals were clearly entitled to State protection from abuse in the form of an effective deterrent; that protection was afforded by the criminal law which clearly made it a very grave offence which carried severe maximum penalties. In addition, civil remedies were available but subject to the statutory time-limits in place.

One example of an area where a positive obligation may well arise in due course is in relation to the right to private life of transsexuals who, having undergone gender reassignment surgery, seek to alter their name and sex on their birth certificate and thereby all other official records. The refusal by the UK to allow such change came under serious criticism in *Rees v UK*.[1] In this case, a female to male transsexual sought to achieve a change in the recorded sex on his birth certificate. The Commission held that there had been a violation of Article 8 in the UK's refusal to allow such a step which could not be justified on any public interest ground. The argument that the birth register provides a historic record which is relevant for the purposes of succession and legitimacy was not seen as a sufficient justification. The European Court held that there had not been a breach of Article 8 on the basis that any other decision would have had the effect of compelling the UK to take the positive step of amending the law and the entire system of registering births and determining civil status. Such a requirement on the UK would be unacceptable. This will no doubt be a matter that arises again and may eventually lead to a positive obligation to change the relevant law in the UK.[2]

In the context of family life, there are perhaps more positive obligations on public authorities. This can already be witnessed in UK domestic law, for example, in the recognition of contact between a child and the absent parent as being the natural and essential right of the child. Further, by virtue of s 34 of the Children Act 1989, it is the duty of any public authority who has care of a child by virtue of a care order, to promote and encourage contact between that child and his parents.

A further aspect of obligations involved in respecting the right to family life is in the sphere of immigration law where there can be a duty to allow an individual to enter or remain in the country in order to properly respect that individual's family life. This is an extremely contentious area and there is a marked tension between the need to comply with Article 8 obligations and the need to maintain some effective power to limit entrance into the UK or to remove entrants in

---

1   Application No 9532/81, (1984) 36 DR 78, 6 EHRR 603.
2   See also *Cossey v UK* (1991) Series A No 184, 13 EHRR 622 where *Rees* was followed but with growing reluctance.

circumstances of some illegality. In *Gul v Switzerland,*[1] the European Court, stated the following principles:

> '(i)   the extent of a State's obligations to admit to its territory relatives of settled immigrants will vary according to the particular circumstances involved and the general interest;
>
> (ii)   as a matter of well established international law and subject to its treaty obligations, a State has the right to control the entry of non-nationals into its territory; and
>
> (iii)   where immigration is concerned, Article 8 cannot be considered to impose on a State a general obligation to respect immigrants' choice of the country of their matrimonial residence and to authorise family reunion in its territory. Accordingly, in order to establish the scope of the State's obligations, the facts of the case must be considered.'

In *Ahmut v The Netherlands,*[2] a father with Dutch and Moroccan nationality resident in The Netherlands claimed that the Dutch authorities' refusal to grant his son a residence permit constituted a violation of Article 8. It was held that family life was established between father and son on the basis that from the moment of birth and by the very fact of it, there exists between a child and his parents a bond amounting to family life. In complying with Article 8 obligations, the European Court considered whether there was a duty on the Dutch authorities to allow the son to reside with his father in The Netherlands, thus enabling the father to maintain and develop family life in that country. On the basis of the decision in *Gul,* it was held that a fair balance had been struck between the father's interests and the State's own interest in controlling immigration. The particular facts were looked at and much weight was given to the fact that the father still had strong cultural and linguistic links with Morocco, as well as the right to live there unhindered and could therefore pursue and develop family life in his country of origin if he so chose. It was said clearly that Article 8 does not guarantee the right to choose the most suitable place to develop family life.

In *Berrehab v The Netherlands,*[3] the decision, on the particular facts of the case, went the other way. A Moroccan father who had lived in The Netherlands for many years and was married to a Dutch woman with whom he had a young daughter was refused a new residence permit and was expelled from the country. The expulsion was held to be a violation of his Article 8 right to respect for family life. In the particular circumstances of this family, it was held that the means employed and the legitimate aim pursued by the State were disproportionate. Much weight was attached to the fact that the father had maintained close links with the child and that the child needed regular contact with her father which would otherwise be denied.

In *R v Secretary of State for the Home Department, ex parte Gangadeen and Jurawan* and *R v Secretary of State for the Home Department, ex parte Khan,*[4] the Court of Appeal was invited to consider whether there had been a violation of Article 8 where it

---

1   RJD 1996-I 159, (1996) 22 EHRR 93.
2   RJD 1996-VI 2017, (1996) 24 EHRR 62.
3   (1988) Series A No 138, 11 EHRR 322.
4   [1998] INLR 207.

was intended to enforce the deportation of parents who were illegal entrants in circumstances where their children were to remain in the UK. Consideration was given to the decisions of the European Court and it was held that the general approach in each individual case was a balancing exercise which started with the scales being even, and with the balance being altered only according to the individual circumstances of that case. Furthermore, it was held that the interests of the child are not paramount in that consideration and preference should not be given to the interests of the child in the balancing exercise. However, where children were involved, their position had to be carefully and separately considered.

JUSTIFIED INTERFERENCE

2.139   By virtue of Article 8(2), there shall be no interference by a public authority with the exercise of any Article 8(1) right unless two conditions are fulfilled. First, the interference must be in accordance with the law and, secondly, it must be necessary in a democratic society in the interests of national security, public safety or the economic well-being of the country, for the prevention of disorder or crime, for the protection of health or morals or for the protection of the rights and freedoms of others.

An individual seeking to argue any violation of Article 8 will first have to establish that there has been an interference with one of his Article 8(1) rights. This should in most cases be relatively easy to determine. There are, however, some more subtle ways of interference. For example, in *Dudgeon v UK*,[1] the claimant had been involved in sexual relations with persons over 21 years of age. He had acted contrary to the national law of the time applicable in Northern Ireland which did not recognise as legal the private homosexual acts of males over 21. It was argued on behalf of the Government that as he had not been prosecuted and as prosecutions statistically were never pursued, there had been no interference. The European Court held that there had been an interference with Mr Dudgeon's right as the potential for a prosecution was ever present and it was the very existence of the legislation which directly affected his private life. Further, it could not be said that prohibiting homosexual conduct in private between consenting males over the age of 21 was justifiable as being necessary in a democratic society.

If medical treatment is administered in circumstances where it is said that the patient was not in a state of mind such as to give informed consent, the treatment is unlikely to constitute an interference. There are wider questions of policy involved in considering whether medical treatment of a mental patient is an interference, particularly if it has the effect of depriving the patient of the right to found a family as in the case of imposed sterilisation.

'In accordance with the law'

2.140   In order to even mount an argument for justified interference, the relevant public authority will firstly have to demonstrate that the interference

---

1   (1981) Series A No 45, 4 EHRR 149.

was one allowed by the provisions of the law of England and Wales. The law has itself evolved partly in response to decisions of the European Court. For example, following the decision in *Malone v UK*[1] referred to above, the Interception of Communications Act 1985 was passed providing for the regularisation and control of telephone tapping and introducing a system of obtaining a warrant from the Home Secretary to allow the tapping to take place. This would seem in the main to have answered the criticisms in *Malone*. An application on the basis that there was no control over abusive applications for warrants to permit the tapping has failed.[2]

Another area in which the law has been evolving has been in the sphere of child care where there are now in existence the most comprehensive statutory provisions to date governing the protection of children by local authorities and the bases upon which the courts can act and interfere in family life and private life by taking children into care or monitoring their development within the family home. These provisions are in Part IV of the Children Act 1989. Any argument that a local authority has acted outside of the law has in the main been dealt with in the care proceedings themselves without any recourse to the European Court.

'Necessary in a democratic society'

2.141   Having established that it has acted in accordance with the law, a public authority seeking to justify interference will then have to establish both the necessity for the interference and its objective. The European Court has been prepared to accept that there are varying degrees of protection that should be afforded to the various Article 8(1) rights. For example, in *Dudgeon*, the right to private enjoyment of sexual relations was held to be a right requiring particularly serious reasons before an interference would be justified. A similar view has been expressed in the case of prisoners' rights to communicate with their legal advisers.[3]

The interference must be necessary in the interests of one of the factors listed in Article 8(2). The interests of national security are most often relied on in complaints as to surveillance, entry and search and interception of correspondence.

In the discharge of their duties to protect children and in the process of applying for and implementing care orders, local authorities are likely to be open to criticism that the right to family life has been interfered with. The wording of Article 8(2) does not sit happily with the conditions needed for a care or supervision order to be made as set out in s 31(1) of the Children Act 1989. Once the Human Rights Act 1998 is in force, it will be interesting to see if parents or indeed children themselves argue a violation of Article 8 rights in the course of the proceedings. The wording of Article 8(2) in the context of child care proceedings will then need considered interpretation. The most likely justification for action will be the necessity to protect health or morals. It

---

1   (1984) 4 EHRR 330.
2   Application No 21482/93, (1994) 78 DR 119.
3   *Golder v UK* (1975) Series A No 18, 1 EHRR 524.

will also be interesting to see whether the paramountcy of the child's interests will be conclusive in determining whether a local authority has been justified in interfering with the right to family life and privacy. A denial of contact with a parent has in the past been held to constitute a breach of Article 8(1) but one that can be justified as being in the best interests of the child.[1]

There will be interesting arguments too over whether medical intervention in the case of incapable or mentally ill patients is justified and, if so, under which element in Article 8(2). The most likely would be again the protection of health or morals, but that could lead to further interesting debate about whose health is being protected, for example by a sterilisation procedure.

Immigration law and policy has undergone some changes by virtue of the growing number of cases involving challenges to removal from the jurisdiction of illegal entrants or overstayers such that family ties are severed. Much of course depends on the extent and significance of the tie being severed by removal, and a pertinent factor is whether or not it would be possible for the remaining family member(s) to travel with the member who is being removed in order to maintain the family life elsewhere, it being accepted that there is no positive duty to allow the family to establish itself in a particular country. However, as has been seen in *Berrehab v The Netherlands*,[2] there was a positive duty on the State to allow a father to stay so that his ties with his daughter could be maintained.

CONCLUSION

2.142   The various rights protected by Article 8 are extremely wide and varied. There will probably be many instances where a violation of Article 8 will be argued either against public authorities or in response to their court action taken against individuals. In all likelihood, it will prove to be a major 'growth area' as domestic courts struggle to pay regard to Article 8 rights and to interpret existing legislation so as to be compatible with those rights. A body of domestic case-law, as guided by the decisions of the Commission and the European Court will not take long to develop, providing further definition of the many fundamental rights and concepts enshrined in Article 8.

---

1   *Gribler v UK* (1988) 10 EHRR 546.
2   (1988) Series A No 138, 11 EHRR 322.

ARTICLE 9 – FREEDOM OF THOUGHT, CONSCIENCE AND RELIGION

2.127   *'Article 9*

Freedom of thought, conscience and religion

1. Everyone has the right to freedom of thought, conscience and religion; this right includes freedom to change his religion or belief and freedom, either alone or in community with others and in public or private, to manifest his religion or belief, in worship, teaching, practice and observance.
2. Freedom to manifest one's religion or beliefs shall be subject only to such limitations as are prescribed by law and are necessary in a democratic society in the interests of public safety, for the protection of public order, health or morals, or for the protection of the rights and freedoms of others.'

INTRODUCTION

2.144   If a court's or tribunal's determination of any question arising under the Act might affect the exercise by a religious organisation (itself of its members collectively) of the Convention right to freedom of thought, conscience and religion, it must have particular regard to the importance of that right.[1] Article 27 of the International Covenant of Civil and Political Rights provides as follows:

> 'In those States in which ethnic, religious or linguistic minorities exist, persons belonging to such minorities shall not be denied the right, in community with the other members of their group, to enjoy their own culture, to profess and practice their own religion, or to use their own language.'

Article 27 of this Covenant is notably expressed in more general terms than Article 9 of the Convention. However, Article 9 of the Convention is framed in not dissimilar language to Article 27 of the Covenant.

RIGHTS CONFERRED BY ARTICLE 9

2.145   The rights conferred under Article 9 clearly include an individual's freedom to manifest his religion in public worship and in teaching alongside the rest of the community. These rights are also entrenched in conjunction with differing aspects of the other Convention rights and in some cases the freedom of religion has to be balanced against the limitations allowed in Article 9(2), which are 'prescribed by law and are necessary in a democratic society in the interest of public safety' etc.

When considering whether the freedom of religion has been engaged, the European Court will also consider in tandem whether other Convention rights may be invoked. For example, Article 8 (respect for private and family life) may be relevant in a case where a Bhuddist prisoner is refused permission to grow a beard because this would disrupt prison rules.

---

1   Section 13.

Article 9 and the margin of appreciation

2.146 The principles of margin of appreciation are fully considered under Article 10 but, generally speaking, in the case of interference in freedom of religion designed to regulate religious conduct, the margin of appreciation accorded to the European Court is a narrow one.[1]

Where the interference arises from generally applicable, neutral laws, the margin of appreciation accorded to public authorities or the courts is a wide one.[2] Some aspects of what constitutes generally applicable, neutral laws are discussed below.

The convictions under Article 9 must be serious

2.147 The term 'belief' appears in Article 9 in the context of the right to freedom of thought, conscience and religion. The concept of 'religious and philosophical convictions' appears in Article 2 of the First Protocol which provides that a State has to respect, in the exercise of any functions that it assumes in relation to education and teaching, the right of parents to ensure that such education and teaching is in conformity with their religious and philosophical convictions. These 'convictions' imply views 'that attained a certain level of cogency, seriousness, cohesion and importance'.[3] For these views to qualify for protection under Article 9(1), they must be coherent views on fundamental problems.

Applying the above criteria, the European Court has held that Jehovah's Witnesses enjoy both the status of a 'known' religion and the advantages flowing from that as regards observance.[4] On the other hand, the Commission has not been prepared to accept a simple assertion that certain kinds of religions exist.[5]

---

1   *Kokkinakis v Greece* (1993) Series A No 260-A, 17 EHRR 397.
2   *Håkansson and Sturesson v Sweden* (1990) Series A No 171, 13 EHRR 1. See also s 13(1) of the Act.
3   *Campbell and Cosans v UK* (1982) Series A No 48, 4 EHRR 293: the expression 'philosophical convictions' in the present context denotes such convictions as are worthy of respect in a democratic society and are not incompatible with human dignity.
4   *Kokkinakis v Greece* (1993) Series A No 260-A, 17 EHRR 397, para 32.
5   A prisoner who was refused permission to register in the prison record his religion as belonging to the 'Wicca Religion' was unsuccessful in proving the existence of a religion as no facts were submitted to establish its existence: *X v UK* Application No 7291/75, (1977) 11 DR 55. The Commission was prepared, however, to accept that Druidism was a religion or belief protected under Article 9: *Chappel v UK* Application No 12587/86, (1987) 53 DR 241.

Nature of rights

Absolute rights

2.148   The right to freedom of thought, conscience and religion is one of the foundations of a 'democratic society'. The right to hold religious belief is almost absolute, but the right to manifest such beliefs, as is seen below, is not absolute. It is, in its religious dimension, one of the most vital elements that go to make up the identity of believers and their conception of life.[1] Article 9 protects primarily the sphere of personal beliefs and religious creeds and, in addition, it protects acts which are intimately linked to these attitudes, such as acts of worship or devotion which are aspects of the practice of a religion or belief in a generally recognised form.[2] Article 9 does not guarantee the right to behave in the public sphere in a manner dictated by a religion or a conviction.[3]

Nor does Article 9 confer a right to exemption from disciplinary rules which apply generally and in a neutral manner.[4] Some examples of European Court cases concerning such laws touch on corporal punishment of children by parents,[5] maintenance payments to children following divorce,[6] and objection to working on Sundays.[7] These cases concluded that there had been no interference with freedom of expression because Article 9 did not always guarantee the right to behave in the public sphere in a way which is dictated by one's religion or belief. The acts in question were not acts which actually expressed a religion or belief but, rather, were motivated or influenced by a religion or belief.[8]

There are a few cases, however, which indicate that some generally applicable neutral laws have violated Article 9(1) particularly when a prisoner is deprived from carrying out religious worship.[9] On the other hand, laws which are not 'religiously neutral', such as a law punishing proselytism,[10] or requiring places of worship to obtain prior approval from a minister,[11] or laws which discriminate against particular religious denominations might well be considered to be non-neutral religious laws which fall foul of Article 9(1).[12] The view is that when a 'law is shown after close scrutiny to be truly general and neutral, it should be immune from challenge under Article 9'.[13]

---

1   *Kokkinakis v Greece* (1993) Series A No 260-A, 17 EHRR 397, para 31.
2   *Vereniging Rechtsinkels Utrecht v The Netherlands* (1986) 46 DR 200.
3   *C v UK* (1983) Application No 10358/83, (1983) 37 DR 142.
4   *Valsamis v Greece* RJD 1996–VI 2312, (1996) 24 EHRR 294 at 317, para 36.
5   *Seven Individuals v Sweden* Application No 8811/79, (1982) 29 DR 104.
6   *Karakuzey v FRG* Application No 26568/95, (1996, unreported).
7   *Stedman, Louise v UK* Application No 29107/95, (1997) 23 EHRR CD 168; see below.
8   *Arrowsmith v UK* Application No 7050/75, (1978) 19 DR 5.
9   See, for example, *Chester v UK* Application No 9488/81 where a prisoner who was in solitary confinement was excluded from collective worship; on the other hand see *X v UK* Application No 5442/74, (1974) 1 DR at 41–42.
10   *Kokkinakis v Greece* (1993) Series A No 260-A, 17 EHRR 397.
11   *Mannoussakis and Ors v Greece* RJD 1996-IV 1346, (1997) 23 EHRR 387.
12   *Church of Lukum v City of Hialeah* 124 L Ed 2d 472.
13   See Stephanos Stavros '*Freedom of Religion*' (1997) EHRLR 627.

Non-absolute rights

2.149   There is a distinction between acts which actually express a religion or belief and which are considered to fall under the scope of Article 9(1) and those which are simply motivated or influenced by religious opinions or beliefs and which are considered not to fall within the scope of Article 9(1). Thus, an act of worship or devotion falls within the first category; whereas, for example, the objection to paying tax because it is used to fund the army or armaments falls under the second category, which is usually associated with beliefs which have no exact conscientious base. Thus, a Quaker who objects to paying income tax because the money is used to finance weapon research, may find that his or her freedom guaranteed under Article 9(1) has not been violated.[1] In considering this issue (objection to paying taxes), the Commission has taken into account the effect of Article 1 of the First Protocol which expressly provides for Member States to raise taxes. As stated above, Article 9 does not confer on a person the right to refuse, on the basis of his or her convictions or belief, to comply with legislation or laws which are themselves neutral and generally in a public sphere.

APPLICATION OF ARTICLE 9

2.150   Article 9 of the Convention has been raised in several different contexts before the European Court and some are considered below.

Criminal law

2.151   The European Court has considered the following cases.

(a) A Sikh wearing a turban because of his religious beliefs claimed that a prosecution and conviction for failing to wear a crash helmet while riding a motorbike on a public road infringed his freedom of religion. The Commission ruled that there was no violation of Article 9 because the wearing of crash helmets while riding a motorbike on a public road was a necessary safety measure for the protection of health within the scope of Article 9(2).[2]

(b) Article 9 does not extend to guaranteeing a right to bring a prosecution for blasphemy against those authors or publishers who offended the religious sensitivities of minority groups.[3]

(c) A pacifist who distributed leaflets to soldiers in Northern Ireland encouraging them to disaffect because of his pacifist views and who was punished for inciting disaffection within the armed forces could not claim protection under Article 9.[4]

---

1   *Arrowsmith v UK* Application No 7050/75, (1978) 19 DR 5.
2   *X v UK* Application No 7992/77, (1978) 14 DR 234. The Motor Cycle Crash Helmets (Religious Exemption) Act 1976 now exempts Sikhs from wearing crash helmets.
3   *Choudhury v UK* (1991) 12 Human Rights LJ 172.
4   *Arrowsmith v UK* Application No 7050/75, (1978) 19 DR 5.

(d) A conviction of an applicant for failing to obtain an authority's permission for running a place of worship amounted to a violation of Article 9(1). In this case, the domestic law clearly intended to regulate the manifestation of religious worship.[1]

Prisoners

2.152 The freedom of religion, as guaranteed by Article 9, is not absolute, but subject to the limitations set out in Article 9. The following cases are relevant.

(a) The Commission ruled that the objections of a Sikh to cleaning his prison cell on grounds that it was contrary to his religious beliefs did not violate Article 9 because the requirement to clean the cells was justified on health grounds.[2]

(b) The modality of a particular religious manifestation (eg attending a mosque for prayer) may be influenced by the situation of the person claiming that freedom. Thus a prisoner who wishes to exercise the freedom of religion by attending a mosque may be restricted by the fact of his imprisonment.[3]

Employment

2.153 In the sphere of employment relations, several cases have concerned religious convictions.

(a) The right to manifest one's religious beliefs or convictions also includes a right not to join a trade union.[4] As it stands, compulsion to join a trade union may be a violation of human rights under Article 9 and Article 11.[5]

(b) A school teacher who resigns from full-time employment because he is refused permission by a local authority to attend a mosque for the purposes of worship during hours of employment may not have his freedom of religion violated. Provision for worship by the individual, alone, at his place of employment does not necessarily satisfy Article 9(1).

(c) The right to exercise freedom of religion may be limited by contractual obligations, including those of employment and by the requirements of the education system as a whole, provided that the employer gives due consideration to the religious position of the employee and does not[6] arbitrarily disregard his freedom of religion.

---

1 *Manoussakis v Greece* RJD 1996-IV 1346, (1997) 23 EHRR 387.
2 *X v UK* (1982) 28 DR 5, para 38.
3 *X v UK* Application No 5442/74, (1974) 1 DR at 41–42.
4 *Chauhan v UK* (1990) 65 DR 41 at 45: an appeal by a Hindu employee who refused to renew his trade union membership on grounds of religious convictions was declared admissible by the Commission but subsequently settled by consent. It is unlawful to refuse a person employment because he is not a member of a trade union or because he is unwilling to remain a member of a trade union: see, for example, s 137 and s 146 of the Trade Union and Labour Relations (Consolidation) Act 1992 and also see *Young, James and Webster v UK* [1981] IRLR 408, ECHR (merits), [1983] IRLR 35, ECHR (compensation) in relation to a complaint under Article 11 where it was held that the dismissal for refusal to join a trade union was contrary to Article 11 (freedom of association).
5 See, for example, *Young, James and Webster v UK* [1981] IRLR 408, ECHR (above).
6 *Ahmad v UK* (1981) 4 EHRR 126, paras 5, 11–19. See s 146 of the Education Act 1996 which restricts the measures which may be taken in relation to teachers on religious grounds. No

(d) Regulations restricting the participation in forms of political activity of certain local government officers because of the nature of their duties was justifiable in order to preserve political neutrality and this was within a State's margin of appreciation. The Regulations were intended to limit political comment likely to link a politically restricted post-holder with a particular party political line and such limitations imposed were limited.[1]

Education

2.154   The suspension of a school child, belonging to the Jehovah's Witnesses, for a day, for refusing to take part in a school parade because it was against her religious belief violated the freedom of religion combined with Article 2 of the First Protocol. This Article enjoins the State to respect parent's convictions, be they religious or philosophical, throughout the entire State education. This duty is a broad one and it applies not only to the content of education and the manner of its provisions but also to the performance of all the functions assumed by the State. But the obligation to take part in a school parade was not such as to offend the parents' religious convictions and therefore did not interfere with her right to freedom of religion.[2]

Planning

2.155   Planning conditions will not violate Article 9 if they are not disproportionate. A planning law restriction or enforcement notice which ostensibly curtailed the freedom of public worship at a temple amounted to an interference with rights under Article 9(1) of the Convention. However, such interference may not be disproportionate to the aim being pursued under Article 9(2), namely, seeking to protect the rights of others. Article 9 may not be used to circumvent existing planning legislation providing the local authority and the planning inspector gave sufficient weight to the religious needs and interest of the applicants and any such interference with Article 9(1), therefore, would not be disproportionate.[3]

Right to marry (Article 12)

2.156   In this context, the European Court has to balance the rights of the individual against the public interest.

(a) The right to marry cannot be considered simply as a form of religious practice and is regulated by Article 12 of the Convention, which leaves the national requirements to be stipulated by domestic law. Thus, the refusal of permission under English law for a Muslim man to marry a 14-year-old

---

teacher shall be disqualified by reason of his religious opinions, or of his attending or omitting to attend religious worship; no teacher shall be required to give religious education. This section does not permit a teacher to break his contract of employment to attend a religious service: see *Ahmad v ILEA* [1978] QB 36 and the European Court agreed with this view (above). Note that the definition of 'racial grounds' does not include religion: s 3(1) of the Race Relations Act 1976 (England and Wales).

1   *Ahmad v UK* (1981) 4 EHRR 126.
2   *Valsamis v Greece* RJD 1996-VI 2312, (1996) 24 EHRR 294, para 37.
3   *ISKCON v UK* (1994) 76 A DR 90.

Muslim girl as permitted by the man's religious law (Islamic law), could not be said to violate his freedom of religion.[1]

(b) Article 9 could not be relied upon by a Quaker who complained that, as under Irish laws he was not allowed to obtain a divorce, he was thereby compelled to cohabit with a person outside marriage and that this was against his conscience.[2]

From these cases, it can be discerned that Article 9 cannot be relied upon to assert the validity of marriages conducted according to special religious rituals (freedom of religion), but which is not recognised according to the domestic marriage laws of the place in which the married parties live or where the marriage is conducted; nor can Article 9 be relied upon to circumvent the domestic laws governing divorce.

National service or armed forces

2.157 Conscientious objectors to national or military service have an additional hurdle to meet. The Commission will consider the effect of a breach of Article 9(1) alongside Article 4(3)(b) of the Convention, which provides that forced or compulsory labour does not include any service of a military character or, in the case of conscientious objectors in countries where they are recognised, service exacted instead of compulsory military service. Thus Article 9 will be interpreted in the light of Article 4.

The compulsory retirement of an army officer for having expressed fundamentalist views did not amount to an interference with his right to freedom of religion because the compulsory retirement was not directed at his beliefs but at his conduct and attitude which transgressed military discipline.[3]

Freedom to manifest religion

2.158 The following cases have sought to define the parameters of the freedom to manifest religion.

(a) Commercial advertisements promoting sales of religious artefacts were clearly not within the scope of Article 9 as the purpose of such advertisements was to market goods for profit rather than the 'manifestation of a belief in practice'.[4]

(b) An applicant who was convicted for disorderly behaviour in a public place for bellowing godly tenets against fornication and alcoholism no doubt had his freedom of religion interfered with, but a criminal conviction was justified for the protection of public order and of the rights and freedom of others, given that his bellowing disturbed the sensitivities of members of the public.[5]

(c) A Buddhist prisoner who objected to a prison rule forbidding him to grow his beard in prison because it contravened his religious practice which required him to grow a beard, had his freedom to manifest his religion

---

1 *Khan v UK* (1986) 48 DR 253.
2 *Johnston and Ors v Ireland* (1986) Series A No 112, 9 EHRR 203, para 63.
3 *Kalac v Turkey* Application No 20704/92.
4 *X and the Church of Scientology v Sweden* Application No 7805/77, (1979) 16 DR 68.
5 *Håkansson v Sweden* (1983) 5 EHRR 297.

interfered with. However, such a measure was justified in the interest of public order.[1]

Welfare benefits

2.159 An unemployed applicant, in receipt of State benefits, who suffered a reduction in his State benefits because he claimed that he was unable to take up any employment due to his conscientious objections, could not rely on Article 9 together with other Articles of the Convention. This was because he was not forced to perform any kind of labour.[2]

The margin of appreciation granted to local authorities in this context is wide and the court will not readily substitute its own assessment for that of the local authority's assessment of what might be the best possible policy in this context. The court will only examine whether the local authority in imposing the sanction or restriction, arbitrarily disregarded the applicant's freedom of religion.[3]

Application to private concerns

2.160 Article 9 applies horizontally providing the interference is first established. The UK's obligations to ensure the enjoyment of rights under Article 9 could be engaged where the actions of a private company are concerned. Thus, even if an employee is not directly employed by the government but her right to freedom of religion is violated by her private employers because the UK government has failed to legislate in a manner which protects that right, then there might well be an interference by the government providing the interference is first established.[4] The dismissal of an employee for refusing to work on a Sunday, because of her religious convictions, did not violate Article 9 because her dismissal was owing to her failing to work certain hours rather than because of her religious beliefs. Therefore, even if she had been employed by the government, no violation of Article 9 could have occurred because there was no evidence that she was dismissed because of her religious belief.[5]

The main principles (such as margin of appreciation) which apply to Article 9 also apply to Article 10. These common principles are discussed in greater detail under Article 10.

---

1 Application No 1753/63, Dec 15.2.65 Collection 16, at 20.
2 Under reg 13(2) of the Jobseeker's Allowance Regulations 1996, SI 1996/207, a person can restrict the nature of the work he is available for on the grounds of a sincere religious belief or conscientious objection, as long as he still has a reasonable chance of finding employment despite that restriction and any other restrictions allowed under the regulations.
3 *Ahmad v ILEA* [1978] QB 36, para 19.
4 *Young, James and Webster v UK* [1981] IRLR 408, para 49 ECHR; and *Stedman, Louise v UK* Application No 29107/95, (1997) 23 EHRR CD 168.
5 *Stedman, Louise v UK* Application No 29107/95, (1997) 23 EHRR CD 14.

SUMMARY

2.161 Freedom of thought, conscience and religion, which is safeguarded under Article 9 of the Convention, is one of the foundations of a 'democratic society' within the meaning of the Convention. It is, in its religious dimension, one of the most vital elements that go to make up the identity of believers and their conception of life. Those who choose to exercise the freedom to manifest their religion, irrespective of whether they do so as members of a religious majority or a minority, cannot reasonably expect to be exempt from all criticism. They must tolerate and accept the denial by others of their religious beliefs and even the propagation by others of doctrines hostile to their faith. However, the manner in which the religious beliefs and doctrines are opposed or denied is a matter which may engage the responsibility of the State, notably its responsibility to ensure the peaceful enjoyment of the right guaranteed under Article 9 to the holders of those beliefs and doctrines. Indeed, in extreme cases the effect of particular methods of opposing or denying religious beliefs can be such as to inhibit those who hold such beliefs from exercising their freedom to hold and express them.

The respect for the religious feelings of believers as guaranteed in Article 9 can legitimately be thought to have been violated by provocative portrayals of objects of religious veneration; any such portrayals can be regarded as malicious violations of the spirit of tolerance, which must also be a feature of democratic society.[1]

Article 2 of the First Protocol must be read in the light of Article 9 of the Convention. The term 'belief' appears in Article 9 in the context of the right to freedom of thought, conscience and religion. 'Convictions' taken on its own is not synonymous with the words 'opinions' and 'ideas'. Article 9 did not confer a right to exemption from disciplinary rules which applied generally and in a neutral manner. Article 9 protected only aspects of religious practice in a generally recognised form which were strictly a matter of conscience.[2]

Military discipline by its nature implies that certain limitations will be imposed on the rights and freedoms of military personnel which cannot be imposed upon those of civilians. These limitations could include one prohibiting the military from engaging in Islamic fundamentalism, in view of its quasi-political aims.[3]

Article 9 protected behaviour which was the direct expression of a religious or of a philosophical conviction, but its protection did not extend to all acts done in the name of those freedoms.[4]

The rights of worship, either alone or in community with others, are not mutually exclusive. Provision for worship by the individual, alone, at his place of employment does not necessarily satisfy Article 9(1). The right to exercise freedom of religion may be limited by contractual obligations, including those

---

1   *Otto-Preminger Institut v Austria* (1994) Series A No 295-A, 19 EHRR 34.
2   *Valsamis v Greece* RJD 1996-VI 2312, (1996) 24 EHRR 294.
3   *Yanasik v Turkey* Application No 14524/89 CD 5, (1993) 16 EHRR.
4   *Fadini v Switzerland* Application Nos 17003/90 and 18206/91 CD 13, (1993) 16 EHRR DC.

of employment, and by the requirements of the education system as a whole, provided the employer gives due consideration to the religious position of the employee and does not arbitrarily disregard his freedom of religion.[1]

---

1   *Ahmad v UK* (1981) 4 EHRR 126.

ARTICLE 10 – FREEDOM OF EXPRESSION

2.162   *'Article 10*

Freedom of expression

1.   Everyone has the right to freedom of expression. This right shall include
      freedom to hold opinions and to receive and impart information and ideas
      without interference by public authority and regardless of frontiers. This
      Article shall not prevent States from requiring the licensing of broadcasting,
      television or cinema enterprises.
2.   The exercise of these freedoms, since it carries with it duties and responsibil-
      ities, may be subject to such formalities, conditions, restrictions or penalties as
      are prescribed by law and are necessary in a democratic society, in the
      interests of national security, territorial integrity or public safety, for the
      prevention of disorder or crime, for the protection of health or morals, for
      the protection of the reputation or rights of others, for preventing the
      disclosure of information received in confidence, or for maintaining the
      authority and impartiality of the judiciary.'

INTRODUCTION

2.163   Article 10(1), unlike Article 19 of the International Covenant on Civil
and Political Rights, does not mention the freedom to seek information.
However, it embodies one of the pillars of fundamental rights and freedom of
expression: '[it] constitutes one of the essential foundations of a democratic
society and one of the conditions of its progress'.[1]

Freedom of the press

2.164   In *Castells v Spain*,[2] the European Court stated:

'Freedom of the press affords the public one of the best means of discovering and
forming an opinion of the ideas and attitudes of their political leaders. In
particular, it gives politicians the opportunity to reflect and comment on the
preoccupations of public opinion; it thus enables everyone to participate in the
free political debate which is at the very core of the concept of a democratic
society.'

Protecting violation of freedom of expression

2.165   When there is a violation of freedom of expression, the examining
court must ask a number of questions:

(1) is the interference in question prescribed by law? (The expression 'law'
     covers not only statute, but also common law.);[3]

---

1   *Handyside v UK* (1976) Series A No 24, 1 EHRR 737.
2   (1992) Series A No 236, 14 EHRR 445 at 476.
3   See *Tolstoy Miloslavsky v UK* (1995) Series A No 323, 20 EHRR 442, para 37: 'the expression
     firstly requires that the impugned measures should have a basis in domestic law. A law

(2) does the interference have aims that are legitimate under Article 10(2)?;

(3) is the interference necessary in a democratic society?

FAR-REACHING APPLICATION OF ARTICLE 10(1)

2.166 Article 10(1) is not only applicable to the press, but also to the reception of ideas and information which are favourably received or regarded as inoffensive or as a matter of indifference, or which offend, shock or disturb. Freedom of expression, as enshrined in Article 10, is subject to a number of exceptions which, however, must be narrowly interpreted and the necessity for any restriction must be convincingly established.[1] Article 10 has been relied upon where access to the media by a prisoner had been restricted by prison rules.[2]

Article 10 has a wide-ranging application covering not only relationships between private individuals but also between public authorities and individuals. It affects working relationships between public sector employers and employees where the former seek to restrain the latter from disclosing confidential information obtained in the course of employment. It affords defences against criminal charges for inciting racial hatred.

RESTRICTIONS IN ARTICLE 10(2) MUST BE CONVINCINGLY ESTABLISHED

2.167 The restrictions contained in Article 10(2) must be convincingly established because of the importance of the fundamental right of freedom of expression. Article 15 of the Convention provides a derogation from this Article: 'in time of war or other public emergency which threatens the life of a nation, a government may take measures that derogate from certain of the rights guaranteed by the Convention'.[3] In time of war, any reporting restrictions in the press should be strictly necessary.

---

which confers a discretion is not in itself inconsistent with this requirement, provided that the scope of the discretion and the manner of its exercise are indicated with sufficient clarity, having regard to the legitimate aim in question, to give the individual adequate protection against arbitrary interference'.

1   *Handyside v UK* (1976) Series A No 24, 1 EHRR 737, para 49.

2   *Bamber v UK* Application No 33742/96: the prison Standing Order prevented prisoners contacting the media by telephone except with permission given in exceptional circumstances. The Commission held that where the State imposes restrictions on a prisoner's access to a particular medium of communication, which he would have enjoyed in normal circumstances had he not been a prisoner, then such restriction might constitute an interference with the right to freedom of expression. In this case, the restriction was justified because the prison authority was not able to effectively control and monitor the telephone communication between prisoner and the media.

3   In *Ireland v UK* (1979–80) 1 EHRR 15, the Court held that where Article 15 was relied upon then a wide margin of appreciation would be credited to the State as the national authorities would be in a better position. However, the Court does not grant unlimited discretion.

The public authority will bear the burden in discharging the derogation relied upon in Article 10(2). The public authority will have to demonstrate to the requisite degree the 'pressing social need' for the interference in question.

DOCTRINE OF MARGIN OF APPRECIATION

Public bodies have a discretion

2.168   The doctrine of margin of appreciation allows a public authority the following options.

(1) A latitude in the application of restrictions on the Convention right in question.
(2) To opt for a course of conduct in carrying out its duties under statute. This course of conduct or range of options may infringe Convention rights if they fall outside the range of permissible options; that is, outside their 'margin of appreciation'.
(3) To choose the measures which it considers appropriate in those matters which are governed by the Convention. The domestic courts have long made it clear that, although they will readily review the way in which decisions are reached, they will respect the margin of appreciation or discretion which the decision-maker has.[1]
(4) Although judicial review does not require or permit a primary fact finding enquiry, it does envisage a fresh appreciation or evaluation or assessment of the facts established by the decision-maker.[2]

The margin of appreciation is a doctrine consisting of judicial restraint

2.169   The measures or actions undertaken by a public authority which falls within the range of permissible options will not be held to be contrary to the Convention by a domestic court or tribunal on the basis that it is not that which the court or tribunal thinks would have been best in the circumstances of the case. The margin of appreciation is a doctrine consisting of judicial restraint. If a domestic court is faced with a complaint that a public authority has acted incompatibly with Article 10(1), it will examine the facts for itself but it is empowered to give the final runing on whether a 'restriction' or 'penalty' is reconcilable with freedom of expression as protected by Article 10.

Judicial restraint

2.170   The measures or actions undertaken by a public authority which fall within the range of permissible options will not be held to be contrary to the Convention by a domestic court or tribunal on the basis that they are not what the court or tribunal thinks would have been best in the circumstances of the case. The margin of appreciation is a doctrine consisting of judicial restraint. If a domestic court is faced with a complaint that a public authority has acted

---

1   *R v Chief Constable, ex parte ITF* (HL(E)) [1998] 3 WLR 1260 at 1268F.
2   *Upjohn v Licensing Authority* Case C 120/97; opinion of Advocate-General Leger.

incompatibly with Article 10(1), it will examine the facts for itself, but it is empowered to give the final ruling on whether a 'restriction' or 'penalty' is reconcilable with freedom of expression as protected by Article 10.

Judicial restraint is not judicial reluctance

2.171 If a person is charged with an offence, for example under the Obscene Publications Act 1959 for having in his possession books considered to be obscene, a criminal court would have to determine whether the charge is an interference which is necessary in a democratic society for the protection of morals.

Whilst the prosecuting authority has a margin of appreciation whether to prosecute or charge an alleged offender, the criminal court will also have a margin of appreciation to determine whether the charge is reconcilable with the freedom of expression as protected by Article 10.

The function of the court obliges it to pay the utmost attention to the principles characterising a 'democratic' society. Consequently, every 'formality', 'condition', 'restriction' or 'penalty' imposed in this sphere must be proportionate to the legitimate aim pursued. The court is required to consider all relevant arguments and must view the decision in the light of the case as a whole, including whether the reasons given by the public authority are relevant and sufficient under Article 10(2).[1]

APPLICATION OF THE DOCTRINE OF MARGIN OF APPRECIATION

2.172 When Article 10 arguments are raised in any court or tribunal, it is essential that the doctrine of margin of appreciation is properly utilised and transposed into domestic law.

The Divisional Court has frequently used the concepts of margin of appreciation depending on the subject matter under review. The Divisional Court's traditional approach is based on the *Wednesbury* principle, namely, that it will not substitute its decision for that of the decision-maker and will only consider whether the decision-maker has failed to take into account relevant matters or failed to consider relevant matters. In a recent judgment of the House of Lords, it was stated that although the distinction between the *Wednesbury* and proportionality test is different, the distinction in practice is in any event much less than is sometimes suggested. The cautious way in which the European Court usually applies this test, recognising the importance of respecting the national authority's (ie decision-maker) margin of appreciation, may mean that whichever test is adopted, and even allowing for a difference in onus, the result is the same and the decision-maker must enjoy a margin of appreciation or discretion that cannot differ according to whether its source is linked to purely domestic principles or European Court principles.[2]

---

1 *Handyside v UK* (1976) Series A No 24, 1 EHRR 737, para 50.
2 *R v Chief Constable, ex parte ITF* (HL(E)) [1998] 3 WLR 1260 at 1277C and 1289D.

There is a difference between the European Court applying the doctrine when supervising a breach of the Convention by a national organ and a domestic court supervising a breach of the Convention by a public authority. One view is that the doctrine of margin of appreciation has no role to play in domestic law. Another view is that the doctrine of margin of appreciation finds no justification when the matter is being examined by a domestic court because domestic courts are better placed to evaluate and determine the necessity or otherwise of an interference of Article 10(1).

However, the suggested view is that all courts and tribunals, when confronted with an argument that there has been a violation of Article 10(1), should not consider the issues as a *reviewing* body, but adopt an equivalent approach to that undertaken by the European Court in similar situations. In making its judgment as to whether sufficiently strong reasons are shown in any particular case to outweigh the important public interest in the press being able to protect the anonymity of its sources, the domestic court will give great weight to the judgments, in particular recent judgments, of the European Court in cases where the facts are similar to the case before the domestic court. The tests which the European Court and the House of Lords apply in considering Article 10 are substantially the same.[1]

Doctrine of proportionality in use

2.173 Alternatively, 'the doctrine of proportionality' may be one useful approach of a judicial examination in scrutinising whether a restriction or penalty or condition is 'necessary in a democratic society'. As applied in the European context, proportionality is a legitimate technique of review and not an appeal process (particularly in a judicial review context). The courts are used to applying the doctrine of proportionality when applying EC law and there is no reason why a similar approach cannot be adopted in the context of human rights.[2]

The doctrine of proportionality as applied by UK courts may be summarised as follows:

(1) the administrative decision must be justified by some imperative require-
     ment in the general interest;
(2) it must be suitable for securing the attainments of the objects which it
     pursues; and
(3) it must not go beyond what it is necessary to attain that objective.[3]

The approach under the doctrine of proportionality is to determine the lawfulness of a public authority's decision and to ensure that excessive measures are not used to achieve given ends. 'Sledgehammers should not be used to crack nuts when ordinary nutcrackers will do.'[4] The fundamental

---

1   See *Camelot Group Plc v Centaur Ltd* [1998] 2 WLR 379 at 388B and 389D–F.
2   The doctrine of proportionality was rejected in *R v Secretary of State for the Home Department,
     ex parte Brind* [1991] 1 AC 679 at 767.
3   See *R v Human Fertilisation and Embryology Authority, ex parte Blood* [1997] 2 WLR 806, at
     819G; and *U v W* [1997] 3 WLR 739 at 751E.
4   See J Jowell and A Lester 'Proportionality: Neither Novel nor Dangerous' in J Jowell and D
     Oliver (eds) *New Directions in Judicial Review* (1988) at p 51.

objection to the utilisation of the doctrine of proportionality is that it invites a review of the merits of the case on a threshold of reasonableness which is much lower than the traditional *Wednesbury* approach (ie irrationality), whereas proportionality demands that the examining court should resolve the differences between competing interests. Therefore, a proportionality test is a much lower test than the *Wednesbury* threshold of unreasonableness. In a number of domestic cases the courts have taken the view that proportionality is another aspect of *Wednesbury* unreasonableness.[1] One view is that the margin of appreciation 'does not cover so many degrees of latitude as that afforded by the traditional *Wednesbury* doctrine'.[2]

PART 2
THE ARTICLES

VARIABLES OF THE DOCTRINE OF MARGIN OF APPRECIATION

2.174 Within the context of Article 10(1), the following variables to the doctrine may occur.

(1) The derogations contained in Article 10(2) must be interpreted narrowly or restrictively.[3] Article 10(1) applies to both spoken and written text.

(2) Freedom of expression under Article 10 is not protected in absolute terms. Where a public authority seeks to muzzle the press, its power to limit the freedom of expression is to be construed narrowly and the public authority will enjoy only a narrow discretion to interfere with this Convention right. Whilst the press must not overstep the bounds set in the interest of the protection of the reputation and rights of others, it is nevertheless incumbent on it to impart information and ideas of public interest even if, for example, the ideas conveyed are 'racist' ones.[4]

(3) Restriction of publication of confidential information concerning commercial matters may well justify an interference of the right to freedom of expression particularly if the information is distributed to a limited circle of tradespeople and does not directly concern the public as a whole.[5]

(4) Where a public authority's decision infringes Article 10(1) but is intended to defend moral values then it enjoys a wide margin of appreciation and a court will more readily find that an interference of this nature is justifiable

---

1   *R v General Medical Council, ex parte Coleman* [1990] All ER 489; the GMC prevented a medical practitioner from advertising his services of a holistic persuasion under the provisions of s 35 of the Medical Act 1983. The European Court dismissed his application and refused to apply Article 10(1) of the Convention; see also *R v Secretary of State for the Home Department, ex parte Brind* [1990] Admin LR 785 at 798.

2   *R v Secretary of State for the Environment, ex parte NALGO* [1993] Admin LR 785 at 798.

3   *Klass and Others v FRG* (1978) Series A No 28, 2 EHRR 214 at 231.

4   *Jersild v Denmark* (1994) Series A No 298, 19 EHRR 1 at 31; *Goodwin v UK* RJD 1996–II 483, (1996) EHRR 420.

5   *Markt Intern and Beermann v FRG* (1989) Series A No 165, 12 EHRR 161 at 171, para 26. See also *Jacubowski v FRG* (1994) Series A No 291–A, 18 EHRR 64, paras 26–27: A certain margin of appreciation is to be left to the State in assessing whether and to what extent interference is necessary, but this margin goes hand-in-hand with European supervision covering both the legislation and the decisions applying it, even those given by an independent court. Such a margin of appreciation appears essential in commercial

under Article 10(2).[1] But the protection of morals must still be within the scope of restraints permitted under the Convention.

(5) Freedom of expression also includes both artistic and cultural expression. That being so, as a matter of principle it may be considered necessary in a democratic society to sanction or even prevent improper attacks on objects of religion.[2]

(6) Where there is a conflict of two fundamental freedoms, that is on the one hand a right of free speech and on the other hand the right of other persons to their freedom of thought, conscience or religion (Article 9) or the right to respect for family or private life (Article 8), then regard must be had to the margin of appreciation left to the public authority, whose duty it is in a democratic society also to consider, within the limits of their jurisdiction, the interest of society as a whole.[3] It may be necessary in a democratic society to set limits to the fundamental freedoms where the exercise of such rights causes offence to others.[4] One view is that the need for repressive action against the freedom of expression is justified if the offensive behaviour of the person exercising this right 'reaches a high level of abuse and comes so close to a denial of the freedom' of another person's fundamental rights.[5] It may be lawful under the Convention for an authority to restrict freedom of expression in order to protect the rights of others not to be offended by insults and abuse directed at their religious or deep-seated beliefs. Any such restriction which the authority imposes must be applied in a non-discriminatory way because Article 14 (which prohibits discrimination) can be infringed if a restriction under Article 10(2) is imposed in a discriminatory manner.[6] To restrict a company's freedom of expression by extending a right to privacy to a corporation would be in conflict with Article 10 because a corporation has no right to private life under Article 8.[7]

---

matters, especially in an area as complex and fluctuating as unfair competition. The European Court must confine its review to the question whether the measures taken at national level are justifiable in principle and proportionate.

1   *Handyside v UK* (1976) Series A No 24, 1 EHRR 737, para 48; *Müller v Switzerland* (1998) Series A No 133, 13 EHRR 212.

2   *Otto-Preminger Institut v Austria* (1994) 19 EHRR 34, para 49.

3   Ibid, at paras 55 and 59.

4   Section 12(4): the court must have particular regard to the importance of the Convention right to freedom of expression and, where the proceedings relate to material which the respondent claims, or which appears to the court, to be journalistic, literary or artistic material (or to conduct connected with such material) (i) the extent to which the material has, or is about to, become available to the public; or (ii) it is, or would be, in the public interest for the material to be published; (iii) any relevant privacy code.

5   See dissenting Opinion of Judges Palm and Pekkanen and Makarczyk in *Otto Preminger* (above), paras 7–8.

6   *Gay News Ltd v UK* (1982) 5 EHRR 123: the applicants could not complain of discrimination because the law of blasphemy protects only the Christian and no other religion; at 131.

7   *R v Broadcasting Standards Commission, ex parte British Broadcasting Corporation* (1999) *The Times*, 9 July.

EMPLOYMENT, CONTRACT AND BREACH OF CONFIDENCE

2.175   In matters of national security or economic and social policy, the public authority possesses a wide margin of appreciation.[1] The Official Secrets Act 1989, s 1(1), makes it unlawful for an ex-security or intelligence member without lawful authority to disclose information etc which has been in his possession by reason of his position as a member of the services. This may well be compatible with the restrictions in Article 10(2) (in the interests of national security) but the common law would no more impose on such service members a duty of non-disclosure that would represent an infringement of his rights of free expression than it would impose a duty that would represent an unreasonable restraint on his ability to earn his living.[2] A court would be reluctant to readily imply a term in a contract which would have the effect of restricting freedom of expression, but the court might well grant an injunction to restrain a defendant from receiving any payment or other benefit from the exploitation of a book or of any information obtained from a position as a member of the Secret Intelligence Service. The domestic court takes the view that such an injunction can readily be justified under Article 10(2) of the Convention as being a necessary and proportionate measure adopted in the interest of national security.[3]

Where a public sector employee is dismissed for a reason which infringes his fundamental rights of free speech or expression, this may well constitute an unnecessary infringement of his rights.[4] The current European Court case-law relates primarily to public sector employment, but there is scope for arguing that such rights also apply in private sector employment, particularly in claims for unfair dismissal, because an industrial tribunal is a public body (see below).

In deciding whether a dismissal or some other action short of dismissal is proportionate to the legitimate aim pursued, a tribunal may have to examine the nature of the freedom of expression (was it political or was it a disclosure of confidential commercial information), the nature of the applicant's job and the potential damage done to an employer's own fundamental rights (including a breach of Article 1 of the First Protocol).

Article 10 applies to the workplace (albeit in a limited sense).[5] An employee might be dismissed or disciplined for exercising free speech in an employment context. A dismissal is an infringement of Article 10(1) if it results from the employee exercising free speech on matters of public concern, but not if the free speech is a criticism of the employer's private rights or workplace.[6] Where the freedom of expression concerns political debate then it will more readily be

PART 2
THE ARTICLES

---

1   But see *Chahal v UK* RJD 1996–V 1831, (1996) 23 EHRR 413 in an Article 3 context; and also see *Klass and Others v FRG* (1978) Series A No 28, 2 EHRR 214.

2   *Attorney-General v Blake* [1996] 3 WLR 741, at 747D–H; which was overturned in the Court of Appeal [1998] 2 WLR 805.

3   *Attorney-General v Blake* [1998] 2 WLR 805 at 824F. The domestic court did not make a full record of the contrary submissions if there were any.

4   *Vogt v FRG* (1995) Series A No 323, 21 EHRR 205.

5   *Ibid.*

6   *Lingens v Austria* (1986) Series A No 103, 8 EHRR 407; *Thorgierson v Iceland* (1992) Series A No 239, 14 EHRR 843; *Jacubowski v FRG* (1994) Series A No 291–A, 19 EHRR 64.

seen that an interference with this right constitutes a disproportionate interference.[1]

Employment tribunals, being included in the definition of public bodies,[2] will have to consider whether there has been an infringement of Article 10(1) and whether such action is justified with regard to Article 10(2). The tribunal is under a positive obligation to ensure that private employers as well as public sector employers do not penalise employees for exercising their Convention rights under Article 10(1). It is well established in European Court jurisprudence that the State (public authorities, including the tribunals and courts) may have positive obligations under the Convention to take positive steps to protect an individual even when public authorities are not themselves responsible for causing the breach of the Convention.[3] Public authorities are required to apply the Convention rights horizontally, that is, in the sphere of individual relations. Most of the European Court case-law, as stated, concerns public sector employees, but it is suggested that the same approach be extended to private employees when fundamental rights are engaged. The tribunal may have to investigate whether the dismissal was because of the employee exercising free speech or whether it was owing to a breakdown of trust and confidence.[4] If an employment tribunal concludes that a public employee has been reprimanded because, in breach of his contract, he has participated in a television or radio programme and that the reprimand is justified in order to protect the rights of the employer, then this may be justified under Article 10(2).[5] Also, if an employer suppresses the freedom of expression of an employee in order to protect the rights of fellow employees, then this is capable of being a legitimate interest within Article 10(2).[6] Where an employer imposes a sanction on an employee for exercising free speech in circumstances where the employee accuses the employer of discrimination, then dismissal may well be in pursuance of a legitimate aim, namely the protection of the reputation of the employer who is accused of discrimination.[7]

Each case will have to be investigated in order to determine whether the infringement of Article 10(1) is justified or not; that is, whether the interference is necessary in a democratic society.

A tribunal will be required to consider a number of factors in deciding whether the interference with free speech etc is justified. These factors include:

---

1   *Castells v Spain* (1992) Series A No 236, 14 EHRR 445; and *Oberschlick v Austria* (1991) Series A No 204, 19 EHRR 389 at 432; freedom of political debate is at the very core of the concept of a democratic society which prevails throughout the Convention.
2   Human Rights Act 1998, s 6(3).
3   See *X and Y v The Netherlands* (1985) Series A No 91, 8 EHRR 235.
4   *Kosiek v FRG* (1986) Series A No 105, 9 EHRR 328.
5   *B v UK* (1985) 45 DR 41.
6   *X v UK* (1979) 16 DR 101.
7   But see the anti-victimisation provisions both in the Sex Discrimination Act 1975, s 4 and s 2 of the Race Relations Act 1976.

(1) the duties, responsibilities and nature of the particular employment; an employee holding a responsible post accepts the attendant restrictions on the right of freedom of expression that are inherent with the job;[1] and an employee's freedom of expression may well have to be curtailed because it conflicts with the nature of his duties;[2]

(2) if the employee's freedom of expression concerned matters of public concern rather than private matters, then it is more likely than not that dismissal or a sanction may not be justified;[3]

(3) if the freedom of expression is abusive or gross, the action taken against such an employee may well be justified;[4]

(4) whether the expressions of the employee are based on evidence or made in good faith.

Article 10(1) has also been used in cases where the 'right to freedom of expression may include the right for a person to express his ideas through the way he dresses'.[5] English courts have so far decided cases involving dress codes in an employment context with singular attention to the Sex Discrimination Act 1975 and unfair dismissal provisions.[6]

CRIMINAL LAW

2.176 Where a sanction against free speech results in a criminal charge or conviction, a domestic court will more readily conclude that the freedom of speech or expression has been infringed. Article 10(1) will have a significant role to play in cases either where there is statutory control of the publication of offensive material or brought under the Indecent Displays (Control) Act 1981, the Incitement of Disaffection Act 1934 (seducing members of the armed forces from their allegiance),[7] the Suicide Act 1961 (forbidding the counselling or procuring of suicide) and other related statutes.

---

1   *Morissen v Belgium* (1988) 56 DR 127: a teacher suspended without pay for exercising her freedom of expression was reasonably justified for the protection of other teachers and the establishment.

2   *Van der Heijden v The Netherlands* (1985) 41 DR 264: the dismissal of an employee working for an immigration institution for being a member of a political organisation hostile to immigrant workers was justified; see also *X v UK* (1979) 16 DR 101: a dismissal of a teacher employed by a non-denominational school for expressing religious beliefs was justified.

3   *Barthold v FRG* (1985) Series A No 90, 7 EHRR 383: proceedings against an employee for informing the public via a newspaper article about the veterinary services at a time when there was public concern were unjustified.

4   In *Grigoriades v Greece* (1995) 20 EHRR CD 92, the Commission declared the complaint admissible notwithstanding that the article against the army was venomous.

5   *Stevens v UK* (1986) 46 DR 245.

6   See *Schmidt v Austicks Bookshops* [1977] IRLR 395; *Smith v Safeway Plc* [1996] IRLR 456, CA: the rules concerning appearance will not be discriminatory because their content is different for men and women if they enforce a common principle of smartness or conventionality, and taken as a whole and not garment by garment or item by item, neither gender is treated less favourably.

7   In an Article 9 context, see *Arrowsmith v UK* Application No 7050/75, (1978) 19 DR 5, para 71: punishing a person for distributing leaflets advising soldiers to go absent without leave or openly to refuse to serve in Northern Ireland did not amount to an interference in

Where disciplinary proceedings are taken against lawyers for criticising the judiciary in a press conference, the interference with freedom of expression is prescribed by law if it is aimed at maintaining the authority and impartiality of the judiciary. Lawyers hold a particular position in the administration of justice and have freedom to criticise the judiciary as long as the criticism is expressed according to the proper procedures. But an interference with the freedom of expression in such cases could reasonably be considered 'necessary in a democratic society'.[1]

The European Court has held that the Obscene Publication Acts have a legitimate aim under Article 10(2), namely, the protection of morals in a democratic society, but the restriction of freedom of expression must be proportionate to the legitimate aim pursued.[2]

Free speech includes not only the inoffensive but also the irritating, the contentious, the eccentric, the heretical, the unwelcome, and the provocative, as long as such speech does not tend to provoke violence.[3]

A prisoner has a right to seek, through oral interviews, to persuade a journalist to investigate his allegations of miscarriage of justice in the hope that his case might be reopened.[4]

LIBEL CASES

2.177   Article 10 has been raised in libel cases where the European Court has to conduct a balancing exercise in setting the rights of one individual or group of individuals against those of others. The libel rule is only an instance of a 'general principle in our law that the expression of opinion and the conveyance of information will not be restrained by the courts save on pressing grounds'.[5]

As far as the freedom of expression is concerned, the European Court has sought to draw a distinction between political and private libels. Political speeches enjoy greater protection under Article 10 than non-political speeches, because the former are part of a democratic process and politicians are accountable to the electorate. Greater weight is attached to free speech in the context of political criticism directed at the government. In a majority of democratic countries, primacy is given to the protection of political speech. While politicians are required to sustain a higher degree of criticism than other

---

manifesting one's beliefs under Article 9. The advice given to soldiers not to serve in Northern Ireland was not done in order to further the applicant's pacifist ideas.

1   *Alois Schopfer v Switzerland* Application No 25404/94.
2   *Handyside v UK* (1976) Series A No 24, 1 EHRR 737, paras 46 and 49.
3   *Redmond-Batel v DPP* (1999) *The Times*, 28 July.
4   *R v Secretary of State for the Home Department, ex parte Simms and Another* [1999] 3 WLR 328. (The value of free speech in a particular case must be measured in specifics. Not all types of speech have an equal value; for example, no prisoner would ever be permitted to have interviews with a journalist to publish pornographic material or to give vent to so-called hate speech: at 337D.)
5   *R v Advertising Standards Authority Ltd, ex parte Vernons Organisation* [1992] 1 WLR 1289 per Laws J, at 1293. The applicant was refused a temporary order seeking to restrict publication of a decision of the respondent pending the outcome of the judicial review proceedings.

people, there are nevertheless limits to such criticism. Whilst a politician must be prepared to accept even harsh criticism of his public activities and statements, such criticism may not be understood as defamatory unless it throws a considerable degree of doubt on his personal character and good reputation.[1]

The domestic courts will have to consider in due course the extent to which freedom of expression governs the relationship between private individuals and how far disputes may be resolved by applying the restrictions contained in Article 10(2). For example, should a court grant an injunction to restrain publication of a leaflet in a picketing case, having in mind the principles of freedom of expression discussed above?[2]

Recent European Court and Court of Appeal cases suggest that all libel plaintiffs can expect to receive lower awards of damages than previously was the case.[3]

ARTICLE 10 AND THE INTERPRETATION OF STATUTES

2.178 The Human Rights Act 1998 requires statutes to be interpreted in accordance with the Convention[4] and there will be cases where this applies to Article 10. In particular, discretionary powers conferred on bodies in wide terms (such as 'they think fit') would have to be given a meaning which is compatible with Article 10. The power to provide advice on professional conduct which previously has been relied upon to prohibit medical practitioners from advertising the nature and availability of holistic medicine, may now have to be construed in accordance with the principles of Article 10 as discussed above.[5] In future, it would be possible to argue that the directives issued under the Broadcasting Act 1981 to the BBC and IBA to refrain from broadcasting the direct spoken words of the members of Sinn Fein were:

(a) contrary to Article 10; that is, such directives issued under statutory power are contrary to Article 10 (subject to any permissible restrictions as are necessary in a democratic society in the interests of national security etc); and

(b) unreasonable because they, inter alia, constituted an unjustified interference with freedom of expression where there was no pressing social need;

---

1 See *Lingens v Austria* (1986) Series A No 103, 8 EHRR 103; and *Oberschlick v Austria* (1991) Series A No 204, 19 EHRR 389 at 405.

2 See *Middelbrook Mushrooms v TGWU* [1993] IRLR 232. The Court of Appeal considered the application of Article 10 of the Convention.

3 *Rantzen v MGN* [1993] 3 WLR 953; *Elton John v MGN* [1996] 2 All ER 35; *Tolstoy Miloslavsky v UK* (1995) Series A No 323, 20 EHRR 442, para 51.

4 Human Rights Act 1998, s 3.

5 See in particular *R v GMC, ex parte Coleman* [1990] 1 All ER 489; s 35 of the Medical Act 1983 was relied upon to prevent a medical practicioner from advertising his holistic persuasion.

(c) were disproportionate to the mischief which the public authority was seeking to prevent.[1]

ARTICLE 10 AND NATIONAL SECURITY

2.179 Article 10 applies to everyone including members of the civil service and security services. The press has a duty to impart information and ideas on matters of public interest given that it is a 'public watchdog'.[2] An authority's restriction of the distribution within army barracks of magazines which were critical of the army was contrary to Article 10. The information conveyed in the magazines to members of the armed forces was in accordance with Article 10 and engaged the responsibilities of the State.[3]

The restrictions of freedom of expression must, even in national security cases, fulfil the tests referred to above, namely:

(1) the sanction must be prescribed by law;[4]
(2) the sanction must pursue a legitimate aim; and
(3) the sanction must be necessary in democratic society.

The State must show that there is a pressing social need for the restriction and that it is proportionate to the threat of national security.

In national security cases, the State has a wide margin of appreciation and may be reluctant to disclose sensitive information regarding national security measures. However, the European Court has emphasised that the margin of appreciation is still subject to its monitoring supervision.[5] The European Court will be prepared, if necessary, to carry out the relevant balancing exercise (subject to the discussion on margin of appreciation above) in determining whether the public interest in disclosure outweighs the State's interest in non-disclosure.[6] In a case where a teacher was dismissed for membership of a political party which was believed to be incompatible with her status as a civil servant and her duty of loyalty owed to the State, the European Court held that

---

1   Effectively the argument set out above would lead to the reversal of *R v Secretary of State for the Home Department, ex parte Brind* [1991] 1 AC 696 (above). This case went to the European Court. The Commission accepted that the ban constituted an interference with the applicant's freedom of expression, although of a limited kind, but that the ban did not exceed the margin of appreciation which the Convention provided to the State to combat terrorism: *Brind v UK* (1994) 18 EHRR CD 76.

2   *Observer and Guardian v UK* (1991) Series A No 216, 14 EHRR 153, para 59(b).

3   *Vereinigung Demokratischer Soldaten Osterreichs and Gubi v Austria* (1994) 20 EHRR 56: the European Court found that Austria had failed to demonstrate that the restriction of the distribution of the magazine within the army barracks was necessary.

4   See *Malone v UK* (1984) 7 EHRR 14 as to the precise terms as to what is meant by 'prescribed by law' (supra).

5   *Observer and Guardian v UK* (1991) Series A No 216, 14 EHRR 153 in *Vereniging Weekblad Bluf v The Netherlands* (1995) 20 EHRR 189 the European Court found that an order withdrawing magazines from sale amounted to a violation of Article 10. In both these cases, the European Court was primarily concerned with the distribution of magazines/books.

6   *Hadjianastassiou v Greece* (1992) Series A No 252–A, 16 EHRR 219: a Greek army officer sold information about military equipment to a private company for money. The State had a

the dismissal was disproportionate.[1] This example, although not directly raising the issue of national security nevertheless reveals that the European Court will investigate a defence raised by a State on the grounds that interfering with fundamental rights is based on national policy.

It remains to be seen how Article 10 will apply in cases where whistleblowers seek to disclose information under the Official Secrets Act 1989 on the grounds of public interest. Currently, there is no defence available in such cases. More interestingly, it may be argued that, when there is a violation of Article 10 and the public authority pleads national security by way of justification, then the domestic courts should be prepared to investigate the justification in the light of the principles adumbrated above. The current position (that is in relation to Article 10) is that in cases relating to national security, the domestic court is not normally inclined to examine the material before the public authority to determine whether its decision was correct and such reluctance also extends to 'other reason of a political nature'.[2] One may expect a shift in the court's attitude in that it may be required to conduct a type of investigation along the principles referred to above.[3] It is desirable to entrust supervisory control to a judge since judicial control offers the best guarantee of independence, impartiality and a proper procedure, particularly if there is no other independent body vested with sufficient powers to investigate a violation of Article 10 on national security grounds.[4]

Article 10 and disclosure of sources of information

2.180 Protection of journalistic sources is one of the basic conditions for press freedom; without such protection, sources may be deterred from assisting the press in informing the public on matters of public interest. It follows that an order for source disclosure cannot be compatible with Article 10 unless it is justified under Article 10(2).[5]

The law does not, however, enable the press to protect the anonymity of the source in all circumstances and much will depend on the particular facts of the case. For example, the public interest in enabling an employer to discover a

---

legitimate interest to preserve the secrecy of its weapon system. But the European Court applying the test concluded that Article 10 had not been infringed. See also *Vogt v FRG* (1995) Series A No 323, 21 EHRR 205 (above) which concerned national security issues.

1   *Vogt v FRG* (1995) Series A No 323, 21 EHRR 205.

2   In an immigration context see *R v the Secretary of State for the Home Office, ex parte Raghbir Singh* [1996] Imm AR 507 at 508. In an Article 3 context, the court would be required to follow the approach set out in *Chahal v UK* RJD 1996–V 1831, (1996) 23 EHRR 413. The Special Immigration Appeals Commission Bill is currently before Parliament. The Bill will provide a right of appeal to a very limited category of persons excluded on grounds of national security etc who have no rights of appeal.

3   In a non-national security case, an administrative decision impinging upon the freedom of individuals to adopt, practise and change their religion must be justified by a sufficiently weighty competing interest of which, in immigration cases, the Secretary of State is the primary judge, but as to which the court exercises a secondary supervisory jurisdiction: *R v Secretary of State for the Home Office, ex parte Moon* [1997] INLR 165.

4   In the context of national security infringing Article 8 rights see *Klass v FRG* (1978) Series A No 28, 2 EHRR 214, paras 55–56.

5   *Goodwin v UK* RJD 1996–II 483, (1996) 22 EHRR 123 at 148–9, para 2.

disloyal employee who leaked confidential information may be greater than the public interest in enabling him to escape detection.[1]

SUMMARY OF CASES

Handyside v UK[2]

2.181   The Obscene Publication Acts have a legitimate aim under Article 10(2), namely, the protection of morals in a democratic society. Each State has the initial task to secure its rights and freedoms. There is no uniform conception of morals. State authorities are better placed than the international judge to assess the necessity for a restriction designed to protect morals. Article 10(2) is applicable not only to 'information' or 'ideas' that are favourably received or regarded as inoffensive or as a matter of indifference, but also to those that offend, shock or disturb the State or any section of the population. This means that every formality, condition, restriction, or penalty imposed in this sphere must be proportionate to the legitimate aim pursued.

Markt Intern Verlagh and Beermann v FRG[3]

2.182   Articles of a commercial nature cannot be excluded from the scope of Article 10(1) which does not apply solely to certain types of information or ideas of forms of expression. As the interference was intended to protect the reputation and rights of others, it had legitimate aims. A margin of appreciation accorded to States in assessing the existence and extent of the need for an interference was essential in commercial matters and, in particular, in an area as complex and fluctuating as that of unfair competition. Even the publication of items which were true and described real events might under certain circumstances be prohibited.

The Observer and Guardian v UK[4]

2.183   An interference intended to maintain the authority of the judiciary pending trial and to protect national security in the sense of the integrity of the Security Service pursued legitimate aims. An interference by way of an injunction intending to preserve the Attorney-General's case at the trial and to protect interests of national security was necessary in a democratic society. Once material in question was no longer confidential, the remaining aim of preserving confidence in the Security Service had already been achieved by initiating proceedings and was not sufficient to interfere with the right protected by Article 10.

---

1   *Camelot Group Plc v Centaur Communications Ltd* [1998] 2 WLR 379.
2   (1976) Series A No 24, 1 EHRR 737.
3   (1989) Series A No 165, 12 EHRR 161.
4   (1991) Series A No 216, 14 EHRR 153.

Ezelin v France[1]

2.184   The right to freedom of expression is one of the foundations of a society. Article 10 is to be regarded as a *lex generalis* in relation to Article 11. Since the protection of personal opinions, secured by Article 10, is one of the objectives of the freedom of peaceful assembly, Article 11 had to considered in the light of Article 10. The prevention of disorder was a legitimate aim pursuant to which interference with the freedom of peaceful assembly might be justified. To be necessary in a democratic society, the interference must be proportionate to its aims, as listed in Article 11(2). This means that the balance has to be struck between such aims and the special and very important rights of free expression and freedom of peaceful assembly. It is therefore not necessary in a democratic society to restrict those freedoms in any way unless the person in question has committed a reprehensible act when exercising his rights.

Oberschlick v Austria[2]

2.185   Article 10 protects not only the substance of the ideas and the information expressed, but also the form in which they are conveyed. Whilst the press must not overstep the bounds set for the protection of the reputation of others, nevertheless its task is to impart information and ideas on political issues and other matters of general interest. Freedom of the press affords the public one of the best means of discovering and forming an opinion of the ideas and attitudes of political leaders. More generally, freedom of political debate is at the very core of the concept of a democratic society which prevails throughout the Convention. The limits of acceptable criticism are accordingly wider with regard to a politician acting in his public capacity than in relation to a private individual. The former inevitably and knowingly lays himself open to close scrutiny of his every word and deed by other journalists and the public at large, and he must display a greater degree of tolerance, especially when he himself makes public statements that are susceptible to criticism. A politician is certainly entitled to have his reputation protected, even when he is not acting in his private capacity, but the requirements of that protection have to be weighed against the interest of open discussion of political issues.

Jersild v Denmark[3]

2.186   The public also have a right to receive ideas of public interest. In considering the duties and responsibilities of a journalist, the potential impact of the medium concerned is an important factor. Article 10 protects both the content and the form of expression. In considering whether the interference complained of was necessary, the courts will look at it in the light of the case as a whole, and will determine whether the reasons adduced by the national authorities are relevant and sufficient, and whether the means employed were proportionate to the legitimate aim pursued. An important factor would be whether the item in question, when considered as a whole, appeared from an objective point of view to have had as its purpose the propagation of racist views

1   (1991) Series A No 202, 14 EHRR 362.
2   (1991) Series A No 204, 19 EHRR 389.
3   (1994) Series A No 298, 19 EHRR 1.

and ideas. News reporting based on interviews constitutes one of the most important means whereby the press is able to play its vital role of public watchdog. The punishment of a journalist for assisting in the dissemination of statements made by another person in an interview would seriously hamper the contributions of the press to matters of public interest and should not be envisaged unless there are particularly strong reasons for doing so.

Otto-Preminger Institut v Austria[1]

2.187 Respect for the religious feelings of others could legitimately be thought to have been violated by the provocative portrayal of objects of religious veneration in a film and such portrayals could also be regarded as malicious violation of the spirit of tolerance, which is a feature of democratic society. There may legitimately be an obligation to avoid, as far as possible, expressions that are gratuitously offensive to others, and thus an infringement of their rights, and which therefore do not contribute to any form of public debate capable of further progress in human affairs. It may be considered necessary to sanction or even prevent improper attacks on objects of religious veneration, provided always that any formality, condition or restriction or penalty be proportionate to the legitimate aim pursued. Since there is no discernible consensus throughout Europe of the significance of religion in society, it is impossible to define comprehensively what interferences with anti-religious speech are permissible. A certain margin of appreciation is therefore left to the national authorities in assessing the existence and extent to the necessity of such interference. This margin is not unlimited, and supervision of a State must be strict because of the importance of the freedoms in question, and the necessity for any restriction must be convincingly established.

Tolstoy Miloslavsky v UK[2]

2.188 An interference which entails a violation of Article 10 must be prescribed by law, must pursue an aim that is legitimate under Article 10(2) and must be necessary in a democratic society. The expression 'prescribed by law' requires first that the impugned measures should have a basis in domestic law. It also refers to the quality of the law in question, requiring that it be accessible to the person concerned and formulated with sufficient precision to enable them to foresee, to a degree that is reasonable in the circumstances, the consequences which a given action may entail. A law which confers a discretion is not in itself inconsistent with this requirement, provided that the scope of the discretion and the manner of its exercise are indicated with sufficient clarity, having regard to the legitimate aim in question, to give the individual adequate protection against arbitrary interference. The word 'law' covers not only statute but also common law.

---

1   (1994) Series A No 295–A, 19 EHRR 34.
2   (1995) Series A No 323, 20 EHRR 442.

Wingrove v UK[1]

2.189   Whereas there is little scope under Article 10 of the Convention for restrictions on political speech or debate of questions of public interest, a wider margin of appreciation is generally available to the Contracting States when regulating freedom of expression in relation to matters liable to offend intimate personal convictions within the sphere of morals or, especially, religion. Moreover, as in the field of morals, and perhaps to an even greater degree, there is no uniform European conception of the requirements of the 'protections of the rights of others' in relation to attacks on their religious convictions. What is likely to cause substantial offence to persons of a particular religious persuasion will vary significantly from time to time and from place to place, especially in an era characterised by an ever-growing array of faiths and denominations.

Piermont v France[2]

2.190   Expulsion measures coupled with a ban on re-entering a State which is intending to censor political opinions and the expression of them amounts to an interference by public authorities with the exercise of the right to freedom of expression. An exclusion order for the same reason contravenes Article 10. While freedom of expression is important for everybody, it is especially so for an elected representative of the people. Accordingly, interference with freedom of expression calls for the closest scrutiny on the part of the European Court. Freedom of political debate is not absolute in nature. A State may impose certain restrictions or penalties on such rights, but it is for the European Court to give a final ruling on the compatibility of such measures with the freedom of expression.

Vereniging Weekblad 'Bluf' v The Netherlands[3]

2.191   The European Court recognises that the proper functioning of a democratic society based on the rule of law may call for surveillance institutions, which in order to be effective must operate in secret and be afforded the necessary protection. In this way, a State may protect itself against the activities of individuals and groups attempting to undermine the basic values of a democratic society. The argument that Article 10 precludes ordering the seizure and withdrawal from circulation of printed matter other than in criminal proceedings cannot be accepted. Because of the nature of the duties performed by the internal security service, such an institution must enjoy a high degree of protection where the disclosure of information about its activities is concerned. Nevertheless, it is open to question whether the information in its report is sufficiently sensitive to justify preventing its distribution. It is unnecessary to prevent the disclosure of information which has already been made public or which has ceased to be confidential.

---

1   RJD 1996–V 1937, (1996) 24 EHRR 1, para 58.
2   (1995) Series A No 314, 20 EHRR 301.
3   (1995) Series A No 306–A, 20 EHRR 189.

ARTICLE 11 – FREEDOM OF ASSEMBLY AND ASSOCIATION

2.192   '*Article 11*

Freedom of assembly and association

1.   Everyone has the right to freedom of peaceful assembly and to freedom of association with others, including the right to form and to join trade unions for the protection of his interests.

2.   No restrictions shall be placed on the exercise of these rights other than such as are prescribed by law and are necessary in a democratic society in the interests of national security or public safety, for the prevention of disorder or crime, for the protection of health or morals or for the protection of the rights and freedoms of others. This Article shall not prevent the imposition of lawful restrictions on the exercise of these rights by members of the armed forces, of the police or of the administration of the State.'

INTRODUCTION

2.193   Article 11 creates fundamental rights. One such right in a democratic society is that of peaceful assembly and, like the right to freedom of expression, is one of its foundations.[1] Usually, Article 11 is considered in the light of Article 10. The right of peaceful assembly includes with it the right of peaceful protest by an individual, particularly against the government.

FREEDOM OF PEACEFUL ASSEMBLY

2.194   The right of freedom of assembly is exercised by persons taking part in public processions. Freedom of assembly is guaranteed to anyone who has the intention of organising a peaceful demonstration. The possibility of violent counter-demonstrations, or the possibility of extremists with violent intentions, not members of the organising association, joining the demonstration, cannot as such take away that right.[2]

Article 11 confers a 'right to freedom of peaceful assembly' and then entitles the State to impose restrictions on that right. The common law recognises that assembly on the public highway may be lawful because not to do so results in the denial of the right contained in Article 11(1). The right may be subject to reasonable restrictions such as that the use of the highway for purposes of assembly must be reasonable and non-obstructive, and must not contravene the

---

1   *Rassemblement Jurassien Unité Jurassienne v Switzerland* Application No 8191/78, (1979) 17 DR 93. There is a difference of opinion as to whether the restrictions imposed by ss 68 and 69 of the Criminal Justice and Public Order Act 1994 are proportionate to the legitimate aim pursued. Cases on this subject are awaited.

2   *Christians Against Racism and Facism v UK* Application No 8440/78, (1980) 21 DR 138.

criminal law of wilful obstruction of the highway. The starting point must be that the assembly on the highway will not necessarily be unlawful.[1]

The right of *peaceful assembly* may be exercised freely:

(1) so long as no wrongful act is done; and
(2) as long as all is done peaceably; and
(3) without violence or threat of violence; and
(4) without obstructing traffic.[2]

Article 11 is frequently invoked in conjunction with Article 10 particularly when the issue concerns an interference with the freedom of peaceful assembly.[3] The protection of personal opinions, secured by Article 10, is one of the objectives of the freedoms of assembly and association as enshrined in Article 11. The basic requirements for the justification of measures restricting rights under Article 11(1) are analogous to those governing restrictions under Article 10(2) of the Convention, the only exception being where the last sentence of Article 11(2) is applicable. Reference should be made to the derogations explained in full under Article 10(2).[4]

Rights of peaceful protest and assembly are amongst our fundamental freedoms: they are numbered among the touchstones which distinguish a free society from a totalitarian one.[5] These are rights which it is in the public interest that individuals should possess; and indeed, that they should exercise without impediment. So long as no wrongful act is done and as long as all is done peaceably and in good order without threats or incitement to violence or obstruction to traffic, an assembly is not prohibited.[6]

Domestic law[7] suggests that members of the public have the right to use the public highway for passing and repassing and any such uses ancillary thereto which are usual and reasonable. However, such right does not include the holding of a peaceful assembly on the highway, even if it causes no obstruction.[8] The view expressed by the European Court is that it is compatible with Article 11 of the Convention. The reality is that peaceful and non-obstructive assemblies on the highway are normally permitted. That is as it should be, since, in the absence of any obstruction or threat of disorder, there is no reason why anyone having the legal right to do so should take any action. A meeting held on the highway is not for that reason alone necessarily to be regarded as an

---

1   *DPP v Jones* [1999] 2 WLR 625 at 634G–635B: the public had the right to use the highway for reasonable and usual activities, including peaceful assembly within the meaning of the Public Order Act 1986, s 14A as inserted by s 70 of the Criminal Justice and Public Order Act 1994.

2   The Lord Chancellor stated that the public highway is a public place which the public may enjoy for any reasonable purpose, provided the activity in question does not amount to a public or private nuisance and does not obstruct the highway by impeding the primary right of the public to pass and repass: within these qualifications there is a public right of peaceful assembly on the highway.

3   *Ezelin v France* (1991) Series A No 202, 14 EHRR 362, para 37.

4   *Vogt v FRG* (1995) Series A No 323, 21 EHRR 205, paras 64 and 66. See also Article 10(2).

5   White Paper *Review of Public Order* 1985 Cmnd 9510, para 17.

6   *Hubbard v Pitt* [1975] 3 All ER 1, at 10.

7   Section 70 of the Criminal Justice and Public Order Act 1994.

8   *DPP v Jones* [1997] 2 WLR 578.

unlawful meeting.[1] The subjection of meetings in public thoroughfares to an authorisation procedure does not normally encroach upon the essence of the right.[2] The right of a person to attend and be present at a Druidic ceremony at Stonehenge on 21 June does not offend Article 11(2) in that the need to protect this historical site fell within the aim pursued by the restriction in Article 11(2).[3]

FREEDOM OF ASSOCIATION

Formation and membership of trade unions

2.195   The right of *freedom of association* includes the following:

(1) the right to form and join a political party[4] or other non-political association such as a trade union or other voluntary group which has a common objective or goal;

(2) the right not to join and not be a member of an association or other voluntary group. This means that an individual cannot be compelled to join an association or trade union for example. Any compulsion to join a trade union may infringe Article 11. Freedom of assembly or freedom of association incorporates the right not to take part in an assembly or association against one's will.

Article 11(1) expressly provides the right of workers to form and join trade unions for the protection of their own interests. Article 11(2) sets out the restrictions which may be imposed on members of the armed forces, or the police or for the administration of the State. Whether a worker is a member of the administration of the State as described in Article 11(2) depends on all the circumstances of a case. For example, civil servants and local government employees, police officers, army personnel and emergency services may fall under this definition so that a ban on trade union membership may not amount to a violation of Article 11(1). Any restrictions imposed on these groups to form and join trade unions are permitted if prescribed by law. Such restrictions are necessary in a democratic society and seek to achieve one of the legitimate aims set out in Article 11(2), ie prevention of disorder or crime.

Collective bargaining

2.196   The right to negotiate via collective bargaining is not a right which is inherent in the right to form and join a trade union. Thus the refusal by an

---

1   *DPP v Jones* [1997] 2 WLR 578 at 587 as *per* Collins J. For a critical view of this case, see an interesting article by Ben Fitzpatrick and Nick Taylor 'Trespassers Might Be Prosecuted' [1998] EHRLR at 292: the authors argue 'that the new powers conferred by the 1994 Act (above at n 9) to restrict assemblies pose a considerable threat to the right to engage in even the most peaceful of gatherings, and contend that these powers represent an inappropriate balance between the rights of those seeking to participate in assemblies and the rights of the community within which the assembly takes place'.

2   *Rassemblement Jurassien Unité Jurassienne v Switzerland* Application No 8191/78, (1979) 17 DR 93.

3   *Pendragon v UK* Application No 31416/96.

4   *Vogt v FRG* (1995) Series A No 323, 21 EHRR 205 at 85 (Opinion).

employer to enter into collective agreements with an employee union does not of itself constitute a breach of Article 11(1).[1] However, trade unions should be enabled, in conditions not at variance with Article 11, to strive for the protection of their members' interests including the right to hold a membership card and the right to be heard. The State has a wide margin of appreciation in deploying methods of achieving this.[2] It is arguable that any bar preventing workers from striking in order to be heard is contrary to Article 11(2). The term 'association' presupposes a voluntary grouping for a common goal.[3]

Protection of the individual

2.197   However, this Article cannot be construed as permitting every kind of compulsion in the field of trade union membership. The State should be prepared to protect an individual against any abuse of a dominant position by trade unions. Therefore, abuse might occur, for example, where the consequences of failure to join a trade union result in exceptional hardship such as dismissal.[4] The European Court has stated that compulsion to join a particular trade union may not always be contrary to the Convention, but if the compulsion takes a form which 'strikes at the very substance' of the freedom of association, there may be a violation of Article 11.[5]

Article 11 must be considered to protect also the negative freedom of association, ie the right not to join and not be a member of an association,[6] although the scope of this protection remains to be defined.[7] While Article 11 mainly requires that States should not interfere with the freedom of individuals to join with others, or not to join with others, in trade unions or other associations, it also imposes on States a duty to take certain positive steps in order to ensure that the freedom to which the Article refers can be effectively enjoyed and exercised.[8]

Article 11 requires that trade unions as well as associations of employers should enjoy a wide freedom to promote their interests and those of their members. In practice, many matters regarding labour relations are left to be regulated by the parties on the labour market and State interference is kept to a minimum. This is in line with the general ideas behind Article 11. However, if the freedom enjoyed by these parties is abused then the State has a duty to provide protection against such abuses.[9] If there is some abuse against an individual party present then the State must offer some legal protection which must be

---

1   *Swedish Engine Drivers' Union v Sweden* (1976) Series A No 20, 1 EHRR 617, para 41.
2   Ibid, (1976) 1 EHRR 617, para 40.
3   *Young, James and Webster v UK* (1981) Series A No 44, 4 EHRR 38.
4   Ibid, paras 53–55; *Sibson v UK* (1993) Series A No 258-A, 17 EHRR 193; see s 152(1)(c) of the Trade Union Labour Relations (Consolidation) Act 1992 which accords with the Convention.
5   Ibid, para 55.
6   *Sigurour Sigurjonsson v Iceland* (1993) Series A No 262, 16 EHRR 462, para 35.
7   *Gustafsson v Sweden* (1996) 22 EHRR 409 at 41, para 70 (Opinion).
8   *Arzte für das Leben v Austria*, (1991) 13 EHRR 204, para 32 and *Young, James and Webster v UK* (1981) Series A No 44, 4 EHRR 38, para 49.
9   *Gustafsson v Sweden* (1996) 22 EHRR 409 at 42, para 77 (Opinion).

proportionate, such as an assessment of whether the action against the claimant had such serious consequences for him that it could not be justified.

Right to strike

2.198   The European Court has decided that the right of groups of employees to strike is not embodied in the freedom of association and a State is free to restrict this right to strike according to its discretion.[1]

VIOLATION OF ARTICLE 11

2.199   If there is a violation of Article 11, then the first step is to establish whether the exercise of one of the protected rights has been interfered with. For example, if a worker (who is not part of the administration of the State, ie a civil servant) is dismissed from employment on account of joining a trade union, it is relatively clear that Article 11 is prima facie applicable.

The second step is to establish whether the interference with the exercise of the right protected by Article 11 falls within the exceptions in Article 11(2). These exceptions are to be narrowly interpreted, and the necessity of imposing any restrictions on the exercise of the rights must be convincingly established. There are a number of considerations which arise in determining whether the interference is justified or not.

(1) It has to be determined whether the interference is 'prescribed by law'; that is, whether the interference is in accordance with the law. This means that the law which governs the interference has to be readily accessible and sufficiently clear so as to allow the employee to regulate his or her conduct accordingly and to foresee the consequences which will ensue if the employee pursues the activity in question.

(2) It has to be determined whether the interference has a legitimate aim under Article 11(2). This is not a difficult enquiry. A dismissal for joining a particular party may be intended to protect national security or to prevent disorder or crime. An employer in such a case may rely on one or more of the aims set out in Article 11(2). Equally, the Ministry of Defence may rely on the last sentence of Article 11(2) in imposing lawful restrictions on the members of the armed forces in exercising these rights under Article 11(1).

(3) It has to be determined whether the interference could be regarded as being 'necessary in a democratic society' in the interest of national security or the prevention of disorder or crime; that is whether the interference corresponds to a 'pressing social need'. The level of this requirement is not as high as a measure which is indispensable, but exceeds that which is merely useful or reasonable or desirable. For example, whether an employee's dismissal (the interference) is really necessary in the sense that it represents a 'pressing social need', in view of the relationship between the way the job was done and the way the freedom of association was exercised.

---

1   *Schmidt and Dahlstrom v Sweden* (1979–80) 1 EHRR 632, para 36.

(4) The decision-maker responsible for assessing the necessity of a given interference enjoys a 'margin of appreciation'. The scope of the 'margin of appreciation' varies depending upon the aim which is being protected under Article 11(2). The decision-maker will have a certain margin of appreciation in assessing whether such a need to act exists, but the European Court is empowered to give the final ruling on whether a restriction is reconcilable with the freedom protected by Article 11. It therefore falls to the European Court, having regard to the circumstances of each case, to determine whether a fair balance has been struck between the fundamental right of the individual and the legitimate interests being pursued.

Finally, this does not mean that the European Court is limited to ascertaining whether the decision-maker or employer exercised its discretion reasonably, carefully and in good faith. What the European Court has to do is to look at the interference complained of in the light of the case as a whole and determine whether it was 'proportionate to the legitimate aim pursued' and whether the reasons given by the decision-maker or employer to justify its act are 'relevant and sufficient'. In this regard the European Court has to satisfy itself that the decision has applied standards which conform with the principles contained in Article 11 and that the decision was based on an acceptable assessment of the relevant facts.

SUMMARY OF CASES

Ezelin v France[1]

2.200 To be necessary in a democratic society, the interference must be proportionate to its aims, as listed in Article 11(2). This means that a balance must be struck between such aims and the special and very important rights of free expression and freedom of peaceful assembly. It is therefore not 'necessary' in a democratic society to restrict those freedoms in any way unless the person in question has committed a reprehensible act when exercising his rights.

A Contracting State would be responsible for a violation of Article 11 if it failed to secure the applicant's rights under that Article as a matter of domestic law.

Although the essential object of Article 11 is to protect the individual against arbitrary interference with his protected rights by the public authorities, there may in addition be positive obligations to secure the effective enjoyments of these rights.

Article 11 encompasses not only the positive right to form and join an association, but also the negative right not to join, or to withdraw from, an association.

The European Court does not decide whether the negative right is to be considered on an equal footing with the positive right.

1   (1991) Series A No 202, 14 EHRR 362, paras 51–53.

Although compulsion to join a particular trade union may not always be contrary to the Convention, a form of such compulsion which strikes at the foundation of the right to freedom of association will constitute an interference with that right.

In certain circumstances, domestic authorities may be obliged to intervene in relationships between private individuals.

The Convention also safeguards the freedom to protect the occupational interests of trade union members by permitting trade union action. In this respect the State has a choice as to the means to be used, including collective agreements.

Gustafsson v Sweden[1]

2.201   Article 11 does not, as such, give the right to not enter into a collective agreement. Any compulsion that operates in the circumstances does not significantly impinge upon the enjoyment of the right of freedom of association even if it causes economic damage, and cannot, therefore, give rise to any positive obligations on the part of the State. There is no reason to doubt that the union collective agreements pursued legitimate aims consistent with Article 11.

The Socialist Party and Others v Turkey[2]

2.202   The dissolution of a political party amounted to an interference with the right to freedom of association under Article 11. Article 11 has an autonomous role but it must still be considered in the light of Article 10. Political parties have a fundamental role to play in a democracy. The freedom of association does not merely concern the right to form a political party, but also guarantees that, once such a party has been formed, it has the right to carry on its political activities in freedom. The exceptions under Article 11 have to be construed strictly and the Contracting States enjoy only a limited margin of appreciation. A measure which constitutes an interference will be necessary only if there is a 'pressing social need'.

---

1   (1996) 22 EHRR 409.
2   (1998) 27 EHRR 51.

ARTICLE 12 – RIGHT TO MARRY

2.203
'Article 12

Right to marry

Men and women of marriageable age have the right to marry and to found a family, according to the national laws governing the exercise of this right.'

PART 2
THE ARTICLES

THE RIGHT TO MARRY

2.204   It is submitted that incorporation of Article 12 into domestic law will not add any further right than already exists as far as marriage is concerned. The right is afforded to men and women only and is a right afforded to those of marriageable age as defined by domestic laws. The right, therefore, is governed by domestic laws as to age (16 to 18 with parental consent, then 18) and as to capacity and formality.

Marriage of prisoners and patients

2.205   In the normal course of events, there is no duty on the State or public authority to facilitate a marriage. The exception to this exists in the case of prisoners. Prior to 1983, it was not possible for prisoners to be married in prison. In two particular cases,[1] the restriction on prisoners' rights to marry was challenged successfully with the European Court deciding against the State's argument that considerations of security precluded arrangements being made for serving prisoners to marry. The European Court held that the obstacles in the way of prisoners were such as to effectively prevent them exercising the right to marry at all. As a direct consequence of these decisions, the Marriage Act 1983 was passed allowing the marriage of prisoners in prisons. This statute also contains provisions allowing mental patients to be married in the institutions in which they may be resident and for house-bound persons to be married in their homes. The fact that cohabitation or consummation may not be possible for a long time after marriage in these situations does not alter the level of respect to be afforded to the right to marry.

The position with the right of patients to marry is now similar even if detained under the mental health legislation. The only requirement is that there should be sufficient understanding of the contract of marriage such as to give the patient the requisite capacity.

Transsexuals

2.206   Article 12 is limited to 'men and women'. This limitation has been challenged by transsexuals and homosexuals. In the case of transsexuals, the European Court in *Rees v UK*[2] accepted the UK government's arguments

---

1   *Hamer v UK* Application No 7114/75, 24 DR 5; and *Draper v UK* Application No 8186/78, 24 DR 72.

2   Application No 9532/81, (1984) 36 DR 78, 6 EHRR 606.

against allowing a female to male transsexual to change the record of his sex on his birth certificate. According to English law, a marriage can take place only between a male and a female and will be void if this is not the case.[1] Birth status remains irrespective of gender reassignment surgery with the result that the applicant in *Rees* was effectively denied the right to marry. In examining the complaint, the European Court was anxious to uphold traditional values and to protect the traditional concept of marriage, stating

> '... the right to marry under Article 12 refers to traditional marriage between persons of the opposite biological sex.... Article 12 is mainly concerned to protect marriage as the basis of the family.'

It was further held that the State was clearly afforded a margin of appreciation inherent in the wording of Article 12 in governing the exercise of the right to marry through domestic law. That domestic law could not so limit the right so as to '... reduce or restrict the right in such a way that the very essence of the right is impaired'. The UK was found not be in violation of Article 12 as the obstacle posed by domestic law was only that marriage between persons of the same biological sex was void and as such was not a domestic limitation that could be said to impair the very essence of the right under Article 12. In *Cossey v UK*,[2] the decision of the European Court was the same in very similar circumstances involving a male to female transsexual who wished to marry a male in the UK. It was again held there was no violation of Article 12, although the European Court was more ready to accept that there may be different situations in a changing world and that such marriages may in fact now be more readily recognised. However, the acceptance of such marriage by some Contracting States did not constitute a general abandonment of the traditional concept of marriage requiring a new interpretation of Article 12. In its decision, the European Court made the following key statement:

> '... attachment to the traditional concept of marriage provides sufficient reason for the continued adoption of biological criteria for determining a person's sex for the purposes of marriage, this being a matter encompassed within the power of the contracting states to regulate by national law the exercise of the right to marry.'

It is noteworthy that both *Rees* and *Cossey* were considered and followed in the recent case of *Sheffield and Horsham v UK*.[3] The facts were similar in that two transsexuals were seeking to challenge the refusal to amend their birth certificates to reflect their change of sex to female, those birth certificates showing their registration as male at birth. It therefore followed that they were not allowed to contract a marriage with a male. It was alleged that their rights under Articles 8 and 12 had been violated. The European Court held that there had been no violation and that in the absence of any shared approach among Contracting States towards the complex issues raised by transsexualism, individual States were entitled to rely on a margin of appreciation to defend a refusal to recognise in law a post-operative transsexual's sexual identity. In respect of Article 12, the UK position was upheld on the basis of the prior two cases and the traditional recognition of marriage as the basis of the family:

---

1   See *Corbett v Corbett* [1970] 2 WLR 1306.
2   (1990) Series A No 184, 13 EHRR 622.
3   [1998] 2 FLR 928.

'... attachment to the traditional concept of marriage which underpins Article 12 of the Convention provides sufficient reason for the continued adoption by the [UK] of biological criteria for determining a person's sex for the purposes of marriage, this being a matter encompassed within the power of the Contracting States to regulate by national law the exercise of the right to marry.'

Although no breaches of Articles 8 and 12 were found, there was strong criticism of the UK government in not keeping the need for appropriate legal measures under review in the following terms:

'... the Court cannot but note that despite its statements in the *Rees* and *Cossey* cases on the importance of keeping the need for appropriate legal measures in this area under review, having regard in particular to scientific and societal developments ... it would appear that the [UK] has not taken any steps to do so ... Even if there have been no significant scientific developments since the date of the *Cossey* judgment which make it possible to reach a firm conclusion on the aetiology of transsexualism, it is nevertheless the case that there is an increased social acceptance of transsexualism and an increased recognition of the problems which post-operative transsexuals encounter ... the Court reiterates that this area needs to be kept under review by Contracting States.'

Homosexuals

2.207 It follows that in respect of homosexuals, there is no recognised right to marry in domestic law by reason of the very definition of marriage. No greater right or protection is afforded to them by Article 12. Furthermore, as has been examined elsewhere in this book, homosexual relations come within the scope of private life in Article 8 and not within family life. It is submitted that homosexual relationships, alongside the transsexual cases, will pose the greatest challenge to the concept and definition of marriage. So far, however, there is little assistance given by the decisions of the European Court which seem to have upheld the traditional concept and the UK position. Of some interest will be the recent attempt in New Zealand[1] by three lesbian couples to challenge the refusal to issue them with marriage licences. The New Zealand Marriage Act 1955 provides no definition of marriage, but the licences were refused on the basis that marriage was a traditional female–male partnership. The couples sought to rely on the New Zealand Human Rights Act 1993, s 19 of which guarantees the right to protection from discrimination on the grounds of sexual orientation. It was argued that the traditional understanding of marriage was unjustifiably discriminatory against homosexuals. The traditional concept was upheld by the Court of Appeal and the argument that the Marriage Act 1955 should be interpreted so as to be in line with the right under the Human Rights Act 1993 was rejected on the grounds that such a re-interpretation would in fact mean a repeal as, without question, the Marriage Act 1955 reflected and was based on the common law meaning of marriage as a male and female union. There can be no doubt that similar challenges will follow in the UK alleging violations of Article 12 and discriminatory treatment so as to constitute a violation of Article 14.

---

1   *Quilter v Attorney-General* [1998] 1 NZLR 523, discussed in an article by Andrew Butler in [1998] *Public Law* at 396.

Divorce

2.208 It has been held that Article 12 does not encompass a right to a divorce even when it may be a necessary pre-requisite to a further marriage. So encountering difficulty or delay in obtaining a divorce will not afford grounds for arguing a violation of the right to marry under Article 12.[1]

Religious belief

2.209 Article 12 should be read in conjunction with ss 2(4) and 7(8) of the Human Rights Act 1998. Section 2(4) provides for a defence that can be used wherever an issue in connection with a Convention right is being determined by a court or tribunal:

> '. . . it shall be a defence for a person to show that he has acted in pursuance of a manifestation of religious belief in accordance with the historic teaching and practices of a Christian or other principal religious tradition represented in Great Britain.'

Section 7(8) provides:

> 'Nothing in this Act shall be used to compel any minister, official or other person acting on behalf of a Christian or other principal religious tradition represented in Great Britain to administer a marriage contrary to his religious doctrines or convictions.'

It would therefore seem that a violation of the right to marry will not be found in circumstances where a minister has refused to conduct a ceremony of marriage on religious grounds, for example, due to the previous divorce of one party to the proposed marriage. In any event, in that scenario, it is unlikely that the right will be found to have been violated as it would be said that the possibility to marry by way of a civil registry office ceremony had not been affected.

Location of marriage

2.210 Just as the right to family life does not encompass the right to choose where to establish and develop that family life, so too with Article 12 the right to marry does not include the right to choose the geographical location of the marriage itself. So, for example, if a deportation were to take place preventing a proposed marriage in the UK, it is unlikely that this will be a violation of Article 12.

THE RIGHT TO FOUND A FAMILY

Application to married or unmarried couples

2.211 This right is not strictly limited to a family in the context of marriage, but there has been an unwillingness on the part of both the Commission and the European Court to admit that the right to found a family can exist outside of marriage. It thus remains to some extent unclear whether an unmarried

---

1   See *Johnston v Ireland* (1986) Series A No 112, 9 EHRR 203, Com Rep (92–102).

couple who have a family or who are trying to have a family will bring their grievances under Article 8 or Article 12. The scope of Article 12 remains open to expansion and no doubt will be expanded domestically if not also in the European Court case-law. As yet, however, there is no decision which makes plain that unmarried couples have the same right to found a family under Article 12 as do married couples. Article 12 provides for the right to marry and found a family to be enjoyed or respected according to the national laws governing the exercise of those rights. Therefore, insofar as national UK law treats married and unmarried couples and legitimate and illegitimate families differently, there is scope for arguing discrimination under Article 14. It is important to note, however, that in *Marckx v Belgium,*[1] the European Court held that Article 12 did not require that all the legal effects attaching to marriage should apply equally to situations that are comparable to marriage.

Sterilisation, abortion and adoption

2.212   Arguments against sterilisation and abortion have been mounted as violations of Article 12. Further, adoption as a means of achieving a family falls within Article 12 and domestic laws governing adoption are therefore open to debate and argument. Article 12 cannot, however, be said to oblige a State to provide adoption opportunities and procedures. Artificial and assisted reproduction also fall within Article 12. Similarly, there seems no obligation to provide for these procedures to take place. However, as they grow more widespread and as the variety of such measures widens, there is much scope for argument that a denial of such treatment to married and even unmarried couples constitutes a breach of Article 12.

Conjugal rights

2.213   The right to marry, as considered above, is respected even when there is no prospect of cohabitation or procreation. Men and women still have the choice and freedom to enter into marriage in those circumstances. However, once the choice has been made and the marriage contracted, there is no duty on the State to allow consummation of the marriage. It would therefore seem there is no duty to provide conjugal rights in respect of serving prisoners.[2] It remains open whether this lack of obligation would also extend to sexual relations between serving prisoners and their spouses (where some rights are in any event allowed in the UK) and to sexual relations between mental patients or between patients and their spouses.

CONCLUSION

2.214   There remain a number of uncertainties as to how Article 12 may in fact be litigated. Decisions of the European Court are few and seem to leave open

---

1   (1979) Series A No 31, 2 EHRR 330.

2   See *X and Y v Switzerland* (1979) 13 DR 242 where the European Court rejected a complaint by two fellow prisoners that they were being denied conjugal rights and that therefore their right to found a family under Article 12 was being violated.

the possibility of limitation of the right to found a family to men and women only. There will no doubt be much interesting argument and litigation which will seek to extend the boundaries of Article 12, particularly in relation to the rights of transsexuals and homosexuals and the 'unmarried family'.

ARTICLE 14 – PROHIBITION OF DISCRIMINATION

2.215   *'Article 14*

Prohibition of discrimination

The enjoyment of the rights and freedoms set forth in this Convention shall be secured without discrimination on any ground such as sex, race, colour, language, religion, political or other opinion, national or social origin, association with a national minority, property, birth or other status.'

GENERAL PRINCIPLES OF APPLICATION

2.216   The European Court has stated on numerous occasions that, if Article 14 is not a fundamental aspect of the case, it will not consider it necessary to deal with it separately.[1]

Article 14 affords protection against different treatment, without an objective and reasonable justification, of persons in similar situations.[2]

Article 14 cannot be relied upon on its own. This provision may be invoked only in conjunction with another provision of the Convention which establishes a right or freedom. Thus, a right to nationality and the right to obtain specific nationality are not among the rights and freedoms recognised by the Convention. Article 14 prohibits discrimination only in regard to the enjoyment of the rights and freedoms guaranteed by the Convention. Therefore, Article 14 cannot be invoked where the issue concerns the right to obtain a specific nationality, which is not one of the Convention rights even though the denial of such right might amount to discriminatory treatment.[3]

Once difference of treatment has been established, such a difference of treatment is discriminatory in the absence of an objective and reasonable justification; that is, if it is not justified by a legitimate aim and if there is no reasonable relationship of proportionality between the means employed and the aim sought to be realised.[4]

Where the European Court finds a breach of a substantive right guaranteed under the Convention, it will not reach a decision on the Article 14 claim.[5] Where no breach of a substantive right under the Convention has been established, the European Court may go on and find that a breach of Article 14 in conjuction with a Convention right has been established.[6]

---

1   *Airey v Ireland* (1979) Series A No 32, 2 EHRR 305, para 30; and *Castells v Spain* (1992) Series A No 236, 14 EHRR 445, para 52.
2   *Fredin v Sweden* (1991) 13 EHRR 784, para 60.
3   *Beldjoudi v France* 14 EHRR 801, paras 76–78.
4   *Darby v Sweden* (1991) Series A No 187, 13 EHRR 774, para 31; and *Hoffmann v Austria* 17 EHRR 293, para 33.
5   *VDSO v Austria* (1995) 20 EHRR 56.
6   *Abdulaziz, Cabales and Balkandali v UK* (1985) Series A No 94, 7 EHRR 471.

PART 2
THE ARTICLES

Where difference of treatment is on grounds of sex, the European Court will require weighty reasons.[1]

Where indirect discrimination is established, the European Court may be prepared to find that there is a breach of Article 14. Thus, rules which are on their face neutral but have an adverse impact on particular groups, may infringe Article 14 taken in conjuction with other Convention rights.[2]

The European Court has stated that negative attitudes towards those of a different race, origin or colour could not justify an interference with respect for private life under Article 8 but that such a complaint under Article 14 may not give rise to any issue separate to that considered under Article 8.[3]

---

1   *Abdulaziz, Cabales and Balkandali v UK* (1995) Series A No 94, at note 6.
2   See an interesting article by Stephen Livingstone 'Article 14 and the Prevention of Discrimination in the ECHR' [1997] EHRLR 31.
3   *Lustig-Prean and Becket v UK* Application No 314117/96, (1999) *The Times*, 11 October.

ARTICLE 16 – RESTRICTIONS ON POLITICAL ACTIVITY OF ALIENS

2.217
'Article 16

Restrictions on political activity of aliens

Nothing in Articles 10, 11 and 14 shall be regarded as preventing the High Contracting Parties from imposing restriction on the political activities of aliens.'

Article 16 of the Convention allows a potential wide-ranging interference with the political rights of aliens. Ultimately, a State has the power to deport aliens to whose activities it objects and the Convention provides no direct protection against the use of that power.

The case of *Piermont v France*[1] was the first case in which the Commission had to give serious consideration to Article 16. The Commission indicated that it regarded the provision as expressing an outdated view of the rights of aliens. Article 16 applies expressly only to the 'political activities' of aliens which, if interpreted to include only matters directly relating to political processes may narrow the applicability of the Article and so confine the State's ability to restrict its obligations under the Convention.

---

1   (1995) Series A No 314, 20 EHRR 301. The applicant was a member of the European Parliament, elected in Germany. By invitation of groups opposed to French nuclear testing the applicant visited the French overseas territories in the South Pacific. Having participated in demonstrations against such testing the applicant was expelled from French Polynesia and forbidden to re-enter. The applicant's claims that her rights under Article 10 and/or 14 had been infringed were met with assertions of justification under Article 16. The Commission concluded that the applicant could not be regarded as an 'alien' in light of her elected status as a member of the European Parliament and her presence in the French territories in an official capacity (the people of French Polynesia voting in European elections).

ARTICLE 17 – PROHIBITION OF ABUSE OF RIGHTS

2.218   '*Article 17*

Prohibition of abuse of rights

Nothing in this Convention may be interpreted as implying for any State, group or person any right to engage in any activity or perform any act aimed at the destruction of any of the rights and freedoms set forth herein or at their limitation to a greater extent than is provided for in the Convention.'

Article 17 may be invoked by an individual against a State, but may also be used by a State to justify its interference with the rights of an individual. The aim, when the Article is invoked by the State, is to prevent a situation where the rights of its members under the Convention would be destroyed. Such an example may arise where a State wishes to prevent the dissemination of racist material or campaigning on a racist platform. In exercising rights under Article 17, consideration must be given to the seriousness and duration of the threat to the State and its response proportionate to that threat. With the incorporation of the Convention into domestic legislation, questions as to whether there has been a breach of an individual's rights under the Act may be brought more easily and readily in domestic courts at all levels. It will no longer be necessary for an individual to exhaust domestic legal remedies (including the House of Lords) before proceeding to the European Court.

ARTICLE 18 – LIMITATION ON USE OF RESTRICTIONS ON RIGHTS

2.219   *'Article 18*

Limitation on use of restrictions on rights'

The restrictions permitted under this Convention to the said rights and freedoms shall not be applied for any purpose other than those for which they have been prescribed.

Article 18 may be invoked only by an applicant who asserts that a restriction permitted by the Convention on the enjoyment of his rights has been used other than one for which it has been authorised. Article 18 can be applied only in conjunction with other Articles of the Convention. In *De Becker v Belgium*,[1] the Commission said that Article 18 was a bar to relying on derogations legitimately made under Article 15 once the emergency had passed.

---

1   Application No 214/56 B 2 (1960) Com Rep. The Commission held that the State's power under Article 17 must be exercised 'to an extent strictly proportionate to the seriousness and duration of [the threat to the democratic system]'.

THE FIRST PROTOCOL – ARTICLE 1 – PROTECTION OF PROPERTY

'THE FIRST PROTOCOL
Article 1

Protection of property

Every natural or legal person is entitled to the peaceful enjoyment of his possessions. No one shall be deprived of his possessions except in the public interest and subject to the conditions provided for by law and by the general principles of international law.

The preceding provisions shall not, however, in any way impair the right of a State to enforce such laws as it deems necessary to control the use of property in accordance with the general interest or to secure the payment of taxes or other contributions or penalties.'

INTRODUCTION

2.220　　Article 1 of the First Protocol has a bearing upon every instance where interference with private property by the State or a public body is permitted by domestic legislation. Under the broad wording of the Human Rights Act 1998, it remains to be seen whether interference with property by any private person which is otherwise lawful would fall within the scope of the Article if it contravenes the principles therein set out as there is relatively little precedent in the decisions made under the Convention.[1]

Structure of Article 1 of the First Protocol: three rules in one

2.221　　Article 1 of the First Protocol is in substance guaranteeing the right of property.[2] The right guaranteed by the Article is tri-partite. Each of the three sentences in the Article sets out a distinct rule.[3]

(1) Rule 1: This rule is contained in the first sentence of the first paragraph. It is of a general nature and provides for the principle of peaceful enjoyment of property.

(2) Rule 2: This rule is contained in the second sentence of the first paragraph and concerns deprivation of possessions which is subject to certain conditions.

(3) Rule 3: This rule is obtained in the second paragraph. It recognises that the State is entitled to control the use of property in accordance with the general interest or to secure certain payments by enforcing such law as is deemed necessary.

1　　See, for example, *James v UK* (1986) Series A No 98, 8 EHRR 123, on leasehold enfranchisement.

2　　*Marckx v Belgium* (1979) Series A No 31, 2 EHRR 330.

3　　*Sporrong & Lönnroth v Sweden* (1982) Series A No 52, 5 EHRR 35.

Priority between the three rules

2.206   The three rules are inter-connected. Rules 2 and 3 are concerned with particular instances of interference, and should be construed in the light of the general principle enunciated in rule 1.[1] Analytically, a court should determine whether the second or third rule is applicable before considering whether the first rule has been complied with.[2] However, there is no need to show a deprivation or a control of use under rule 2 or 3 in order to establish a breach of rule 1. Nor is there necessarily a breach of rule 1 where property has been interfered with in a way which does not fall within the ambit of rules 2 and 3.[3]

Principle of fair balance

2.223   The governing principle is that of 'fair balance'. A fair balance has to be struck between the protection of an individual's fundamental rights and the demands of the general interests of the community. The individual should not have to bear too heavy a burden in the pursuit of the public interest. The whole Article is structured so as to reflect this approach.[4]

MEANING OF 'POSSESSIONS'

2.224   The word 'possessions' is to be given a broad definition. 'Possessions' has an autonomous meaning.[5] Under the Convention it has included financial interests and advantages which do not fall within any definition of 'property' in English law. By s 2 of the Act, case-law on the Convention is to be heeded in interpreting the Schedule, so the wider approach will be applied to the Act.

Examples of 'possessions'

2.225   The following instances show what falls within the meaning of 'possessions':

(1)   interests in land (eg, freehold, title absolute, leases[6]);
(2)   tangible property such as aircraft, books;
(3)   intangible property such as shares and securities; the value of a business, credit-worthiness, clientele and goodwill;[7] patents; the economic benefit of outline planning permission; the economic value of a licence to serve

---

1   *Air Canada v UK* (1995) Series A No 316, 20 EHRR 150, para 22; *Lithgow v UK* (1986) Series A No 102, 8 EHRR 329, para 106.
2   *Sporrong & Lönnroth v Sweden* Application No 24484/94, [1998] HRCD Vol X, No 3, para 61.
3   *Sporrong & Lönnroth v Sweden* (1983) Series A No 52, 5 EHRR 35, para 69.
4   *Holy Monasteries v Greece* (1994) Series A No 301-A, 20 EHRR 1, para 70.
5   *Matos e Silva, Lda and Others v Portugal* (1997) 24 EHRR 573, para 75.
6   But not a tenancy of 5 months standing, see *Pentidis and Others v Greece* (1997) 24 EHRR CD 1.
7   *Van Marle v The Netherlands* (1986) 8 EHRR 483.

alcohol;[1] contractual rights such as licences of land; a right to compensation; judgment debts;

(4) the civil rights and obligations protected by Article 6. A civil claim exists prior to legal proceedings and is a concept independent of them.[2] A claim for damages may be a possession;[3] but not a claim to an equitable or discretionary award.[4]

Examples which are not possessions

2.226 By contrast, it has been held that income is not a possession (as opposed to any property interest from which it is derived);[5] but the revenue derived from working certain disputed land may qualify (the European Court did not find it necessary to decide).[6]

Property not yet acquired

2.227 The applicant must already have acquired the property in question. Article 1 of the First Protocol does not apply to property which a person wants or hopes to acquire, whether on intestacy or through voluntary dispositions,[7] or through the operation of law where there is no existing entitlement.

For example, the Article did not help a same-sex partner trying to establish succession rights to a secure tenancy under the Housing Act 1980, because she did not have any existing right to the disputed tenancy.[8]

Undistributed property

2.228 However, property is covered where it is merely undistributed, and not yet in the custody of the owner; for example, an inheritance where a certain share of an estate has been acquired but has not yet been assigned.[9] A share of a fund where an identifiable and specific portion of the fund has been acquired, such as a pension fund,[10] may amount to a possession. The Article can provide protection only for a specific share of a pension fund, or a portion of a contributory social security fund, not a guarantee to a pension nor to a general insurance where there is no direct link between the level of contributions paid and the benefit to be awarded.[11]

Unattributed funds

2.229 A right to emergency assistance can be a pecuniary right and therefore a 'possession' for the purposes of Article 1 of the First Protocol, but the basis on

---

1   *Tre Traktörer Aktiebolag v Sweden* (1991) Series A No 159, 13 EHRR 309.
2   *Golder v UK* (1975) Series A No 18, 1 EHRR 32.
3   Application No 10138/82, (1986) 8 EHRR 252.
4   *Leutscher v Netherlands* Application No 17314/90, (1997) 24 EHRR 181.
5   Application No 8003/77, (1981) 3 EHRR 285, Commission.
6   *Matos e Silva, Lda and Others v Portugal* (1997) 24 EHRR 573.
7   *Marckx v Belgium* (1979) Series A No 31, 2 EHRR 330, para 50.
8   *S v UK* Application No 11716/85, (1986) 47 DR 274 (application refused by the Commission).
9   Application No 8695/79, (1986) 8 EHRR 498.
10   Application No 5849/72, (1986) 8 EHRR 269.
11   *Starman v Netherlands* Application No 10503/83, (1986) 8 EHRR 73.

which this was held was that an applicant was entitled to that assistance only where he or she had made certain minimum contributions to the unemployment insurance fund and had already exhausted an entitlement to unemployment benefit.[1]

WHOSE RIGHTS ARE PROTECTED?

2.230 The property rights protected under Article 1 of the First Protocol are those of individuals, corporations and companies, legal owners, trustees[2] and beneficial owners.

The complainant must be the owner of the relevant property; there is no scope for action in the name of an agent or third party.

A complainant who acquires an interest which is already subject to or held upon certain conditions, and in that sense 'comes to' the interference, is not a victim of any violation if those conditions are enforced. For example, the rights of a purchaser of land designated for proposed motorway construction were not interfered with by those proposals because the designation was in place before the purchase[3] (but a landlord by the purchase of rent-controlled property could be a victim' of rent control laws[4]).

RULE 1 – PEACEFUL ENJOYMENT

2.231 Rule 1 of Article 1 of the First Protocol provides a general, residual right to peaceful enjoyment of property without interference. It is not concerned with enjoyment in the sense of amenity or freedom from noise as it does not guarantee a right to the enjoyment of possessions in a pleasant environment.[5] Peaceful enjoyment connotes the right to use, sell, develop, destroy or otherwise deal with property, including the right to dispose of it by will or other voluntary disposition.[6]

The meaning of 'enjoyment'

2.232 The meaning of 'enjoyment' varies according to the property in question. Where the property was land, denial of access which in turn prevented the owner from dealing with the land amounted to an interference with her enjoyment; hindrance can amount to a violation of Article 1 just like a legal impediment.[7] However, the right to peaceful enjoyment of possessions does not include as a corollary the right to freedom of movement.[8]

---

1   *Gaygusuz v Austria* (1997) 23 EHRR 364, paras 39–41.
2   *James v UK* (1986) Series A No 98, 8 EHRR 123.
3   Application No 10390/83, v UK (1986) 8 EHRR 301.
4   *X v Austria* Application No 8003/77, (1981) 3 EHRR 285, Commission.
5   Application No 13728/88, (1990) and *Rayner v UK* Application No 9310/81, (1986) 47 DR 5.
6   *Marckx v Belgium* (1979) Series A No 31, 2 EHRR 330.
7   *Loizidou v Turkey* (1997) 23 EHRR 513 (merits judgment).
8   *Loizidou v Turkey* (1995) Series A No 310, 20 EHRR 99, Commission.

Interference with enjoyment

2.233   Interference may amount to a continuing violation of rights, or may be construed as a single and finite event, depending on the circumstances.[1] It is important, however, to distinguish between a continuing interference and a single act with continuing consequences or effects.[2] The distinction has particular relevance with regard to issues of limitation.

Fair balance

2.234   For the purposes of rule 1, the court must determine whether a fair balance has been struck between the demands of the general interest of the community and protection of the individual's fundamental rights.[3] Where the individual has had to bear an excessive burden of hardship or inconvenience such that the fair balance is upset, the Article is violated.[4]

The general interest

2.235   Identifying the general interest of the community is initially the task of the relevant public authority, and will typically require the exercise of discretionary judgment. Insofar as the exercise of discretion involves a multitude of factors, there will be a wide 'margin of appreciation'[5] allowed, but it is submitted that the courts will apply a close scrutiny to the exercise of that judgment. It is relevant to consider whether there is a coherent strategy underlying the steps taken which it is said amount to an interference.[6]

The need for proportionality

2.236   In order for a fair balance to be struck, there must be a reasonable relationship of proportionality between the means employed and the aim pursued.[7] The court will look to see whether the interference corresponds to the objective, or whether, with regard to the aim pursued, it amounts to a disproportionate and intolerable interference with the rights of the owner, impinging on the very substance of the right to property.[8]

The significance of compensation

2.237   The burden to be borne by the individual in the pursuit of the general interest can be considerably mitigated if the individual can claim compensation, and if there is an effective route by which the individual can challenge the interference.[9] The procedural safeguards available to the individual will be especially material in determining whether the margin of appreciation has been overstepped.[10] Compensation can constitute adequate reparation only

---

1   *Papamichalopoulos and Others v Greece* (1993) 16 EHRR 440.
2   See dissenting judgments in *Loizidou v Turkey* (1997) 23 EHRR 513 at 536–552.
3   *Sporrong & Lönnroth v Sweden* (1983) Series A No 52, 5 EHRR 35, para 69.
4   *Matos e Silva, Lda and Others v Portugal* (1997) 24 EHRR 573.
5   *Buckley v UK* RJD 1996–IV 1271, (1997) 23 EHRR 101, para 75.
6   *Matos e Silva, Lda and Others v Portugal* (1997) 24 EHRR 573 at para 87.
7   *Air Canada v UK* (1995) Series A No 316, 20 EHRR 150, para 36.
8   *Hamer v Land-Rheinland* (1981) 3 EHRR 140.
9   *Sporrong & Lönnroth v Sweden* (1983) Series A No 52, 5 EHRR 35.
10 *Buckley v UK* RJD 1996–IV 1271, (1997) 23 EHRR 101, para 76.

where it also takes into account the damage arising from the length of any deprivation, and must be paid within a reasonable time.[1]

The significance of other remedies

2.238 The legitimacy of the interference itself is affected by whether the individual has any fair means of objecting to it, as an unfair procedure may be invoked to show that the 'fair balance' principle has been offended against.[2] It follows that, for example, any internal appeals procedures ought to be exhausted before turning to the Act for a remedy under Article 1 of the First Protocol.

The availability of judicial review

2.239 Under the Convention, the availability of judicial review in the UK courts has been enough to satisfy the requirement for fair process as an ingredient of the 'fair balance' (notwithstanding the reluctance of the UK courts to adopt 'proportionality' as a principle of judicial review).[3] It would seem to follow that if judicial review as a remedy is available in respect of an alleged interference with property, the interference may fall within the margin of appreciation on that basis.

RULE 2 – DEPRIVATION

2.240 Under rule 2 of Article 1 of the First Protocol, a person is deprived of his or her property only where he or she is deprived of ownership by the operation of law.[4] Nothing short of an expropriation or a transfer or extinguishment of ownership will do. If no legal transfer of ownership has occurred the court will look to see whether a *de facto* deprivation of ownership has taken place.[5]

'De facto' deprivation

2.241 A *de facto* deprivation occurs where the applicant has no means whatsoever of dealing with the property, not where he is merely prevented from dealing with it in any particular way.[6]

Examples of deprivation

2.242 The creation of a presumption of title in favour of the State, which left an applicant unable to maintain a centuries-old claim to adverse possession of land, amounted to a deprivation.[7] However, it was not a deprivation of property to restrict the rent which a landlord was allowed to charge and to provide tenants with statutory security of tenure as the landlord was still able to deal

---

1   *Guillemin v France* (1998) 25 EHRR 435 at 54.
2   See eg *Erkner & Hofauer v Austria* (1987) Series A No 117, 9 EHRR 464.
3   See eg *Air Canada v UK* (1995) Series A No 316, 20 EHRR 150.
4   *Handyside v UK* (1976) Series A No 24, 1 EHRR 737.
5   *Sporrong & Lönnroth v Sweden* (1983) Series A No 52, 5 EHRR 35.
6   *Matos e Silva Lda and Others v Portugal* (1997) 24 EHRR 573; *Papamichalopoulos v Greece* (1993) 16 EHRR 440, para 45.
7   *Holy Monasteries v Greece* (1994) Series A No 301–A, 20 EHRR 1.

with the property;[1] it did not amount to a deprivation to seize publications pending trial for obscenity, but it was a deprivation to forfeit and destroy them afterwards.[2]

When deprivation is permitted by Article 1 of the First Protocol

2.243 Deprivation is permissible under two conditions; where it is carried out: (i) in the public interest; and (ii) subject to the control of law. When considering the public interest, the court is concerned with the justification and motives for actual taking.[3] The conditions provided for by law are examined to ensure that the process is fair.

Meaning of the 'public interest'

2.244 The 'public interest' does not bear a different meaning from the 'general interest' in rule 3 of the Article.[4] In rule 2, however, there is no test of 'necessity' before a deprivation can be permissible in the public interest. A measure need not benefit the majority of the population in order for it to be in the public interest. The public interest can be identified with the interests of one person[5] (where there was a public health issue but only one neighbour could be shown to be affected). Steps to preserve public morals,[6] to enhance social justice by the redistribution of interests in land[7] and to assist in the prevention of tax evasion[8] have been held to be in the public interest.

The fair balance principle

2.245 Throughout the Article the guiding principle is that of 'fair balance' between individual and community interests. In striking such a balance, the court will pay particular attention to the question of proportionality of the means employed, ie whether the deprivation of the individual's property corresponds to the public interest objective, and to the question of compensation.

The significance of compensation

2.246 There is no express reference to any right to compensation in the Article. However, the availability of appropriate compensation goes a long way towards determining whether an interference is proportional and whether the balance has properly been struck between the individual and the public interest. The taking of property without payment of an amount reasonably related to its value will normally constitute a disproportionate interference,

---

1   *X v Austria* Application No 8003/77, (1981) 3 EHRR 285.
2   *Handyside v UK* (1976) Series A No 24, 1 EHRR 737.
3   *Lithgow v UK* (1986) Series A No 102, 8 EHRR 329.
4   *Handyside v UK* (1976) Series A No 24, 1 EHRR 737.
5   Application No 10968/84, (1986) 8 EHRR 80.
6   *Handyside* (above), and see the particular instances of interference with freedom of expression under Article 10.
7   *James v UK* (1986) Series A No 98, 8 EHRR 123.
8   *Hentrich v France* (1994) Series A No 269–A, 18 EHRR 440.

and a total lack of compensation can be considered justifiable only in exceptional circumstances.[1] Where the public interest is particularly strong, a lesser amount of compensation may be appropriate.[2]

Subject to the control of law

2.247 Deprivation may only be made subject to the conditions provided for by law. It must be lawful in itself, and the concept of lawfulness connotes precision, foreseeability, lack of arbitrariness, and a means for the complainant to challenge the deprivation by adversarial means with equality of arms.[3] International law is not available as a recourse to a British national making a claim under the Human Rights Act 1998. However, under the Convention, the European Court has on occasion looked at the principles of international law as a measure against which to test the fairness and proportionality of the safeguards offered by domestic law.[4]

RULE 3 – CONTROL OF USE

2.248 On the face of it, rule 3 of Article 1 of the First Protocol concerns itself only with direct interference by a State; however, the effect of s 6 of the Act will be such as to regulate the enforcement by any public body of the laws permitting interference with property in this context.

The scope of rule 3

2.249 Rule 3 does not extend the circumstances in which interference with property is presently lawful. It renders such lawful interference subject to a test of necessity, and brings it within the scope of the 'fair balance' principle including the notion of proportionality. It may be noted that rule 3 does not extend to any interference with property which is not provided for by law; it does not, for example, extend to any administrative or policy action unless it is founded upon law.

The meaning of 'necessary'

2.250 'Necessary' does not entail that a measure can be shown to be 'indispensable' nor that it is merely 'useful or reasonable'.[5] The test which has emerged from decisions in the European Court is whether a State can demonstrate that the measure in question corresponds to a pressing social need.

Controlling the use of property

2.251 As noted above, there may be an interference with the peaceful enjoyment of property which does not fall within the scope either of rule 2 or of

PART 2
THE ARTICLES

---

1   *Holy Monasteries v Greece* (1994) Series A No 301–A, 20 EHRR 1.
2   *James v UK* (1986) Series A No 98, 8 EHRR 123.
3   *Hentrich v France* (1994) Series A No 269–A, 18 EHRR 440.
4   *Stran Greek Refineries and Stratis Andreadis v Greece* (1995) Series A No 301–B, 19 EHRR 293, para 72.
5   *Handyside v UK* (1976) Series A No 24, 1 EHRR 737.

rule 3. In some circumstances, the European Court has considered that a step which might on the face of it seem to amount to a 'deprivation' (see rule 2 at **2.240**) is better treated as a control of use; for example, the seizure and permanent confiscation of texts found to be obscene.[1] Where a transfer of ownership has not taken place, but property is detained, this may constitute a control of use.[2]

Examples of control of use

2.252   Examples of control of use include: seizure of property, as noted at **2.235**; preventative seizure to avoid disposal of property believed to be the fruits of crime;[3] restrictions upon the use which may be made of property, for example the level of rent which may be charged;[4] restrictions on development and planning;[5] restrictions on import;[6] and constraints upon the inheritance of property. Control of use may entail the imposition of positive requirements on a property owner, for example a requirement that certain land be planted with trees.[7]

The general interest

2.253   In rule 3 of Article 1 of the Firt Protocol, the phrase 'general interest' has not been defined differently from 'the public interest' in other Articles contained in Sch 1 to the Act and, as noted previously, it is possible for the general interest to be reflected by the particular interests of only one person.[8] Given the overriding principle of 'fair balance' throughout interpretation of the Act, and the governing principle provided by rule 1 of this Article, it is submitted that identifying where the general interest lies will not be a matter exclusively for the public body which proposes to control the use of the property in question, notwithstanding the apparently unfettered discretion offered by rule 3.

The significance of compensation

2.254   The European Court has suggested that the availability of compensation may have a lesser part to play under rule 3 than rule 2 when considering whether a measure imposes a disproportionate burden upon an individual.[9]

Securing the payment of taxes etc

2.255   The other part of rule 3 preserves the right of a State to enforce laws so as to secure the payment of taxes or other contributions or penalties. Such laws must still satisfy the requirement to be 'necessary' with the particular meaning

---

1   *Handyside v UK* (1976) Series A No 24, 1 EHRR 737.
2   *Air Canada v UK* (1995) Series A No 316, 20 EHRR 150; *Sporrong & Lönnroth v Sweden* (1983) Series A No 52, 5 EHRR 35.
3   *Raimondo v Italy* (1994) 18 EHRR 237.
4   *Kilbourn v UK* (1986) 8 EHRR 81; *Scheibl v Austria* (1981) 3 EHRR 285.
5   *Pine Valley Developments Ltd v Ireland* (1991) Series A No 222, 14 EHRR 319.
6   *AGOSI v UK* (1986) Series A No 108, 9 EHRR 1.
7   *Denev v Sweden* Application No 127570/86, (1989) 59 DR 127.
8   Eg Application No 10968/84, (1986) 8 EHRR 80.
9   *Baner v Sweden* Application No 11763/85, (1989) 60 DR 128.

given to that term in the context of the Act, but by and large the cases under the Convention have demonstrated that the European Court's concern has been with the 'fair balance' principle, ie to ensure that procedural guarantees are available, and that the burden on the individual is not so excessive as to be disproportionate or so as to 'fundamentally interfere with (the taxpayer's) financial position'.[1] Where a social security contribution scheme was discriminatory as between men and women, with no compelling reason for the discrimination, a violation of Article 14 (prohibition of discrimination), taken together with Article 1 of the First Protocol, was made out.[2]

RELATIONSHIP WITH OTHER ARTICLES

2.256   Interference with property can arise in circumstances where the real substance of the objection falls within the scope of another Article. Under the Convention, the Commission has on occasion refused to examine an issue said to arise under Article 1 of the First Protocol because it has said that it adds nothing to the complaint; for example, where the complaint concerned the basis on which a pension entitlement was calculated, the Commission decided that the true claim was one of unfairness in determination of the entitlement, thereby falling within Article 6 (right to a fair trial).[3] There are obvious links between the right to enjoy one's possessions and the right to respect for one's home under Article 8.[4] Conversely, the European Court has on occasion not proceeded to deal with a complaint under Article 14 (prohibition of discrimination) because it has already found a violation of Article 1 of the First Protocol.[5]

---

1   *Wasa Liv Onsesidigt v Sweden* Application No 13013/87, (1998) 58 DR 163.
2   *Van Raalte v The Netherlands* RJD 1997–I 173, (1997) 24 EHRR 503.
3   *Lobo Machado v Portugal* (1997) 23 EHRR 79, para 34.
4   See for example *Gillow v UK* (1986) Series A No 109, 11 EHRR 335; and *Buckley v UK* RJD 1996–LV 1271, (1997) 23 EHRR 101.
5   *Matos e Silva, Lda and Others v Portugal* (1997) 24 EHRR 573.

THE FIRST PROTOCOL – ARTICLE 2 – RIGHT TO EDUCATION

THE FIRST PROTOCOL
Article 2
Right to education

No person shall be denied the right to education. In the exercise of any functions which it assumes in relation to education and to teaching, the State shall respect the rights of parents to ensure such education and teaching in conformity with their own religious and philosophical convictions.'

INTRODUCTION

2.257   The right to an education of one's choice is not absolute. The State is not required to guarantee that all children will be taught according to the wishes of their parents. The State is not obliged to provide or subsidise any particular form of education in order to conform with the religious or philosophical convictions of the parents. The Education Acts recognise the general principle that pupils are to be educated in accordance with their parents' wishes if to do so is compatible with efficient instruction and training, and not unreasonably expensive.[1]

There is a reservation, under Part II of the Human Rights Act 1998, in that the principle affirmed in the second sentence of Article 2 of the First Protocol is accepted by the UK only so far as it is compatible with the provisions of efficient instruction and training, and the avoidance of unreasonable public expenditure. This reservation reflects the principle enshrined in domestic legislation, namely that the cost of providing education is a relevant factor.

Education involves not only the right to impart knowledge but also the right to receive knowledge and information. The imparting of such information must accord with the religious and philosophical convictions of the child's parents. Education embraces the whole process where adults seek to transmit their beliefs, culture and other values to children.

EDUCATION MUST RESPECT PARENTS' WISHES

2.258   Education is not only confined to teaching in a classroom. It may include wider aspects of religious or philosophical convictions. For example, participation in a procession celebrating Independence Day may be part of the education given to a pupil. But the compulsory requirement of school children to participate in a procession which is against their parents' pacificist convictions infringes Article 2 of the First Protocol. The important point is that Article 2 requires the State to respect parents' convictions, be they religious or philosophical, throughout the entire education programme. This duty of the

---

1   Education Act 1996, s 9.

State or school is a broad one and it applies not only to the content of education and the way the curriculum is implemented but also to the setting and planning of the curricula.

The State or school may not pursue an aim of indoctrination that might be regarded as not respecting parents' religious and philosophical convictions. This limit must not be exceeded.

It is not every conviction of the parents which will be respected by the State or school. Therefore, if a parent has a firm conviction that his child should not wear prescribed uniform, this does not necessarily mean that the school should educate the child in accordance with that conviction. In such an instance, conviction is not taken to mean simply 'opinions' or 'ideas'. To require a school to abide by the parents' convictions, the convictions must have attained a certain level of cogency, seriousness, cohesion and importance. Thus, Rastafarians or Jehovah's Witnesses enjoy a status of a 'known religion' and such parents are entitled to rely on the right to respect for their convictions. Rastafarians may insist that their school children do not cut their hair and these parents may rely on the right to respect for their religious convictions within Article 2 of the First Protocol. Similarly with the Sikh pupils. Such parents may therefore insist that their children are to be provided with education according to their convictions. On the other hand, a parent may have a pacifist conviction and may insist that his child does not engage in violent contact sports set by the school.

As an adjunct to the fundamental right to education guaranteed by the first sentence of Article 2 of the First Protocol, there is the right set out in the second sentence, which aims at ensuring that the information or knowledge included in the school curriculum is conveyed in an objective, critical and pluralistic manner.

This means that a parent may not insist that his child is not provided, through teaching or education, with information or knowledge of a directly or indirectly religious or philosophical kind. Parents may not object to the fact that part of the education content consists of religious teachings which they do not approve of otherwise teaching would be impracticable. It is very difficult for many subjects taught in school not to have, to a greater or lesser extent, some philosophical or religious implications. So, for example, non-Christians may not object to being taught something simply because part of the subject refers to Christianity.

The fact that a parent's wishes form the minority view does not necessarily mean that the majority view prevails. A balance must be achieved which ensures a fair and proper treatment of minority views and any abuse of a dominant position is to be avoided.

PUNISHMENT IN SCHOOLS

2.259 Schools may legitimately impose penalties (not ill-treatment) on pupils disobeying their instructions. Discipline is an integral part of the educational process because it seeks to achieve the development and moulding of the character and mental powers of its pupils. But physical punishment may not be accepted and the States' obligation to take measures designed to ensure that individuals (and schools for that matter) will not be ill-treated in breach of Article 3 (prohibition of torture) and that children are entitled to protection, through effective deterrence, against such treatment. If the penalty is purely an educational measure (eg, suspension) and is of a temporary nature and does not have a psychological impact on the pupil, it may well be acceptable within the terms of Article 2 of the First Protocol providing the penalty (suspension) does not breach the right of the pupil's parents to ensure the education conforms with their own religious and philosophical convictions. Thus, a one-day suspension imposed on a pupil who fails to attend a school parade may well infringe Article 2 if the requirement to attend the parade does not conform with the parents' religious and philosophical convictions (eg, Jehovah's Witnesses).

In order to determine whether the penalty imposed on a pupil is justified under Article 2, the question arises whether the penalty or punishment was 'necessary in a democratic society'; that is, whether there was a 'pressing social need' for the penalty or punishment. The State or school has a margin of appreciation in assessing the existence and extent of such a necessity, but this margin of appreciation is subject to a supervision by the court. Any penalty or punishment (eg, suspension) which affects the exercise of a right guaranteed or protected by Article 2 cannot be justified under its terms unless the penalty is proportionate to the legitimate aim pursued. What the court has to do is to look at the penalty complained of (suspension or exclusion) in the light of the case as a whole and determine whether it was 'proportionate to the legitimate aim pursued' (whether a school's decision to suspend or expel a pupil was proportionate to his or her behaviour) and whether the reasons given by the decision-maker or school to justify its act are 'relevant and sufficient'. In this regard, the court has to satisfy itself that the decision-maker or school has applied standards which conform with the principles contained in Article 2 and that the decision was based on an acceptable assessment of the relevant facts.

Article 2 of the First Protocol may also be employed in conjunction with the other Convention rights. Therefore, a pupil who is punished for writing a newspaper article about the school or for speaking to the press about the school may invoke Article 10 (freedom of expression) in addition. This will involve asking the question whether the suspension of a pupil for writing a critical article about the school curriculum or speaking to the press about the school teaching methods denied his right to education and his or her right to freedom of thought or expression protected by Article 10.

Children attending a school where corporal punishment was practised have been treated by the Commission as having a direct and immediate personal interest in complaining about such punishment, even though they have not been punished.

PART 3

COMMENTARY

COMMERCIAL DISPUTES

INTRODUCTION

3.1 Companies may rely on the Human Rights Act 1998 in several respects. First, a public limited company may well be a public body for the purposes of the Act. The large public utilities are clearly within the scope of being public bodies and have specific responsibilities, because it is unlawful for a public authority[1] to act in a way which is incompatible with one or more of the Convention rights.

Secondly, a company may also be a victim within the meaning of the Act. The European Court has on numerous occasions received petitions from companies claiming to be victims. Whether a company can establish it is a victim within a commercial context will depend on a number of factors including the nature of the complaint. The question whether a shareholder may claim to be a victim of measures affecting a company cannot be determined solely on the basis of whether he is a majority shareholder (although this provides an important, objective indication), but other considerations may also be relevant according to the specific circumstances of each case.[2] A company shareholder may have a ground of complaint that he is a victim because an interference by a public authority has caused an adverse alteration in his financial circumstances due to a fall in the value of his shares resulting in violation of his right to personal enjoyment of his possessions. Article 1 of the First Protocol (protection of property) applies both to natural and to legal persons. Companies and their shareholders therefore have the right to peaceful enjoyment of possessions. A shareholder has rights under the Convention and may rely on the fundamental rights more readily in cases where the company cannot do so. A shareholder, however, may not obtain the 'piercing of the corporate veil' or the disregarding of the company's legal personality unless in exceptional circumstances.[3]

---

1   Public authority is to be given a wide meaning. This term will include not only central government, the police, but also privatised utilities, the City Takeover Panel, the BBC, the Advertising Standards Authority, Railtrack, British Telecom etc. It is suggested that one test to ascertain whether a body is public or private arises from the dicta in the ECJ: *Foster v British Gas* [1990] IRLR 353 (a body, whatever its legal form, which has been made responsible, ... for providing a public service under the control of the State and has for that purpose special powers going beyond those which result from the normal rules applicable in relations between individuals). A body which falls under the control of the State, directly or indirectly, or which has special statutory or other powers beyond those of a private individual is to be viewed as a public authority: also *Marshall v Southampton and SW Hampshire AHA* [1986] IRLR 140.
2   *Agrotexim and Others v Greece* (1996) Series A No 330, 21 EHRR 250.
3   Ibid.

ARTICLE 8 – RIGHT TO RESPECT FOR PRIVATE AND FAMILY LIFE

3.2   Not only will the Human Rights Act 1998 affect public companies per se, but it will also affect the relationship between private companies (which are not public bodies) and individuals, because many of the protected rights have horizontal effect. For example, by reason of the horizontal effect, Article 8 will secure protection of interception of telecommunications between competitors, employers, and those receiving services from companies. Article 8 will also protect confidentiality of messages between Internet users (e-mail etc). The right to respect for private life includes the right to develop relationships with others and professional or business activities are not excluded from the notions of home and private life because this would otherwise lead to inequality of treatment under Article 8. Interpreting private life and home as including certain professional or business premises is consistent with the object and purpose of Article 8.[1] Similarly, intercepting an office telephone would infringe Article 8 and such a complainant would be entitled to an effective remedy under Article 13 (right to an effective remedy).[2] Any intervention by the public authorities in the sphere of private activities of any person, whether natural or legal, must have a legal basis and be justified on the grounds laid down by law.[3]

Public companies, such as waste-treatment plants, must also have regard to whether their activities affect the private rights of individuals. Thus, if the fumes and smells emanating from the activities affect the health of those residents living nearby, such residents may have a complaint under Article 3 (prohibition of torture) and Article 8 (right to respect for private and family life) of the Convention. Severe environmental pollution may affect an individual's well-being and prevent him from enjoying his home in such a way as to affect his private and family life adversely without, however, seriously endangering his health.[4] The applicability of Article 8 will herald a new approach to an interference with an individual's private life such as interference with the reception of television broadcasts, nuisance caused by traffic congestion or smells emanating from a pig farm granted planning permission.[5] A company or body corporate does not enjoy a right to privacy. This is because the right to privacy is exclusively limited to human and natural persons. Article 8 was not intended to protect corporations or companies. Therefore, the Human Rights Act 1998 is not intended to confer a wider concept of privacy on corporations.[6]

---

1   *Niemietz v FRG* (1992) Series A No 251–B, 16 EHRR 97, paras 29–31.
2   *Halford v UK* [1997] IRLR 471, para 62.
3   *Hoechst v Commission* [1989] ECR 449 referred to in *Niemietz v FRG* (1992) Series A No 251–B, 16 EHRR 97, para 22.
4   *López Ostra v Spain* (1995) Series A No 303–C, 20 EHRR 277.
5   *Hunter v Canary Wharf Ltd* [1997] AC 655; *Wheeler v JJ Saunders Ltd* [1995] 3 WLR 466.
6   *R v Broadcasting Standards Commission, ex parte British Broadcasting Corporation* (1999) *The Times*, 9 July.

ARTICLE 1 OF THE FIRST PROTOCOL – PROTECTION OF PROPERTY

3.3 Companies seeking restitution of moneys from the tax authorities which were paid under invalidated tax provisions should be aware that Article 1 of the First Protocol guarantees in substance the right to peaceful enjoyment of their property and may be applicable for the purposes of examining whether there was an interference with their legal claims.[1] A revocation of a permit to mine or exploit pits may well amount to an interference with a right to peaceful enjoyment of property.[2] Companies seeking compensation from public authorities for interference with their trading activities or because of a tortious act by public authorities can legitimately expect that there will be no retrospective deprivation of the compensation claim by the public authorities because this will not be compatible with the Article.[3]

There is inherent in Article 1 of the First Procotol a right to compensation for the taking of anyone's property, where and insofar as the payment of compensation is necessary to preserve the appropriate relationship of proportionality between the interference with the individual's rights and the public interest. The UK government has a wide discretion to determine when interference with property rights is required in the national interest. The justification of such interference in the case of a company or shareholder will depend on whether the terms and conditions of the taking, including the compensation terms, impose an excessive or disproportionate burden on the company or individual in relation to what may reasonably be considered justifiable in the public interest. A taking of property for public purposes without payment of compensation reasonably related to its value would normally constitute a disproportionate interference justifiable under Article 1 of the First Protocol, but only where the element of disproportion is real and substantial.[4] Differences of treatment in the exercise of rights and freedoms guaranteed will violate Article 14 (prohibition of discrimination) if they have no objective and reasonable justification. Those in comparable situations must be treated similarly.[5]

In one case, a withdrawal of a company's liquor licence affected its capability to run its restaurant. There was a private commercial activity based on a contractual relationship between the licence holder and its customers. The economic interest connected with the running of a restaurant was possession and therefore the withdrawal of the licence interfered with the peaceful enjoyment of the company's possession.[6]

PART 3
COMMENTARY

---

1   *The National & Provincial Building Society v UK* (1997) 25 EHRR 127.
2   *Fredin v Sweden* (1991) Series A No 192, 13 EHRR 784; *Håkansson and Sturesson v Sweden* (1990) Series A No 171, 13 EHRR 1.
3   *Pressos Compania Naveria and Others v Belgium* (1995) Series A No 322, 21 EHRR 301.
4   *Lithgow v UK* (1986) Series A No 102, 7 EHRR 56.
5   *Darby v Sweden* (1991) Series A No 187, 13 EHRR 774.
6   *Tre Traktorer Aktiebolag v Sweden* (1991) Series A No 159, 13 EHRR 309.

ARTICLE 6 – RIGHT TO A FAIR TRIAL

3.4   Article 6(1) (fair and public hearing) applies where the subject matter of an action is 'pecuniary' in nature and is founded on an alleged infringement of rights which are likewise pecuniary or where its outcome is decisive for private rights and obligations. Companies, directors and shareholders may resort to Article 6 and the principle of equality of arms implies that each party to litigation should be afforded a reasonable opportunity to present his case under conditions that did not place him at a substantial disadvantage vis-à-vis his opponent.[1] It is necessary in a democratic society that governments exercise supervisory controls over large commercial activities in order to ensure good management practices and transparency of honest dealings, but the principles of Article 6 will apply if relevant. A shareholder will find it difficult to invoke Article 6 or Article 13 (right to an effective remedy) in seeking an injunction or damages in respect of an act or omission that is prejudicial to their company.[2] Article 6 also extends to a company director who is compelled to give statements to government inspectors. Such compulsion infringes a right to a fair hearing by the use of the statements given to the inspectors in criminal proceedings.[3] The right to defend oneself is a fundamental right irrespective of guilt so that legal expenses incurred as a result of preserving the business reputation is a deductible expense providing it has been incurred wholly and exclusively for the purposes of the trade.[4]

ASSOCIATIONS

3.5   A refusal of a licence by an authority to an association seeking[5] to set up and operate a private radio station may constitute an unjustified interference with the right to impart information under Article 10 (freedom of expression).

Some organisations which are established under private law and enjoy full autonomy in determining their own aims, organisation and procedure and have power to negotiate their own wages and rates with their members or to seek to maintain limitations on the number of members may well be an 'association' for the purposes of Article 11 (freedom of assembly and association). Any rule made by such a non-political organisation which, for example, makes it a prerequisite of membership for a person to acquire a taxi-cab driver's licence may infringe Article 11 and Article 9 (freedom of thought, conscience and religion). Association also includes a negative aspect, namely, the freedom not to join or to withdraw from an association. Hence, an obligation of membership of an association which an applicant must endure

---

1   *Dombo Beheer BV v The Netherlands* (1994) Series A No 274–A, 18 EHRR 213, paras 32–33. Also see *Fayed v UK* (1994) Series A No 294–B, 18 EHRR 393; *Ruiz Mteos v Spain* (1993) Series A No 262, 16 EHRR 505; *Sramek v Austria* (1985) 7 EHRR 351.
2   *Agrotexim and Others v Greece* (1996) Series A No 330, 21 EHRR 250.
3   *Saunders v UK* RJD 1996–VI 2044, (1997) 23 EHRR 313; and see *R v Morrisey and Staines* (1997) *The Times*, 1 May.
4   See *McKnight (Inspector of Taxes) v Sheppard* [1999] 1 WLR 1333 at 1338H.
5   *Radio ABC v Austria* (1998) 25 EHRR 185.

might go further than is required to achieve a proper balance between the conflicting interests of those involved and might not be regarded as proportionate to the aim being pursued.[1]

A health trust will have to consider the implications of Article 2 of the First Protocol and will have to act in accordance with it, taking steps to protect and save life. A shortage of resources may not be a defence in refusing to fund expensive treatment for cancer patients or to save the life of a child because it would prolong his life for a few years or more. The turning off of the life support machine of a patient in a persistent vegetative state will have to be reconsidered in the light of Article 2 hereafter. The closing of a nursing home or the refusal to provide health care to a chronically sick person will be in breach of Article 8 (right to respect for private and family life) and is not justifiable under Article 8(2).[2]

ARTICLE 10 – FREEDOM OF EXPRESSION

3.6   Freedom of expression in its true dimension is the right to receive and to impart information and ideas. Commercial speech is directly connected with that freedom. The great issues of freedom of information, of a free market in broadcasting and of the use of communication satellites cannot be resolved without the freedom of advertising and a total restriction on advertising would amount to a prohibition of those freedoms set out in Article 10.[3] Therefore, any restriction imposed on professional bodies from advertising is inconsistent with the principle enshrined in Article 10. To restrict a company's freedom of expression by extending a right to privacy to a corporation would be in conflict with Article 10 because a corporation has no right to private life under Article 8 (right to respect for private and family life).[4]

OTHER ARTICLES: A BRIEF RESUMÉ

3.7   Public bodies include companies which provide public functions[5] or perform acts of a public nature. The large utilities, housing associations, quangos or private companies subcontracting work for local authorities would have to consider the application of the Convention in a number of areas.

(a)   Article 2 (right to life): public bodies creating dangerous environments;
(b)   Article 3 (prohibition of torture): residential homes ill treating their elderly or young residents;

---

1   *Sigurour A Sigurjonsson v Iceland* (1993) Series A No 262, 16 EHRR 462, para 31.
2   *R v North and East Devon Health Authority, ex parte Coughlan* (1999) *The Times*, 20 July.
3   *Barthold v FRG* (1985) Series A No 90, 7 EHRR 383; *X and Church of Scientology v Sweden* (1979) 16 DR 68 at 72–74.
4   *R v Broadcasting Standards Commission, ex parte British Broadcasting Corporation* (1999) *The Times*, 9 July.
5   Section 6(5): In relation to a particular act, a person is not a public authority by virtue only of subs (3)(c) if the nature of the act is private.

(c) Article 8 (right to respect for private and family life): companies causing nuisance to residential occupiers in the immediate neighbourhood or causing environmental pollution;

(d) Article 1 of the First Protocol (protection of property): companies interfering with the property rights of individuals;

(e) Article 2 of the First Protocol (right to education): private schools expelling pupils where such expulsion is not proportionate to the behaviour complained of.

These are but a few examples of how the Convention may be breached.

CASE EXAMPLE

3.8 A client complains that his business has been searched by the police or Customs & Excise under a search warrant issued by the relevant court (see for example, ss 15–16 of PACE 1984). The client asks you to advise him specifically on his rights under the Convention on the grounds that the search has affected his business activities and impaired the business goodwill and his own reputation.

The arguments available to the client in both criminal and civil proceedings will include that there has been a violation of:

(1) Article 8;

(2) a violation of Article 1 of the First Protocol;

(3) that there is a potential claim for damages for just satisfaction.

The pleadings will include the following matters:

(a) the full facts relating to the infringement of the Articles in question including the full description of the searches and seizures of documents;

(b) the relevant domestic law should be set out supporting the search;

(c) the relevant principles of each Article relied upon should be set out by the appropriate party:

    (i) the right to respect for private life includes business relationships;[1]

    (ii) the fact that correspondence is of a professional nature in no way renders Article 8 inapplicable;[2]

    (iii) the search of business premises constitutes an interference with the rights set out in Article 8;

    (iv) a company may be a victim of the infringement;[3] the shareholder has locus standi to bring proceedings;[4]

    (v) the interference is not necessary as the search is not proportionate to the legitimate aims sought to be achieved; in particular, the search was not accompanied by any special procedural safeguards etc and, more importantly, the search impinged on the confidential trade secrets or professional integrity of the applicant etc;

---

1 *Niemietz v FRG* (1992) 16 EHRR 97, paras 29–30.
2 Ibid, para 32.
3 *Agrotexim and Others v Greece* (1996) 21 EHRR 250.
4 Article 6(1) and Article 25.

(vi)   the confiscation of the documents and interference with the business constitutes an interference with Article 1 of the First Protocol; such search affects the goodwill and reputation of the business and there has been loss caused by the search;

(vii) damages are claimed for pecuniary loss and non-pecuniary loss. Details of such loss are to be pleaded;

(viii) the interference is prescribed by law because of the domestic statutory provisions which allow the search to take place;

(ix)   the interference is for a purpose which is legitimate under Article 8(2) since it is to protect others and to prevent crime.

PART 3
COMMENTARY

CONSUMER LAW AND SALE OF GOODS

INTRODUCTION

3.9   The areas of consumer law and sale of goods are already substantially codified by EC Directives. In a human rights context, it is submitted that there will be little impact by the 1998 Act on these areas of law. Consumer law and sale of goods are areas governed largely by market forces, competition and financial profit. As a result, they do not lend themselves to the notion of fundamental human rights. Notwithstanding that, what follows is a summary of those Articles which it is submitted might have some impact upon these areas of law.

However, in addition to the wealth of protection afforded by EC Directives, the 1998 Act will ensure that where the consumer is dealing with a public body, that public body must act in a manner compatible with the Convention.

ARTICLE 2 – RIGHT TO LIFE

3.10   Product liability is a significant part of consumer law and is the subject of much litigation. Again, it is an area that has seen much regulation since the UK entered the European Union. If death results from the use of a dangerous product or substance, it may be argued that the right to life has been infringed.

The wording of Article 2 would appear to rule out accidental death as a potential breach. Of course, the majority of deaths resulting from the use of a defective product would be accidental and would fall outside the Article. However, the Article does expressly state that 'everyone's right to life should be protected by law'.

So if a dangerous product has made its way onto the market as a result of some loophole in the law then it could be argued that the State has breached the right to life. Similarly, where the organs of the State have failed properly to regulate potentially dangerous products resulting in death, then this too could amount to a breach.

These potential arguments appear as yet to be untested by the European Court. It remains to be seen therefore if they have any merit.

ARTICLE 6 – RIGHT TO A FAIR TRIAL

3.11   Since consumer law and sale of goods fall within the category of 'civil rights and obligations', people who have disputes arising out of these areas of law will have a right to have the issues determined by an independent and impartial tribunal.

Disputes concerning consumer law and sale of goods will commonly be determined by small claims arbitration in the county court or the normal procedure in the county court depending upon the value of the claim.

However, some agreements in these areas of law, especially sale of goods, will provide for arbitration in the event of a dispute. Whether the arbitration hearing concerned affords the parties the guarantees contained within Article 6(1) will of course depend upon the individual facts of the case. The arbitrator will have to be impartial and fair in conducting the hearing. The arbitrator must also be independent.

Can such an arbitration be described as a tribunal? If so, then the arbitrator must act in a way that is compatible with the Convention. It can be said that an arbitrator is performing a function of a public nature.[1]

It should be borne in mind that as the issues to be determined are classed as civil rights and obligations, there will be no breach of Article 6 if there is a right of appeal to a tribunal bearing all the hallmarks of a court-like body.

PART 3
COMMENTARY

---

1   See s 6(3)(b) of the Act.

CORONER'S COURT

ADVISING THE CLIENT

3.12 Coroners' courts have jurisdiction to conduct inquests into deaths, industrial accidents, railway accidents and treasure trove. The court's powers in relation to treasure trove are now obsolete. Its most common function is the inquest into death.

The coroner's court is an inferior court of record. None the less, it is still a tribunal that determines issues. However, over the years, the role of the coroner's court has changed. It no longer has the power to name persons it finds responsible for the death of the deceased. Essentially, the coroner's court is an inquest into the facts and nothing else. It has been expressly stated that it is not the role of the coroner's court to gather evidence for pending or future criminal or civil proceedings.[1]

APPLICATION OF THE CONVENTION

Article 6 – right to a fair trial

3.13 Findings of fact made by the coroner's court can be used in subsequent civil actions. In fact the Broderick Committee on Death Certification and Coroners[2] stated that the coroner's enquiry should, inter alia, preserve the legal interests of the family of the deceased, heirs or other interested persons.

Although the coroner can no longer name a person as being responsible for the death of a deceased, he can make a finding of fact which is such that it inevitably points to a person or persons as being responsible for the death. However, this fact does not entitle the implicated person to the safeguards guaranteed under Article 6(2). Such a person cannot be said to be 'charged with a criminal offence'.[3]

The coroner's findings are often used in subsequent civil proceedings, which are directly decisive of civil rights or obligations. In relation to the issue of the reasonableness of the length of proceedings, it has been held that proceedings before a constitutional court are relevant as the result of those proceedings may influence the outcome of the proceedings in ordinary courts.[4] Applying this reasoning to coroners' courts, it is arguable that given the influence which the outcome before that court may have on subsequent civil proceedings then Article 6(1) should apply.

Given the above, it is submitted that in certain circumstances the coroner's court can be seen as being determinative of civil rights and obligations at the

---

1   *R v Poplar Coroner, ex parte Thomas* [1993] 2 WLR 547.

2   1971 Cmnd 4810.

3   *EL v Switzerland* (1997) 3 BHRC 348.

4   *Pammel v FRG* (1998) 26 EHRR 100.

very least. For example, the family of a deceased man may wish to make a claim on his life insurance. A finding of suicide would invalidate the policy. It is submitted that in such circumstances the findings of the coroner's court would be determinative of civil rights and obligations. Accordingly, the safeguards under Article 6(1) would apply.

Right to a fair hearing

3.14   The coroner has a duty to inform persons whose conduct may be called into question as to the time and the place of the inquest. Such persons may also be required to give evidence. Where the conduct of a particular person is being called into question in this manner, Article 6(1) should apply. It could be argued that the fact that a person's conduct has been implicated in the death of another puts them in jeopardy of criminal or civil proceedings.

The spouses or personal representatives of the deceased (interested persons) must be notified if their whereabouts is known. The coroner is not under any obligation to notify other persons unless those persons have provided their name, address and telephone number.

The coroner is under no duty to inform interested persons as to their right to be represented and to ask questions of witnesses called. The coroner alone has the right to call witnesses. He alone decides who can give relevant evidence and interested persons cannot call their own witnesses. However, if the coroner refuses to hear relevant evidence from a potential witness, this can be challenged by way of judicial review proceedings. The inability of interested persons to call their own witnesses is arguably another breach of the principle of fairness.

Interested persons are not entitled to receive any evidence or documents to be used at the hearing in advance.[1] Nor are such persons entitled to see any witness statements in advance. Once the hearing is under way, interested persons can see any documents placed into evidence and any statements used to refresh a witness's memory. Interested persons can obtain evidence and documents after the conclusion of the proceedings.

It should be noted that, whilst an interested person may get advice from a solicitor under the Green Form Scheme, there is no legal aid available for representation at the hearing.

The effect of all these factors discussed above is that the hearing may not be a fair one. However, domestic courts have found no breach of natural justice where an interested party was not supplied with witness statements before the inquest.[2] Notwithstanding the decision in *ex parte Peach*, the cumulative effect of all these shortcomings is a denial of the right to a fair trial.

---

1   *R v Southwark Coroner, ex parte Hicks* [1987] 1 WLR 1624, [1987] 2 All ER 140.
2   *R v Hammersmith Coroner, ex parte Peach* [1980] 2 WLR 4690.

PART 3
COMMENTARY

A public hearing

3.15   Coroner's proceedings are held in public[1] and so to that extent the proceedings comply with the publicity requirement in Article 6.

Independent and impartial tribunal established by law

3.16   A coroner who might have an interest in the outcome of the inquest cannot of course be an impartial and independent tribunal. Where a coroner expresses a view during the inquest which suggests bias, then those proceedings are likely to be quashed on a judicial review of the proceedings.[2]

It should be noted that where a tribunal which complies with Article 6(1) can review the decision, there will be no breach.[3] In addition, legal representation is payable under Advice By Way Of Representation (ABWOR) for judicial review proceedings.

Article 2 – right to life

3.17   As the coroner's court is concerned primarily with the inquest into death, the right to life protected under Article 2 is highly relevant. As will be seen below, the court is under a duty to apply this Article and the rights guaranteed thereunder.

PROCEDURE

3.18   A coroners' court is a public authority within the meaning of the 1998 Act. It must take into account Convention jurisprudence and must not act in a way which is incompatible with the Convention.[4]

Accordingly, the coroner's court is bound by s 6 of the Act to apply the Articles of the Convention along with European jurisprudence. In interpreting any legislation, the coroner's court must as far as possible read the legislation so as to give effect to the Convention.[5] Sections 3 and 6 of the Act impose positive duties upon tribunals with regard to applying the Convention. In the example given of a family seeking a finding which would not invalidate an insurance policy, the coroner must have regard to Article 1 of the First Protocol. The right to claim the proceeds of an insurance policy in the name of the deceased and other rights and property which form part of the deceased's estate can be described as 'possession' for the purposes of Article 1 of the First Protocol.

Any potential Convention points should be argued before the coroner's court so that the issue can be further argued before a higher court. If it is alleged that a particular statute is incompatible with the Convention, a coroner's court would not have the power to make a declaration of incompatibility. The

---

1   Coroner's Rules 1984, SI 1984/552, r 17.
2   *R v HM Coroner for Inner West London, ex parte Dallaglio* [1994] 4 All ER 139.
3   *Stefan v UK* Application No 29419/95; (1998) 125 EHRR CD 130.
4   See s 6 of the Act.
5   Section 3 of the Act.

proceedings would have to be adjourned while a declaration is sought in a higher court.

If it is argued that the hearing itself (as opposed to a statute) was in breach of the Convention then this may be a breach of s 3 or s 6 of the Act and the aggrieved party can bring proceedings in respect of that breach.[1] Alternatively, the aggrieved party can rely on the Convention right concerned in judicial review proceedings.[2]

By s 8 of the Act, an applicant may be granted such relief, remedy or order that the court in question considers just and appropriate. In relation to hearings before the coroner, the only relevant remedy would be to quash the findings of the hearing and to order a fresh hearing.

PART 3
COMMENTARY

---

1   Section 7 of the Act.
2   Section 7(1)(b).

COURTS MARTIAL

ADVISING THE CLIENT

3.19   Hearings before courts martial are governed by the Army Act 1955 as amended by the Armed Forces Act 1996. Undoubtedly, Article 6 (right to a fair trial) applies to these proceedings as they concern criminal charges. Further, the protection afforded by Article 6 extends to the sentencing procedure that takes place after conviction.[1]

Article 6 operates to ensure that the accused gets a fair hearing within a reasonable time. In addition, the hearing must be before an impartial and independent tribunal.

APPLICATION OF THE CONVENTION

Independence and impartiality

3.20   The amendments to the Army Act 1955 arise out of the decision in the case of *Findlay v UK*.[2] Mr Findlay was charged with various offences under the 1955 Act and civilian criminal law. The investigation into these offences was conducted by a commanding officer. The commanding officer was also responsible for deciding whether the charges would proceed to trial and for the drafting of the charges. The commanding officer was also charged with the duty of convening the court martial. In addition, all the officers sitting on the court martial were subordinate in rank to the commanding officer. The decision of the court martial was not effective until ratified by the commanding officer. He also had the power to vary the sentence imposed.

After sentence, the convicted person had the right to have the sentence or conviction reviewed. This review was dealt with administratively. If the review was unsuccessful, the convicted person did not have the reasons disclosed to him.

The European Court found that there was an appearance of impartiality and a lack of independence contrary to Article 6.

This position has now been altered by the Armed Forces Act 1996. This Act created a separate and permanent prosecuting authority similar to the Crown Prosecution Service. The commanding officer still has the duty of investigating the matter but is no longer involved in the convening of the court martial. There is now a judge advocate who has the power to give rulings and directions as to the law.

A reviewing authority has now been established and will give reasons for their determinations. In addition, there is now a right of appeal to the (civilian) Court Martial Appeal Court.

---

1   *Findlay v UK* RJD 1997-I 263, (1997) 24 EHRR 221.
2   Ibid.

Notwithstanding these welcomed changes in procedure, the very nature of army life may mean that in individual cases there will be evidence of a lack of independence and impartiality. The practitioner in this area must always be alive to the requirements of Article 6.

A fair hearing

3.21 The notions of fairness and impartiality are closely linked. However, the notion of fairness is wider than that of independence and impartiality. For example, the opportunity to know in advance the case against you is an aspect of fairness.[1] This is also known as the principle of equality of arms. The principle dictates that an accused be given a reasonable opportunity to present his case under conditions that do not place him in a position of disadvantage vis-à-vis his opponent.[2] If an accused before a court martial is not given reasonable time to prepare his defence or is denied access to the evidence against him, then the subsequent hearing is likely to be deemed unfair under Article 6.[3]

Fairness also dictates that the hearing takes place in the presence of the accused with a view to adversarial argument.[4] Normally, the accused should be told the identity of witnesses who should give their evidence in the presence of the accused. This procedure can be departed from only if there is evidence that the life, liberty or the security of the witness is at stake.[5] Where it is necessary and appropriate to depart from this normal procedure the court must ensure that the consequent difficulties faced by the defence are properly counterbalanced by established procedures.

The accused must be given the opportunity to reply to submissions made against him. Further, an accused must be given adequate and proper opportunity to challenge and question a witness against him.[6]

The European Court has held that the right against self-incrimination is a concept central to the issue of a fair hearing under Article 6.[7] If admissions are gained in breach of the right against self-incrimination, and are used as evidence against the accused in subsequent criminal proceedings, this will amount to a breach of Article 6. However, it should be noted that it is not necessary for the right against self-incrimination to be in an unqualified form.[8] It would appear that the ability to draw an adverse inference from the exercise of the right to silence would not necessarily lead to a breach of the right to a fair trial.

The decision in the *Saunders* case (above) focused upon interviews conducted by the Department of Trade and Industry inspectors. Persons so interviewed

PART 3 COMMENTARY

---

1   See the decisions in *Lobo Machado v Portugal* (1997) 23 EHRR 79 and *Niderost-Huber v Switzerland* (1998) 25 EHRR 709.
2   *Ankerl v Switzerland* (1996, unreported).
3   *Foucher v France* (1998) 25 EHRR 234.
4   See Article 6(3)(b); *Van Mechelen v The Netherlands* (1998) 25 EHRR 647.
5   *Doorson v The Netherlands* (1996) 22 EHRR 330.
6   *Delta v France* (1993) 16 EHRR 574.
7   *Saunders v UK* RJD 1996-VI 2044, (1997) 23 EHRR 313.
8   Ibid.

are obliged to answer questions put to them or face contempt proceedings. In the context of military law, the role of the commanding officer as investigator requires scrutiny. The commanding officer will nearly always be of a superior rank to the officer under investigation. Given the culture of army life and the notion of the line of command, it is unrealistic to suggest that officers under investigation would exercise their right to silence. If admissions extracted in such an atmosphere are then used as evidence against an accused officer, there would appear to be a strong argument that the right to fair trial has been breached.

A public hearing: judgment should be pronounced publicly

3.22   Court martial hearings do not appear to be conducted publicly. This again would appear to be in breach of Article 6.

Again, there appears to be no provision for the court martial to pronounce its judgment publicly. There would appear to be no explanation linked to the prejudice of the proceedings to excuse the public pronouncement.

Right to be informed promptly of accusation

3.23   The client has the right to be told in language that he understands the nature and cause of the accusation. Sufficient detail of the charges must be given and arguably this should be explained in ordinary language to ensure that the accused understands fully.

Adequate time and facilities for preparation of defence

3.24   The right to a fair trial must logically afford the accused a right to have the evidence against him disclosed in advance of his trial. Along with appropriate disclosure, the accused must also be given sufficient time before the trial to prepare his defence. An application for an adjournment to facilitate preparation, which is unreasonably refused, will amount to a breach.

Legal assistance

3.25   Legal aid is available for proceedings before a court martial. If the accused cannot afford to pay for representation, the Legal Aid Board will pay for it. Legal aid should also be available before any appellate court or procedure. If legal aid is denied in circumstances where the accused cannot afford to pay for his own representation then this would clearly amount to a breach. Further, where legal aid is denied on the basis that there is no merit in the defence or the appeal, this may be a breach of Article 6(3)(c). In considering whether denial of legal aid amounts to a breach, the nature of the proceedings, the powers available to the court, the limited capacity of an unrepresented defendant and the importance of the issue at stake must be carefully examined.[1]

---

1   *Boner v UK* (1995) 19 EHRR 246.

Examination and calling of witnesses

3.26   The accused has the right, either himself or through his representative, to examine witnesses called to give evidence against him. In addition, he can call witnesses to give evidence on his own behalf. The examination of witnesses and the calling of evidence are governed largely by relevance and subject to this an accused should be free to ask such questions and to call such witnesses as he chooses.

Summary matters

3.27   Although much of the procedure in relation to court martials has been changed, the procedure in relation to summary matters remains largely unaltered. For example, the commanding officer investigates and charges the accused. In addition, if the accused pleads guilty or the commanding officer considers there is sufficient evidence to support a conviction then the same commanding officer will sentence the accused.

The commanding officer has the power to refer the charge to a higher authority if he considers this appropriate and he does so before the charge is proved. The effect of referral would be for the charge to be heard before a court martial.

If the commanding officer considers the charge proved, the accused can elect trial before the court martial before a finding of guilty is formally recorded.

It should be noted that a commanding officer could impose a sentence of detention of up to 60 days or a fine.

It appears that this procedure falls foul of Article 6 in that there is undoubtedly an appearance of partiality. The commanding officer has a central role as investigator, tribunal and in sentencing. For the same reasons as pointed out in the *Findlay* decision, this summary procedure cannot be described as independent or impartial.

As this summary procedure concerns the determination of criminal charges, the accused has a right to be tried before a tribunal at first instance. The commanding officer's role cannot be described as a tribunal as it lacks all the hallmarks of a court-like body. The accused can of course elect trial before a court martial but this right is only exercisable after the commanding officer has decided he is guilty of the charge. This would appear to offend against the principles of fairness and the presumption of innocence enshrined within Article 6(3), as the issue of guilt has already been determined to some extent.

Although these summary decisions are subject to a reviewing procedure, the accused is entitled to all the guarantees of Article 6 at first instance as the charges are criminal in nature.[1]

PART 3
COMMENTARY

---

1   *De Cubber v Belgium* (A/86), (1985) 7 EHRR 236, paras 31–32.

PROCEDURE

3.28   The court martial as a court or a tribunal will fall under s 6 of the 1998 Act and so will be under a duty to act in a manner which is compatible with the Convention.

Any potential Convention arguments should be raised at first instance before the court martial. If the defence intend to argue that a particular statute is in conflict with the Convention, then it seems that the court martial will have to adjourn while the point is argued before a higher court with jurisdiction to issue a declaration of incompatibility.

By s 4(5) of the 1998 Act, the Courts-Martial Appeal Court has the power to make a declaration of incompatibility.

If the court martial hearing is conducted in a manner that can be said to be incompatible with the Convention, then the defendant may bring action under the Act in the appropriate court or tribunal. What will be an appropriate court or tribunal is yet to be determined but it seems likely to be the Courts-Martial Appeal Court since this tribunal also has jurisdiction to deal with alleged incompatibility.

The commanding officer in his role under the summary procedure also has duties under the Act. The commanding officer falls under s 6(3)(b) of the Act in that he is a person who is carrying out a function of a public nature and must act in a manner that is compatible with the Convention.

CRIMINAL PROCEEDINGS

INTRODUCTION

3.29   The effect of the Human Rights Act 1998 on domestic criminal proceedings is likely to be significant. Defendants in domestic courts will be able to rely on Convention rights to mount challenges to substantive and procedural aspects of criminal law. Examples of such challenges include applications to exclude evidence obtained in violation of a Convention right or submissions that the prohibition of certain conduct contravenes individual rights protected by the Convention. In such circumstances, the court may be requested either to exercise its discretion or to interpret legislation in light of the Act.

In cases where it is not possible to construe a statute so as to avoid violation of a defendant's Convention rights, a declaration of incompatibility may be sought on appeal to the higher courts. Following such a declaration, domestic courts would be able to grant remedies within their powers which are deemed just and appropriate. They may for instance quash a conviction or substitute an absolute discharge for the original sentence imposed. Other effective remedies may include adjourning proceedings, releasing the defendant on bail and staying other cases raising the same point as an abuse of process pending ministerial consideration of the impugned legislation in light of the declaration.

The remainder of this chapter provides an outline of the sorts of issues which, following incorporation, may arise within the context of domestic criminal proceedings by reference to some of the Convention Articles.

THE RELEVANT ARTICLES

Article 3 – prohibition of torture

Detention during Her Majesty's Pleasure
3.30   The sentencing of minors to lengthy detention for punitive purposes may constitute inhuman treatment contrary to Article 3. Support for this notion is found in cases such as *Hussain v UK*[1] where the European Court took the view that a sentence of detention at Her Majesty's Pleasure, imposed on a juvenile murderer as a punitive life sentence, could potentially violate Article 3. Similarly, in the earlier case of *Weeks v UK*,[2] the European Court expressed the view that a punitive sentence of life imprisonment imposed on a 17-year-old offender convicted for robbery would also potentially violate Article 3.

---

1   (1996) EHRR 1; see *Venables and Thompson v UK* Application Nos 24724/94 and 24888/94 declared admissible by the Commission. The applicants also complain that it is inhuman and degrading treatment to put a child on trial in an adult court in the full glare of publicity. A further complaint made is that the fixing of the length of the punitive phase of detention for a child held at Her Majesty's Pleasure by the Home Secretary rather than by a judge violates Articles 5 and 6 of the Convention.
2   (1987) Series A No 114, 10 EHRR 293.

Automatic life sentences
3.31 The imposition of an automatic life sentence on an offender may in certain circumstances also raise issues under Article 3. Section 2 of the Crime (Sentences) Act 1997 introduced a novel approach to automatic life sentences whereby, in the absence of exceptional circumstances, an offender with a prior conviction for a sexual or violent offence who is then subsequently convicted of another such offence, must be sentenced to life imprisonment or custody. It is arguable that, were a court to find that exceptional circumstances do not exist, the imposition of a life sentence on an offender who does not represent a danger to society and who is unlikely to re-offend would be arbitrary[1] and could constitute inhuman treatment in breach of Article 3.

Article 4 – prohibition of slavery and forced labour

Community service order
3.32 Article 4(2) of the Convention provides that 'no one shall be required to perform forced or compulsory labour'. It is arguable that the abolition by s 38 of the Crime (Sentences) Act 1997 of the requirement that an offender should consent to a community service order may lead to a breach of Article 4(2) in circumstances where a court order requires an offender who is not subject to imprisonment or custody to perform unpaid work.

Article 5 – right to liberty and security

Bail
3.33 Section 25 of the Criminal Justice and Public Order Act 1994 prohibits the granting of bail to defendants who have previously been convicted of murder, manslaughter or rape, if they are facing a similar charge. It is likely that this provision as it stands is in breach of the Convention because it denies domestic courts the jurisdiction to ask, as required by Article 5, whether a defendant falling within the terms of s 25 should be detained pending trial or released on bail.[2]

Article 6 – right to a fair trial

Compulsory questioning
3.34 The use of answers against a defendant in criminal proceedings is likely to violate the Convention if these answers were obtained from the defendant during the course of compulsory questioning at a prior stage. In *Saunders v UK*,[3] the European Court found that the admission in evidence of transcripts of interviews with Department of Trade and Industry inspectors violated Article 6

---

1   Contrary to Article 5; see also *R v Secretary of State for the Home Department, ex parte Pierson* [1997] 3 WLR 492, which provides support for the argument that judges rather than the executive should fix tariffs for offenders sentenced to mandatory life imprisonment, in accordance with the provisions of Articles 5 and 6.
2   See *BH v UK* Application No 30307/96 and *CC v UK* Application No 32819/96 – two cases concerning s 25 which the Commission has declared admissible. An amendment to the Crime and Disorder Bill has now been tabled which would require bail to be granted 'only if the court ... is satisfied that there are exceptional circumstances which justify it'.
3   RJD 1996-VI 2044, (1997) 23 EHRR 313.

because a failure by the applicant to answer the inspectors' questions would have been enforceable by criminal sanctions. The European Court held that:

> 'the privilege against self-incrimination is an important element in safeguarding an accused from oppression and coercion during criminal proceedings. The very basis of a fair trial presupposes that the accused is afforded the opportunity of defending himself against the charges brought against him. The position of the defence is undermined if the accused is under compulsion, or has been compelled to incriminate himself.'

In *R v Morrissey* and *R v Staines*,[1] the Court of Appeal held that domestic courts cannot disapply the legislation or exclude the evidence under s 78 of PACE 1984 and thereby give effect to the judgment in *Saunders v UK*. Following incorporation, a declaration of incompatibility is likely to be sought from the Court of Appeal on this issue.

Right to silence

3.35   In *Murray v UK*,[2] the European Court did not find that the drawing of adverse inferences on the facts of the case was in violation of Article 6. This was on the basis of 'the formidable case against the applicant' which called for an explanation, the safeguards contained in the legislation, the fact that the inferences had been drawn by a judge sitting without a jury and whose reasons for drawing inferences could be reviewed on appeal. However, the European Court did find that the adverse inferences drawn in the applicant's case contributed to a violation of Article 6 which arose from the delayed access to a solicitor at the police station. Several other cases concerning the drawing of adverse inferences from silence during questioning have been declared admissible by the Commission. In *Quinn v UK*,[3] the applicant had been denied access to a lawyer before being questioned but had given evidence at trial and, in *Hamil v UK*,[4] the applicant had given an explanation before and after his arrest but did not give evidence at trial.

Disclosure

3.36   Under the Criminal Procedure and Investigations Act 1996 (CPIA 1996), a defendant in the magistrates' court has the right to primary disclosure which might undermine the case for the prosecution against the accused. However, where the offence in question is a summary offence only, the prosecution does not have to serve the defendant with advance information in the form of statements taken from the Crown's witnesses.[5] Hence, since under CPIA 1996 the defendant's right to secondary disclosure of material which may advance the defence case is contingent upon the service by the defendant of a statement setting out the matters on which he takes issue with the prosecution witnesses and the reasons he takes issue with them, this essentially means that the defendant cannot exercise his right to secondary disclosure if he has not had disclosure of the prosecution evidence.

---

1   (1997) *The Times*, 1 May.
2   (1996) 22 EHRR 29.
3   (1996) 23 EHRR CD 41.
4   [1997] EHRLR 169.
5   Magistrates' Courts (Advance Information) Rules 1985, SI 1985/601.

This position was reinforced in *R v Kingston upon Hull Justices, ex parte McCann*[1] where the Divisional Court held that the right to a fair trial did not demand that a defendant charged with a summary offence have advance disclosure of the prosecution witness statements. Further, in *R v Stratford Justices, ex parte Lambert*,[2] the Divisional Court stated that it is not a consequence of Article 6 that prosecution witness statements in summary proceedings had to be disclosed to the defence before the trial. However, in spite of this, it remains arguable that the duty under Article 6 of the Convention is a broad one which is not contingent on the disclosure of a defence statement even if the requirement to serve such a statement should in itself not be in breach of Article 6.

In *Jespers v Belgium*,[3] for example, the Commission held that a defendant must 'have at his disposal, for the purposes of exonerating himself or of obtaining a reduction in his sentence, all relevant elements that have been or could be collected by the competent authorities'. Similarly, in *Edwards v UK*,[4] the European Court held that 'it is a requirement of fairness under Article 6(1) ... that the prosecution authorities disclose to the defence all material evidence for or against the accused and that the failure to do so in the present case gave rise to a defect in the trial proceedings'.

Public interest immunity

3.37 In *Rowe and Davis v UK*,[5] the applicants complained that Article 6 prohibits the withholding of relevant evidence from a defendant on the grounds of public interest and the failure of the *ex parte* procedure established in *R v Johnson and Rowe*[6] to provide the defence with sufficient opportunity to make informed representations contravenes the *audi altarem partem* principle and breaches Article 6. The complaint was declared admissible and cases such as this one may therefore result in a decision of the European Court on the compatibility with Article 6 of withholding material from the defence in criminal proceedings on grounds of public interest immunity.

Article 7 – no punishment without law

Non-retrospectivity

3.38 Under Article 7, the imposition of a heavier penalty than the one applicable at the time the criminal offence was committed is prohibited. The compatibility of the confiscation provisions under the Drug Trafficking Offences Act 1986 with Article 7 of the Convention was challenged in *Welch v UK*.[7] The European Court found that a confiscation order was a penalty and held that the retrospective application of the provisions to offenders who committed offences before the 1986 Act came into force contravened Article 7. Similarly, in *R v Secretary of State for the Home Department, ex parte Pierson*,[8] it was

---

1   (1991) 155 JP 569.
2   (1999) *The Times*, 25 February.
3   (1981) 27 DR 61.
4   (1992) Series A No 247-B, 15 EHRR 417.
5   (1998) EHRLR 92.
6   [1993] 97 Cr App R 110.
7   (1995) Series A No 307-A, 20 EHRR 247.
8   [1997] 3 WLR 492.

held that a mandatory lifer's tariff could not be increased once it had been fixed and communicated.

Article 8 – right to respect for private and family life

Homosexual conduct

3.39 Article 8 requires that interference by a public authority with the exercise of the right to respect for private and family life should be necessary in a democratic society in pursuit of a legitimate aim. In *Dudgeon v UK*,[1] the European Court held that legislation which prohibited homosexual conduct committed in private by consenting males over the age of 21 constituted an interference with the respect for private life guaranteed by Article 8 and was not justifiable as being necessary in a democratic society. Similarly, in *Sutherland v UK*,[2] the Commission found that the prohibition under UK law of sexual relations between men under the age of 18 in contrast to the minimum age of 16 for heterosexual sexual relations was discriminatory, violated the applicant's right to respect for his private life, and was not justifiable as being necessary in a democratic society.

Sado-masochism

3.40 In *Laskey, Jaggard and Brown v UK*,[3] the applicants complained that prosecution and convictions for acts committed in the course of consensual sado-masochistic activities between adults contravened Article 8. The European Court disagreed and held that 'one of the roles which the state is unquestionably entitled to undertake is to seek to regulate, through the operation of the criminal law, activities which involve the infliction of physical harm. This is so whether the activities in question occur in the course of sexual conduct or otherwise'.

Covert surveillance

3.41 In *Govell v UK*,[4] the police had drilled a hole into the applicant's living room wall from an adjoining house to enable them to hear what was being said in the house and had also installed camera equipment in the next-door property. The Commission found that this intrusive surveillance which was carried out prior to the coming into force of the Police Act 1997 violated Article 8 and that it was not in accordance with the law. The 1997 Act does not generally require that prior independent authorisation be obtained before intrusive surveillance is carried out; this may arguably be incompatible with Article 8.

Interception of telephone calls

3.42 In *R v Effick*,[5] it was held that portable telephones are not covered by the Interception of Communications Act 1985 (ICA 1985). Hence, since the

---

1   (1981) Series A No 45, 4 EHRR 149; see also *Norris v Ireland* (1988) Series A No 142, 13 EHRR 186.
2   [1998] EHRLR 117.
3   RJD 1997-I 120, (1997) 24 EHRR 39.
4   [1997] EHRLR 438.
5   [1995] 1 AC 309.

interception of calls on such telephones is not regulated by statute, any such interceptions are likely to breach Article 8. The interception of private telephones from within the premises of the person conducting the interception is also not covered by ICA 1985. Accordingly, in *Halford v UK*,[1] the European Court found that an internal telephone interception by the police of the private office telephone of a senior police officer was in breach of Article 8.

Article 10 – freedom of expression

Blasphemy
3.43   In *Wingrove v UK*,[2] the applicant complained that the British Board of Film Classification's refusal to classify his film violated Article 10. The European Court disagreed and held that respect for the religious feelings of believers could move a State legitimately to restrict the publication of provocative portrayals of objects of religious veneration and, further, that the State had a wider margin of appreciation in regulating such matters.

Prosecution for election expenditure
3.44   Section 75 of the Representation of the People Act 1983 (RPA 1983) prohibits unauthorised persons from spending more than £5 on conveying information to electors with a view to promoting or procuring the election of a candidate. In *Bowman v UK*,[3] the applicant complained that the prosecution brought against her under this section violated Article 10. The European Court found that s 75 of RPA 1983 operated for all practical purposes as a total barrier to the applicant publishing information with a view to influencing certain voters; further, that it constituted a restriction on the applicant's freedom of expression which was disproportionate to the aim pursued.

Arrest of demonstrators
3.45   In *Steel and Others v UK*,[4] the European Court found that the arrest of demonstrators who were involved in peaceful protest and against whom proceedings were subsequently withdrawn, constituted a breach of Article 10. The European Court considered that the removal of the applicants from the scene of the protest interfered with their freedom of expression given the peaceful nature of their protest and the fact that they had not caused any significant obstruction.

Article 11 – freedom of assembly and association

Trespassory assembly
3.46   Under the Public Order Act 1986, as amended by the Criminal Justice and Public Order Act 1994, orders banning all trespassory assemblies in an area within a five-mile radius for a period of up to four days may be sought by the police who also have the power to stop and direct people from going to such assemblies. In *DPP v Jones*,[5] the divisional court held that the offence of

---

1   (1997) 24 EHRR 523.
2   RJD 1996-V 1937, (1997) 24 EHRR 1.
3   (1998) 26 EHRR 1.
4   (1998) *The Times*, 1 October.
5   [1997] 2 All ER 1191.

trespassory assembly was committed even in the event of a peaceful and non-obstructive demonstration. Defendants in such circumstances will potentially be able to argue a violation of the right to freedom of assembly contrary to Article 11 of the Convention.

CONCLUSION

3.47   An exhaustive overview of the issues likely to arise in criminal proceedings following incorporation is beyond the scope of this chapter. It is merely intended to convey an appreciation of the substantial impact which the Human Rights Act 1998 is likely to have on this area of law as practitioners become more familiar with the wealth of Convention case-law already in existence and the development of a body of domestic case-law raising Convention issues begins to take place.[1]

PART 3
COMMENTARY

---

1   Sources relied upon for this chapter include Ben Emmerson, 'The Human Rights Bill: its effect on Criminal Proceedings'; David Feldman, 'Remedies for Violations of Convention Rights under the Human Rights Act' (1998) EHRLR; David Thomas, 'Incorporating the European Convention on Human Rights; its impact on sentencing law'.

DISCRIMINATION AND EMPLOYMENT

INTRODUCTION

3.48   The areas of employment law and discrimination generally have already seen substantial input from Europe. EC Directives have the status of domestic UK legislation without further enactment. So how will the Human Rights Act 1998 affect these areas of law? Notwithstanding the regulation of these areas to bring domestic law into line with the rest of Europe, the new Act may still prove to be an important last resort for those charged with the task of advising in employment and discrimination law. In some circumstances, the Act may be the first port of call.

ARTICLE 2 – RIGHT TO LIFE

Basic principles

3.49   The following basic principles apply to Article 2.

(1) Article 2 is a fundamental provision and therefore requires strict interpretation.[1]
(2) The act complained of which leads to the loss of life must be deliberate. This follows from the use of the word 'intentionally' in the Article.
(3) Where a direct link can be established between the act complained of and potential risk to life this may constitute a breach.[2]
(4) No actual loss of life is necessary to found breach.

Application of Article 2 to employment

3.50   Article 2 will have little operation in employment law within this jurisdiction. Where a death occurs in the context of employment, it will rarely be intentional. Notwithstanding this, practitioners need to be aware of the principles under Article 2.

Even with today's standards of health and safety at work, deaths due to dangerous working conditions and or dangerous systems of work do still occur. If death occurs as a result of an employer's breach of the domestic laws, then arguably the victim's right to life has not been protected by the law falling foul of Article 2. Similarly, where, as a result of some loophole in the law, a death occurs then again this may amount to a breach.

Similarly, where death occurs as a result of deliberate flouting of the law as opposed to mere negligence, then this may also amount to a breach. Of course, one does not have to wait for a death to occur. Any conditions that can be shown to be a threat to life will also be a breach of the Article.

---

1   *McCann v UK* (1996) Series A No 324, 21 EHRR 97.
2   *Balmer-Schafroth v Switzerland* (1998) 25 EHRR 598.

Where working conditions are such that employees risk their life and eventually lose it, the bereaved family will in addition to their claim in negligence have a claim founded on the breach of Article 2.

It seems likely that claims for breach of Article 2 may be pleaded alongside negligence in much the same way as breach of statutory duty is pleaded concurrently with negligence claims. Circumstances leading to the death of an employee that cannot be described as negligent will rarely amount to a breach of Article 2 unless the death resulted from some deliberate action. There can be no breach in cases of tragic or freak accidents.

ARTICLE 3 – PROHIBITION OF TORTURE

Basic principles

3.51 The following basic principles apply to Article 3.

(1) Article 3 constitutes an absolute right to have one's life protected by law and an absolute prohibition on deprivation of life intentionally save in certain prescribed situations. There can be no exceptions or derogations to this Article. Further, everyone is afforded this right irrespective of any alleged wrongdoing.

(2) The ill-treatment complained of must attain a minimum level of severity to constitute a breach.[1]

(3) All the circumstances of the case must be considered in order to establish whether a breach has occurred. Relevant considerations include duration of treatment, physical and mental effects and at times the sex, age and state of health of the victim will be relevant.[2]

(4) It is likely that only treatment that causes intense physical and mental suffering and acute psychiatric disturbances will amount to inhuman treatment.[3]

(5) Treatment that arouses feelings of fear, anguish and inferiority capable of humiliating and debasing and possibly breaking the victim's physical or moral resistance will constitute degrading treatment.[4]

(6) Whether the treatment complained of amounts to torture, inhuman or degrading treatment will depend upon the intensity of suffering inflicted.[5]

(7) The term 'torture' has attached to it a special stigma as deliberate inhuman treatment causing very serious and cruel suffering.[6]

Application of Article 3 to employment

3.52 The average complaint from an employee about bad treatment will not fall within Article 3. Treatment that results in injury to feelings and may, for

---

1   *Ireland v UK* (1978) Series A No 25, 2 EHRR 25.
2   Ibid.
3   Ibid.
4   Ibid.
5   Ibid.
6   Ibid.

example, amount to discrimination on the grounds of sex or race will not usually amount to degrading treatment.[1]

The ill-treatment that is the subject of complaint must attain a minimum level of severity if it is to fall within the scope of Article 3.[2] In *Hector v UK*,[3] the ECJ held that where a man was refused entry to a private club on the grounds of race this did not constitute degrading treatment. The ECJ was of the opinion that the treatment complained of did not reach such a level of severity as to make it a breach of Article 3. Although the standard for breach of this Article is a high one, it should be borne in mind that the Convention is a living instrument and it must be interpreted according to current day situations.

Arguably, working conditions that are in breach of domestic health and safety laws and constitute a threat to life and limb may amount to inhuman or degrading treatment if the conditions complained of fall to the requisite standard of severity, for example, staff toilets or changing facilities that are unclean or do not afford employees adequate privacy.

It is suggested that conditions prevailing in establishments better known as 'sweat shops' commonly operating in the clothing trade may be an example of the kinds of conditions that will amount to a breach of Article 3. In such establishments, those employed are commonly required to work long hours without breaks under crowded and dangerous conditions. Such conditions when compared to those that are commonplace in the UK could be described as inhuman or degrading and therefore amount to a breach.

ARTICLE 4 – PROHIBITION OF SLAVERY AND FORCED LABOUR

3.53   Again, it is suggested that there will be few cases in the UK which would amount to a breach of Article 4.

However, cases reported in the media some time ago in relation to au pairs and nannies may have constituted a breach of Article 4. In some of the cases reported, women were brought to the UK specifically to work as child-carers for particular families. Their entry to the UK was tied to their employment with a particular family. It was reported that some families stopped paying their 'employees' and virtually kept them prisoner. These families ensured continued work from these women by keeping their travel documents and threatening to have them sent back to their countries of origin.

It is suggested that cases such as these may amount to slavery, servitude or at the very least forced labour as there is no contract of employment in the true sense. Such conditions may also be of sufficient severity to amount to a breach of Article 3.

---

1   *Paruszweska v Poland* Application No 33770/96 (1998).
2   *Ireland v UK* (1978) Series A No 25, 2 EHRR 25, para 162.
3   (1990) *The Guardian*, 20 April.

ARTICLE 6 – RIGHT TO A FAIR TRIAL[1]

3.54   Article 6(1) applies to any tribunal or decision-making tribunal that is charged with determining 'civil rights and obligations'. For example, proceedings before the Health Committee which decide a doctor's fitness to practice must conform with Article 6.[2]

In order for the civil limb of Article 6(1) to be applicable, there must be a 'dispute' over a right that could be said, at least arguably, to be recognised under domestic law. In addition, the 'dispute' has to be genuine and serious, and the outcome of the proceedings directly decisive of the right in question.[3]

Therefore, bodies that regulate professions deciding upon expulsion or disqualification will, as a general rule, have to comply with Article 6. Examples include The Law Society, the Bar Council, the Jockey Club and the Football Association.

Such a tribunal does not fall foul of Article 6 if it is comprised of members of the same profession as that of the person who is being 'judged'. In the *Stefan* case, it was not a breach of Article 6 for the Health Committee to be made up in part by doctors. The Committee was still capable of being an independent tribunal.

However, if any of the members of the tribunal were also involved in the investigation process that led to the hearing, this would lead to an appearance of bias. Even an appearance of bias is sufficient to impugn the entire proceedings.

Even where the hearing before the tribunal had some shortcomings, providing these are cured by appeal to another tribunal possessing all the hallmarks of independence, impartiality and the other guarantees under Article 6(1), there will be no breach. In the *Stefan* case, the legislation provided for appeal from the Health Committee to the Privy Council and no breach of Article 6 was found, despite the Committee lacking some of the characteristics of a 'court-like' body.

Pension rights have been held to be civil rights under Article 6(1) and proceedings carried out in determination of those rights should have all the guarantees under the Article.[4]

It must be noted that although Article 6(1) applies to a tribunal determinative of civil rights and obligations, it does not apply to tribunals that merely evaluate qualifications, and interviewing panels and other recruitment methods might be outside the scope of the Article. If the interviewing body can also properly be described as a public body then the guarantees under this Article may be applicable. By virtue of s 6 of the Human Rights Act 1998, it is unlawful for a public body to act in a way which is incompatible with the Convention, so if a public body also happens to be the interviewer, they are under an obligation to comply with the Articles of the Convention.

---

1   For application to employment tribunals see **3.64**.
2   *Stefan v UK* Application No 29419/95 (1997).
3   *Balmer-Schafroth v Switzerland* (1998) 25 EHRR 598.
4   *Pauger v Austria* RJD 1997-III 881, (1998) 25 EHRR 105.

Similarly, disputes relating to the recruitment or termination of service of public servants or other employees generally do not need to comply with the provisions of Article 6(1) (see the decision in *Paruszweska* (see **3.52**)).

ARTICLE 8 – RIGHT TO RESPECT FOR PRIVATE AND FAMILY LIFE

Private life

3.55 The use of the word 'respect' in Article 8 implies some positive obligation on behalf of the State.[1] Consequently, positive action from the State in the form of legislation will from time to time be necessary in order to comply with this Article.

It is becoming increasingly common in some professions for prospective employees to undergo and pass a medical examination before starting a job. How much the employer or prospective employer is entitled to know must be considered.

Not every aspect of an individual's physical health will be an indicator of their lifestyle or other aspects of their private life. It is not unreasonable for an employer to know whether or not an employee is fit for work. However, requirements to be tested for HIV or drug use, or genetic testing are matters that go beyond the merely physical and delve into the realms of private life.

It is a breach of the right to private life for a prospective employer (and it follows that this must also apply to employers generally) to test a candidate for HIV without their consent.[2] Similarly, any covert methods of testing would also amount to a breach. In the *X* case, the applicant refused to be tested for HIV, but his blood sample was subjected to a T-cell count, another way of determining HIV status.

However, the decision in the *X* case does not prohibit all such testing. An employer may request that a candidate undergoes a blood test, if the test is considered necessary in order to determine a candidate's suitability for the post. In those circumstances, if the candidate then refuses to consent to the test and the employer refuses to recruit him as a result, there is no breach.

The crucial factor is whether the test in question is considered necessary for the post. Testing for evidence of sexually transmitted diseases, other diseases or illnesses can be justified only if there is a risk of infection to people whom the candidate is likely to come into contact with. Such testing or a condition of employment that requires such testing will amount to a breach of the right to private life if the disease or illness does not affect the ability to work.

Random testing, provided it is done with consent and is necessary to determine suitability, will not amount to a breach.

Whether a test will be deemed necessary will vary according to the profession concerned and the duties to be carried out in furtherance of that profession.

---

1   *Campbell and Cosans v UK* (1982) Series A No 48, 4 EHRR 293.
2   *X v Commission of the European Communities* [1995] IRLR 320.

For example, it is unlikely that there will be a breach of the right to private life if a doctor is to be tested for HIV. But to impose such a requirement upon a receptionist would almost certainly amount to a breach.

Similarly, testing for drug or alcohol use with consent will not be in breach of Article 8 if it is necessary in the same sense as discussed above. It is unlikely to be a breach for a train driver to be so tested as this could be justified on public safety grounds under Article 8(2). Again, whether the test is truly necessary will depend on the nature of the work to be carried out.

The following basic principles can be taken from the decision in the *X* case:

(1) there is no breach if the employee consents to testing;
(2) surreptitious testing is likely always to amount to a breach;
(3) if the testing in question is necessary, there will be no breach;
(4) what is necessary will depend on the circumstances of the case including the nature of the employment and the testing concerned.

Family life

3.56 It has been held that with respect to migrant workers, conditions imposed on their residence should not hinder their families' ability to come and join them. To do so would amount to a breach of Article 8, the right to family life.[1]

Less favourable treatment in the work place of pregnant women, expectant fathers or those with families may amount to a breach of the right to family life if the result is to make establishing a family more difficult or less advantageous. This breach would be in addition to breaches of the Sex Discrimination Act 1986 and the Employment Rights Act 1996 and a potential applicant could argue all three breaches in support of a claim at an employment tribunal. For example, if a female employee takes maternity leave and as a result is passed over for promotion, this may amount to a breach as it hinders the exercise of the right or makes it appear a less attractive option to start a family.

Could the lack of adequate child care facilities provided by an employer or the State amount to a breach? Arguably, if the lack of such services resulted in the right to family life being hindered, then it should follow that there would be a breach. Similarly, lack of availability of job shares or flexi-time making it difficult for parents to pick their children up from school or nursery may for the same reasons amount to a breach of Article 8.

ARTICLE 9 – FREEDOM OF THOUGHT, CONSCIENCE AND RELIGION

Basic principles

3.57 The following basic principles apply to Article 9(1).

(1) The religion concerned must have the status of a 'known religion' as advantages of observance flow from such a status.[2]

---

1   *Commission of the European Communities v FRG* [1993] CMLR 540.
2   *Kokkinakis v Greece* (1994) Series A No 260, 17 EHRR 397.

(2) Freedom of religion implies a right to try to convert one's neighbours to that religion.[1]

(3) The Contracting States are given a margin of appreciation to allow them to ensure peaceful enjoyment of the freedoms guaranteed under the Convention for all citizens.[2]

Application of Article 9 to employment

3.58 A dismissal that is on the grounds of a view held or expressed by an employee may amount to unfair dismissal under domestic law. In addition, a dismissal for such reasons may also amount to a breach of this Article. The same principle applies if the dismissal is as a result of an employee's religious beliefs. Where the reason for dismissal is clearly an employee's religious or other beliefs, this will amount to a breach.

However, it is not necessary for an employer to endure an employee who openly expresses racist or sexist views. Article 9(2) expressly limits the exercise of this right as it carries with it duties and obligations and an employer does not breach Article 9(1) if, for example, an openly racist employee is dismissed for that reason.

There may well be a different result if the employee merely holds such views without expressing them openly. It is submitted that such an individual would enjoy protection from the right to freedom of thought and conscience.[3]

Similarly, if an employee was known to be a member of a group or organisation that held certain views about minority groups (for example, the British National Party) provided he kept this separate from his work-life, he would be protected from dismissal on the grounds of such membership. A dismissal in the above circumstances would amount to a breach of both Article 9(1) and Article 8.

It becomes more difficult to find a breach if there is no dismissal involved. However, any work conditions or terms of employment that make the exercise of the right protected more difficult, would also amount to a breach. So, for example, a work place that did not provide for halal, kosher or vegetarian food in the staff canteen may be committing a breach. Factors such as the percentage of the work force affected and the cost of providing the facilities would appear to be irrelevant as they do not come under the prescribed excuses under Article 9(2).

Further, employers that employ Muslims should allow them time off during the day where possible for daily prayers. Arguably, the exercise of the right to religion may extend to the provision of a quiet place where Muslim employees can carry out daily prayers.

Conditions of employment that cannot be met or are more difficult to meet by members of certain religious groups are already legislated against in domestic

---

1   *Kokkinakis v Greece* (1994) Series A No 260, 17 EHRR 397.
2   Ibid.
3   See below the discussion of the decision in *Vogt v FRG* (1996) Series A No 323, 21 EHRR 205.

race discrimination laws. However, if the condition in question is a necessary requirement of the position, then there is no breach of the anti-discrimination laws. This rule echoes that expressed in the *X v Commission of the European Communities* decision.[1]

Conditions that are not necessary may amount to a breach of the right to freedom of religion if the condition is one that members of a particular religious group would find it difficult to comply with. For example, a requirement to have short or shaven hair would be impossible for observers of the Sikh religion to comply with without breaking their religious beliefs. A requirement that female employees should wear skirts and not trousers would be a requirement that some Muslim women would find offensive to their religious convictions.

Perhaps a more frequent and recent problem is that of Sunday trading. A condition of employment that compelled a Christian to work on a Sunday would amount to a breach of this Article. The same principle must also apply to observers of the Jewish faith whose Sabbath falls on Friday; for Seventh Day Adventists the relevant day would be Saturday.

There appears to be an overlap between this Article and Articles 8 and 10. If the factual circumstances permit an applicant is likely to argue breach of several Articles.

ARTICLE 10 – FREEDOM OF EXPRESSION

Basic principles

3.59   The following basic principles apply to Article 10.

(1) Where a legitimate aim can be shown, interference with the right may be justifiable in a democratic society.[2]
(2) The action complained of must be proportionate to the pursuit of a legitimate aim.[3]
(3) Article 11(1) by its very nature seeks to protect the rights secured under Article 10.

Application of Article 10 to employment

3.60   The rights guaranteed under Article 10 and those protected by Article 9 will commonly have to be balanced out against each other. This is known as the doctrine of proportionality. Although everyone enjoys freedom of expression, this is only to the extent that the exercise of the right does not infringe someone else's human rights.

Any unnecessary infringement of this right will amount to a breach. Prohibition of meetings, speeches, lectures, interviews with the media and publication of articles may all amount to a breach unless the employer can point to some

---

1   [1995] IRLR 320.
2   *Vogt v FRG* (1995) Series A No 323, 21 EHRR 205 and see also the terms of Article 10(2).
3   See decision in *Vogt* (above).

genuine reason in support of the prohibition under attack. (For example, members and former members of MI5 are prohibited from communicating with the media under the Official Secrets Act 1989, the reason for the infringement being national security.)

In a recent decision of the European Court, it was held that the dismissal of a teacher from a German State school amounted to a breach of Articles 10 and 11, as the reason for the dismissal was the teacher's membership of the German Communist Party.[1]

In *Attorney-General v Barker*,[2] the defendant was a former employee of the Royal household who wished to publish his experiences. The contract of employment included a term prohibiting publication of any information, conversations etc gained or heard in the Royal household. The Queen applied for an injunction restraining publication of the defendant's book. The defendant argued that the injunction was, inter alia, a breach of his right as protected by Article 10. The court upheld the grant of the injunction holding that the sanctity of the employment contract was more important than 'foreigners' having the opportunity to read the book. The court did not specifically address the Convention point raised. However, it seems that the decision is correct in that to allow publication would also be to allow a breach of the right to privacy and family life of the Royal family. Again, a balancing exercise must be carried out.

ARTICLE 11 – FREEDOM OF ASSEMBLY AND ASSOCIATION

Basic principles

3.61 The following basic principles apply to Article 11(1).

(1) The right to strike is by implication protected by Article 11.
(2) A compulsion to join a trade union or group would amount to a breach of Article 11.
(3) Any unnecessary restrictions placed upon the calling of meetings etc within the working environment would amount to a breach.
(4) This Article also protects the right to join a trade union.
(5) A straightforward prohibition on union membership would of course constitute a breach. But any unnecessary interference or hindrance with the exercise of the right would also be a breach.

Application of Article 11 to employment

3.62 In *The National Association of Teachers in Further and Higher Education (NATFHE) v UK*,[3] a requirement under s 226A of the Trade Union and Labour Relations (Consolidation) Act 1992 to serve an employer with a notice before a strike ballot was examined. The notice had to contain the names of all employees eligible to vote.

---

1 See decision in *Vogt* (above).
2 [1990] 3 All ER 257.
3 Application No 28910/95, 16 April 1998.

It was argued on behalf of NATFHE that the requirement of a notice infringed the right to strike, which was by implication protected under Article 11. However, the Commission held that the requirement did not amount to a breach in the particular circumstances of that case. However, the Commission accepted that in certain circumstances such a requirement could amount to a breach. For example, where the employer concerned is known to have anti-trade union tendencies and would use the details contained within the notice to persecute employees, then there would be a breach of Article 11(1).

Given the decision in the *NATFHE* case, s 226A of the Trade Union and Labour Relations (Consolidation) Act 1992 would appear to conflict with Article 11. The 1998 Act should provide for an exception to the notice provisions where it can be shown that the employer concerned has anti-trade union tendencies.

Does Article 11 protect an individual's right not to join a trade union? In *Gustafsson v Sweden*,[1] it was held that compulsion to join a trade union would not always be contrary to the Convention. However, where the form of compulsion used strikes at the very substance of freedom of association, it would constitute an interference with that freedom. The notion of a negative right to freedom of association is well established and may in certain circumstances require State intervention to protect that right.

Article 11 does not protect the right not to enter a collective agreement and so the decision in *Swedish Engine Drivers' Union v Sweden*[2] is wrong to this extent.

PART 3
COMMENTARY

---

1   (1996) 22 EHRR 409; see also the decision in *Sibson v UK* (1993) Series A No 258-A, 17 EHRR 193.
2   (1976) Series A No 20, 1 EHRR 617.

EMPLOYMENT TRIBUNALS

ADVISING THE CLIENT: PROCEDURE

3.63 Employment tribunals will be under a duty to construe domestic legislation so that it is compatible with the Convention[1] and also to act in a manner that is compatible with the Convention.[2]

Employment tribunals will not have the jurisdiction to declare a statute to be incompatible with the Convention. If a party alleges before a tribunal hearing that a particular statute is incompatible with the Convention, the matter will have to be pursued before a higher court.[3] The proceedings before the tribunal will either have to be adjourned pending the outcome of the incompatibility issue or a party may choose to conclude the proceedings before the tribunal and then pursue a finding of incompatibility.

The notice of application in proceedings before the tribunal should disclose any allegations of infringement of Convention rights. If it is alleged that a particular statute is incompatible with the Convention, this too should be cited on the face of the application. In addition, these should be argued orally before the tribunal.

APPLICATION OF THE CONVENTION

A fair hearing

3.64 The rules of procedure for industrial tribunals provide for discovery of evidence and exchange of witness statements. In addition, the tribunal also has the power to order a party to give details of their allegations or grounds of resistance. Failure to comply with a direction by either party could lead to an award of costs against them.

The parties should be given reasonable opportunity to prepare their case[4] and so application for adjournments or to break a trial fixture should not be unreasonably refused.

Each party should know in advance the case against them. This is known as equality of arms and dictates that a party should not be placed in a position of disadvantage vis-à-vis their opponent.[5] Every party to proceedings before the tribunal should as far as possible be made to give details of their case. A failure to comply with such a direction should be punished accordingly. Where a party refuses to comply, arguably that party should be debarred from arguing his case at the final hearing because to proceed to trial in these circumstances would mean unfairness to the other party.

---

1   Section 3 of the Act.
2   Section 6 of the Act.
3   Section 4(5) of the Act.
4   *Niderost-Huber v Switzerland* (1998) 25 EHRR 709.
5   *Ankerl v Switzerland* (1996, unreported).

Both parties should be afforded the opportunity to comment upon the evidence and cross-examine witnesses.[1]

A public hearing

3.65   Hearings before employment tribunals are open to the public and to the media. However, the tribunal has the power to restrict access to the hearings if the interests of justice so dictate. For example, it might be considered undesirable to allow the media to have access when the tribunal is hearing evidence that might affect national security. A hearing in camera for these reasons would not amount to a breach of the right to a public hearing.

Reasonable time

3.66   The parties are entitled to a fair hearing within a reasonable time. In fact, the time aspect of Article 6 can be seen as an element of the right to a fair hearing.[2] Whether the proceedings (including any appeal hearings to the Employment Appeals Tribunal) are unfair due to unreasonable delay depends upon the complexity of the case concerned and the conduct of the parties.[3] The delay caused by any one party or the State authorities must be looked at in the context of the overall length of the proceedings. The European Court has held that where the overall length of the proceedings was four years there was a breach of Article 6(1) when the State authorities were responsible for only 26 months of that period.[4] Further, a chronic backlog of cases cannot justify excessive length of proceedings.[5]

Independence and impartiality

3.67   Where there is evidence to suggest that any member of the tribunal has an interest in the outcome of the proceedings, this would be a breach of this aspect of Article 6. There need not be any real impartiality on behalf of a tribunal member, an appearance is sufficient for the proceedings to fall foul of Article 6.

Any comments made by a member of a tribunal tending to suggest bias or impartiality will lead to the proceedings being deemed a breach of Article 6(1).

Legal aid

3.68   There is no legal aid available for hearings before the tribunal. However, this is not a breach of Article 6 as the entitlement to free legal representation is provided only if a person is facing a criminal charge.

A potential applicant in employment tribunal proceedings will be entitled to free initial advice under the Green Form Scheme.

PART 3
COMMENTARY

---

1   *Delta v France* (1993) 16 EHRR 574.
2   *Darnell v UK* (1993) Series A No 272, 18 EHRR 205.
3   *Sussmann v FRG* (1998) 25 EHRR 64.
4   *Robins v UK* RJD 1997-V 181, (1997) *The Times*, 24 October.
5   *Pammel v FRG* (1998) 26 EHRR 100.

EXTRADITION, EXPULSION/REMOVAL AND ADMISSION

EXTRADITION

3.69   The Commission has stated that:

> 'although extradition and the right of asylum are not, as such, among the matters governed by the Convention ... the Contracting States have nevertheless accepted to restrict the free exercise of their powers under general international law, including the power to control the entry and exit of aliens, to the extent and within the limits of the obligations which they have assumed under the Convention.'[1]

In the context of extradition, the European Court considered and reinforced this principle when it stated that:

> 'the decision by a Contracting State to extradite a fugitive may give rise to an issue under Article 3, and hence engage the responsibility of that State under the Convention, where substantial grounds have been shown for believing that the person concerned, if extradited, faces a real risk of being subjected to torture or to inhuman or degrading treatment or punishment in the requesting country. The establishment of such responsibility inevitably involves an assessment of conditions in the requesting country against the standards of Article 3 of the Convention. ... In so far as any liability under the Convention is or may be incurred, it is liability by the extraditing Contracting State by reason of its having taken action which has as a direct consequence the exposure of an individual to proscribed ill-treatment.'[2]

Liability for potential violations

3.70   The European Court has explained that:

> 'it is not normally for the Convention institutions to pronounce on the existence or otherwise of potential violations of the Convention. However, where an applicant claims that a decision to extradite him would, if implemented, be contrary to Article 3 by reason of its foreseeable consequences in the requesting country, a departure from this principle is necessary, in view of the serious and irreparable

---

1   *X v Austria* Application No 2143/64, (1964) 7 YB 314, at 328; *Atun v FRG* Application No 10308/83, (1983) 36 DR 209, at 232–233 (The extradition of the applicant for a political offence did not constitute a violation, but the Commission indicated that extradition of an applicant to face prosecution in a requesting State 'simply because of his political opinions' may amount to inhuman treatment because of the risk that proceedings would lead to an 'unjustified or disproportionate sentence'.)

2   *Soering v UK* (1989) Series A No 161, 11 EHRR 439, para 91 (The extradition of the 18-year-old West German applicant was sought from the UK to face capital charges of murder in the American State of Virginia which had the death penalty for murder. The European Court held that 'having regard to the very long period of time spent on death row in such extreme conditions, with the ever-present and mounting anguish of awaiting execution of the death penalty, and to the personal circumstances of the applicant, especially his age and mental state at the time of the offence,' the extradition would breach Article 3. In reaching this decision, the European Court was also influenced by the fact that because the applicant could have been removed to West Germany to face trial, 'the legitimate purpose of extradition could be achieved by another means which would not involve suffering of such exceptional intensity or duration.').

nature of the alleged suffering risked, in order to ensure the effectiveness of the safeguard provided by that Article.'[1]

EXPULSION/REMOVAL

3.71 The principles derived from extradition cases apply in cases relating to expulsion. In this context, the European Court has stated that:

'Contracting States have the right, as a matter of well-established international law and subject to their treaty obligations including the Convention, to control the entry, residence and expulsion of aliens. Moreover, it must be noted that the right to political asylum is not contained in either the Convention or its Protocols. However, it is well established in the case law of the Court that expulsion by a Contracting State may give rise to an issue under Article 3, and hence engage the responsibility of that State under the Convention, where substantial grounds have been shown for believing that the person in question, if expelled, would face a real risk of being subjected to treatment contrary to Article 3 in the receiving country. In these circumstances, Article 3 implies the obligation not to expel the person in question to that country.'[2]

Assessment of the risk of ill-treatment

3.72 The European Court has stated that:

'in determining whether substantial grounds have been shown for believing the existence of a real risk of treatment contrary to Article 3 the Court will assess the issue in the light of all the material placed before it or, if necessary, material obtained *proprio motu.*'[3]

In cases where expulsion of the applicant has already occurred, the European Court has said that:

'the existence of the risk must be assessed primarily with reference to those facts which were known or ought to have been known to the Contracting State at the time of the expulsion; the court is not precluded, however, from having regard to information which comes to light subsequent to the expulsion.'[4]

PART 3 COMMENTARY

---

1   *Soering v UK* (1989) Series A No 161, 11 EHRR 439, para 90.
2   *Chahal v UK* RJD 1996-V 1831, (1996) 23 EHRR 413, paras 73–74. See also *Cruz Varas and Others v Sweden* (1992) Series A No 201, 14 EHRR 1. (A Chilean applicant was deported back to Chile after his asylum claim was refused; his wife and child went into hiding in Sweden. The European Court held that the decision to deport him did not violate Article 3 on the basis that substantial grounds had not been established for believing that he would face a real risk of being subjected to ill-treatment contrary to Article 3 on his return to Chile.) See also *Vilvarajah and Others v UK* (1993) Series A No 215, 14 EHRR 248. (Five Sri Lankan Tamils were refused asylum in the UK and returned to Sri Lanka. The European Court held that Article 3 had not been breached on the basis that although the situation in Sri Lanka was still unsettled and there was the possibility that the applicants might be detained and ill-treated, a mere possibility of ill-treatment is not sufficient to give rise to a breach of Article 3. As to three of the applicants who were said to have in fact been subjected to ill-treatment after their return to Sri Lanka, the European Court said that 'there were no special distinguishing features in their cases that could or ought to have enabled the Secretary of State to foresee that they would be treated in this way.')
3   Eg *Vilvarajah and Others v UK* (1991) Series A No 215, 14 EHRR 248, para 107.
4   Ibid; see also *Cruz Varas and Others v Sweden* (1992) Series A No 20, 14 EHRR 1.

The European Court has also stated that:

> 'in order to assess the risks in the case of an expulsion which has not yet taken place, the material point in time must be the Court's consideration of the case. Although the historical position is of interest in so far as it may shed light on the current situation and its likely evolution, it is the present conditions which are decisive.'[1]

Applicant's conduct/national security

3.73 The European Court stated that:

> 'whenever substantial grounds have been shown for believing that an individual would face a real risk of being subjected to treatment contrary to Article 3 if removed to another State, the responsibility of the Contracting State to safeguard him or her against such treatment is engaged in the event of expulsion. In these circumstances, the activities of the individual in question, however undesirable or dangerous, cannot be a material consideration. The protection afforded by Article 3 is thus wider than that provided by Articles 32 and 33 of the UN Convention on the Status of Refugees.'[2]

In relation to national security the European Court stated specifically that there is no room:

> 'for balancing the risk of ill-treatment against the reasons for expulsion in determining whether a State's responsibility under Article 3 is engaged. It follows from the above that it is not necessary for the Court to enter into a consideration of the Government's untested, but no doubt *bona fide* allegations about the first applicant's terrorist activities and the threat posed by him to national security.'[3]

---

1   *Ahmed v Austria* RJD 1996-VI 2195, (1996) 24 EHRR 278, para 43. (The European Court held that the expulsion of a Somali national who had been convicted of attempted robbery and had as a consequence lost his refugee status in Austria would be in breach of Article 3. The present conditions in Somalia were such that 'the country was still the theatre of a fratricidal war between rival clans' and the applicant still faced a serious risk of being subjected to treatment contrary to Article 3 if he was returned there.) See also *Chahal v UK* RJD 1996-V 1831, (1996) 23 EHRR 413, para 86.

2   *Chahal v UK* RJD 1996-V 1831, (1996) 23 EHRR 413, para 80; *Ahmed v Austria* RJD 1996-VI 2195, (1996) 24 EHRR 278, para 41. See also *Nasri v France* (1995) 21 EHRR 458 (Commission held in the particular circumstances of the case that the deportation to Algeria, of a deaf mute who had lived for most of his life in France, on the basis of various criminal offences which he had committed would violate Article 3. Having concluded that the deportation would violate Article 8, the European Court did not examine the complaint under Article 3); *D v UK* RJD 1997-III No 37, (1997) 24 EHRR 423. (The European Court held that the threatened deportation to St Kitts of the applicant following his conviction and release from prison for importing heroin would violate Article 3. The decision was based on the fact that the applicant was terminally ill with AIDS and St Kitts lacked proper medical or social facilities needed by the applicant. The European Court stated that 'in the very exceptional circumstances of this case and given the compelling humanitarian considerations at stake, the implementation of the decision to remove the applicant would be a violation of Article 3.)

3   *Chahal v UK* RJD 1996-V 1831, (1996) 23 EHRR 413, paras 81–82. (The European Court ruled that the proposed expulsion to India of the applicant who was an Indian citizen and a Sikh militant for reasons of national security would be contrary to Article 3. Following the Home Secretary's decision that he should be deported, the applicant had unsuccessfully applied for asylum in the UK on the basis that he would be subjected to torture and persecution in India especially in light of his detention and torture when he was last in India.)

ADMISSION

3.74   The Commission has stated that, although a State has a sovereign power to admit persons to its territory, by virtue of Article 3:

'the state's discretion in immigration matters is not of an unfettered character, for a state may not implement policies of a purely racist nature, such as a policy prohibiting the entry of any person of a particular skin colour.'[1]

The Commission has further stated that:

'as generally recognised, a special importance should be attached to discrimination based on race; that publicly to single out a group of persons for differential treatment on the basis of race might, in certain circumstances, constitute a special form of affront to human dignity; and that differential treatment of a group of persons on the basis of race might therefore be capable of constituting degrading treatment when differential treatment on some other ground would raise no such question.'[2]

The Commission has also explained that violation of Article 3 could occur in this context only where:

'there is a substantiated level of intense physical and mental suffering as a direct result of the implementation of the immigration measure or where there was a particularly aggravating factor such as discrimination.'[3]

CONCLUSION

3.75   In recent cases, the European Court has emphatically reinforced the principle of absolute prohibition under Article 3. In the *Chahal*[4] judgment, the issue of national security, non-justifiable in UK courts, was deemed by the European Court to be an immaterial consideration in the face of a real risk of treatment contrary to Article 3. Significantly, as the European Court recognised, the protection afforded by Article 3 in the context of expulsion is now wider than that provided by the United Nations Convention on the Status of Refugees 1951. In the case of *D v UK*,[5] the European Court radically broadened the concept of State responsibility as it stated in that case:

---

1   *Abdulaziz, Cabales and Balkandali v UK* (1985) Series A No 94, 7 EHRR 471.
2   *East African Asians v UK* (1981) 3 EHRR 76, para 207. (The applicants who were UK citizens were refused admission into the UK despite the fact that they had been reduced to second-class citizens in their East African countries of residence. The Commission stated that 'the racial discrimination, to which the applicants have been publicly subjected by the application of the [UK] immigration legislation constitutes an interference with their human dignity which in the special circumstances [of the case] amounted to degrading treatment in the sense of Article 3 of the Convention'.) See also *Abdulaziz, Cabales and Balkandali v UK* (1985) Series A No 94, 7 EHRR 471. (The applicants, settled permanently in the UK, were refused permission to be joined by their husbands who were not British nationals. The European Court concluded that the difference of treatment occasioned by the Immigration Rules was not degrading because 'it was not designed to, and did not, humiliate or debase but was intended solely to achieve legitimate immigration measures'.)
3   *Poku v UK* (1996) *The Times*, 28 November (the deportation of the mother of children with rights to remain in the UK was not contrary to Article 3).
4   *Chahal v UK* RJD 1996-V 1831, (1996) 23 EHRR 413.
5   *D v UK* RJD 1997-III No 37, (1997) 24 EHRR 423.

'given the fundamental importance of Article 3 in the Convention system, the Court must reserve to itself sufficient flexibility to address the application of that Article in other contexts which might arise.'

In light of this statement, it remains to be seen whether the State will be obliged to ensure that individuals are not subjected by other individuals to treatment which is incompatible with Article 3.

FAMILY PROCEEDINGS

INTRODUCTION

3.76   The Human Rights Act 1998, s 6 makes it unlawful for public authorities to act in a way which is incompatible with Convention rights. Section 6(3) defines a public authority as a court or tribunal and any person who performs certain functions of a public nature. Section 6(7) makes it clear that to act can include a failure to act. The remedy is provided by s 7, which provides that a person who claims that a public authority has acted in a way that is unlawful according to s 6(1) can either bring proceedings against the authority involved or rely on the Convention rights in any legal proceedings. This is subject to the condition that it must be established that such a person was or would be a victim of the unlawful act complained of. It is important to note that the legal proceedings referred to in which Convention rights can be invoked include, by virtue of s 7(5), proceedings brought by the public authority concerned and also an appeal against the decision of a court or tribunal so providing a ground of appeal.

Section 8 empowers the court to award such remedy, within its normal powers, as may be appropriate in the circumstances. The courts have no more power to set aside Acts of Parliament than presently exist. However, by virtue of s 3(1), legislation must be interpreted in such a way as to be compatible with Convention rights. The higher courts have the power to make a declaration of incompatibility. Further, by virtue of s 2(1), any court or tribunal determining any question which has arisen in connection with a Convention right must take into account judgments and decisions of the European Court, and opinions and decisions of the Commission.

In the family law context, the Act and Convention rights will mostly be invoked by those who can establish they are the victims of the actions of local authorities in their child protection activities. If the local authority involvement is without formal court proceedings, decisions can be challenged by way of judicial review where it is claimed the authority has acted in a way that is incompatible with the 'victim's' Convention rights. If the involvement is also by way of court proceedings, any claimed violation of Convention rights can be raised in the proceedings and argued there. If it is claimed that the court deciding the issue has acted in a way that is incompatible with that victim's Convention rights, there is a ground of appeal of the decision on that basis.

CONVENTION RIGHTS

3.77   Whilst Articles 8 and 12 of the Convention are most specifically concerned with family situations and directed at family law, other Convention rights will be of relevance and will often be invoked. The family lawyer who is properly briefed to consider whether there is any cause of action under the

PART 3
COMMENTARY

Human Rights Act 1998 will need to be mindful of the rights guaranteed under Articles 2, 3, 5, 6, and 14 as well as Articles 8 and 12.

Article 2 – right to life

3.78 Article 2 guarantees the right to life. In the family context, this Article may be invoked in cases involving the withdrawal of life supporting treatment, for example, where patients in a persistent vegetative state are concerned. Since the House of Lords' decision in *Airedale NHS Trust v Bland*,[1] allowing for the judicial authorisation of the discontinuance of life sustaining treatment in cases where the diagnosis is unanimously that of persistent vegetative state, it has been the practice of health authorities to apply to the President of the Family Division of the High Court for authorisation to discontinue treatment. In such situations, there is scope for argument that Article 2 is breached by the withdrawal of treatment. As to who can argue the contravention, it can only be the 'victim' who must be the person whose life is to be thereby terminated. In practice, the only way such a representation could be made is by the practice of appointing the Official Solicitor to represent the patient, as presently happens. It would not be open to relatives to argue a contravention of Article 2. It may, however, be possible for a relative to argue that the withdrawal of treatment will amount to an interference with their family life with the patient in contravention of Article 8.

Article 3 – prohibition of torture

3.79 Article 3 of the Convention prohibits torture, inhuman or degrading treatment. This may be invoked in cases involving children where the level of their care is at issue. In particular, it may be invoked by local authorities as a justification for their involvement and ultimate removal of children from their natural parents or other carers in extreme cases of ill-treatment or over-chastisement. It may further be invoked against a local authority where a parent or other interested person complains of the ill-treatment a child receives within the care of the local authority, whether in a residential home, or at the hands of carers with whom the authority places the child. The complaint against the authority may be that, through their agents, they are acting in contravention of Article 3 or even that they are failing to act so as to prevent a contravention of Article 3.

Article 5 – right to liberty and security

3.80 Article 5 seeks to protect the liberty of the individual and security of the person subject to the specific conditions stated. This may be invoked where a local authority seeks or obtains a secure accommodation order in respect of a minor under the provisions of the Children Act 1989, s 25.

Article 6 – right to a fair trial

3.81 Article 6 seeks to protect the right to a fair trial. It applies whether the trial relates to the determination of civil rights and obligations or is the trial of a

---

1   [1993] 1 FLR 1026.

criminal charge. In any family context where there are court proceedings, this right must be respected and borne in mind. A contravention of Article 6 can be invoked, for example, by parents or other carers against whom accusations of neglect of children are levelled by the local authority, who believe that they have not had a fair hearing. This may be based on the procedure adopted at the hearing itself or even on the failure to provide full documentary evidence before a court hearing so as to cause prejudice. It can also be invoked where the person aggrieved has been denied the time and opportunity to obtain some evidence in rebuttal of the allegations levelled against him. Most commonly, this may be where a request to obtain expert forensic evidence of, for example, the cause of injury to a child is refused. Another example would be where the opportunity to instruct a further child psychiatrist to examine the child and report is refused. It is arguable that Article 6 may even be invoked where the complainant is excluded from the decision-making meeting of a local authority where decisions are often made as to removal of children and the instigation of court proceedings, involving discussion in detail about the alleged conduct of the excluded party. This would most often happen in the case of an unmarried father who does not have parental responsibility and against whom there are allegations of abuse or other ill-treatment or neglect of the child. Quite often such a parent will be excluded from case conferences at which key decisions concerning the future of the child are made and although the meeting is not a hearing as such, it may be possible to invoke Article 6 in that the decision will be made on the basis of evidence which excludes the viewpoint of the 'accused' parent.

Article 8 – right to respect for private and family life

3.82 Article 8 guarantees the right to respect for private and family life. It is likely that for family lawyers this will be the most frequently invoked and argued provision of the Convention. This will be mostly in the public law context where local authorities will clearly be interfering with family life in their child protection activities. There will no doubt be much discussion over the justification for such interference and whether it falls within the margin of appreciation recited in Article 8(2). The detailed provisions of Article 8 have been considered in Part 2 and particular instances of its application will be considered below.

Article 12 – right to marry

3.83 Article 12 guarantees that men and women of marriageable age shall have the right to marry and to found a family. The right to marry has so far been interpreted quite restrictively in decisions of the European Court. This has been considered in the analysis of Article 12 in Part 2 of this book. It is likely that this interpretation will change only if the law changes to reflect and give some recognition to the change in legal status of post-operative transsexuals and to same sex marriages. There is limited scope at present for arguing that the UK law preventing such marriages is in contravention of Article 12 rights on the basis of the European Court decisions. Perhaps this is an area in which campaigning and lobbying with the aim of extending the legal boundaries will achieve more than legal argument. There is more scope for arguing a contravention of the right to found a family and there is no reason why there should not be persistent challenges by aggrieved 'victims' in relation to the administering of assisted reproduction techniques and by those who have had or face an enforced sterilisation. A complaint that there has been a denial of available treatment would properly be mounted as a contravention of Article 12, even in the context of a single parent or an unmarried couple.

Article 14 – prohibition of discrimination

3.84 Article 14 prohibits discrimination on the grounds of sex, race, colour, language, political or other opinion, national or social origin, association with a national minority, property, birth or status. In the family context, there may well be situations in which there is complaint that a person has been discriminated against on any one or more of these grounds by, for example, a local authority in its choice of carers for children, in its decision to instigate removal procedures, in the denial of assisted reproduction, even in the refusal to recognise same sex marriages. Further, there may well be situations in which it is argued that an unmarried couple have been treated differently to a married couple. In *Marckx v Belgium*,[1] there was a very strong indication that there was no expectation on States to treat married and unmarried couples in the same way and afford them the same legal recognition. We can see this already in one example of domestic law and that is in relation to the position of unmarried fathers who are not automatically accorded parental responsibility but need to obtain it in accordance with the Children Act 1989, s 4. This very point arose in *McMichael v UK*[2] where the European Court considered whether there was a violation of Article 14 in the requirement that an unmarried father must acquire parental responsibility whereas it attaches automatically to mothers and married fathers. It was held that the difference in treatment of married and unmarried fathers was not discriminatory as the purpose behind it was to provide a mechanism for identifying meritorious fathers who might be accorded parental rights. Therefore, the legislation had a legitimate aim and the principle of proportionality had been respected in terms of the means employed in achieving that aim. However, it does remain the case that only an unmarried father faces the possibility of having parental rights, once acquired, removed from him again under the provisions of the Children Act 1989. Whilst it has been clearly decided that such a measure is an extreme and Draconian last resort, it is submitted that such provision does constitute a breach of Article 14. It cannot be said that such a provision continues to provide a method for distinguishing the meritorious from the unmeritorious father. Argument may be advanced along these lines in domestic law possibly leading to the conclusion that this provision of the Children Act 1989 cannot be interpreted in a way which is compatible with Convention rights.

---

1   (1979) Series A No 31, 2 EHRR 330.
2   (1995) Series A No 307–B, 20 EHRR 205.

ARTICLE 8 AND THE CONCEPT OF FAMILY LIFE

3.85 In order to mount an argument that there has been a breach of the right to respect for family life, the first stage will be to establish the existence of family life. It is only where it can be shown to have existed that the second stage of whether there has been an interference can be explored because, as discussed previously, the Convention does not seek to guarantee the right to acquire family life, only the maintenance of it once achieved. Although examined in the detailed consideration of Article 8 in Part 2 of this book, the following is intended to provide an overview of those categories of relationships where family life has been held to exist.

Same-sex relationships

3.86 Partners in a same-sex relationship have been held not to have family life with each other. This is so whether the relationship is of a homosexual nature or where post-operative transsexuals are concerned whose gender is not recognised in legal terms as having changed from their birth gender. Such relationships fall within the category of private life and not of family life: see the cases of *Dudgeon v UK*,[1] *Cossey v UK*,[2] *Rees v UK*,[3] and *Johnston v Ireland*.[4] It would be open on that basis to argue a breach of the right to respect for private life in Article 8 in appropriate cases.

Legitimacy

3.87 A child 'born of a lawful and genuine marriage' has, from the very moment of birth, a relationship of family life with his parents.[5] Further, it has been held that a child born of a marital union has, from the moment of birth, a bond amounting to family life with his parents as do the parents, from the moment of birth, with the child.[6] Despite the emphasis on a child born of a marital union, it has also been held that Article 8 makes no distinction between legitimate and illegitimate families.[7]

Father's rights

3.88 Further, it was held in *Keegan v Ireland*[8] that a father and child have a relationship of family life from the moment of birth where the relationship between the mother and father is not one of marriage but is of sufficient constancy and of significant duration involving some cohabitation. This was in the context of a father who had separated from the mother prior to the child's birth after a two-year relationship in which plans to marry had been made. Since the child's birth, the father had seen the baby only once. It was held that

PART 3 COMMENTARY

---

1   (1981) Series A No 45, 4 EHRR 149.
2   (1990) Series A No 184, 13 EHRR 622.
3   Application No 9532/81, (1984) 36 DR 78.
4   (1986) Series A No 112, 9 EHRR 203.
5   *Berrehab v The Netherlands* (1988) Series A No 138, 11 EHRR 322.
6   *Boughanemi v France* RJD 1996–II 593, (1996) 22 EHRR 228; and *Ahmut v The Netherlands* RJD 1996–VI 2017, (1996) 24 EHRR 62.
7   *Marckx v Belgium* (1979) Series A No 31, 2 EHRR 330.
8   (1994) Series A No 290, 18 EHRR 342.

the nature of the relationship which had existed between the parents was such that family life existed between the father and the child since his birth. In contrast, in *MB v UK*,[1] it was held that there was no family life between a father and child born out of a six to seven-month relationship between the parents who had not cohabited during their relationship and where the mother gave birth after separation. In *M v Netherlands*,[2] a man donating sperm to enable a woman in a lesbian relationship to have a baby did not have family life with that child despite the fact that he baby-sat on a weekly basis. So it does seem that in respect of the existence of family life between parents and children in the unmarried context there is a marked difference between a child born of a casual relationship and/or one who is unintentionally conceived and a child born into an established relationship. At the least there must be some demonstrated interest in and commitment to the child by the unmarried father for him to successfully assert family life with his child. It remains to be seen how this will be interpreted and expanded in domestic law.

Near relatives

3.89 Family life includes the ties between near relatives, for example, between grandparents and their grandchildren.[3] This seems to have been reasoned on the basis that these near relatives are likely to play a considerable role in family life.

In *Moustaquim v Belgium*,[4] the European Court included the relationship between siblings in the concept of family life. As for other family members, they have been included very much on the facts surrounding the particular relationship concerned rather than the fact of the relationship itself. The relationship of, for example, uncle and nephew or aunt and niece or wider family members will depend on the reality of the relationship, how often there is contact and the bond which exists between the individuals. No doubt there will be much argument on this point as the categories are challenged and expanded. It is unlikely that wider family members who have only occasional contact with each other will be held to have family life.

PUBLIC LAW AND JUSTIFIED INTERFERENCE

3.90 If family life exists then it will be necessary to examine whether there has been an interference with the right to respect for it. The clearest and most frequently encountered interference of this kind is in the public law context in the child protection activities of local authorities. This usually involves a removal of a child from parents or other carers or a restriction of contact. Domestic law provides for the making of care or supervision orders if the strict threshold requirements of the Children Act 1989, s 31 are satisfied. In all such applications, the interests of the child are paramount. It will almost certainly be

1 (1994) 77 DR 108.
2 (1993) 74 DR 120.
3 *Marckx v Belgium* (1979) Series A No 31, 2 EHRR 330.
4 (1991) Series A No 193, 13 EHRR 802.

the case that local authority intervention, if the s 31 criteria are satisfied, is in accordance with the law and/or that it is interference which is necessary for the protection of health or morals. It may therefore be those cases where the grounds for intervention are weak which can be successfully challenged by invoking Article 8 rights or those cases where there are procedural irregularities or unfairness in the decision-making process both before and during trial.

Once a care order is made, the implementation of the care plan by the local authority will be susceptible to challenge on Article 8 grounds. Further, the obligation provided by domestic law on local authorities by virtue of the Children Act 1989, s 34 to promote contact between a child in care and that child's natural parents will likewise be susceptible to such challenge if the local authority prevents contact without court sanction.

In those cases where local authority intervention has been with the consent of the parent and no recourse has been made to the court, as for example where a parent has agreed to the voluntary accommodation of a child, the actions of the local authority will be susceptible to challenge on Article 8 grounds. This will be by way of judicial review of their actions.

PRIVATE LAW

3.91 Disputes between private individuals in the family context will not provide much scope for argument over Convention rights. It is only where the dispute ends up in court for judicial determination that there will be a duty on that court to determine the dispute in accordance with Convention rights. If it is said that the judicial process has not involved a consideration of the right to family life, an appeal may lie on this ground. In the context of a contact dispute between parents where one partner is being denied contact with a child by the other parent, it will be possible to argue that a judicial sanction of that denial amounts to a breach of Article 8 rights.

It is worth noting that Article 5 of the Seventh Protocol of the Convention provides for the equality of private law rights and responsibilities between spouses. This will have the greatest bearing on the manner in which the domestic courts deal with financial disputes between spouses. Presently, in considering ancillary relief applications, there is no duty on the domestic courts to promote financial equality.

PART 3
COMMENTARY

HOUSING

SCOPE OF THIS CHAPTER

3.92   This chapter considers topics arising in the field of residential property and how the Act may have a bearing upon them.

THE ACQUISITION OF HOUSING

3.93   The Act, like the Convention upon which it is based, does not create nor guarantee a right to a home,[1] in contrast to other treaties to which the UK is a signatory or a party.[2] Throughout the Articles, notably Article 1 and Article 8 of the First Protocol, advantages which an applicant hopes to acquire are not protected but only those which he already has.

In the absence of a substantive right to housing, the procedural and 'fair process' implications of the Act may have the greatest significance. In the field of housing, a great many decisions are made by bodies which will fall within the definition of 'public authority' under s 6 of the Act, but whose decisions may previously have been open to challenge only upon narrow grounds of error of law, or *Wednesbury* unreasonableness in judicial review. Other bodies, such as housing associations, will find those decisions which entail the exercise of a public function susceptible to challenge for the first time if they fail to act compatibly with Convention rights (for example, in the disposition of property acquired with Housing Corporation funds).

Public authorities must not discriminate in relation to the rights and freedoms secured by the Convention on grounds such as race or sex,[3] or on the grounds of property ownership, or perhaps most significantly, on the grounds of national or social origin.[4] Where an applicant has a civil right, such as an entitlement to be offered accommodation, he has a procedural right to a fair and public hearing; Article 6 might be used, for example, to challenge the number of 'points' awarded on a housing allocation scheme or the outcome of a medical assessment of need.

As noted above, the Act does not offer protection for an advantage which the applicant wants to acquire. To date, this has been the stumbling block for attempts to extend a right of succession to same-sex partners.[5] Under the Act, however, the courts must act in accordance with Convention principles in

---

1   *X v FRG* (1956) No 159/56 1 YB 202.
2   Eg United Nations International Covenant on Economic Social and Cultural Rights: '... the Parties recognise the right of everyone to ... adequate food, clothing and housing ...', and the European Social Charter: 'everyone has a right to housing'.
3   Article 14.
4   See the various developments in the treatment of asylum seekers in their eligibility for State assistance.
5   See *S v UK* (1986) 47 DR 274; *Fitzpatrick v Sterling Housing Association Limited* 30 HLR 576, CA, particularly per Ward LJ.

interpreting legislation, which emphatically will include the phrase 'member of the family'.

THE PRESERVATION OF OCCUPATION

3.94   Where occupiers have statutory security of tenure, the criteria for bringing occupation to an end often include considerations of 'reasonableness'.[1] Courts are expressly included within the definition of public authorities, and must therefore apply the Convention principles to the determination of reasonableness. Notably, Article 1 of the First Protocol requires that a person may be deprived of a tenancy only if it is in the 'public interest', as an interest in land falls within the definition of a possession.

Persons in unlawful occupation of land will have protection under the Act if they can demonstrate that what they occupy is their 'home'. The Court of Appeal was prepared in February 1997 to acknowledge the principle enshrined in Article 8 in relation to a defaulting mortgagor who had no defence to a claim for possession, but whose wife was entitled to remain in occupation for the time being; the solution was for the Court to adjourn proceedings generally pending the determination of the wife's defence.[2]

Respect for the home entails protection for occupation of and access to the home,[3] and against intrusion into it for purposes such as search or seizure; any such interference must be justified to the extent of being necessary for various specific public objectives.[4] These rights may, for example, come to the aid of squatters faced with removal under the various criminal statutes dealing with trespass.[5]

Where what is occupied is a mobile home or caravan, the European Court has not ruled out complaints on the basis that the 'home' in question is mobile and not necessarily fixed at a particular address;[6] the case-law emphasises the concern behind Article 8 to protect home life whereas Article 1 of the First Protocol is more concerned with housing as property.[7]

Premises which an applicant intends to occupy or wants to occupy can fall within the meaning of 'home',[8] subject to the existence of some sort of proprietary right in those premises.

---

1   Eg Housing Act 1988, s 7; Housing Act 1985, s 84.
2   *Albany Home Loans v Massey* 29 HLR 902.
3   *Wiggins v UK* Application No 7456/76, (1978) 13 DR 40; *Cyprus v Turkey* (1976) 4 EHRR 482.
4   Article 8.
5   Eg Criminal Law Act 1977, s 7; Criminal Justice and Public Order Act 1994, ss 61, 68, 76.
6   *Buckley v UK* RJD 1996-IV 1271, (1996) 23 EHRR 101; *Smith v UK* (1994) 18 EHRR CD 65.
7   See, for example, *James v UK* (1986) Series A No 98, 8 EHRR 123.
8   See, for example, *Gillow v UK* (1986) Series A No 109, 11 EHRR 335, where the applicants were away from the premises for 19 years during which Housing Laws were passed, but their furniture remained there.

THE QUALITY OF ACCOMMODATION

3.95   Given the broad definition of 'home' in Article 8, it may be possible to use this Article in relation to unsatisfactory accommodation where there is no other statutory basis for complaint, such as inappropriate accommodation provided in discharge of a statutory housing duty.[1] This argument entails the imposition upon a public authority of a positive duty to promote the Article 8 rights; an approach which has been upheld in the Court.[2]

A further positive duty arises under Articles 2 and 3 which supplement existing duties of care such as the duty under the Occupiers' Liability Act 1984. It is arguable that the protection afforded by Article 3 against inhuman or degrading treatment extends to housing conditions, perhaps only in circumstances where the applicant has had no choice but to accept the accommodation; but it is important to note that the cases upheld by the European Court have concerned severely unsatisfactory premises in which the applicant was detained.[3]

There is no right under Article 1 of the First Protocol to housing in pleasant circumstances or with pleasant amenities, but interference which disturbs home or family life may be challenged under Article 8.[4]

STATE POWERS AND PRIVATE PROPERTY

3.96   Direct intervention by public authorities in the use of private property plainly must be justified within the provisions of the Act. The European Court has considered examples of interference, such as the exercise of compulsory purchase order powers[5] and the imposition of rent control on private landlords' dealings with their tenants,[6] and has by and large upheld the same in the public interest.

An important component of the public interest test is the requirement for proportionality, such that an individual must not be expected to bear a disproportionately heavy burden in order to gratify the objectives of the public authority.[7] The availability of compensation for the individual's inconvenience, and whether compensation is adequate, is a significant consideration in deciding whether a measure satisfies the need for proportionality.[8]

---

1   See, for example, *Lismane v Hammersmith & Fulham LBC* (1998) *The Times*, 27 July, CA.
2   See, for example, *X and Y v The Netherlands* (1985) Series A No 91, 8 EHRR 387, para 23; *Osman v UK* (1998) *The Times*, 5 November.
3   See, for example, prisoners in *The Greek Case* 12 YB 1 (1969) Com Rep; and *Guzzardi v Italy* (1980) Series A No 39, 3 EHRR 333; *B v UK* (psychiatric hospital) (1981) 32 DR 5, Com Rep 29.
4   *Rayner v UK* Application No 9310/81, (1986) 47 DR 5; *Arrondelle v UK* Application No 7889/77, (1982) 26 DR 5; *López-Ostra v Spain* (1995) Series A No 303-C, 20 EHRR 277.
5   *Howard v UK* Application No 10825/84, (1985) 52 DR 198; *X v UK* Application No 2261/81, (1982) 28 DR 177.
6   *James v UK* (1986) Series A No 98, 8 EHRR 123.
7   See, for example, *Sporrong & Lönnroth v Sweden* (1983) Series A No 52, 5 EHRR 35.
8   See, for example, the discretionary and mandatory provisions of the Land Compensation Act 1973.

Likewise, public authorities must ensure that they operate in accordance with Convention principles in granting or withholding rights or licences to deal with private property; it would not, for example, be lawful to discriminate on any ground set out in Article 14 upon an application for planning permission. Notably, there is no provision in the Act against discrimination on the basis of disability or age, but existing UK legislation in relation to the former has still to make its mark.[1]

REMEDIES

3.97　The Act provides for damages to be available in certain circumstances where existing UK law has denied them,[2] but only under restrictive conditions.[3] The principles applied by the European Court must be taken into account by the UK courts, but these principles hardly amount to a coherent code for awards of damages. Where there is an existing basis for an award of damages, such as a cause of action in tort or contract, the Act is unlikely to affect traditional approaches to quantum.[4]

Declarations of incompatibility may be made, but by no court lower than the High Court or Court of Appeal. It follows that a challenge based upon any legislation which cannot be read and given effect to in a way which is compatible with a Convention right must be pursued at least to this level for such a remedy to be available.

PART 3
COMMENTARY

1　Disability Discrimination Act 1995.
2　See, for example, *O'Rourke v L B Camden* (1997) 29 HLR 793.
3　Human Rights Act 1998, s 8.
4　Ibid, s 11.

IMMIGRATION

3.98   The Convention does not guarantee the right of an alien to enter or reside in any particular country, nor a right not to be expelled from there.[1]

LIBERTY (ARTICLE 5)

3.99   There are various provisions in the Immigration Acts allowing for a person who is refused leave to enter or who is deemed to be an illegal entrant to be detained pending his removal from the country. Article 2 of the Fourth Protocol guarantees the right of liberty only in the case of persons lawfully within the territory of a State. Article 5(1)(f) of the Convention expressly refers to the detention of a person to prevent his effecting an unauthorised entry into the country. This provision is aimed at a person who has been detained for the sole purpose of excluding him from the State in question. Everyone has the right to liberty and security of person. No one shall be deprived of his liberty save in the lawful arrest or detention of a person to prevent his effecting an unauthorised entry into the country or a person against whom action is being taken with a view to deportation or extradition in accordance with a procedure prescribed by law.

Deprivation of liberty under Article 5(1)(f) will be justified only for as long as extradition or deportation proceedings are being conducted. Thus, if such proceedings are not being prosecuted with due diligence, the detention will cease to be justified under Article 5(1)(f).[2]

FAMILY LIFE (ARTICLE 8)

3.100   There is no right of an alien to enter, remain or reside in a particular country guaranteed by the Convention. If a person is refused entry to a country where his close family resides, an issue may arise under Article 8 of the Convention. As a matter of international law, the State has the right to control entry of non-nationals into its territory, but the extent to which the State is obliged to admit into its territory relatives of settled immigrants will vary according to the particular circumstances of the case and the general public interest.[3] The Immigration and Asylum Act 1999 confers on the adjudicators and Tribunal jurisdiction to allow appeals if the immigration officer or

---

1   *Amuur v France* (1996) 22 EHRR 533 (Opinion); and Application No 12461/86, (1986) DR 51 at 258.

2   *Quinn v France* (1995) Series A No 311, 21 EHRR 529 at 550, para 48. The delays of some three and ten months between stages of extradition proceedings made the total duration of detention excessive.

3   *Gul v Switzerland* RJD 1996-I 159, (1996) 22 EHRR 93, para 38; and *Abdulaziz, Cabales and Balkandali v UK* (1985) Series A No 94, 7 EHRR 471, paras 67–68.

entry clearance officer has acted in breach of the appellant's human rights.[1]

For example, a child born of a marital union is part of the family from the moment of birth and by the very fact of its birth. There exists between child and parent a bond amounting to family life which cannot be broken save in exceptional circumstances.[2] But there is nothing in the Convention which requires the UK courts to act otherwise than in accordance with the interests of the child.[3]

The concept of family life on which Article 8 is based embraces, even where there is no cohabitation, the tie between parent and child regardless of whether or not the child is legitimate.[4] The tie can be broken only in exceptional circumstances.

The essential purpose of Article 8 is to protect the individual against arbitrary interference in his family life by public authorities including immigration authorities in deportation cases. Article 8 does not impose a general obligation upon a State to authorise family reunion upon its territory.[5] Thus, there is no obligation imposed on the authority to respect the choice by married couples of the country of their matrimonial residence and to authorise family reunion in its territory. All the facts of the case must be considered. For example, in a deportation case the following factors might be relevant:

(i) any obstacles preventing the deportee from developing family life in the country to which he is to be returned;

(ii) whether a family member has spent all his life in the country from which he is to be removed.[6] This means that the court will examine whether the immigrant has a real family life in the UK (his family is in the UK or that he has a stable relationship and social ties here);

(iii) whether the immigrant has kept in close contact with his own country and has family members there;[7]

(iv) the seriousness of a criminal offence.[8]

DOES THE DEPORTATION OR OTHER DECISION TAKEN AGAINST THE IMMIGRANT CONSTITUTE A VIOLATION OF HIS RIGHT TO RESPECT FOR HIS PRIVATE LIFE AND FAMILY LIFE AS GUARANTEED BY ARTICLE 8 OF THE CONVENTION?

3.101 If there is an interference by an immigration official of a person's family life (deportation or refusal of entry clearance) then the first step is to

---

1 For example, a person refused leave to enter as a visitor to provide a kidney transplant for a sponsor in the UK may well constitute a breach of Article 3.

2 *Gul v Switzerland* RJD 1996-I 159, (1996) 22 EHRR 93, para 32.

3 *Dawson v Wearmouth* [1999] 2 WLR 960 at 973H.

4 *Boughanemi v France* RJD 1996-II No 8, (1996) 22 EHRR 228, para 35.

5 *Gul v Switzerland* RJD 1996-I 159, (1996) 22 EHRR 93, para 38.

6 *Berrehab v The Netherlands* (1998) Series A No 138, 11 EHRR 322, para 7: a daughter of a Moroccan immigrant had been born in The Netherlands and spent all her life there was a strong factor against deportation of the immigrant father.

7 *Gul v Switzerland* RJD 1996-I 159, (1996) 22 EHRR 93, para 42.

8 *Boughanemi v France* RJD 1996-II No 8, (1996) 22 EHRR 228, para 45.

determine whether such interference is in accordance with the law within the meaning of Article 8(2). This simply means identifying whether the decision taken against the immigrant is taken in accordance with the immigration laws. If the answer is yes then the next step is to determine whether the interference had a legitimate aim (set out in Article 8(2) – national security, public safety or the economic well-being of the country, for the prevention of disorder or crime etc). Finally, a court must examine whether the interference is necessary in a democratic society.

The decision must be shown to be necessary in a democratic society, that is justified by a pressing social need, and, in particular, proportionate to the legitimate aim pursued. The tribunal or court will have to examine whether in the case before it, a fair balance has been struck between the legitimate aim pursued and the seriousness of the interference with the immigrant's right to respect for his private and family life.[1] Such examination should be scrutinised with particular care. For example, if the immigrant is to be removed to a country where he does not have any social links then in such a situation an order for deportation to that country is frequently a measure of such severity that it cannot be considered as proportionate to the aim pursued under Article 8(2).[2]

Article 3 will apply in cases where the immigrant faces deportation which will result in his facing a real risk of being subjected to ill-treatment or loss of life.[3] A failed asylum seeker who satisfies the tribunal that he might face death or torture in his home country because of civil strife may rely on Article 3. Similarly, a person who is being returned to a country in which he faces a death penalty will be able to invoke Article 3.

Article 1 and Article 13 of the Convention (which have not been incorporated) may be relied upon before a tribunal because it is a public body which has to act compatibly with the Convention[4] in cases involving entry clearance refusals outside the UK.[5]

The Fourth Protocol is not currently incorporated into the Act. This Protocol guarantees, inter alia: a right to internal freedom of movement; a right to non-expulsion from the Home State; a right of entry to the State of which a person is a national; and a prohibition on the collective expulsion of aliens.[6] However, the jurisprudence of the ECJ[7] and Article F of the EC Treaty (introduced by the TEU) requires respect for fundamental rights and an

---

1   *Moustaquim v Belgium* Commission's Opinion of 12.10.89, para 61; and *Boughanemi v France* RJD 1996-II No 8, (1996) 22 EHRR 228 at 241, para 74 (Opinion).
2   *Boughanemi v France* RJD 1996-II No 8, (1996) 22 EHRR 228 at 242, paras 76–78 (Opinion).
3   *Chahal v UK* RJD 1996-V 1831, (1996) 23 EHRR 413.
4   See s 6 of the Act.
5   *D v UK* (1997) 24 EHRR 423, *Loizidou v Turkey* (1997) 23 EHRR 513. Paragraph 26 of HC 395 provides that where appropriate, the term 'Entry Clearance Officer' should be substituted for 'Immigration Officer'. Thus, it is arguable that ECO's decisions will fall under the scrutiny of the Convention as being public officers. The White Paper includes immigration officers, but does not refer to ECOs.
6   These rights are identical to the provisions of the International Covenant on Civil and Political Rights.
7   Case C-260/89 ERT [1991] ECR 1-2925 at 2963-4.

applicant in a case which involves EC law may invoke the Fourth Protocol if necessary on the grounds that it is part of the corpus of law to be taken into account by the European Court in construing the EC Treaty.[1]

The rights set out in the Seventh Protocol will be included at some point in the future. This Protocol seeks to guarantee specific procedural safeguards against arbitrary expulsion of aliens.[2]

Article 14 (non-discrimination) may have some limited application to immigration cases.[3] By and large, this Article will rarely be relied upon in immigration cases with much success unless there is a clear case of discrimination on grounds of race or sex.[4]

The application of the Human Rights Act in the immigration context

3.102 Immigration and entry clearance officers will be required to comply with the Convention in taking immigration decisions.[5]

On appeal, the adjudicator and the tribunal must have regard to the European Court's jurisprudence and will not be required to follow such domestic human rights jurisprudence as preceded the incorporation by the Human Rights Act. Adjudicators and tribunals must interpret primary and subordinate legislation whenever enacted and construe and give effect in a way which is compatible with the Convention rights.[6] But an adjudicator or tribunal may not make a declaration of incompatibility if it is not possible to read or give effect to the legislation in a way which is compatible with the Convention rights. Only the superior courts can do this in an immigration context.[7] The adjudicator or tribunal may declare immigration rules ultra vires on the grounds of

PART 3
COMMENTARY

---

1   *R v Secretary of State for the Home Department, ex parte Manjit Kaur* CO/0985/98 – which concerns the construction to be adopted which entitles a British overseas citizen to enter and remain in the UK.

2   The White Paper at paras 4.14 and 4.15 indicate that this Protocol will be incorporated in the future.

    Article 1 of the Seventh Protocol provides:

1   An alien lawfully resident in the territory of a State shall not be expelled therefrom except in pursuance of a decision reached in accordance with law and shall be allowed:

    a   to submit reasons against his expulsion;

    b   to have his case reviewed; and

    c   to be represented for these purposes before the competent authority or person or persons designated by that authority.

2   An alien may be expelled before the exercise of his rights under paragraphs (a), (b) and (c) of this Article, when such expulsion is necessary in the interest of public order or is grounded on reasons of national security.

3   *Abdulaziz, Cabales and Balkandali v UK* (1985) Series A No 94, 7 EHRR 471.

4   Entry clearance and Immigration officers are required to carry out their duties without regard to the race, colour or religion of persons seeking to enter or remain in the UK: para 2 of HC 395. Given the provisions of Article 14 there is considerable force in arguing that the same anti-discrimination provision should extend to anti-sex discrimination in the immigration field: *Amin v ECO Bombay* [1983] 2 AC 818 may have to be revisited in a relevant case.

5   Section 6(1) and Article 17.

6   Section 3(1) of the Act and as to the principles of 'reading down' see *de Freitas v Ministry of Agriculture* [1998] 3 WLR 675 at 683C, PC. See also s 21 which defines what a tribunal is.

7   Section 4.

incompatibility with the Convention rights.[1] It is important for advocates to argue points of incompatibility before adjudicators so that:

(i) an adjudicator may make recommendations with respect to any other action which the adjudicator considers should be taken in the case under the Immigration Act 1971 in conjunction with the Human Rights Act;

(ii) an appeal to the Court of Appeal or an application for judicial review, whichever is appropriate, can be pursued in this regard.

A person's reliance on a Convention right does not restrict any other right or freedom conferred on him by or under any law having effect in any part of the UK to make any claim or bring any proceedings.[2] Thus asylum seekers, for example, may rely on the 1951 Refugee Convention already encompassed in the domestic law in addition to the Convention rights.

The combined provisions of ss 6 to 9 means that it is unlawful for public bodies to act in a way which is incompatible with the Convention. An adjudicator is also covered by s 6 because:

(i) he is acting as a public body;

(ii) the Government has stated that the effect of an order made by a Minister under s 7(11) of the Act would be to make the European Court's jurisdiction apply to all tribunals and adjudicators.[3]

Section 6, it seems, creates a free-standing jurisdiction. Convention arguments may be advanced before an adjudicator or tribunal notwithstanding that there is no specific provision in the immigration rules governing the case in question. Therefore, an adjudicator or tribunal under s 7 of the Act is required to determine Convention issues and to reach a specific conclusion whether or not the decision being appealed is unlawful because it breaches the Convention in any particular manner. This is because, under s 7, a person who claims that a public authority has acted (or proposes to act) in a way which is made unlawful by s 6(1) may:

(a) bring proceedings against the authority under this Act in the appropriate court or tribunal; or

(b) rely on the Convention right or rights concerned in any legal proceedings,

but only if he is (or would be) a victim of the unlawful act.

---

1 Section 4 does not prohibit this and, further, s 19(1) of the Immigration Act 1971 is to be construed so as to allow an adjudicator or tribunal to declare or, alternatively, recommend that the immigration rule in question is not compatible with the Convention right and therefore not in accordance with the law. Immigration rules are not it appears subordinate legislation: s 21. The adjudicator or tribunal being a public body has to act compatibly with Convention rights: ss 6–7.

2 Section 11(1) of the Act. Thus whilst an appellant may not be able to rely on Article 6 (fair hearing) in an immigration context because European Court jurisprudence suggests that immigration and asylum issues do not concern 'civil rights' he may still rely on the common law right to a fair hearing (eg breach of the rules of natural justice; bias; an adjudicator accused of sleeping).

3 Human Rights Bill (19 January 1998), HL Cols 360–362. Lord Williams of Mostyn: 'The effect of Amendment No 30 is to enable a Minister to confer jurisdiction on a tribunal to determine Convention issues to to grant a remedy where a public authority has acted incompatibly with the Convention rights. The jurisdiction is to be conferred by order. It will be in addition to the existing statutory provisions relating to tribunal jurisdiction'.

An appellant (who is a victim under the meaning of the Human Rights Act) should not only rely on s 6 of the Human Rights Act before an adjudicator but he may also rely on s 19(1)(a)(i) of the Immigration Act 1971 in both asylum and non-asylum appeals where his Convention rights have been breached by an immigration authority's decision. An adjudicator or tribunal would thus have to consider whether the decision being appealed is:

(i)   in accordance with the law or immigration rules and;
(ii) incompatible with the Convention right or jurisprudence.

Therefore, in an asylum appeal, the powers of an adjudicator would not only examine whether the removal of an appellant would be contrary to the UK's obligation under the 1951 Refugee Convention but also examine whether the removal or expulsion or deportation would be contrary to Article 2 (loss of life: ie death penalty), Article 3 (degrading treatment), Article 8 (family and private life) or Article 9 or 10 (in cases where the asylum seeker's post-arrival activities in the UK were conducted pursuance of these rights). Similarly, in deportation cases, an appellant with less than 7 years' residence may submit that there is no power in law to make a deportation order[1] against him on grounds that the deportation infringes his Convention rights under Article 8, for example. In such a case, the right of appeal would not be a restricted right of appeal but a full right of appeal and the previous case-law on this subject would not be followed. The appellant would argue that the power to deport him contravenes a Convention right and that the adjudicator or tribunal must act in accordance with s 6 of the Human Rights Act.

Bail applications made under Sch 2 to the Immigration Act 1971 must be considered in the light of the jurisprudence governing Article 5 of the Convention. For example, the granting or refusal of bail must be assessed with reference to a number of other relevant factors, such as the character of the person involved, his morals, his domicile, his profession, his assets etc.[2] Sections 44 to 54 of the Immigration and Asylum Act 1999 provide new bail schemes for detained persons. If detention of a person is based on arbitrary grounds, the detention may infringe Article 5(1)(f) of the Convention. For example, if the detention of a person is excessive, or if deportation is not intended, or if the deportation proceedings are not pursued diligently.[3] Reasons for refusal of bail must be provided and justified. For example, the reasons should state whether bail is being refused because the detained person may abscond or because he will commit an offence. There must be some evidence for reaching this conclusion.

Remedies under the Human Rights Act 1998 in an immigration context

3.103   Under the Human Rights Act, the Minister who has power to make rules in relation to a particular tribunal may, if he considers it necessary to ensure that the tribunal can provide an appropriate remedy in relation to an

---

1   Section 5(1) of the Immigration Act 1971.
2   *W v Switzerland* (1994) 17 EHRR 60, para 33; and *Yaqci and Sargin v Turkey* (1995) 20 EHRR 505, para 74.
3   Detention of a person pending the outcome of his application for asylum may be said to fall within Article 5(1)(f) because the ultimate decision is to deport him: *X v UK* 7706/76 DS 1, pp 435–436.

act (or proposed act) of a public authority which is (or would be) unlawful as a result of s 6(1), by order add to:

(a) the relief or remedies which the tribunal may grant; or

(b) the grounds on which it may grant any of them.

No doubt there will be specific rules made in relation to the specific remedies the adjudicator or tribunal can invoke. However, under s 8, if a tribunal finds that a decision of an immigration officer is unlawful or would be unlawful then it may grant such relief or remedy, or, make such order, within its powers as it considers just and appropriate. These powers include, with reference to the Immigration Acts, the power to:

(i) issue directions;[1]

(ii) make recommendations on grounds of the Convention;

(iii) declare that an asylum appellant is a refugee from a particular date[2] and if he is not a refugee then to declare that he should not be expelled on Convention grounds.

It may also be proper for an adjudicator or tribunal:

'to make extra-statutory recommendations ... to note any relevant findings or observations on ECHR matters that have not been pertinent in the case in point (eg the existence of a potential "victim of a violation" who is not a party to the appeal before them. One such example might be a family sponsor who is severely disabled.'[3]

Appeals to the Court of Appeal under s 9 of the Asylum and Immigration Appeals Act 1993 will lie in cases:

(i) where a declaration of incompatibility is sought under s 4 of the Human Rights Act which is material to the appeal;

(ii) on any question of law including Convention grounds where they are material to the decision being appealed.

If leave to appeal by the tribunal is refused from a determination of an adjudicator then the only recourse is judicial review. The grounds for judicial review may also include an argument that the determination of the tribunal is unlawful on the grounds that its determination (including refusal of bail) is incompatible with the Convention rights.[4] Proceedings under s 7 (complaint that an adjudicator or tribunal has acted in a way which is made unlawful by s 6 may bring proceedings against the public authority (which includes a court or tribunal and any person certain of whose functions are functions of a public nature))[5] must be brought before the end of the period of one year beginning with the date on which the act complained of took place.[6] On the face of this provision, it seems that the applicable time-limits for bringing proceedings under s 7(1) are not extended in:

---

1 Section 19(3) of the Immigration Act 1971; and see *R v Secretary of State for the Home Department, ex parte Salaka* [1994] Imm Ar 227, CA. For example, an adjudicator may direct that an entry clearance be issued on grounds of the Convention rights.

2 Belvue (11834a) (unreported Immigration Appeal Tribunal Determination).

3 See an excellent article, Dr Hugo Storey 'Implications of Incorporation of ECHR in the Immigration and Asylum Context' [1998] EHRLR 452 at 471.

4 With reference to s 6 of the Act.

5 Section 6(3) of the Act.

6 Section 7(5) of the Act.

(i) appeals against decisions by entry clearance officers and immigration officers which are contrary to Convention rights;

(ii) appeals against the determination of adjudicators to the tribunals where the adjudicator has acted in a way which is incompatible with a Convention right;

(iii) appeals to the Court of Appeal against the tribunal's determination on similar grounds;

(iv) judicial review proceedings against the determinations of adjudicators or tribunals on the grounds that the adjudicator or tribunal has acted in a way which is incompatible with a Convention right because any such proceedings are subject to rules imposing a stricter time-limit in relation to the proceedings in question.

It may be argued that there are no current stricter time-limits applying to proceedings which may be brought in an immigration context under s 7(1) of the Human Rights Act since there are no current procedures applying to post-incorporation proceedings specifically. Pre-incorporation procedures relating to relevant immigration appeals do not provide for appeals on the grounds that it is unlawful for a public authority, adjudicator, tribunal or court to act in a way which is incompatible with a Convention right and therefore the more generous time-limits in s 7(5)(a) apply. In any case, the extension of time provisions in s 7(5)(b) may be invoked notwithstanding the strict time-limits in which to bring an appeal. Thus, for example, it is arguable that a tribunal may have power under s 7(5)(b) to extend the time-limits of an appeal from an adjudicator if it considers it equitable having regard to all the circumstances.

Compensation can be granted only by a court or tribunal with power to make such an award.[1] At present, the adjudicator and immigration appeal tribunal do not have power to award damages or compensation. A Minister may make rules for a particular tribunal to allow it to grant additional remedies to the extent he considers it necessary to ensure that the tribunal can provide an appropriate remedy in respect of a violation of a Convention right.[2] This does not mean that compensation may not be sought in an appropriate case from the relevant authority because there has been a breach of Convention rights (eg from the Secretary of State for the Home Department). Practitioners should be aware that, although the adjudicator or tribunal may not have power to award compensation, currently a victim may still pursue a claim for compensation in judicial review proceedings where the tribunal has refused leave to appeal and possibly also in the appeal proceedings in the Court of Appeal by invoking Article 13 (effective remedy). Compensation for violation of a Convention right is to be governed by the principles developed in the European Court's jurisprudence under Article 41.[3] It may be argued in the superior courts that the immigration authority has violated the appellant's Convention rights and that he has suffered loss or injury as a result and therefore should be compensated adequately.[4]

---

1   Section 8(2) of the Act.
2   Section 7(11).
3   Section 8(4).
4   For example, along the lines of *Francovich and Bonifaci v Italy* [1992] IRLR 840.

Asylum

3.104 Asylum appeals will have to be considered with care, particularly against the following Convention rights.

(i)   Article 2 (right to life). This Article is expressed in absolute terms. If a failed refugee can show that removing him to his country may endanger his life (a real risk as opposed to a mere possibility) because of civil strife then Article 2 is engaged.

(ii)   Article 3 (prohibition of torture). This Article is expressed in absolute terms. It is wider in its application than the terms of the Refugee Convention. Thus serious ill-treatment which does not constitute persecution under the Refugee Convention may satisfy the requirements of Article 3. For example, an applicant who does not succeed under the Refugee Convention in establishing that she is a refugee by reason of being raped by a soldier in the country from which she has fled, will most certainly succeed in establishing that her removal from the UK to the country from which she has fled will breach Article 3 of the Convention.[1] In an Article 3 case, there is no requirement for the Special Adjudicator to conduct a balancing exercise between the needs of the claimant and the interests of the expelling State.[2] Thus, matters of immigration control and policy will not outweigh the safety interests of the claimant. Similarly, if the failed refugee demonstrates that he or she is suffering from AIDs (HIV positive) and there are inadequate medical facilities in the country to which she is being removed, then an expulsion to that country may well constitute a breach of Article 3.[3] The prospect of facing prosecution for desertion from the armed forces or for committing criminal activity may not constitute inhuman or degrading treatment in the country to which a person is to be removed.[4]

(iii)   Article 5 (right to liberty and security) and Article 6 (right to a fair trial) may also be applicable if a person can demonstrate that, if expelled to his country, there is a real risk that he will be detained and tried for offences in breach of these Articles (lack of a fair trial or arbitrary pre-trial detention).[5] A person's detention pending deportation may infringe Article 5(1)(f) if it is excessive or if the deportation proceedings are not pursued diligently and expeditiously.[6]

(iv)   Article 7 may apply if the person sought to be removed can show that he will be sentenced to a greater term of imprisonment than the term which applied at the time the offence was committed in his country.

---

1   The accumulation of acts of physical violence inflicted on the applicant and the especially cruel act of rape to which she was subjected amounts to torture in breach of Article 3 of the Convention: *Aysin v Turkey* (1997) 25 EHRR 251, para 86 of judgment and para 189 of opinion. Torture includes both mental and physical harm. Also see *Soering v UK* (1989) 11 EHRR 439 (it will be a breach of Article 3 to remove a person to a country where she would be at risk of torture or inhuman or degrading treatment).
2   *Chahal v UK* (1996) 23 EHRR 413, para 80.
3   *D v UK* (1997) 24 EHRR 423.
4   *X v FRG* Application No 7334/76.
5   Article 5(1)(f) is most appropriate in this case.
6   *Chahal v UK* (1996) 23 EHRR 413, paras 112–113.

(v) Article 8 has been widely relied upon by immigrants and asylum seekers. A failed asylum seeker whose family is settled in the UK will have good grounds for claiming that to remove him from the UK will mean separating him from the rest of his family thereby constituting a breach of Article 8 and that there is no pressing social need justifying the decision. A detailed analysis of the case-law on this subject is set out under Article 8.

(vi) Articles 9, 10 and 11 have little scope for application in immigration or asylum cases.

(vii) Article 12 (right to marry) may assist a detainee wishing to marry while in detention.[1]

(viii) Article 14 is not free standing and is usually invoked in conjunction with the other Articles cited above.

PART 3
COMMENTARY

---

1   *Hamer v UK* (1979) 24 DR 5; *Draper v UK* (1980) 24 DR 72.

PLANNING

INTRODUCTION

3.105 The European Court's jurisprudence discloses many instances where town and country planning controls of Member States have been challenged, and the European Court and the Commission have been willing on occasion to hold that planning activities have violated Convention rights. In this area the principle of maintaining a fair balance between the rights and needs of the individual and the general or public interest has been a matter of foremost consideration.

In addition to remedies sought through the courts, issues arising under the Human Rights Act 1998 will need to be raised and considered at the planning inquiry stage. Ministers, civil servants and local authorities are all public authorities which must act compatibly with Convention rights (subject to primary legislative incompatibility). Bodies such as urban development corporations and housing action trusts must act compatibly when exercising those functions which are of a public nature.

ARTICLE 1 OF THE FIRST PROTOCOL – PROTECTION OF PROPERTY

3.106 It is perhaps self-evident that the property rights preserved by Article 1 of the First Protocol will be relevant to applications of the Human Rights Act 1998 in the field of planning control, occasionally as to deprivation, but more usually as to control of use or interference under the first paragraph.

In the first place, the definition of 'possessions' under Article 1 of the First Protocol is capable of encompassing the economic value of outline planning permission upon which purchasers of land relied,[1] and similarly the economic interests connected with the running of a restaurant while it had a licence to serve alcohol which was subsequently revoked.[2] The 'value added' by the existence of planning permission is accordingly capable of recognition as a possession in itself.

However, withdrawal of such permission may be more susceptible to challenge as a control of use (unless perhaps it renders the land valueless, or where the complainant has no other property right but a profit or similar right to benefit from use in that way[3]). A deprivation may occur where the consequences of revocation of a permit to use land are so serious as to amount to a *de facto* deprivation.[4]

---

1   *Pine Valley Developments Ltd v Ireland* (1991) Series A No 222, 14 EHRR 319; and *Fredin v Sweden* (1990) Series A No 192, 13 EHRR 784.
2   *Tre Traktorer Aktiebolag v Sweden* (1991) Series A No 159, 13 EHRR 309.
3   See *Fredin v Sweden* (1990) Series A No 192, 13 EHRR 784.
4   Ibid.

Where the planning decision itself is not impugned, but it has the effect of rendering property subject to uncertainty for lengthy periods, this in itself may contravene the principle of 'fair balance', by causing the individual to bear a disproportionate burden, the more so where compensation is not available.[1] Given the restricted circumstances in which compensation is available under English planning legislation, it is likely that development of the law under the Act will pay particular attention to the significance of compensation in the balancing process.

ARTICLE 6 – RIGHT TO A FAIR TRIAL

3.107   Article 6(1) guarantees a fair trial in the determination of civil rights. Many decisions affecting 'civil rights' are made in the administrative sphere. In addition to the remedies which may be available directly against a public authority decision-maker, there may be recourse under this Article for a person who is affected indirectly by planning control but who has no locus under planning legislation.[2]

ARTICLE 8 – RIGHT TO RESPECT FOR PRIVATE AND FAMILY LIFE

3.108   Article 8 (everyone has the right to respect for his private and family life, his home and his correspondence) has featured in European Court and Commission decisions. 'Home' is not restricted to the place of residence, as it may include an office.[3] Control of use preventing occupation of a dwelling may be an interference with one's home under Article 8;[4] the particular lifestyle of the complainant (eg a gypsy) may make planning control an interference where it would not be so for another intended occupier.[5] Land use proximate to a home may give rise to a breach of Article 8.[6]

---

1   *Sporrong & Lönnroth v Sweden* (1983) Series A No 52, 5 EHRR 35.
2   See, for example, *Zander v Sweden* (1993) Series A No 279–B, 18 EHRR 175.
3   *Niemietz v FRG* (1992) Series A No 251–B, 16 EHRR 97.
4   *Gillow v UK* (1986) Series A No 109, 11 EHRR 335.
5   See *Buckley v UK* RJD 1996–IV 1271, (1997) 23 EHRR 101; the complaint was not upheld because the interference was not disproportionate and there were adequate safeguards.
6   *López Ostra v Spain* (1995) Series A No 303–C, 20 EHRR 277.

POLICE: CIVIL ACTIONS AGAINST THE POLICE

INTRODUCTION

3.109   The police authority is a public authority and the police are required to act in a way which is compatible with rights under the Convention in carrying out their duties under the Human Rights Act 1998, their statutory and common law powers.[1]

The Convention rights which apply to police activity are as follows:

(a) right to life under Article 2;
(b) prohibition of torture under Article 3;
(c) liberty and security under Article 5;
(d) respect for private and family life including home and correspondence under Article 8;
(e) freedom of assembly and association under Article 11;
(f) prohibition of discrimination on grounds of sex, race, colour etc under Article 14.

ARTICLE 2 – RIGHT TO LIFE[2]

3.110   Article 2 ranks as one of the most fundamental provisions of the Convention.[3] It is not exclusively concerned with the intentional killing of a suspect. Any force used by police to apprehend or maim or kill a suspect must be no more than absolutely necessary for the achievement of one of the purposes set out in subparas (a), (b) or (c) of Article 2(2).[4] In particular, the force must be strictly proportionate to the achievement of those aims. The domestic provisions allowing the use of force and the test applied under Article 2 are no different in essence.[5] In assessing whether the force used constitutes a breach of Article 2, the domestic court must not only examine what the police believed, but it must examine all the circumstances surrounding the killing of the suspect.[6] But the use of force by police in killing a suspect may be justified under Article 2 where their belief is based on an honest belief which is perceived, for good reasons, to be valid at the time but which subsequently turns out to be mistaken.[7]

Where there is an allegation that the authorities had violated their positive obligation to protect the right to live in the context of the duty to prevent and suppress offences against the person, it must be established to the court's satisfaction that the authorities knew or ought to have known at the time of the

---

1   Section 6(1) of the Human Rights Act 1998.
2   For a full and detailed commentary, see Part 2, Article 2.
3   *McCann v UK* (1995) Series A No 324, 21 EHRR 97, paras 146–7.
4   Ibid, paras 148–150.
5   Section 117 of the Police and Criminal Evidence Act 1984 (PACE 1984).
6   *McCann v UK* (1996) Series A No 324, 21 EHRR 97, para 173.
7   Ibid, para 200.

existence of a real and immediate risk to the life of an identified individual from the criminal acts of a third party and that they failed to take measures within the scope of their powers which, judged reasonably, might have been expected to avoid that risk.[1] A claim of negligence against the police will require a court to adjudicate on the admissibility of the merits of the claim that there was a relationship of proximity between the claimant and the police, that the harm caused was foreseeable and that in the circumstances it was fair, just and reasonable not to apply the exclusionary rule outlined.[2] Any such assertion by a claimant of such a right invokes the applicability of Article 6(1) of the Convention.[3] Thus, a claimant has a right to go to court for a declaration that, irrespective of public policy preventing claims against the police, the claimant would have a claim in negligence against the police and that it is not fair, just and reasonable in the circumstances of the case to apply the 'exclusionary rule' excluding negligence claims against the police. The applicability of the 'exclusionary rule' has to be decided afresh in each individual case. If the police are granted a 'blanket immunity' against suit, this will offend Article 6(1) and will be disproportionate and unjustifiable. A balance has to be struck between the hardship suffered by the individual claimant and the damage done to the public interest if an order is made against the defendant police.[4] If the relationship between the claimant and the police defendant is not proximate, it will be difficult to establish a claim against the defendant.[5]

PART 3
COMMENTARY

ARTICLE 3 – PROHIBITION OF TORTURE[6]

3.111 In respect of a person deprived of his liberty, any recourse to physical force which has not been made strictly necessary by a suspect's conduct diminishes his human dignity and is in principle an infringement of Article 3 of the Convention. The requirements of an investigation and the undeniable difficulties inherent in the fight against crime cannot justify placing limits on the protection to be afforded in respect of the physical integrity of individuals.[7] Thus, any kind of torture, such as deprivation of sleep, withholding of food or medical treatment may constitute an infringement of Article 3.[8] Torture is the

---

1   *Osman v UK* Application No 87/1997/871/1083.
2   *Hill v Chief Constable of West Yorkshire* [1989] AC 53.
3   *Osman v UK* Application No 87/1997/871/1083.
4   *Barret v Enfield LBC* [1999] 3 WLR 79 at 84. A court will now be reluctant to strike out claims against the police based on a public policy exclusionary rule without first investigating all the facts.
5   *Palmer v Tees Health Authority and Another* (1999) *The Times*, 6 July. It is implicit in *Osman* that it was appropriate to strike out actions on the ground that, in law, proximity is not established without establishing the facts of the case.
6   For a full and detailed commentary, see the annotations to Article 3.
7   In the instant case, the injuries suffered by the applicant showed that he underwent ill-treatment which amounted to both inhuman and degrading treatment: *Ribitsch v Austria* (1996) Series A No 336, 21 EHRR 573 (injuries included punches to the head, kidneys and right arm and kicks to the upper leg and kidneys; he was pulled to the ground by the hair and his head was banged against the floor).
8   *Ireland v UK* (1978) Series A No 25, 2 EHRR 25. *A v UK* Application No 100/1997/884/1096: this case deals with the States' obligation to take measures designed to ensure

most serious kind of ill-treatment. If a suspect is treated badly by the police and such treatment causes either mental or physical suffering or both then there is a clear infringement of Article 3. Domestic courts will have regard to the gender, age and vulnerability of the suspect. Treatment amounts to torture if it has seriously affected the health or well-being of the suspect.

Inhuman treatment includes physical assaults, forced confessions, inhuman detention or a threat of torture.

Degrading treatment is less serious treatment than torture, but may be grossly humiliating. For example, discriminating against a suspect because of his disability, race or gender may amount to degrading treatment.

ARTICLE 5 – RIGHT TO LIBERTY AND SECURITY[1]

Article 5(1) – Loss of liberty

3.112 The right to liberty contemplates the physical liberty of a person and therefore there must be a certain level of physical restraint.[2] There is no requirement that there should be a total restraint of liberty. For a deprivation of liberty to be lawful under Article 5(1), it must at any given moment fall within one of the categories of arrest or detention set out in subparas (a) to (f) of Article 5(1).

A period of detention must be in accordance with a procedure prescribed by domestic legislation and the procedure laid down by it and this requires an examination of the quality of the law in question, requiring it to be compatible with the rule of law.[3] If, for example, the proceedings are not conducted with requisite diligence or if the detention results from some misuse of authority, it ceases to be justifiable under Article 5(1)(f).

A period of detention will in principle be lawful if it is carried out pursuant to a court order. A subsequent finding that the court erred under domestic law in making the order will not necessarily retrospectively affect the validity of the intervening period of detention for the purposes of Article 5(1)(a), (b).[4]

When an arrest is based on reasonable grounds for suspecting a person of having committed an offence, this condition may justify the initial arrest and detention but, after a certain lapse of time, it may no longer suffice.[5] There must be other valid grounds for justifying detention.

---

individuals (and schools for that matter) will not be ill-treated in breach of Article 3 by other individuals and that children are entitled to protection, through effective deterrence, against such treatment. The European Court awarded the applicant in this case a sum of £10,000 by way of just satisfaction in respect of non-pecuniary damages (para 33).

1   For a full and detailed commentary, see Part 2, Article 5.
2   *Amuur v France* (1996) 22 EHRR 533, para 44 (Opinion).
3   Ibid, para 50.
4   *Kryzycki v FRG* (1978) 13 DR 57 and also see *R v Governor of Wandsworth Prison, ex parte Sorhaindo* (1999) TLR, 5 January. *Brogan v UK* (1989) 11 EHRR 117: the fact that a suspect has been detained and then released without charge does not mean without more that the arrest and detention was not in accordance with Article 5(1)(c).
5   *Mitap and Muftuoglu* (1996) 22 EHRR 209 at 215, para 56 (Opinion).

The pre-trial detention of an accused person should not exceed a reasonable time.[1] The requirements set out in Article 5(1) are no different than UK domestic law in this regard.

Article 5(2) – informed promptly

3.113   Article 5(2) requires an arrested person to be informed promptly, in a language which he understands, of the reasons for his arrest. The requirements set out in Article 5(2) are no different from s 28 of PACE 1984.[2]

Section 28(1) of PACE 1984 was intended to put on a statutory footing that a person who is being arrested has to be *informed* that he is being arrested and why. Section 28(1) applies to both private citizens and police constables. Section 28(1) suggests that the arrested person must be told in some form of words that he is arrested regardless of whether the fact of arrest is obvious.

Article 5(4) – lawfulness of detention

3.114   Everyone who is deprived of his liberty is entitled to issue proceedings by which the lawfulness of his detention shall be decided by a domestic court.[3] The determination provided for in Article 5(4) could be incorporated in the decision ordering the arrest or detention, if this decision was taken by a court which provided the fundamental guarantees of procedure.[4]

Article 5(5) – enforceable right to compensation

3.115   Article 5(5) guarantees an enforceable right to compensation but only to those who have been the victims of arrest or detention in contravention of the provisions of Article 5.[5] There is scope for arguing that compensation payable for a breach under Article 3, for example, should be more generous than the guidelines in domestic law.[6]

PART 3
COMMENTARY

---

1   *Kemmache v France* (1992) 14 EHRR 520, para 45 (see the provisions of PACE 1984, ss 41–46 relating to detention).
2   The *common law* position before PACE 1984 was:
   (a)   that the person who was being arrested had to be *told* that he was being arrested and why unless the circumstances were such that he must have known the general nature of the offence for which he was arrested;
      (i)   *Christie v Leachinsky* [1947] AC 573 at 587–8 as per Viscount Simon; 591, 593A;
      (ii)   the simplest thing was for the arrestor to *say* 'I arrest you'; *Alderson v Booth* [1969] 2 QB 216 at 221C–D (per curiam);
      (iii)   *R v Inwood* [1973] 1 WLR 647H at 652H–653B (there is no magic formula; only the obligation to make it plain to the suspect by what is *said* and *done* that he is no longer a free man);
      (iv)   *Abassy v MPC* [1990] 1 WLR 385 at 392D.
3   *De Wilde, Ooms and Versyp v Belgium* (1971) Series A No 12, 1 EHRR 373, para 73.
4   Ibid.
5   *Wassink v The Netherlands* (1990), Series A No 185–A, para 38 and *Benham v UK* RJD 1996–III 738, (1996) 22 EHRR 293, para 50.
6   *Thompson* [1997] 3 WLR 402.

ARTICLE 6 – RIGHT TO A FAIR TRIAL[1]

3.116 There is a right to consult a solicitor when in detention under PACE 1984.[2] The refusal of access to a solicitor might constitute a breach of Article 6(1).[3] The application of the exclusionary rule providing a water-tight defence to a civil action against the police, amounts to disproportionate restriction on the right of access to a court in breach of Article 6(1) of the Convention. The court must have regard to the presence of other public interest considerations which pull in the opposite direction to the application of the rule.[4]

ARTICLE 8 – RIGHT TO RESPECT FOR PRIVATE AND FAMILY LIFE[5]

3.117 Any search and seizures made at a person's house may interfere with his rights to respect for his private life and his home and correspondence as secured in Article 8(1). It is clear from the European Court's case-law that telephone conversations made from the home are covered by the notion of 'private life' and 'correspondence' under Article 8 of the Convention.[6]

There might be an interference with Article 8(1) if:

(i)   the powers of search are very wide when undertaking the search;
(ii) there is the absence of a judicial warrant;
(iii) there are insufficient restraints and conditions provided for in law.[7]

If there is an interference with the home or private life (including subjecting the suspect to degrading treatment – such as taking intimate samples in order to humiliate a suspect) by the police or which is in accordance with PACE 1984, then the next issue is whether the interference is justified under the terms of Article 8(2), notably whether they were 'in accordance with the law' and 'necessary in a democratic society' for one of the purposes enumerated.[8] The interference in question must have some basis in domestic law.[9] There must be a measure of legal protection in domestic law against arbitrary interferences by public authorities with the rights safeguarded by Article 8(1).[10]

In addition, however, an interference must satisfy the test of being necessary in a democratic society to be justified under Article 8(2); that is, whether the interference is justified and proportionate in meeting a pressing social need. The interference in question must strike a fair balance.

---

1   For a full analysis of Article 6, see Part 2, Article 6.
2   PACE 1984, s 58.
3   *Golder v UK* (1975) Series A No 18, 1 EHRR 524; *R v Chief Constable of S Wales, ex parte Merrick* [1994] 1 WLR 663.
4   *Osman v UK* Application No 87/1997/871/1083. This effectively means that *Hill v Chief Constable of West Yorkshire Police* [1989] AC 53 is no longer good law.
5   For a full and detailed commentary, see Part 2, Article 8.
6   *Halford v UK* Application No 20605/92, (1997) 24 EHRR 523.
7   *Funke v France* (1993) Series A No 256–A, 16 EHRR 229, paras 57–59.
8   *Malone v UK* (1984) Series A No 82, 7 EHRR 14, para 65.
9   Ibid, para 66.
10 Ibid, para 67; and see *Klass v FRG* (1978) Series A No 28, 2 EHRR 214.

ARTICLE 11 – FREEDOM OF ASSEMBLY AND ASSOCIATION[1]

3.118 Rights of peaceful protest and assembly are fundamental freedoms.[2] These are rights which it is in the public interest for individuals to possess and exercise without police interference so long as no wrongful act is done by those exercising such rights. As long as it is done peaceably and in good order without threats or incitement to violence or obstruction to traffic, an assembly is not prohibited.[3]

Domestic law[4] suggests that members of the public have the right to use the public highway for passing and repassing and for any such uses ancillary thereto which are usual and reasonable; and that such right does not include the holding of a peaceful assembly on the highway, even if it causes no obstruction.[5] This view is compatible with Article 11 of the Convention.

PART 3
COMMENTARY

---

1   For a detailed analysis of Article 11, see Part 2, Article 11.
2   White Paper *Review of Public Order*, para 17.
3   *Hubbard v Pitt* [1975] 3 All ER 1 at 10.
4   Section 70 of the Criminal Justice and Public Order Act 1994.
5   *DPP v Jones* [1997] 2 WLR 578.

SOCIAL SECURITY

ARTICLE 6(1) – RIGHT TO A FAIR TRIAL

Social security and other welfare benefit hearings

3.119   The general rule is that Article 6(1) (right to a fair and public hearing within a reasonable time by an independent and impartial tribunal) will apply in the field of social security and that this will include welfare benefit.[1] As a consequence, Article 6(1) will apply at social security appeal tribunals (SSATs). Social security is regarded as a civil right.

The factors that are relevant to the application of Article 6(1) at SSATs are:

(a) it will not be enough to show that a dispute is pecuniary in nature, although this will be a factor that can be taken into consideration;
(b) the approach to benefits may be different to the approach to contributions;
(c) a person suffering an interference with their means of subsistence and who is claiming an individual economic right flowing from specific rules will be relevant.

It will follow that not only income support but also payments from the Social Fund will be subject to Article 6(1).

Hearings within a reasonable time

3.120   It is notable that there are no time-limits placed upon SSATs to either convene or to issue their determinations. Article 6(1) will apply where a tribunal fails to sit within a reasonable time or to deliver its determinations. While the complexity of a case will be relevant insofar as the reasonableness of a time scale, it is incumbent upon the authorities to organise legal systems in such a way as to meet their obligations.

Excessive workload of a tribunal cannot be taken as a consideration so as to disapply Article 6(1). Conduct of the parties will be relevant; however, the applicant who is responsible for delay will not forfeit the protection afforded by Article 6(1) where the authority is responsible for further delay.[2]

---

1   In *Schuler-Zgraggen v Switzerland* (1993) Series A No 263, 16 EHRR 405 at 430 the preliminary objection of the Government that the public nature of Social Security disputes precluded the application of Article 6(1) of the Convention was unanimously rejected by the European Court, the reasoning being that the European Court's own case-law and the need for equality of treatment warranted that as a general rule Article 6(1) would apply to social insurance. The definition of social insurance was further developed by the European Court when it held that the general view today should be consistent with *Salesi v Italy* (1993) Series A No 257–E, para 19; that is that Article 6(1) should apply not only to social insurance per se but also to welfare assistance.

2   In *Lombardo v Italy* (1992) Series A No 249-B, 21 EHRR 188 the central issue revolved around the length of time taken by the Court to determine an albeit complex issue of law. The case involved an applicant who claimed entitlement to an 'enhanced ordinary pension' from his previous employers. The substance of the claim was that his enforced

Disputes relating to the recruitment and employment of public/civil servants are, as a general rule, outside of the scope of Article 6(1). This notwithstanding, Article 6(1) will apply where there is an obligation on the State to pay a pension, which is a civil right.[1]

Equality of arms

3.121   There is no right to legal aid for representation at social security appeal tribunals. Further, the appellant at an SSAT has no right of access to documentation or case reports other than those put before the tribunal by a Benefits Agency Presenting Officer, nor to impartial council as to where such information may be acquired. This might be open to challenge within the remit of any Act based upon the Convention.[2]

Oral hearings

3.122   It is not necessarily the case that fair procedure will in every instance require that an oral hearing be held. The issue will therefore be whether an oral hearing is necessary in order that a tribunal may be procedurally fair. With the emphasis on the effects of disability, with regard to the view taken within social security law that disability appeals tribunals should give most weight to the effects that disabilities have upon the individual claimant, rather than on a straightforward examination of medical evidence, it would appear that Article 6(1) will again be of primary importance.

An oral hearing may not be dispensed with in the following circumstances:

(a)   where it has been requested;

PART 3
COMMENTARY

---

invaliding out of the Italian Carabinieri on the twin grounds of an ulcer and neoplasia were both medical conditions which had been caused by work. The Italian Government had allowed an enhanced pension for a period of two years with respect to that part of the claim which related to the ulcer but had rejected the part of the claim relating to the neoplasia. Taking into account that Article 6(1) states that everyone is entitled to a hearing within a reasonable time by a tribunal, the European Court's judgment held that, while all the criteria such as complexity had to be taken into account, it was for the Contracting States to organise their legal systems in such a way as to meet their obligations. Further to this, a Contracting State could not successfully argue that having a heavy workload was a legitimate criteria to be considered nor, indeed, a factor that could take a decision outside the remit of Article 6(1).

1   In *Paccione v Italy* 20 EHRR 396, it had previously been held by the European Court that where some of the delay had been the responsibility of the applicant it did not assist the Government where the Government had not responded adequately and had themselves been responsible for the majority of the delay. In this case, the applicant was 75 years of age when in 1980 his former employer the San Remo District Council had communicated its decision as to the amount of the applicant's ordinary pension. Mr Paccione complained that not all matters relating to his employment had been considered. In April 1985, the applicant requested that matters be dealt with more speedily. In April 1989, when the applicant was 84 years old, the Court of Audit was able to set down a hearing for June of that year. There were further delays before the text of the judgment was finally handed down in March 1993. Whilst, admittedly, some of these later delays were the responsibility of the applicant, the Commission again reiterated that it was for the authorities to organise their legal systems in such a way as to ensure that citizens were guaranteed judgment within a reasonable time.

2   See *Schouten and Meldrum v The Netherlands* (1994) Series A No 304, 19 EHRR 432.

(b) if any waiver of the oral hearing has not been given unequivocally;

(c) where it would run counter to public interest;

(d) where there are matters of public importance.[1]

Conclusion

3.123   The topics covered above should not be seen as exhaustive. There are many areas that have still to be challenged or where final determinations have still to be made. Two which appear ripe for challenge are the non-availability of legal aid and the practice of councillors sitting as judges in their own cause in housing benefit review boards.

Article 6(1) should not be seen as standing alone; as will be discussed below, Article 6(1) is not the only Article which can be invoked.

ARTICLE 9 – FREEDOM OF THOUGHT, CONSCIENCE AND RELIGION

3.124   Article 9(1) guarantees the right to freedom of thought, conscience and religion. The term belief exists in Article 9 with regard to these freedoms, and the concept of religious and philosophical convictions appears in Article 2 of the First Protocol. It is necessary that these words are not seen as synonymous with mere opinions and/or ideas. Rather, they must exist within a higher level of belief.[2]

Democracy must be seen as having a greater meaning than simply that the will of the majority must prevail. Democracy will provide that the interests of the minority will be of consequence. It will therefore follow that there will be occasions when the will of the minority will prevail over the will of the majority. Persons acting out of sincerely held religious and/or moral belief will be able to invoke the protection of Article 9 of the Convention and Article 2 of the First Protocol.

For instance, those who refuse to work on holy days, or who refuse to take up employment for companies whose business infringes upon their own personal beliefs (eg, a Moslem accountant working for a brewery) should succeed in the argument that they have not lost entitlement to job seeker's allowance.

Although provisions in Article 4 specifically envisage the possibility of military service being compulsory, it may still be argued that a pacifist could invoke Article 9 in the event of refusing work in an ordnance factory, if welfare benefits were withdrawn or disallowed. There is further strength to this argument in countries such as the UK where there is no conscripted military service.

ARTICLE 8 – RIGHT TO RESPECT FOR PRIVATE AND FAMILY LIFE

3.125   Article 8 is perhaps the most far reaching of all Convention rights and as such provides possibly the most fruitful means of redress. Article 8(2) is of

---

1   See *Fischer v Austria* (1995) 20 EHRR 3–9.

2   See *Valsamis v Greece* RJD 1996-VI 2312, (1996) 24 EHRR 294 at 294–295.

special significance, simply because any interference with the rights protected by Article 8 has to comply with its very strict conditions. As a result, it will be possible to challenge any number of welfare benefits and pensions withheld from classes of persons if they fall outside formally accepted conventions.

It would seem unlikely that any government would attempt to utilise the protection of morals as a means of circumventing duties to treat its citizens in an equitable fashion. Therefore, it would appear arguable that many groups within society will be able to invoke Article 8.

Widowers should be entitled to the same pension rights as widows, not only for financial reasons but also to give validity to their status as widowers. Similarly, gay couples could argue that their relationships should be given equal status to heterosexual relationships. Finally, both same sex and unmarried heterosexual couples could argue that they should have equal status with married couples in financial matters such as widow's pensions, superannuation transfers and income tax thresholds.

ARTICLE 1 OF THE FIRST PROTOCOL – PROTECTION OF PROPERTY

3.126   The contributions made to pension schemes or unemployment benefit schemes may well fall within the provisions of Article 1 of the First Procotol. This is because the second paragraph of Article 1 establishes that the duty to pay contributions falls within its field of application.[1]

It is also arguable that certain benefits (eg industrial injuries invalidity benefit) might be considered to be a 'possession' within the meaning of Article 1. A suspension of such benefit because of imprisonment may not, however, amount to a violation of Article 1 if the suspension of benefit is in accordance with the domestic provisions.[2]

ARTICLE 14 – PROHIBITION OF DISCRIMINATION

3.127   Article 14 complements the other substantive provisions of the Convention and the Protocols but it has no independent existence. It cannot be applied unless the facts at issue fall within the ambit of one or more of those provisions.[3]

A difference of treatment is discriminatory if it has no objective and reasonable justification, that is, if it does not pursue a legitimate aim or if there is not a reasonable relationship of proportionality between the means employed and the aim sought to be realised.

Thus, for example, a benefits scheme which requires contributions from unmarried childless men aged 45 or over, but not from similarly situated

---

1   *Van Raalte v The Netherlands* RJD 1997-I 173, (1997) 24 EHRR 503, paras 30, 512 and 516.
2   *George Carlin v UK* Application No 27537/95.
3   *Van Raalte v The Netherlands* RJD 1997-I 173, (1997) 24 EHRR 503, para 33.

women, constitutes a difference in treatment between persons in similar situations, based on gender. Article 14 requires that exemptions are applied evenhandedly to both men and women, unless there are compelling reasons justifying a difference in treatment.[1]

Very weighty reasons would have to be put forward before a difference in treatment based exclusively on the ground of sex is held compatible with the Convention.[2]

Damages

3.128   A finding of a violation of Article 14 of the Convention taken together with Article 1 of the First Protocol might not entitle an applicant to retrospective exemption from contributions.[3] There might be an entitlement to damages if such damage is sustained as a result of a violation of the Convention rights.[4]

---

1   *Van Raalte v The Netherlands* RJD 1997-I 173, (1997) 24 EHRR 503, para 41.
2   Ibid, para 39; and see *Schmidt v FRG* (1994) Series A No 291-B, 18 EHRR 513, para 22.
3   *Van Raalte v The Netherlands* RJD 1997-I 173, (1997) 24 EHRR 503, para 50.
4   *Schmidt v FRG* (1994) Series A No 291-B, 18 EHRR 513, para 33.

TORTS

SCOPE OF THIS CHAPTER

3.129 This section addresses torts already existing in English law and proposes ways in which the provisions of the Act may enhance or alter such causes of action.

IMPACT OF THE ACT ON EXISTING LAW

3.130 By ss 2 and 3 of the Act, domestic courts must as far as possible read and give effect to existing legislation in a way which is compatible with the Convention rights, and must have regard to relevant European Court decisions and opinions. Given that the domestic courts are themselves to be regarded as public authorities which must act compatibly with Convention rights, the common law will be susceptible to the same approach.

PARTIES TO PROCEEDINGS

3.131 There are parties of three types envisaged under the Act:[1]

(1) those which in all circumstances constitute public authorities;
(2) those which count as public authorities because some of their functions are functions of a public nature; and
(3) those which are purely private bodies or persons.

Members of the first group may always be defendants to proceedings under the Act;[2] of the second group only when the act in question is an act of a public and not a private character; and of the third group, never. The significance of this approach for the established law of torts will lie primarily in the prospects of enlarging liability for an omission to act, because several of the Convention rights envisage a positive duty to prevent harm,[3] and in the impact upon vicarious liability where the very nature of the act complained of may determine whether a party is capable of bearing liability or not. A putative plaintiff as victim of a tort would seem to fall squarely within the 'victim' test under s 7 of the Act.

REMEDIES

3.132 In addition to the requirement that existing law is construed compatibly with the Convention, the Act offers a cause of action and potentially a line

---

1   See *Hansard* (HL) cols 758/759 (24 November 1997), and (HC) col 775 (16 February 1998).
2   Eg *Schmidt, Dahlstrom v Sweden* (1979) 1 EHRR 632; compare *Jones v Swansea City Council* [1990] 3 All ER 737, HL.
3   For example, Articles 2 and 3 and see *Osman v UK* Application No 87/1997/871/1083 (1998) *The Times*, 5 November.

of defence to a victim of an unlawful act, and expressly creates a right of damages for breaches, although this right is not unrestricted.[1] It is worth noting the one-year period of limitation applicable under the Act, in contrast to the three-year or six-year periods usually applicable to tortious wrongs.

TORTS INVOLVING INTERFERENCE WITH THE PERSON

Assault and battery

3.133   Article 3 prohibits torture or inhuman or degrading treatment. Interference with the person which is insufficiently proximate to found a tort of assault may be actionable here.[2] The doctrine of necessary consent applied by the English courts[3] where a patient is incapable of consenting to medical treatment will need to take Article 3 as a starting point, as the Article 3 right is entirely unqualified.[4] The same issues may well arise in the context of corporal punishment.[5] In cases of the control of fertility by medical intervention, Article 12 (right to found a family) must be considered.

Harassment

3.134   The definition of 'harassment' in the Protection from Harassment Act 1997 must be read so as to incorporate the rights protected by Article 8, and in so far as any common law tort of 'harassment' is thought to have emerged, the same will apply. As against this, the important rights of freedom of thought (Article 9), of expression (Article 10) and of peaceful assembly (Article 11) will have a significant impact upon any attempt further to extend the tort to cover such conduct as protesting against experimentation on animals where no other wrong is committed.[6]

False imprisonment and wrongful arrest

3.135   Plainly, Article 5 has particular resonance here, with its express reference to the need for lawful procedure to be observed. The doctrine of '*volenti non fit injuria*' may become more limited in scope in that the rights prescribed by the Act may be restricted only in the circumstances laid out.[7] Article 3 may play a part in the sense that intolerable conditions may eventually render detention unlawful, a line of thought canvassed by the Court of Appeal

---

1   See ss 7 and 8 of the Act.
2   See, for example, the psychological interrogation techniques found to have been degrading in *Ireland v UK* (1978) Series A No 25, 2 EHRR 25.
3   For example, *F v West Berkshire Health Authority* [1990] 2 AC 1.
4   In *Herczegfalvy v Austria* (1992) Series A No 242-B, 15 EHRR 437, it was held not to be a breach of Article 3 to give food and drugs forcibly to a violent, mentally ill patient on hunger strike; the obligation to preserve life under Article 2 takes priority.
5   See *Costello-Roberts v UK* (1993) Series A No 247-C, 19 EHRR 112; *Y v UK* (1994) 17 EHRR 238; *Warwick (M and K) v UK* Application No 9471/81.
6   And see *Huntingdon Life Sciences Ltd v Curtin* [1998] 1 *Current Law* 112, (1997) *The Times*, 11 December, QBD.
7   See, for example, *Herd v Weardale Steel Co* [1915] AC 67, inviting the question of whether *de facto* detention falls within the scope of Article 6.

in *R v Deputy Governor of Parkhurst Prison, ex parte Hague/Weldon* although rejected by the House of Lords.[1] It is also worth bearing Article 6 in mind which establishes an entitlement to a hearing within a reasonable time.

Malicious prosecution

3.136   By s 6 of the Act, domestic courts and tribunals are included within the definition of public authorities, and their actions are susceptible to litigation. The scope of judicial immunity may be curtailed, and the remedy for judicial acts done ultra vires may extend beyond an entitlement to have the act set aside or any remedy such as habeas corpus, to a new cause of action including a claim for damages. The implications of the Act are primarily as to the parties to, and remedies for, any claim under this tort.

TORTS INVOLVING INTERFERENCE WITH PROPERTY OR ECONOMIC INTERESTS

Wrongful interference with goods

3.137   The code provided by the Torts (Interference with Goods) Act 1977 is unlikely to be substantially affected by the Act, save in that the definition of 'goods' shall be read in the light of Article 1 to the First Protocol. Under that Article, 'possessions' is given a broad and autonomous meaning which can encompass any interest in property to which a definite entitlement has been established. Depending upon the context, Article 8 (respect for home and correspondence) may have a part to play.[2] The Act may also have implications for the conduct of execution of judgment against goods.

'Economic torts' and intellectual property

3.138   As noted above, the definition of 'possessions' provided under Article 1 of the First Protocol offers an enlargement of the various interests protected at law.[3] The Court of Appeal has considered the implications of Article 10 and the tensions which may arise between the protection of economic rights and the right to disseminate opinions and information.[4] Similar tensions may arise in the context of Article 11 (free assembly and trade unions).[5]

PART 3
COMMENTARY

---

1   [1992] 1 AC 58, HL.
2   See *McLeod v UK* (1998) *The Times*, 1 October, and see further the sections on trespass, below, and on housing at **3.92**.
3   See also decisions in Part 2, Article 10 such as *Müller v Switzerland* (1988) Series A No 133, 13 EHRR 212, but compare *Autronic AG v Switzerland* Series A No 178, 12 EHRR 485.
4   *Middlebrook Mushrooms v TGWU* [1993] ICR 612.
5   See, for example, *Ezelin v France* (1991) Series No A 202-A, 14 EHRR 362; *Otto-Preminger Institute v Austria* (1994) Series A No 295-A, 19 EHRR 34.

TORTS RELATING TO THE USE AND OCCUPATION OF LAND

Trespass to land

3.139   Article 1 of the First Protocol encompasses deprivation of land, but where procedural safeguards are available in the existing law and are sufficient, it is unlikely that the Act will contribute much.[1] There may be scope for addressing the lacunae which exist in the context of re-entry upon land without court process,[2] or for challenging the propriety of criminal process against unlawful residential occupiers,[3] with the assistance of Articles 8 and 11.

Nuisance

3.140   It is important to note that Article 1 to the First Protocol does not guarantee a right to enjoyment of property in pleasant surroundings. By contrast, complaints of disturbance from aircraft noise have been framed under Article 8.[4] The right to respect for private and family life and for the home (Article 8) may establish a locus standi against interference of the sort which was unable to succeed in *Hunter v Canary Wharf Ltd*[5] due to the absence of sufficient property interest in the complainant's home.[6] Again, a tension may arise between the right to respect for the home and the rights provided under Article 10 to freedom of expression and the imparting of information and ideas, and to the manifestation and observance of belief under Article 9.

Occupiers' liability and health and safety provisions

3.141   Given the positive duty which arises upon public authorities in some circumstances (eg, to preserve life under Article 2) the test of liability for injury caused to entrants upon land may entail a heavier burden for the occupier to discharge. The Health and Safety Executive would appear to be a public authority of the first category[7] and susceptible to proceedings for a failure to act. None the less, constraints imposed by an occupier upon the conduct of entrants upon land (such as restrictions upon dress for safety reasons) may require justification under the terms of Articles 9, 10 and 13. Control of use under Article 1 of the First Protocol is subject to a justification of necessity and proportionality, and 'the general interest' may plainly encompass measures taken for the preservation of safety.

---

1   But see *Mcleod v UK* (1998) *The Times*, 1 October.
2   For example, by a public authority mortgagee, or against non-residential property.
3   Criminal Law Act 1977, Part V as amended; Criminal Justice and Public Order Act 1994, ss 61, 68.
4   *Rayner v UK* Application No 9310/81, (1986) 47 DR 5; *Arrondelle v UK* Application No 7889/77, (1982) 26 DR 5; and see *López Ostra v Spain* (1994) Series A No 303-C, 20 EHRR 277.
5   [1997] 2 All ER 426.
6   See particularly the judgment of Lord Cooke in *Hunter* (above) at 459.
7   See **3.131**.

SPECIAL DUTIES OF CARE

Medical negligence

3.142 The European Court jurisprudence under Article 2 envisages a positive duty to take steps to protect life.[1] Against this, the 'reasonable care' test for negligence may prove to be insufficient. The scope of the duty may extend to the provision of information for the making of informed choices as to treatment,[2] and raises important issues as to whether the availability of resources can be taken into account.[3] Inadequate medical care may be encompassed within the scope of inhuman or degrading treatment under Article 3,[4] as may experimental treatment.[5] Article 8 raises potentially significant issues pertaining to the disclosure of medical records.

Professional negligence of lawyers

3.143 Articles 5 and 6 with their associated rights to speedy and fair trial may raise issues against the legal organs of the State. As noted above, Article 8 may colour the extent of the duty to make disclosure of documents, and lawyers need to take care to advise fully as to the duty to disclose.

Duties owed to prisoners and other detainees

3.144 The special circumstances of people in lawful custody will potentially attract the provisions of many of the Articles.[6] It has been noted above[7] that, on one view, inhuman or degrading treatment under Article 3 can render unlawful a detention which was otherwise lawful. The positive duty to protect life under Article 2 and the concomitant obligations to secure proper medical care may have particular impact upon persons lawfully deprived of their liberty. Notably, 'forced or compulsory labour' under Article 4 does not include work required to be done in the ordinary course of legitimate detention, but degrading activity imposed as a punishment will fall within Article 3.

Articles 8 (private life and correspondence) and 10 (freedom of expression) both carry provisos restricting the exercise of the rights, but any such restriction is at least subject to the test of necessity and must be justified by the public authority seeking to restrict the right. Article 5 (right to liberty) provides for a right to speedy determination of the propriety of detention and creates a specific right to damages for contravention of the Article,[8] and Article 6 (fair

---

1 See, for example, *X v UK* Application No 7154/75, (1978) 14 DR 31 where the Commission stated that Article 2 'enjoins the state not only to refrain from taking life intentionally but, further, to take appropriate steps to safeguard life'. See also *Osman v UK* (1998) *The Times*, 5 November.

2 See *X v Ireland* Application No 6839/74, (1976) 7 DR 78.

3 *Airey v Ireland* (1979) Series A No 32, 2 EHRR 305.

4 *Tanko v Finland* Application No 23634/94 (1994, unreported); and see also *Hurtado v Switzerland* (1994) Series A No 280-A.

5 *X v Denmark* Application No 9974/82, (1983) 32 DR 282.

6 See, generally, discussion of Articles 8 and 12, above, and the rights of prisoners to free association, marriage and the right to found a family.

7 At **3.135**.

8 But see the limitations on damages comprised in s 8 of the Act.

trial) offers an extension of the right to be heard in decisions relating, for example, to release on parole or license. It remains to be seen whether detainees can call on Article 2 of the First Protocol to secure the provision of continuing or adult education.

DEFAMATION

3.145   The UK courts have considered the tension arising between Articles 8 and 10 in the context of defamation,[1] and of course the protection of the reputation or rights of others is expressly included within the restrictions to the right of freedom of expression under Article 10. It is possible that the broad scope of Article 13 (prohibition of discrimination) will enable claims for defamation to be made by persons on the basis that they fall within a class which has been defamed if the defamation can be shown to have its basis in discriminatory treatment.

---

1   See, for example, *Rantzen v Mirror Newspapers* [1993] 3 WLR 953; *Derbyshire CC v Times Newspapers* [1992] 3 All ER 65; *Attorney-General v Guardian Newspapers (No 2)* [1990] 1 AC 109, CA; [1993] 2 WLR 449, HL.

PART 4

CASE STUDY

CASE STUDY

INTRODUCTION

4.1 The following problem is considered under the Human Rights Act 1998 (the Act). First, a vertical application of the Act is considered and, secondly, a horizontal application of the Act.

THE PROBLEM

4.2 The client is a teacher who has been dismissed for teaching pupils in school about homosexuality and providing the pupils with books on the subject. The local authority dismissed the client because he could not continue to work in the position which he held without contravention (either on his part or on that of his employer) of a duty or restriction imposed by or under an enactment and therefore the dismissal was fair.[1] The local authority dismissed the client because they considered his teaching activities contravened s 28 of the Local Government Act 1988 (LGA 1988). The client now seeks advice in relation to bringing a complaint against the school and the local education authority and wishes to:

(a) pursue a remedy in the employment tribunal or county court for unfair dismissal and/or breach of contract (horizontal challenge); and

(b) challenge the legality of s 28 of LGA 1988 (vertical challenge).

VERTICAL AND HORIZONTAL ARGUMENTS

4.3 A vertical challenge or application is one where an individual enforces a Convention right against a State (ie Government or public authority as defined). The Human Rights Act 1998, according to some sources,[2] confers rights on individuals against the State, but does not confer rights on individuals to bring actions against other individuals (not a public body under the Act) on Convention grounds. However, it is suggested for reasons expressed elsewhere[3] that the Human Rights Act 1998 applies horizontally as well as vertically. By horizontally, it is meant that one individual may rely on the Convention rights against another individual where there has been an infringement of such Convention rights. The Convention applies both to statutory law and common

---

1   Employment Rights Act 1996 (ERA 1996), s 98(2)(d).

2   In the White Paper, *Rights Brought Home*, at para 1.18, it was stated that 'the time has come to enable people to enforce their Convention rights against the State in British courts, rather than having to incur the delays and expense which are involved in taking a case to the European Court ... Our aim is a straightforward one. It is to make more directly accessible the rights which the British people already enjoy under the Convention'.

3   See the Introduction.

law (which governs the behaviour between private individuals, eg tort).[1] This means that the domestic court or tribunal must interpret, apply and develop the common law compatibly with the Convention case-law including, for example, the case-law on the freedom of expression and private life. There are some Convention rights which impose positive obligations on the State to protect individuals against interference with those rights by other individuals (which may not be public bodies), so that the State may be liable for the infringement of the guaranteed Convention rights by an individual. For example, the State has to take steps to protect life under Article 2. The above factors strongly suggest that the Convention, as implemented by the Act, applies both vertically and horizontally even in cases where the opponent is not a public body.[2]

CHALLENGING THE DISMISSAL IN AN EMPLOYMENT TRIBUNAL (HORIZONTAL CHALLENGE)

Is the dismissal a private act?

4.4 A complaint for unfair dismissal may be brought in the employment tribunal before the end of the period of three months beginning with the effective date of termination.[3] Unfair dismissal on the face of it is a private act by an employer towards his employee.

It is certainly arguable that the local authority is a public authority whose functions are functions of a public nature.[4] But the problem lies in determining whether the dismissal is a private act, because in relation to a particular act, a person is not a public authority if the nature of the act is private.[5]

Is the dismissal an exclusively private act?

4.5 It is arguable that the dismissal is not exclusively a private act as defined. As the local authority dismissed the client because he could not continue to work in the position which he held without contravention of s 28 of LGA 1988,[6]

---

1 An interesting dichotomy is made between direct and indirect horizontal effect: 'The "Horizontal Effect" of the Human Rights Act' by Murray Hunt [1998] PL, at 423. His view is that the Act is not intended to have direct horizontal effect but that the court is obliged to act compatibly with the Convention in administering justice between private litigants, thus rendering an indirect horizontal effect of the Convention.

2 Professor Sir William Wade QC states that s 6 incorporates the Convention rights as equally applicable in all proceedings, in the same sweeping way as the European Union law is incorporated by s 2 of the European Communities Act 1972: 'Opinion: Human Rights and Judiciary' [1998] EHRLR 5 at 525.

3 ERA 1996, s 111(2)(a).

4 By s 6(1) and (3)(b): It is unlawful for a public authority to act in a way which is incompatible with one or more of the Convention rights; public authority includes any person certain of whose functions are functions of a public nature.

5 Section 6(5) of the Human Rights Act 1998.

6 Section 28 of the 1998 Act provides:
   'A local authority shall not –
   (a)   intentionally promote homosexuality or publish material with the intention of

the local authority in dismissing the client was acting in furtherance of a statutory public duty and carrying out a public function. If the dismissal was not a private act, the statutory provisions should be construed as widely as possible in favour of the employee. In determining whether the act complained of is a public or private act, the following should be considered.

(1) Each case should be determined on its own facts.

(2) Does the act complained of have a statutory underpinning?

(3) Are important points of public law involved?

(4) Does the act affect a wider group of people than the victim in question?

(5) What is the nature of the public body?

(6) What is the nature of the act complained of? If it contravenes one of the fundamental rights, it is more likely to be a public act.[1]

(7) What is the nature of the injury or damage suffered by the victim?[2]

(8) Was the act carried out by or on behalf of religious bodies? If so, it may well be a private act.

(9) Is the act exclusively private in nature?

If the dismissal is a private act, should the Convention apply horizontally?

4.6 Even if the local authority is not a public authority under the Act, the client may argue that the tribunal, being a public authority under the Act,[3] should act compatibly with the Convention. Any reliance by the local authority on s 28 of LGA 1988 to justify the dismissal will have to be scrutinised against the client's Convention rights, namely, Article 10. It could be argued that a defence under s 28 should not be available because if the tribunal were to allow such a defence to be relied upon, it would itself be acting contrary to Article 10 and possibly Article 8. Put simply, a dismissal based on s 28 may not be justified in circumstances where the client has sought to exercise his freedom of expression in imparting information to pupils about homosexuality.

The local authority may argue that it could not have acted differently and that it was not acting unlawfully in giving effect to s 28 of LGA 1988.[4]

Time-limits

4.7 If the act complained of is not exclusively private in nature, then the local authority must act in a way which is compatible with the Convention.[5] This means that the victim may bring proceedings against the authority under the Act and rely on the Convention rights in the employment tribunal proceed-

PART 4
CASE STUDY

---

      promoting homosexuality;

    (b)   promote the teaching in any maintained school of the acceptability of homosexuality as a pretended family relationship.'

1   This is because the public body has a duty to act compatibly with the Convention rights. Much will depend on the weight to be attached to the particular right infringed, for example restraint of free speech particularly in a political context may well be said to amount to a public act.

2   A person whose rights may be infringed in future is not excluded if the public body proposes to act in a particular way in the future: s 7(1).

3   Section 6(1) of the Act.

4   Section 6(2) of the Act.

5   Section 6(1).

ings.[1] The time-limit for bringing the Convention proceedings is one year beginning with the date on which the act complained of took place, although the employment tribunal has a discretion to allow a longer period if it considers it equitable having regard to all the circumstances, subject to the time-limits imposed under the employment legislation.[2] It is advisable to bring the Convention complaint at the same time as the claim for unfair dismissal. If judicial review is used to bring a claim under the Act, the three-month time-limit will apply.

Establishing that the client is a victim

4.8   The client may invoke the Convention rights in the employment tribunal if he can demonstrate that he is a victim for the purposes of the Convention.[3] A person can properly claim to be a 'victim' of an interference with the exercise of his rights under the Convention if he has been directly affected by the matters allegedly constituting the interference. There is also scope for arguing before the employment tribunal that the infringement of the Convention rights in this case permits a free-standing complaint under s 6 of the Act, independent of any complaint that may be brought under the employment legislation.

The Convention arguments and pleadings in a horizontal claim

4.9   In addition to the usual domestic arguments that the dismissal of the client is unfair under the employment legislation, in this particular case the following Convention arguments will arise for consideration.

(1) The client was dismissed for distributing literature amongst pupils concerning homosexuality and for expressing views on this subject. The dismissal is contrary to Article 10(1) of the Convention in that it infringes freedom of expression and freedom to impart information. The dismissal does not have aims that are legitimate under Article 10(2) and it is not necessary in a democratic society.[4]

(2) There is a duty not to discriminate under Article 14 read in conjunction with Article 2 of the First Protocol. The duty not to discriminate against teachers in relation to educating and teaching pupils about homosexuality is clearly arguable on grounds that the discrimination is based on expressing particular opinions.

(3) Any reservation contained in Article 2 of the First Protocol should be construed narrowly, particularly if it seeks to infringe fundamental human rights, in this case the livelihood of the teacher.[5]

---

1   Section 7(1). At present, there are no rules in force to ensure that the tribunal can provide a remedy: s 7(11). The employment tribunal is a creature of statute and its remedies are currently limited: ERA 1996, s 205. It is still arguable that even in the absence of rules there is an independent or free-standing right conferred by s 6(1) on tribunals to apply the Convention and have regard to the powers of remedies in s 8.

2   The time-limits in s 111 of ERA 1996 apply only to complaints brought under this Act and not to Convention complaints: ERA 1996, s 205.

3   Section 7(7).

4   See the case-law under Article 10 at **4.15**.

5   Article 8 (private life). See *Holley v Smith* [1998] 1 All ER 866: exceptions must be narrowly interpreted; the necessity for any restrictions must be convincingly established: *The Observer*

The nature of the tribunal's investigative power

4.10   First, the employment tribunal will not only be concerned to establish whether the dismissal is within the range of reasonable responses of a reasonable employer,[1] but must also go on to consider for itself the primary facts which are alleged to constitute an infringement of the Convention rights, in order to assess whether the decision actually taken by the employer falls within a band of reasonable responses. This is because the tribunal has to act compatibly with the Convention[2] and it will not suffice for the tribunal to limit its investigation, where Convention rights are infringed, to whether the dismissal was within the range of reasonable responses. Not to do so may infringe the Convention and the Act.[3] There might be instances where a tribunal will allow a certain margin of appreciation or discretion in the decision-maker if the decision is based on the use of resources or operational reasons or medical or clinical judgements.[4]

Secondly, if it is established that there has been an infringement of the Convention right, the tribunal will have to apply the 'proportionality test'[5] to determine whether the dismissal, which contravenes the Convention in material respects, is fair. The proportionality test and the *Wednesbury* test are not coterminous.[6] Proportionality requires the domestic court or tribunal to judge the necessity of the action taken as well as whether it was within the range of courses of action that could reasonably be followed. Proportionality can therefore be a more exacting test in some circumstances.

Thirdly, the tribunal must first find the facts which contravene the Convention rights and in doing so it will have to make primary findings of fact. This examination is not limited to whether the employer mistakenly believed that there was no infringement of the Convention. The tribunal will also have to establish which Convention rights are engaged. The nature of the Convention rights infringed are important. For example, a breach of Article 3 is more

PART 4
CASE STUDY

---

and Guardian v UK (1991) Series A No 216, 14 EHRR 153 at 191, para 59. See also *Campbell and Cosans v UK* (1982) Series A No 48, 4 EHRR 293, para 37.

1   *Conlin v United Distilleries* [1994] IRLR 169.
2   Section 6(1).
3   Articles 6 and 13.
4   *R v Chief Constable, ex parte ITF Ltd* [1998] 3 WLR 1260 at 1268F–H (HL(E)); *James v UK* (1986) Series A No 98, 8 EHRR 123.
5   (a) The measures adopted must be carefully designed to achieve the objective in question. They must not be arbitrary, unfair or based on irrational considerations. The measures must be rationally connected to the objective.
    (b) The means, even if rationally connected to the objective, should interfere as little as possible with the right or freedom in question.
    (c) There must be proportionality between the effects of the measure and the objective which has been identified as of sufficient importance: see *R v Oakes* (1986) 26 DR 200 at 227–228.
6   *R v Chief Constable, ex parte ITF Ltd* (E) [1998] 3 WLR 1260 at 1277B–C HL: in *Brind* [1991] 1 AC 696 the House treated *Wednesbury* reasonableness and proportionality as being different. Although in some ways they are, the distinction between the two tests in practice is in any event much less than is sometimes suggested. The cautious way in which the Court usually applies this test, recognising the importance of respecting the national authority's margin of appreciation, may mean that whichever test is adopted, and even allowing for a difference in onus, the result is the same. See 1288H–1289E.

serious in that the rights thereunder are absolute. Other Articles (such as Articles 8 to 11 and Article 1 of the First Protocol do not confer absolute rights.

Fourthly, the tribunal will have to embark upon a judgment for itself having regard to the principle of proportionality. In this regard, the tribunal will have to review the decision of the employer against the background information. At this juncture, it is particularly important for the tribunal to have regard to the 'margin of appreciation' precisely because the tribunal is not itself the decision-maker.[1]

Finally, the tribunal will have to consider the nature of the Convention right which is alleged to have been infringed in order to determine the nature of the scrutiny to be applied. In this particular case, as it is alleged that Articles 8, 10 and 14 are contravened, the following factors ought to be considered:

(1) a balance has to be struck between the employee's interests and those of the employer in abiding by any statutory provisions;

(2) whether there are any social, legislative, economic or political considerations which favour one view as opposed to another.[2] In this regard, practitioners are advised to obtain as much information as possible in the form of affidavits from specialist organisations, academics, writers, experts or such bodies which might be able to contribute specialist views on social policies;[3]

(3) regard must be taken of the legislative purpose of the statutory provisions in question, but where fundamental rights are engaged (eg liberty, livelihood or freedom of speech) the tribunal must scrutinise the measure adopted carefully and anxiously and act compatibly with the Convention;

(4) in deciding whether a dismissal or some other action short of dismissal is proportionate to the legitimate aim pursued, a tribunal may have to examine the nature of the freedom of expression (was it political or was it a genuine imparting of educational information), the nature of the job and the potential damage done to an employer's own fundamental rights.

---

1   *R v Chief Constable, ex parte ITF Ltd* [1997] 3 WLR 132 at 149C, CA. See also 'Principles of interpretation of Convention rights under the Human Rights Act and the discretionary area of judgment' by David Panick QC [1998] PL 545 at 548. 'The doctrine of margin of appreciation does not apply when a national court is considering the Human Rights Act. However, a similar doctrine should be recognised by the courts ... national courts will accept that there are circumstances in which the legislature and the executive are better placed to perform those functions. The manner in which the domestic court exercises its responsibilities will depend on the nature of the dispute ... There are circumstances in which the court will defer to the opinion of the legislature, executive or other relevant person or body.'

2   In order to maintain the balance between the individual and society as a whole, rigid and inflexible standards should not be imposed on the legislature's attempt to resolve the difficult and intransigent problems with which society is faced when seeking to deal with serious crime: *Hong Kong v Lee Kwong-kut* [1993] AC 951 at 975A–G.

3   If the Convention were to be made part of our domestic law, then in the exercise of the primary jurisdiction the court (occupying, for it, a relatively novel constitutional position) might well ask for more material than the adversarial system normally provides, such as a 'Brandeis brief': *R v MOD, ex parte Smith* [1996] QB 517 at 564F.

Article 10 – freedom of expression

4.11 In this case, the following matters need to be considered both from the employers' and employees' point of view and a fair balance has to be struck between the competing considerations.

(1) Is the interference in question prescribed by law?

4.12 The answer to this is clearly yes, because the employer is acting in accordance with the terms of the contract that he will dismiss the employee for conduct which affects the employer's business. The actions of the employee in teaching pupils about homosexuality contravenes s 28 of the 1988 Act.[1] The expression 'law' covers not only statute, but also common law.[2]

(2) Does the interference have aims which are legitimate under Article 10(2)?

4.13 In this regard, the employer will contend that the dismissal does pursue legitimate aims under Article 10(2), namely the protection of the morals of its pupils. The employee will seek to argue that none of the restrictions contained in Article 10(2) apply and that, in any case, the restrictions contained in Article 10(2) must be convincingly established because of the importance of the fundamental right of freedom of expression.

(3) Is the dismissal necessary in a democratic society?

4.14 It is this area which requires a careful balancing exercise to be undertaken by a tribunal. In deciding whether the dismissal is proportionate to the legitimate aim pursued, a tribunal may have to examine:

(a) the nature of the freedom of expression (in this case the employee will contend that he was expressing his political or genuine beliefs that homosexuality is to be treated no differently than heterosexuality);

(b) the nature of the employee's job and the potential damage done to an employer's own fundamental rights (the employer may well argue that the school will lose parental support and trust if the employee is allowed to continue teaching pupils about homosexuality and this for example constitutes a breach of Article 1 of the First Protocol);

(c) the duties and responsibilities and nature of the particular employment; an employee's freedom of expression may well have to be curtailed because it conflicts with the nature of his duties;[3]

---

1 Section 98(2)(c) of ERA 1996: the employee could not continue to work in the position which he held without contravention on the part of the employer of a duty imposed by s 28 of the Local Government Act 1988.

2 See *Tolstoy Miloslavsky v UK* (1995) Series A No 323, 20 EHRR 442, para 37: the expression first requires that the impugned measures should have a basis in domestic law. A law which confers a discretion is not in itself inconsistent with this requirement, provided that the scope of the discretion and the manner of its exercise are indicated with sufficient clarity, having regard to the legitimate aim in question, to give the individual adequate protection against arbitrary interference.

3 *Van der Heijden v The Netherlands* (1985) 41 DR 264: the dismissal of an employee working for an immigration institution because of being a member of a political organisation hostile to immigrant workers was justified; see also *X v UK* (1979) 16 DR 101: a dismissal of a teacher employed by a non-denominational school for expressing religious beliefs was justified.

(d) whether the employee's freedom of expression was concerned with matters of public concern rather than private matters; if so then it is more likely than not that dismissal or a sanction may not be justified;[1]

(e) whether the freedom of expression was abusive or gross; if so, the action taken against such an employee may well be justified;[2]

(f) whether the expressions of the employee are based on evidence or made in good faith.

Case-law

4.15 The tribunal must have regard to the court's case-law on this subject when examining the complaint of unfair dismissal.[3]

Tribunal's power with regard to Convention rights

4.16 The tribunal does not have the power to declare the statutory provision as being incompatible with the Convention.[4] An attempt should be made to persuade the tribunal that the statutory provision (s 28 of the 1988 Act), should be interpreted in such a way as to make it compatible with Convention rights. It could also be argued that in this case there is no statutory bar on an employee teaching pupils about homosexuality particularly if the teaching does not seek to encourage pupils to engage in any proscribed sexual practice. The employer, on the other hand, will seek to argue that s 28 of the 1988 Act should be construed in accordance with its own fundamental rights (Articles 1 and 2 of the First Protocol). The tribunal has to choose an interpretation between these two competing rights. This is clear from the wording of s 3 of the Act, which provides that the legislation must be read and given effect in a way which is compatible with *the* Convention rights and not *merely* one individual's Convention rights.

If the tribunal is unable to interpret the statutory provisions compatibly with the Convention rights then it does not have power to make a declaration of incompatibility. Depending on the nature of the claim, it might be possible to seek an adjournment of the proceedings and seek leave to move for judicial review to challenge the validity of the statutory provisions under the Act.[5] The other alternative is to request the tribunal to express a view as to the compatibility of the statutory provision in question and to then pursue an appeal to the appropriate higher court for a declaration of incompatibility.[6] There is an important decision to make here:

---

1   *Barthold v FRG* (1985) Series A No 90, 7 EHRR 383: proceedings against an employee for informing the public via a newspaper article about the veterinary services at a time when there was public concern was unjustified.

2   In *Grigoriades v Greece* (1995) 20 EHRR CD 92 the Commission declared the complaint admissible notwithstanding that the article against the army was venomous.

3   Section 2(1) of the Act and see Part 2, Article 10.

4   Section 4(1)(5). A tribunal may grant such relief or remedy, or make such order, within its powers as it considers just and appropriate: s 8(1).

5   See below.

6   In this case the Court of Appeal: s 4(5).

(1) if a declaration of incompatibility is sought in judicial review proceedings then it should be remembered that, like all declarations, it will be discretionary;[1]

(2) if a statutory right of appeal is pursued to the Court of Appeal on a point of law then it is arguable that the Court on such an appeal does not have the residual discretion which it has on an application for judicial review to limit the circumstances in which it grants leave or relief;[2]

(3) if the declaration of incompatibility will not benefit the victim, there might be difficulties in obtaining legal aid;

(4) if the tribunal expresses a view that the statutory provision is incompatible with the Convention right, the Employment Appeal Tribunal (EAT) may be persuaded to grant leave to appeal on a point of law because:

  (a) a person may rely on the Convention rights in any legal proceedings;[3]

  (b) a complaint that a statutory provision is incompatible with the Convention right ought to be treated as a point of law on appeal even though the EAT may not make a declaration of incompatibility;[4] otherwise a victim may never proceed to the Court of Appeal seeking a declaration of incompatibility in an employment context;

  (c) if a person succeeds in his claim before a tribunal on non-Convention grounds that the dismissal was unfair, then it might be difficult to continue proceedings either by way of judicial review or on appeal to the Court of Appeal on the grounds that the statutory provision is incompatible with Convention rights because he may cease to be a victim under the Act.[5]

Furthermore, if a case is adjourned before a tribunal pending a declaration of incompatibility by a superior court, advisers should be prepared to persuade a court to issue a declaration relating to the future of the case on the ground, for example, that a declaration would have a significant impact on the course of the proceedings and therefore a declaration relating to the incompatibility of the statutory provision is not academic or hypothetical.[6]

---

1 Section 4(4); it may make a declaration of that incompatibility. If the courts were to undermine the principle of *ultra vires* by making it discretionary, no victim of an excess or abuse of power could be sure that the law would protect him: *Bugg v DPP* [1993] QB 473 at 499–500.

2 See, for example, *Mallinson v Secretary of State for Social Security* [1994] 1 WLR 630 at 638H, HL.

3 Section 7(1)(b), (6).

4 Section 21(1) of the Employment Tribunals Act 1996.

5 Article 25 (now Article 34) does not permit individuals to complain against a law in abstract because they felt that it contravened the Convention. It does not suffice for an applicant to claim that the mere existence of a law violated his rights under the Convention. The law must be applied to his detriment. A law might, however, violate the rights of an individual if he was directly affected by the law in the absence of any specific measure of implementation: *Klass and Others v FRG* (1978) Series A No 28, 2 EHRR 214, para 33. Article 25 entitles an individual to contend that a law violates his rights by itself in the absence of an individual measure of implementation: *Marckx v Belgium* (1979) Series A No 31, 2 EHRR 330, para 27.

6 See, for example, *Mercury Ltd v Telecommunications Director* [1996] 1 WLR 48 at 59 (HL(E)). A declaration may be given if the question is not entirely academic or hypothetical.

Tribunal must give reasons for its decision

4.17   What the tribunal has to do is to look at the dismissal complained of in the light of the case as a whole and determine whether it was 'proportionate to the legitimate aim pursued' (whether the employer's decision to dismiss was proportionate to the employer's behaviour) and whether the reasons given by the employer to justify its act are 'relevant and sufficient'. In this regard the tribunal has to satisfy itself that the employer has applied standards which conform with the principles contained in Articles 8, 10, etc and that the decision was based on an acceptable assessment of the relevant facts. Thus, it is important to stress to the tribunal that the reasons for its decision are set out comprehensively. Reasons should be stated with sufficient clarity as that is one of the factors which makes it possible for a person to exercise the rights of appeal.[1] Article 6(1) imposes an obligation on the court to provide reasons for its decision.[2]

Damages

4.18   Compensation for an infringement of the Convention may be awarded only by a court or tribunal which has power to award damages.[3] If the tribunal finds that the dismissal violates Articles 8 and 10 of the Convention, it is arguable that under its current statutory structure it has power to award damages for breach of the Convention under the Act since it is adjudicating a civil dispute.[4] Such a view is consistent with Article 13 of the Convention.[5]

However, the Minister may make rules to enable the tribunal to award compensation under the employment legislation.[6]

In awarding compensation the tribunal must take into account the principles applied by the European Court in relation to the award of compensation under Article 41.[7] Damages may be awarded for:

(1)   pecuniary and non-pecuniary loss;

---

1   *Hadjianastassiou v Breece* (1992) 16 EHRR 219 at 237.
2   *Van de Hurk v The Netherlands* (1994) 18 EHRR 481 at 501. See *Stefan v GMC* [1999] 1 WLR 1239 at 1299A–H. The reasons should be adequate: *Norton Tool Co Ltd v Tewson* [1973] 1 WLR 45 at 49.
3   Section 8(2).
4   Under s 123(1) of the Employment Rights Act 1996, the tribunal has power to award compensatory damages in such amount which it considers just and equitable in all the circumstances. Thus, it is arguable that it has power to award damages in civil proceedings for the purposes of s 8(2) of the Human Rights Act 1998.
5   Article 13 has been omitted from the Human Rights Act 1998. This Article provides that everyone whose Convention rights have been violated shall have an effective remedy before a domestic court. Article 13 may still be relied upon by an individual in certain circumstances notwithstanding its absence from the Act. See **1.3**.
6   Section 7(11) of the Act.
7   Previously Article 50. Note that damages under s 9(3) in respect of a judicial act done in good faith is available to compensate a person to the extent required by Article 5(5) of the Convention. A 'right to damages for violation of a Convention right per se could conceivably be extended further, to impose a constitutional liability on the Crown for loss or injury caused by the failure of the law which the State administers to respect the rights contained in the Act': see 'Remedies for Violations of Convention Rights under the Human Rights Act' by David Feldman [1998] EHRLR 6 at 702.

(2) anxiety and distress;[1]

(3) a violation of the Convention rights;

(4) loss of liberty – such as excessive periods of incarceration;

(5) physical assaults;[2]

(6) damage to land;[3]

(7) loss of business opportunities;[4]

(8) interest on late payments.[5]

Damages may not be available in the following circumstances:

(1) those who have committed serious offences;[6]

(2) if the breach of the Convention right is minimal or only procedural in nature.[7]

Costs and expenses which are actually and necessarily incurred and reasonable are recoverable[8] on an equitable basis. However, costs in the employment tribunal are only recoverable in exceptional circumstances.[9]

In claiming damages in the employment tribunal, a clear distinction ought to be drawn between the more favourable domestic principles applying to the award of damages and the Convention principles in the same area. There is no clear formula which can be derived from the Convention jurisprudence in awarding damages. Damages are awarded on an equitable basis. Thus, for example, damages for injury to feelings in sex and race discrimination cases are more ostensibly favourable under domestic principles than damages awarded in respect of the same subject matter in the Convention cases. A complainant must ensure that separate heads of damages are claimed for violation of the Convention in addition to a claim for injury to feelings and or aggravated damages. In this case, therefore, the client should seek not only damages for loss of wages and injury to feelings if possible, but also damages for breach of Articles 8 and 10 of the Convention.[10]

PART 4
CASE STUDY

---

1   *López Ostra v Spain* 20 EHRR 277 (about £1,000).

2   *Ribitsch v Austria* (1996) Series A No 336, 21 EHRR 573; and *A v UK* (100/1997/884/1096) has been decided by the European Court. The States' obligation to take measures designed to ensure individuals (and schools for that matter) will not be ill-treated in breach of Article 3 by other individuals and that children are entitled to protection, through effective deterrence, against such treatment. The European Court awarded the applicant in this case a sum of £10,000 by way of just satisfaction in respect of non-pecuniary damages (para 33).

3   *Hentrich v France* (1994) Series A No 269-A, 21 EHRR 199.

4   *Allenet de Ribemont v France* (1995) Series A No 308, 20 EHRR 557.

5   *Schuler-Zgraggen v Switzerland* (1993) Series A No 263, 21 EHRR 404. After 1 April 1990, tribunals were empowered to award interest: Industrial Tribunals (Interest) Order 1990, SI 1990/479.

6   *Jamil v France* (1996) 21 EHRR 65; and *McCann v UK* (1995) Series A No 324, 21 EHRR 97, para 219 (since the terrorist suspects had been intending to plant a bomb in Gibraltar, the Court did not consider it appropriate to award financial compensation).

7   *Schmautzer v Austria* (1995) Series A No 328-A, 21 EHRR 573.

8   *McCann v UK* (1996) Series A No 324, 21 EHRR 97, para 220.

9   Eg where 'a party has, in bringing or conducting the proceedings, acted frivolously, vexatiously, abusively, disruptively or otherwise unreasonably': Industrial Tribunals (Constitution and Rules of Procedure) Regulations 1993, SI 1993/2687, Sch 1, para 12(1).

10   *López Ostra v Spain* (1995) Series A No 303-C, 20 EHRR 277. Damages had been awarded for violation of Article 8. There was no precise quantification of the heads of damages, but an overall sum of £16,000 was awarded for breach of Article 8.

VERTICAL CHALLENGE AND PRINCIPLES OF CONSTRUCTION

Principles of interpretation

4.19   So far as it is possible to do so, s 28 of the 1988 Act must be read and given effect in a way which is compatible with the Convention rights. The basic principles of interpretation may be summarised as follows.

(1)   There is a strong presumption that those statutes which post-date the Act are intended to be compatible with the Convention rights.[1] Those statutes which pre-date the Act are to be interpreted in accordance with the Act.

(2)   Section 3 will require an 'innovative approach'. Even if there is no ambiguity, the provision will have to be interpreted as far as possible consistently with the Convention unless there is a clear limitation expressed in the provision or statute.

(3)   The emphasis is on what is 'possible' rather than what is 'reasonable'.[2]

(4)   The Convention is a living instrument which must be interpreted in the light of present-day conditions.[3] Certain terms which have originated from the well-established common law background against which the Act was passed might have to be examined in light of the common law and the Convention as a living instrument.

(5)   Construction of statutory provisions which contravene human rights and freedoms gives rise to a presumption of constitutionality and in construing constitutional provisions a liberal,[4] generous and purposive approach is required.[5]

(6)   Legal provisions which interfere with individual rights must be formulated with sufficient precision to enable the citizen to regulate his conduct.[6] The critical question then is whether the proposed interpretation provides a rule sufficiently precise to enable a citizen to regulate his conduct, particularly if the consequence of his actions may lead to criminal prosecution. One principle which has to be observed here is legal certainty.[7] If the proposed interpretation remains too wide in its

---

1   Particularly where the minister has made a statement of compatibility: s 19 of the Act.

2   The Lord Chancellor has stated that s 3(1) will require an innovative approach. If there is no ambiguity, the provision will have to be interpreted consistently with the Convention unless a clear limitation is expressed. However, in *de Freitas v Ministry of Agriculture* [1998] 3 WLR 675 at 681H, PC: 'while it may be justifiable on occasion to imply words into a statute where there is an ambiguity or an omission and the implied words are necessary to remedy such a defect'. If the courts were to hold that more marginal claims of right should enjoy the protection of a rigorous rule of statutory construction not applied in contexts save that of the protection of fundamental rights and freedoms, they would impermissibly confine the powers of the elected legislature: *R v Lord Chancellor, ex parte Lightfoot* [1999] 2 WLR 1126 at 1136H.

3   *Tyrer v UK* (1978) Series A No 26, 2 EHRR 1, para 31.

4   *Attorney-General of the Gambia v Momodou Jobe* [1984] AC 689; and *Minister of Home Affairs v Fisher* [1980] AC 319.

5   *Attorney-General of Hong Kong v Lee Kwong-kut* [1993] AC 951 at 966D–E per Lord Woolf.

6   *G v FRG* Application No 13079/87, (1989) 60 DR 256 at 261: legal provisions which interfere with individual rights must be formulated with sufficient precision to enable the citizen to regulate his conduct.

7   *de Freitas v Ministry of Agriculture* [1998] 3 WLR 675 at 682D, PC.

scope and possible application then this will militate against such an interpretation.[1]

(7) If the reading down of the statutory provision produces an entirely different provision from that which Parliament enacted, such a construction should not be utilised.[2]

(8) Any restriction on the guaranteed right of freedom of expression or other constitutional rights must be narrowly interpreted.[3]

(9) In interpreting the Convention, the courts seek, given the provisions of the Convention, to give the 'fullest weight and effect consistent with the language used and with the rest of the text'.

(10) The English courts should, like the ECJ, apply a teleological rather than a historical method to the interpretation of the Convention. The ECJ seeks to give effect to what it conceives to be the spirit rather than the letter of the Treaties.[4] Therefore, it is suggested that the correct approach and order should be to firstly determine the spirit then the general scheme and finally the wording of the provision. But even in this context the exercise must still be one of construction and it should not exceed the limits of what is reasonable.[5]

(11) More than one Convention right may inform the interpretation of the legislation in question and a balanced view should prevail between the competing rights.

(12) The Convention is not intended to guarantee rights which are theoretical or illusory, but rights which are practical and effective.[6]

(13) The courts must take account of all statutory provisions so as to ensure, wherever possible, that the result prescribed by the Convention rights is attained. This duty applies as regards not only legislation specifically introduced in order to implement the Convention rights but also other

PART 4
CASE STUDY

---

1   *Broadrick v Oklahoma* (1973) 413 US 601 at 432–433.

2   'In the final analysis, a law that is invalid in so many of its applications will, as a result of wholesale reading down, bear little resemblance to the law that Parliament passed and a strong inference arises that it is invalid as a whole ... In my opinion, it is Parliament that should determine how the section should be redrafted and not the court': as per Sopinka J in *Osborne v Canada (Treasury Board)* (1991) 82 DLR (4th) 321 at 347.

    'The real question is whether what remains is so inextricably bound up with the part declared invalid that what remains cannot independently survive or, as it has sometimes been put, whether on a fair review of the whole matter it can be assumed that the legislature would have enacted what survives without enacting the part that is ultra vires at all': *Attorney-General of the Gambia v Momodou Jobe* [1984] AC 689 at 703.

3   *Observer and Guardian v UK* (1991) Series A No 216, 14 EHRR 153 at 191.

4   *Henn and Darby v DPP* [1981] AC 850 at 892 per Lord Diplock which was concerned with the interpretation of the EC Treaty and also see *Van Gend en Loos* Case 26/62 [1963] ECR 1: to ascertain whether the provisions of an international treaty extend so far in their effects it is necessary to consider the spirit, the general scheme and the wording of those provisions.

5   The adoption of a construction which departs boldly from the ordinary meaning of the language of the statute is, however, particularly appropriate where the validity of legislation has to be tested against the provisions of European law. In that context, it is appropriate to strain to give effect to the design and purpose behind the legislation, and to give weight to the spirit rather than the letter. But even in this context the exercise must still be one of construction and it should not exceed the limits of what is reasonable: *Clarke v Kato* [1998] 1 WLR 1647 at 1656A–B.

6   *Airey v Ireland* (1979) Series A No 32, 2 EHRR 305 at 314, para 24.

statutory provisions, including those enacted before the Human Rights Act 1998.[1]

(14) Reading words into statutory provisions is more difficult because it would require judges to choose specific words to add to the gaps in the statutory provision.[2] In choosing between reading specific words into the statutory provision or making a declaration of incompatibility the following factors are important.

(a) Could it be assumed that Parliament would have enacted the suggested missing words in that specific statutory context?

(b) Would Parliament have chosen to include these missing words rather than having no such legislation at all?

(c) Are the suggested missing words sufficiently precise and clear to be read into the statutory provision to enable it to be applied consistently and fairly and to enable the citizen to regulate his conduct?[3]

(d) Does the choice of missing words involve consideration of complex social and political matters?[4]

(e) Do the missing words create a substantial change in the traditional, social, religious, public, philosophical or legal institution?

(f) Do the missing words interfere with the legitimate object and purpose of the statutory provision and if so is the interference major or minimal?

(g) If the words are read into the statutory provision, will this interfere with the central purpose of the whole Act in question?

(h) Would the missing words to be read into the statutory provision have an adverse impact on others or lead to excessive public expenditure?

(i) Is reading words into the statutory provision a better choice than a declaration of incompatibility?

(j) Do the missing words impact on fundamental rights?

(k) Are the missing words warranted in order to ensure that they reflect societal changes, keep abreast with scientific developments and remain in line with present-day conditions?[5]

(l) Is the statutory provision in question the subject of an amendment?

---

1 The same approach found in the European Court of Justice's jurisprudence should apply: 'When applying national law, whether adopted before or after the Directive, the national court that has to interpret that law must do so, as far as possible, in the light of the wording and the purpose of the Directive, so as to achieve the result that it has in view and thereby comply with the third paragraph of Article 189 of the EC Treaty'.
See *Silhouette International v Harlauer* [1998] 3 WLR 1218 at 1232G and 1238G–H.

2 *de Freitas v Ministry of Agriculture* [1998] 3 WLR 675 at 683F, PC.

3 See Canadian case of *Schachter v Canada* [1992] 2 SCR 679; 93 DLR (4th) 1 at DLR 11 and an incisive article by Mary Childs 'Constitutional Review and Underinclusive Legislation' [1998] PL at 647.

4 *Quilter v A-G* [1998] 1 NZLR 523: the term marriage applies to opposite-sex and not same-sex marriages and there was no discrimination in confining marriage to opposite-sex couples.

5 See *Inze v Austria* (1987) Series A No 126, 10 EHRR 394.

(m) Is it appropriate to add words by way of modification of the meaning of a statutory expression in order to find a construction consistent with European law?[1]

(n) Would Parliament prefer no human rights on the particular subject?

(o) A constitution embodies fundamental rights and freedoms, not their particular expression at the time of the enactment. Its terms must be broadly interpreted and the meaning and content of a clause or phrase should not be immutably fixed at the date the constitution came into force.[2]

Applying the above principles to the construction of s 28 of the 1988 Act, it is necessary to consider whether it is possible to construe this provision consistently with Article 10 of the Convention.[3]

The applicant may submit that s 28 of the Local Government Act 1988 is not to be interpreted as justifying the dismissal of a teacher for expressing his genuine views on homosexuality in a classroom, but concerns the promotion of teaching methods generally.

The respondent may submit that the teaching of homosexuality by the teacher in the classroom contravened s 28 which clearly justifies the dismissal of the teacher.

If it is linguistically possible to interpret the provision in the way advanced by each party, particularly if it means redefining the provision so as to make the meaning advanced unreasonable, then this interpretation should not be adopted and a declaration of incompatibility may have to be resorted to in judicial review proceedings. If it is possible to interpret the provision consistently with the Convention rights, but the effect is to fully distort the true meaning of the provision as examined against the statutory scheme, then the court may refuse to interpret the provision in the manner suggested if this were to emasculate the provision of any sensible or practical effect. In short, the court may refuse to adopt a formulated interpretation if it produces an altogether different provision from that which Parliament enacted.[4] The only remedy is to then seek a declaration of incompatibility.

Consideration of consistency with Convention rights

4.20 If the tribunal considers that the applicant's teaching of homosexuality falls within the terms of s 28 of the 1988 Act then it must go on to consider whether the restrictions imposed by this section are consistent with the freedom of expression (and other Convention rights) and whether they are reasonably required for the performance of the duties involved. Furthermore the restrictions must be reasonably justifiable in a democratic society.

---

1 *Clarke v Kato* [1998] 1 WLR 1647 at 1659H as was done in *Litster v Forth Dry Dock and Engineering Co Ltd* [1990] 1 AC 546.

2 *Thomas v Baptiste* [1999] 3 WLR 249 at 2619.

3 Section 3(1) of the Act.

4 *de Freitas v Ministry of Agriculture* [1998] 3 WLR 675 at 683C, PC: '... the principle that an enactment construed by severing, reading down of making implications into what the legislature has actually said should take a form which it could reasonably be supposed that Parliament intended to enact'.

If the tribunal does not accept the construction advanced by the applicant in this case then it will have to consider whether s 28 does impose restrictions on the applicant which are reasonably required for the proper performance of his functions as a teacher and whether the restrictions are reasonably justifiable. The considerations which are relevant to this enquiry are as follows.

(1) Is there an absolute prohibition on the freedom of expression in the class-room (eg the restrictions are not universal and relate only to matters dealing with homosexuality)?[1]
(2) Are the attendant restrictions on the right of freedom of expression inherent with the job?[2]
(3) Is the particular freedom of expression concerned with matters of public concern or private matters?
(4) Are the expressions gross or abusive or educational in content (dismissal action taken against abusive or gross conduct may well be justified)?[3]
(5) Were the expressions made in good faith?[4]
(6) Are the morals of the pupils likely to be corrupted?

Is the restriction on the freedom of expression reasonably justifiable in a democratic society?

4.21 Even if the tribunal is satisfied that the restriction imposed by s 28 was reasonably required for the proper performance of teachers' functions, it will have to consider whether such restriction is reasonably justifiable in a democratic society.

The following principles arise for consideration here:
(1) the burden is on the person asserting that it is justifiable;
(2) the restriction must be demonstrably justified in a free and democratic society;[5]
(3) whether the legislative objective is sufficiently important to justify limiting a fundamental right such as freedom of expression;
(4) whether the measures adopted to meet the legislative purpose or objective are rationally connected to it;
(5) whether the means used to impair the right or freedom are no more than necessary to accomplish the objective. This means that any restrictions on the guaranteed right of freedom of expression must be proportionate to the aims sought to be achieved.[6]

---

1   The freedom of expression can be exercised without restraint other than in matters set out in s 28 of LGA 1988: *Council of Civil Service Union v UK* Application No 11603/85, (1987) 50 DR 228.

2   *Morissen v Belgium* (1988) 56 DR 127: the suspension of a teacher without pay for exercising her freedom of expression was reasonably justified for the protection of other teachers and the establishment.

3   In *Grigoriades v Greece* (1995) 20 EHRR CD 92 the Commission declared the complaint admissible notwithstanding that the article against the army was venomous.

4   For a more detailed commentary on freedom of expression in Article 10, see Part 2, Article 10.

5   *de Freitas v Ministry of Agriculture* [1998] 3 WLR 675 at 684, PC.

6   *James v UK* (1986) Series A No 98, 8 EHRR 123 at 145; *A-G v Guardian Newspapers Ltd (No 2)* [1990] 1 AC 109 at 283–4 per Lord Goff.

In this case, the tribunal will have to consider whether s 28 applies a blanket restriction in all circumstances where teachers are penalised for teaching about homosexuality irrespective of the depth of information conveyed to the pupils (eg whether the restriction applies to all teachers irrespective of their grades).

Appeal to the Court of Appeal

4.22 An appeal to the Court of Appeal on a point of law from the EAT in respect of whether the restrictions imposed are consistent with the freedom of expression, are reasonably required for the performance of the duties involved, and are reasonably justifiable in a democratic society will be on limited grounds. Unless the tribunal or EAT has misdirected itself in law or otherwise fails to have proper regard to the relevant considerations in this field the Court of Appeal (like the EAT) is unlikely to interfere with the findings of the tribunal in this Convention context.

INVALIDITY (DECLARATION OF INCOMPATIBILITY) VERTICAL CHALLENGE

4.23 Only superior courts can make a declaration of incompatibility.[1] If the court is satisfied that primary legislation is incompatible with a Convention right then it may make a declaration of incompatibility.[2] If the court is satisfied that subordinate legislation is incompatible with the Convention and the enabling primary legislation prevents the removal of the incompatibility, it may make a declaration of that incompatibility.[3] But the declaration of the incompatibility does not affect the validity, continuing operation or enforcement of the provision and it is not binding on the parties to the proceedings.[4]

It appears that if the court is satisfied that a subordinate provision is incompatible with a Convention right, but that the enabling primary legislation does not prevent the removal of that incompatibility then the court may make a declaration of the incompatibility not under s 4 of the Act but either under its inherent jurisdiction[5] or under s 8(1) of the Act. Such a declaration is not made under s 4[6] and therefore will affect the validity, continuing operation and enforcement of the provision in question.

If the court is considering making a declaration of incompatibility then the relevant Minister of the Crown is entitled to notice under the rules of the court.[7] Notice may be given at any time during the proceedings.[8] It is advisable

PART 4 CASE STUDY

---

1   Section 4(5) of the Act.
2   Section 4(1)(2) of the Act.
3   Section 4(3)(4) of the Act.
4   Section 4(6) of the Act.
5   Because not to do so means that it will act incompatibly with its Convention obligation: s 6(1) of the Act.
6   See s 4(6).
7   Section 5(1) of the Act.
8   Section 5(3) of the Act.

to notify the relevant Minister as soon as judicial review proceedings are contemplated and seek his view as to whether he should be joined in as a party to the proceedings at an early stage.

In this case, it is important to remember that if a declaration is being sought that s 28 of the 1988 Act is incompatible with Article 10 then a choice has to be made whether to pursue this in the Court of Appeal via the statutory process or by way of judicial review.[1] The time-limit for bringing an application for judicial review proceedings is 'promptly and in any event within three months'.[2] The time-limit applying to a declaration of incompatibility appears to be one year beginning with the date on which the act complained of took place or such longer period as the court considers equitable having regard to all the circumstances.[3] This is because a declaration of incompatibility brought by a victim under the Act is in fact a complaint that a public authority has acted in a way which is made unlawful because it has acted incompatibly with a Convention right.

In this case, the principles which will arise in persuading the High Court to grant leave to move for judicial review on the grounds that s 28 of the 1988 Act is incompatible with Article 10 of the Convention are as follows:

(1) the applicant is a victim under the Act;[4]
(2) s 28 of the 1988 Act cannot be read and given effect in a way which is compatible with the applicant's freedom of expression under Article 10 of the Convention. There is no sensible formulation of words which can be read into the statutory provision which gives the applicant a right to exercise his fundamental right of freedom of expression;
(3) the fact that the applicant is a teacher does not justify a substantial invasion of his basic rights and freedoms;
(4) the blanket restriction imposed by this section affects all teachers irrespective of their grade and irrespective of the degree of information about homosexuality conveyed. Such a restriction is not only excessive, but is too wide in its scope and application. A teacher is left with no clear guidance as to the exercise of his freedom of expression;
(5) the interference is not justifiable.

---

1 *Thomas v Baptiste* [1999] 3 WLR 249 at 2619.
2 RSC Ord 53, r 4.
3 Section 7(1)(5) of the Act.
4 Section 7(1) of the Act.

4.24 PLEADINGS IN THE HIGH COURT (MODEL CLAIM)

There follows a model claim incorporating the facts and issues discussed above.

IN THE HIGH COURT OF JUSTICE
QUEEN'S BENCH DIVISION
CROWN OFFICE LIST
CO NO1234/99

R v THE ABC CITY COUNCIL (1) AND THE SECRETARY OF STATE FOR
THE DEPARTMENT OF ENVIRONMENT (2) EX PARTE XYZ

DECISION CHALLENGED

The compatibility of section 28 of the Local Government Act 1988 with the
Applicant's Convention rights under the Human Rights Act 1998. Section 28
provides:

A local authority shall not:

(a) intentionally promote homosexuality or publish material with the intention of promoting homosexuality;
(b) promote the teaching in any maintained school of the acceptability of
homosexuality as a pretended family relationship.

RELIEF SOUGHT

(1) A declaration under section 4 of the Human Rights Act that section 28 of
the Local Government Act 1988 is incompatible with the Applicant's
Convention rights in particular:

(i) section 28 of the 1988 Act is incompatible with Article 10 on its own or
read in conjunction with Article 2 of the First Protocol and Article 14
of the Convention set out in Schedule 1, Part I and Part II to the
Human Rights Act 1998.

(2) Damages: under section 8 of the Human Rights Act 1998. The Applicant
claims damages on the grounds that section 28 of the 1988 Act contravenes
her fundamental rights and as a consequence she has suffered loss and
damage including injury to feelings. The extent of her losses are set out in
her affidavit.

(3) Interest at such rate as the court considers appropriate in respect of any
award the court may make.

(4) Any other relief including costs.

(5) If permission to move for judicial review is given then an order for
expedition. The Applicant's claim for unfair dismissal before the industrial tribunal sitting at [   ] is adjourned pending this application for
judicial review.

PART 4
CASE STUDY

GROUNDS UPON WHICH RELIEF IS SOUGHT

(1) The first Respondent is a local authority and employer of the Applicant. For purposes of this application the first Respondent is a public authority as defined by section 6(1) of the Human Rights Act 1998 (the 1998 Act).

(2) The second Respondent is the relevant Minister of the Crown responsible for the enforcement of the Local Government Act 1988.

(3) The Applicant was employed as a teacher at the [   ] School which fell within the educational responsibilities of the first Respondent.

(4) On [*date*] the Applicant was dismissed by the first Respondent because the Applicant had been teaching pupils at the School about gays and lesbian relationships. The full facts leading to his dismissal and the reasons for the dismissal are set out in the Applicant's affidavit.

(5) The first Respondent dismissed the Applicant on the grounds that the performance of his duties contravened section 28 of the Local Government Act 1988. The first Respondent has alleged that in so dismissing the Applicant it has not acted unfairly and that it has acted in accordance with section 28. The first Respondent contends that it could not have acted differently given the terms of section 28 of the 1988 Act and that it was acting so as to give effect or enforce section 28.

(6) On [*date*] the Applicant submitted a claim to the Employment Tribunal sitting at [   ] for unfair dismissal.

(7) On the [*date*] the Employment Tribunal made a preliminary ruling that section 28 of the 1988 Act cannot be read or given effect in a way which is compatible with Article 10 of the Convention in Schedule 1 Part I to the 1998 Act and that the first Respondent has not acted in a way which is incompatible with Article 10 of the Convention: section 6(1)(2) of the 1998 Act. The Tribunal concluded that the first Respondent could not have acted differently solely because of the effect of section 28. The Tribunal's reasons for its preliminary decision is at page [   ] of the bundle.

(8) The Tribunal has adjourned the hearing for unfair dismissal pending this Application for Judicial Review.

(9) The Applicant seeks a declaration under section 4 of the 1998 Act that section 28 of the 1988 Act is incompatible with Article 10, Article 2 of the First Protocol and Article 14 of the Convention.

(10) The Applicant avers that he is a victim as defined under section 7(1) of the 1998 Act.

PARTICULARS OF INCOMPATIBILITY

(a) The Applicant was dismissed for distributing literature amongst pupils regarding homosexuality and for expressing views on this subject. The dismissal is contrary to Article 10(1) of the Convention in that it infringes his freedom of expression and to impart information. The dismissal does not have aims that are legitimate under Article 10(2) and it is not necessary in a democratic society;

(b) there is a duty not to discriminate under Article 14 read in conjunction with Article 2 of the First Protocol. To dismiss teachers for educating and teaching pupils about homosexuality is to dismiss them for expressing particular opinions;

(c) section 28 of the 1988 Act cannot be read and given effect in a way which is compatible with the Applicant's freedom of expression under Article 10 of the Convention and therefore it appears that the first Respondent, in dismissing the Applicant with reference to section 28 of the 1988 Act, because he was teaching pupils about homosexuality, was acting so as to give effect to this statutory provision;

(d) the Applicant contends that section 28 contravenes his freedom of expression and this interference is therefore prescribed by law. The first Respondent dismissed the Applicant because they had to do so given the terms of section 28. The dismissal amounts to an infringement of Convention rights particularly Articles 10, 2 of the First Protocol and Article 14;

(e) the Applicant contends that the dismissal with reference to section 28 does not pursue aims that are legitimate under Article 10(2) as contended for by the first Respondent that the dismissal does pursue legitimate aims under Article 10(2) namely the protection of the morals of its pupils;

(f) the Applicant contends that the restrictions imposed by section 28 are inconsistent with the freedom of expression (and other Convention rights) and such restrictions are not reasonably required for the performance of his duties as a teacher. Full details of this contention are explained in the Applicant's affidavit;

(g) furthermore the restrictions imposed by section 28 cannot be reasonably justifiable in a democratic society;

(h) the Applicant contends that the restrictions imposed by section 28 on the guaranteed right of freedom of expression is not proportionate to the aims sought to be achieved under section 28 of the 1988 Act and that the restriction is disproportionate to the mischief which the public authority is seeking to prevent;

(i) the Applicant contends that the effect of section 28 is to discriminate against teachers who genuinely believe that the teaching of homosexuality in schools is in the best interest of pupils and such discrimination is contrary to Article 10, Article 2 of the First Protocol combined with Article 14;

(j) accordingly the Honourable Court is invited to declare that section 28 of the 1988 Act is incompatible with Article 10.

....
Signed

PART 5

HUMAN RIGHTS ACT 1998

Human Rights Act 1998

(1998 c 42)

ARRANGEMENT OF SECTIONS

PART 5
THE ACT

An Act to give further effect to rights and freedoms guaranteed under the European Convention on Human Rights; to make provision with respect to holders of certain judicial offices who become judges of the European Court of Human Rights; and for connected purposes.[1]

[9th November 1998]

---

1   The European Convention on Human Rights, an international treaty elaborated within the Council of Europe, was opened for signature in November 1950. The Court of Human Rights was set up in 1959. The rights and freedoms set out in the Convention rights should be secured to anyone within the jurisdiction of the UK: *Ireland v UK* (1979) 2 EHRR 25. The Act makes the protection of human rights primarily the responsibility of the UK courts. The strong view is that the Convention and the Act are to apply to citizens, or residents, of the UK, as the Convention exists to protect the rights of the individual against the State. Whether the Act has territorial effect remains to be argued. Consequently, whether the Act applies to an immigrant seeking entry into the UK remains to be tested. The European Court has held that a person who has only temporary admission and mere physical presence in the UK was still within the jurisdiction of the ECHR: *D v UK* [1997] EHRLR 534. See also *X v FRG* Application No 1611/62, (1965) YB 158 at 163 which suggests that ECHR applies extra-territorially. A State or local government has never, under the Convention, been able to take action before the Strasbourg Courts.

Article 1 of the Convention imposes an obligation on the Contracting Parties to secure the Convention rights to everyone within the jurisdicion of the State. Article 1 has not been incorporated. It is to be noted that the grant of State immunity in respect of other sovereign acts does not involve a violation of Article 6: *Waite v FRG* Application No 2608/94, 2 December 1997 cited in *Holland v Lampen-Wolfe* [1999] 1 WLR 1888 at 194F.

Introduction

1   The Convention Rights[1]

(1)   In this Act, 'the Convention rights' means the rights and fundamental freedoms set out in—

   (a) Articles 2 to 12 and 14 of the Convention,
   (b) Articles 1 to 3 of the First Protocol, and
   (c) Articles 1 and 2 of the Sixth Protocol,[2]

as read with Articles 16[3] to 18 of the Convention.

(2)   Those Articles are to have effect for the purposes of this Act subject to any designated derogation or reservation (as to which see sections 14 and 15).[4]

(3)   The Articles are set out in Schedule 1.

(4)   The Secretary of State may by order make such amendments to this Act as he considers appropriate to reflect the effect, in relation to the United Kingdom, of a protocol.

(5)   In subsection (4) 'protocol' means a protocol to the Convention—

(a) which the United Kingdom has ratified; or
(b) which the United Kingdom has signed with a view to ratification.[5]

(6)   No amendment may be made by an order under subsection (4) so as to come into force before the protocol concerned is in force in relation to the United Kingdom.

---

1   *General*
      This section specifies those Articles of the Convention and the First Protocol to it (the Convention rights) which are given further effect by the Act. These Convention rights are set out in Sch 1. The Schedule may be amended by order to reflect the effect of a protocol to the Convention which the UK has ratified or signed with a view to ratification. Article 13 of the Convention is omitted. The Act amplifies rights already given by our common law and contributes to the European Convention, and makes the Convention rights enforceable against public authorities in our own courts.
2   Abolition of the death penalty other than in times of war. It would be possible for the death penalty to be reintroduced by a future vote of Parliament, but only by way of an amendment to the Act.
3   Article 16: Nothing in Articles 10, 11 and 14 shall be regarded as preventing the High Contracting Parties from imposing restrictions on the political activity of aliens. Possession of the nationality of a Member State of the European Union and status as a member of the European Parliament do not allow Article 16 to be raised against such a person: *Piermont v France* 20 EHRR 301.
4   Article 15 of the Convention permits a State to derogate from certain Articles in time of war or other public emergency threatening the life of the nation. The UK has one derogation in place in respect of Article 5(3) of the Convention as described in Sch 2, Part I to the Act. Article 64 of the Convention allows a State to enter a reservation when a law in force is not in conformity with a Convention provision. Part II of Sch 2 to the Act contains the reservations.
5   The UK is also a party to the First Protocol to the Convention which guarantees the right to peaceful enjoyment of possessions (Article 1 of the Protocol), the right to education (Article 2); and the right to free elections (Article 3): Part II of Sch 1 to the Act. The Protocols were introduced by the Strasbourg organs to adapt the Convention standards to new situations. The Protocols have been added to the original Convention rights in order to meet new demands. Protocol Nos 1, 4, 6 and 7 have added further rights to those set out in the Convention. Protocol No 1 appears in Part II of the Schedule. Protocol No 4 (not included) guarantees the freedom of movement, Protocol No 6 abolishes the death penalty in times of peace and Protocol No 7 provides for the right of appeal in criminal proceedings.

---

2   Interpretation of Convention rights[1]

(1)   A court or tribunal determining a question which has arisen in connection with a Convention right must[2] take into account any—

(a) judgment, decision, declaration or advisory opinion of the European Court of Human Rights,[3]
(b) opinion of the Commission given in a report adopted under Article 31[4] of the Convention,
(c) decision of the Commission in connection with Article 26 or 27(2)[5] of the Convention, or
(d) decision of the Committee of Ministers taken under Article 46[6] of the Convention,[7]

whenever made or given, so far as, in the opinion of the court or tribunal, it is relevant to the proceedings[8] in which that question has arisen.

(2)   Evidence of any judgment, decision, declaration or opinion of which account may have to be taken under this section is to be given in proceedings before any court or tribunal in such manner as may be provided by rules.

(3)   In this section 'rules' means rules of court or, in the case of proceedings before a tribunal, rules made for the purposes of this section—

(a) by the Lord Chancellor or the Secretary of State, in relation to proceedings outside Scotland;

(b) by the Secretary of State, in relation to proceedings in Scotland; or
(c) by a Northern Ireland department, in relation to proceedings before a Tribunal in Northern Ireland—
    (i) which deals with transferred matters; and
    (ii) for which no rules made under paragraph (a) are in force.

---

1   *General*
  This section provides that a court or tribunal determining a question in connection with a Convention right must take account of relevant judgments, decisions, declarations and opinions made or given by the European Commission and Court of Human Rights and the Committee of Ministers of the Council of Europe. The European Court's judgments are final and binding but they are declaratory in nature. A judgment given by the European Court is binding on the State concerned. If the European Court finds a violation of the Convention, it has no power to quash the decisions of the national authorities or to make consequential orders. Judgments are presented to the Committee of Ministers, which then supervise their implementation. Many of the judgments of the Euroepan Court have led to changes in the legislation. For example, the Contempt of Court Act 1981 was enacted following the complaint to the European Court on restrictions on press comment during the thalidomide proceedings: *Sunday Times v UK* (1979) 2 EHRR 245.
2   The court or tribunal it seems must take into account judgments etc of the European Court of Human Rights without being invited to do so. It has no discretion to ignore such judgments if relevant. The UK government's White Paper states that these decisions or judgments will not be binding. But the court or tribunal is not limited by the principles applied in Strasbourg and might enlarge the principles in favour of an applicant's fundamental rights. The courts will often be faced with cases which involve factors perhaps specific to the UK which distinguish them from cases considered by the European Court. The UK courts are not bound to follow European Court judgments in cases to which the UK has not been a party. It is important that UK courts have the scope to apply discretion so as to develop human rights law in the domestic context: *Hansard* HL cols 1270, 1271 (19 January 1998) as per Lord Chancellor. The doctrine of margin of appreciation means allowing the UK courts a margin of appreciation when it interprets UK law. The UK courts are expected to interpret the Convention in accordance with British and European jurisprudence on human rights.
3   It is appropriate that courts and tribunals should take into account the jurisprudence of the European Court when considering the effect of UK domestic legislation and applying it: *R v Manchester Crown Court, ex parte McDonald* [1999] 1 WLR 832 at 850F.
4   For Article 31, see Appendix 6.
5   For Article 26 and Article 27(2), see Appendix 6.
6   For Article 46, see Appendix 6.
7   Protocol No 11 was opened for signature by Member States on 11 May 1994. The European Court and the European Commission of Human Rights is to be replaced by a single full-time Court. The role of the Committee of Ministers is to be abolished.
8   Proceedings include interlocutory proceedings; eg application for discovery of documents: see *Rantzen v Mirror Group Newspapers* [1994] QB 670; *Mcginley and Egan v UK* Application Nos 21825/93 and 23414/94 concerns an allegation that refusal to disclose documents violates Article 6(1) of the Convention (denial of an effective remedy).

Legislation

3 Interpretation of legislation

(1)   So far as it is possible to do so, primary legislation and subordinate legislation must be read and given effect in a way which is compatible with the Convention rights.[1]

(2)   This section—

(a) applies to primary legislation and subordinate legislation whenever enacted;[2]
(b) does not affect the validity, continuing operation or enforcement of any incompatible primary legislation;[3] and
(c) does not affect the validity, continuing operation or enforcement of any incompatible subordinate legislation if (disregarding any possibility of revocation) primary legislation prevents removal of the incompatibility.[4]

---

1   *General*
  Primary and subordinate legislation, whenever enacted, must as far as possible be read and give effect in a way which is compatible with the Convention rights. This is an interpretative principle. It also provides that this does not affect the validity, continuing operation or enforcement of any incompatible primary

legislation, or any incompatible subordinate legislation if primary legislation prevents the removal of incompatibility. If the courts find it impossible to construe primary legislation in a way which is compatible with the Convention rights, the primary legislation remains in full force and effect. All the courts may do is to make a declaration of incompatibility.

The term 'possible' is different from 'reasonable'. It means, 'what is the possible interpretation?'. The Lord Chancellor maintained that the word 'possible' is the plainest means which can be devised for simply asking the courts to find the construction consistent with the intentions of Parliament. The courts must construe statutes so that they bear a meaning which is consistent with the Convention whenever that is possible according to the language of the statutes but not when it is impossible to achieve that: 583 HL 535 (18 November 1997). This rule of construction means that the courts will be required to interpret legislation so as to uphold Convention rights unless legislation itself is so clearly incompatible with the Convention that it is impossible to do so. This rule of construction is to apply to past as well as future legislation. The courts will not be bound by previous interpretations: *Rights Brought Home: The Human Rights Bill*, Cmnd 3782 (Home Office, 1997), para 2.7.8.

The court or tribunal is required in every case to construe primary or subordinate legislation in a way which is compatible with the Convention rights. It is the duty of the court or tribunal to do this even if it is not requested to do so. This principle of construction applies to legislation whenever enacted.

(a) The words of a statute dealing with the subject-matter of the Convention are to be construed as intended to implement the Convention obligations and not to be inconsistent with it if they are reasonably capable of bearing such a meaning: *Garland v British Rail* [1983] 2 AC 751 at 771 per Lord Diplock; a case dealing with EC law.

(b) A national court which determines that its national law is not compatible with the Convention should in any event interpret that law in such a way that it is in conformity with the provisions of Directives. That obligation also applies in respect of national law which was already in existence before the Directive in any area which was later covered thereby (*Marshall v Southampton (No 2)* [1993] ICR 893, ECJ at 922, para 22). There is no reason why the same approach cannot be adopted as in EC case-law.

(c) There is a difference between European Community law and the Convention because it is a requirement of membership of the European Union that Member States give priority to directly effective EC law in national legal systems but there is no reason why the courts should not construe Convention rights in the same manner. It should be pointed out that the European Community is not a Contracting Party to the European Court, and is not, therefore, subject to the jurisdiction of the Strasbourg organs: *International Handelsgesellschaft* Case C-11/70 [1970] ECR 1125, ECJ.

(d) Constitutional guarantees or fundamental rights (particularly Articles 2 and 3) must not be subjected to the approach applicable to the interpretation of other legislation. What is needed is 'a generous interpretation avoiding what has been called the "austerity of tabulated legalism" suitable to give to individuals the full measure of the fundamental rights and freedoms referred to': *Minister of Home Affairs v Fisher* [1980] AC 319 at 328H.

(e) Article 3 of the Convention, for example, is an unqualified and absolute guarantee of the human rights it protects: *Ireland v UK* (1978) 2 EHRR 25 at 79, para 163. In order to filter out insubstantial complaints the only qualification is that, in order for conduct to be covered by the prohibition, it must 'attain a minimum level of severity'. There is no express or implied derogation in favour of the State: the prohibition is equally applicable during a war or public emergency. There is no derogation in favour of the State in order to enable it to fight terrorism or violent crime: *Fisher v Minister of Public Safety and Immigration* [1998] 3 WLR 201, PC at 215D–H.

(f) In judging cases under Article 3 the domestic court must consider the actual facts of the case in order to assess whether the treatment or punishment in its impact on the individual is inhuman or degrading: *Soering v UK* (1989) 11 EHRR 439 and *Fisher v Minister of Public Safety and Immigration* [1998] 3 WLR 201, PC at 216A–E. In *Soering* (above) at 474, para 104 the Court stated:

'The manner in which the death penalty is imposed or executed, the personal circumstances of the condemned person and a disproportionality to the gravity of the crime committed, as well as the conditions, of detention awaiting execution, are examples of factors capable of bringing the treatment or punishment received by the condemned person within the proscription under Article 3.' If a legalistic interpretation of Article 3 leads to the conclusion that its provision would not be violated, that interpretation must surely give way to an interpretation which protects the individual from such treatment and respects his human rights: *Fisher v Minister of Public Safety and Immigration (No 2)* [1999] 2 WLR 349 at 361F. A constitution is a legal instrument giving rise, amongst other things, to individual rights capable of enforcement in a court of law. Respect must be paid to the language which has been used and to the traditions and usages which have given meaning to that language. It is quite consistent with this, and with the recognition that rules of interpretation may apply, to take as a point of departure for the process of interpretation a recognition of the character and origin of the instrument, and to be guided by the principle of giving full recognition and effect to those fundamental rights and freedoms with a statement of which the Constitution commences: *Minister of Home Affairs v Fisher* [1980] AC 319 at 329 per Lord Wilberforce.

(g) A principle emerging from the jurisprudence of the Strasbourg Courts is the principle of effectiveness, viz that in interpreting the Convention the court seeks, given the provisions of the Convention, to give the 'fullest weight and effect consistent with the language used and with the rest of the text': Merrills, *The Development of International Law by the European Court of Human Rights* (1989), p 98.

(h) In *de Freitas v Ministry of Agriculture* [1998] 3 WLR 653, PC at 683, the House of Lords adopted the principle of 'reading down' a statutory provision espoused by Sopinka J in *Broadrick v Oklahoma* (1973) 413 US 601 at 347:

'... In the final analysis, a law that is invalid in so many of its applications will, as a result of wholesale reading down, bear little resemblance to the law that Parliament passed and a strong inference arises that it is invalid as a whole' (at 683G–H).

At 684 the Court put forward the following propositions in determining whether a limitation is arbitrary or excessive: (i) the legislative objective is sufficiently important to justify limiting a fundamental right; (ii) the measures designed to meet the legislative objective are rationally connected to it; and (iii) the means to impair the right or freedom are not more than is necessary to accomplish the objective.

2   At present, subordinate legislation may be struck down by the courts on the same grounds as in the case of other forms of administrative action. Primary and subordinate legislation are subject to a declaration of incompatibility: 583 HL 544–545 (18 November 1997). Under s 21 of the Act of the Scottish Parliament and the Act of the Northern Ireland Assembly, and Order in Council other than one made in the exercise of HM Royal Prerogative are defined as subordinate legislation.

3   This section provides that where it is not possible to read and give effect so as it is possible to do so in a way that is compatible with the Convention rights, that does not affect its validity, continuing operation or enforcement. This ensures that courts are not empowered to strike down Acts of Parliament which they find to be incompatible with the Convention rights. The Government would wish to respond to a declaration of incompatibility rapidly. A declaration of incompatibility by a higher court does not mean that a lower court would be bound to follow the declaration.

4   The Act is intended to provide a new basis for judicial interpretation of all legislation, not a basis for striking down any part of it. The domestic courts will be able to strike down or set aside secondary legislation which is incompatible with the Convention unless the terms of the parent statute make this impossible. This power is no different than the power of the court to strike down *ultra vires* subordinate legislation. Where the enabling power in primary legislation clearly allows for the relevant provision then it will have to be argued, no doubt, that the enabling provision must be construed in a manner which prevents the enactment of subordinate rules (immigration rules, bye-laws, policies based on statutory powers) which are inconsistent with Convention rights and accordingly the rule in question is *ultra vires* because it is inconsistent with the parent Act. Further see s 4(5) below.

Although the Act does not allow the court to set aside an Act of Parliament or primary legislation it does provide for a fast-track procedure for changing legislation in response either to a declaration of incompatibility by the higher domestic courts or to a finding of a violation of the Convention in Strasbourg: see ss 10–12. A finding by the European Court of a violation of a Convention right does not have an automatic effect of changing UK law. But the UK has agreed to abide by the decisions of the European Court or where the case has not been referred to the European Court, the Committee of Ministers. A relevant Minister will be able to amend the legislation by Order so as to make it compatible with the Convention. The Order will be subject to approval by both Houses of Parliament before taking effect, except where the need to amend the legislation is particularly urgent when the Order will take effect immediately but will expire after a short period if not approved by Parliament.

4   Declaration of incompatibility[1]

(1)   Subsection (2) applies in any proceedings in which a court[2] determines whether a provision of primary legislation is compatible with a Convention right.[3]

(2)   If the court is satisfied that the provision is incompatible with a Convention right, it may[4] make a declaration of that incompatibility.

(3)   Subsection (4) applies in any proceedings in which a court determines whether a provision of subordinate legislation, made in the exercise of a power conferred by primary legislation, is compatible with a Convention right.[5]

(4)   If the court is satisfied—

(a)   that the provision is incompatible with a Convention right, and

(b) that (disregarding any possibility of revocation) the primary legislation concerned prevents removal of the incompatibility,

it may make a declaration of that incompatibility.[6]

(5) In this section 'court' means—[7]

(a) the House of Lords;

(b) the Judicial Committee of the Privy Council;

(c) the Courts-Martial Appeal Court;

(d) in Scotland, the High Court of Justiciary sitting otherwise than as a trial court or the Court of Session;

(e) in England and Wales or Northern Ireland, the High Court or the Court of Appeal.[8]

(6) A declaration under this section ('a declaration of incompatibility')—

(a) does not affect the validity, continuing operation or enforcement of the provision[9] in respect of which it[10] is given; and

(b) is not binding on the parties to the proceedings in which it is made.[11]

---

1 *General*

This section provides that specified courts may make a 'declaration of incompatibility' where they are satisfied that a provision of primary legislation is incompatible with the Convention rights, or that a provision of subordinate legislation is incompatible and the primary legislation under which it was made prevents the removal of that incompatibility. It also provides that such a declaration does not affect the validity, continuing operation or enforcement of the provision in respect of which it is given.

2 Court refers to High Court: s 4(5).

3 If the court determines that it is impossible to interpret an Act in a manner which is compatible with the Convention then the court will be able to make a declaration to that effect. The court will be able to make a declaration in any proceedings before them whether the case originated before them or in considering an appeal from a lower court.

4 The term 'may' should be construed as 'shall' if the court is satisfied that the provision is incompatible with one or more of the Convention rights. See example in Bennion *Statutory Interpretation* 3rd edn (Sweet & Maxwell) at p 34. A court is not precluded before the completion of a trial from considering the compatibility of a provision of primary legislation with the Convention: *R v DPP, ex parte Kebilene* [1999] 3 WLR 175 at 198H.

5 This power is an important one. Therefore if the enabling provision clearly allows for the creation of subordinate legislation or rules (ie which is *intra vires* the enabling provision) which are incompatible with the Convention rights then the court may make a declaration of incompatibility. As an example, an immigration rule, though *intra vires* s 3(2) of the Immigration Act 1971, may still be incompatible with one or more of the Convention rights. However, the Government's view (Hansard, Lords, 24 June 1998, p 1130) is that if subordinate legislation is incompatible with the Convention but cannot be quashed because of the nature of the primary legislation then all the courts can do is to declare its incompatibility. To quash the subordinate legislation in instances where it is *intra vires* but incompatible with the Convention will be to strike at the sovereignty of Parliament.

6 If the Government and Parliament refused to act on a declaration of incompatibility, the victim would most certainly take the case to Strasbourg.

7 Judges who preside over criminal trials do not have the power to make declarations of incompatibility. But judges sitting in judicial review proceedings would have such power.

8 Tribunals and lower courts do not have power to make a declaration of incompatibility. It may be appropriate, in a proper case, for a victim to bring judicial review proceedings if a declaration of incompatibility is sought before the determination of his rights before a tribunal or lower court. It remains to be seen whether a victim should exhaust his appeal rights before seeking judicial review for a declaration of incompatibility from a higher court. Judicial review will be more appropriate in cases where the evidence is not in dispute so that the court will not be required to make further findings of fact and where its prior ruling will produce a clear outcome on the result of the pending appeal. Judicial review may be used expeditiously in such an event.

9 Provision relates to a statutory provision; thus it is arguable that administrative decisions or extra-statutory decisions may be invalid if a declaration to that effect is made and may be binding on the parties.

10 A declaration of incompatibility.

11 It is arguable that a declaration of incompatibility affects the validity of the administrative or other decisions taken under the provision declared to be incompatible with the Convention rights or this would have been expressed to the contrary. It appears that if the court is satisfied that a subordinate provision is incompatible

with a Convention right but that the enabling primary legislation does not prevent the removal of that incompatibility, the court may make a declaration of the incompatibility not under s 4 but either under its inherent jurisdiction or under s 8(1) of the Act. Such a declaration is not made under s 4 and therefore such a declaration will affect the validity, continuing operation and enforcement of the provision in question.

5 Right of Crown to intervene[1]

(1)   Where a court is considering whether to make a declaration of incompatibility, the Crown is entitled to notice in accordance with rules of court.

(2)   In any case to which subsection (1) applies—

(a) a Minister of the Crown (or a person nominated by him),[2]
(b) a member of the Scottish Executive,
(c) a Northern Ireland Minister,
(d) a Northern Ireland department,

is entitled, on giving notice in accordance with rules of court, to be joined as a party to the proceedings.

(3)   Notice under subsection (2) may be given at any time during the proceedings.

(4)   A person who has been made a party to criminal proceedings (other than in Scotland) as the result of a notice under subsection (2) may, with leave, appeal to the House of Lords against any declaration of incompatibility made in the proceedings.

(5)   In subsection (4)—

'criminal proceedings' includes all proceedings before the Courts-Martial Appeal Court; and
'leave' means leave granted by the court making the declaration of incompatibility or by the House of Lords.

1   *General*
    The Crown has the right to have notice that a court is considering whether or not to make a declaration of incompatibility, and entitles the Crown to be joined as a party to the proceedings. Whether the applicant has to bear the costs of the Crown in the event of his being unsuccessful remains to be seen.
2   A nominated person will be joined in his own capacity and would be acting on his own behalf and not on behalf of the Government (Hansard, 17 June 1998, p 396). The Minister will decide who the best person is to speak on the issues under examination. If the measures of the Synod were being considered, then the Synod itself would be nominated by the Minister if it were decided that that was in the public interest. The nominated person would ensure that all relevant information is then placed before the courts for consideration. Such a nominated person should not act as a partisan in the case.

Public authorities

6 Acts of public authorities[1]

(1)   It is unlawful[2] for a public authority[3] to act in a way which is incompatible with a Convention right.[4]

(2)   Subsection (1) does not apply to an act if—

(a) as the result of one or more provisions of primary legislation, the authority could not have acted differently;[5] or
(b) in the case of one or more provisions of, or made under, primary legislation which cannot be read or given effect in a way which is compatible with the Convention rights, the authority was acting so as to give effect to or enforce those provisions.

(3)   In this section, 'public authority' includes—

(a) a court or tribunal, and

(b) any person certain of whose functions are functions of a public nature,[6]

but does not include either House of Parliament or a person exercising functions in connection with proceedings in Parliament.[7]

(4)   In subsection (3) 'Parliament' does not include the House of Lords in its judicial capacity.

(5)   In relation to a particular act, a person is not a public authority by virtue only of subsection (3)(b) if the nature of the act is private.[8]

(6)   'An act' includes a failure to act but does not include a failure to—

(a) introduce in, or lay before, Parliament a proposal for legislation; or

(b) make any primary legislation or remedial order.

---

1   *General*

It is unlawful for a public authority to act in a way which is incompatible with the Convention rights, unless that would be inconsistent with the effect of primary legislation.

2   The term 'unlawful' should be construed as widely as possible having particular regard to the Convention rights and the universally accepted standards of justice. Law includes not only common law and statute law but should invoke the concept of the rule of law itself and the universally accepted standards of justice observed by civilised nations which observe the rule of law: *Thomas v Baptiste* [1999] 3 WLR 249 at 259H and 269D. The High Court has an inherent jurisdiction to prevent the initiation of civil proceedings which were likely to constitute an abuse of the process of the court. As long as the inherent power was exercised only when it was appropriate for it to be exercised, no contravention of Article 6 or common law principle was involved: *Ebert v Birch and Another* (1999) *The Times*, 28 April.

3   Public authority is to be given a wide meaning and is not to be construed narrowly as is evident from s 6(3). This term includes central government, the police, immigration officers, prisons, court officials, courts and tribunals, privatised utilities, the City Takeover Panel, the BBC, the Advertising Standards Authority but possibly not the Football Association or the Jockey Club unless exercising public functions in which case they would fall within s 6(1). The actions of Parliament are excluded: s 6(3). It is suggested that one test to ascertain whether a body is a public or private one gains assistance from the dicta in the ECJ's jurisprudence: *Foster v British Gas* [1990] IRLR 353 'a body, whatever its legal form, which has been made responsible, . . . for providing a public service under the control of the State and has for that purpose special powers going beyond those which result from the normal rules applicable in relations between individuals' and *NUT v Governing Body of St Mary's Church of England (Aided) Junior School* [1997] IRLR 242 (Church of England voluntary aided school held to be a public body). A body which falls under the control of the State, directly or indirectly, or which has special statutory or other powers beyond those of a private individual is to be viewed as a public authority: also *Marshall v Southampton and SW Hampshire AHA* [1986] IRLR 140.

The courts will consider the nature of the body and the activity in question.

A private prosecutor would not be a public authority although the court, as a public authority, would be required to act not incompatibly with the Convention. The Government has suggested that liability in domestic proceedings should lie with bodies in respect of whose actions the UK Government was answerable in Strasbourg. The question is whether the body is sufficiently public to engage the responsibility of the State. The test must relate to the substance and nature of the act, not to the form and legal personality. There are three obvious categories: (i) the first category is the obvious public authorities such as central government, local government and police; (ii) the second category consists of organisations with a mix of public and private functions, ie bodies which are private but have performed public functions partly as a result of privatisation and contracting out (eg Rail Track; the Press Complaints Commission which undertakes public functions whereas the press itself does not); (iii) the third category consists of bodies with no public functions and fall outside this section.

The Government expressed the view (Hansard, 20 May 1998, p 1015) that the Church of England, the Church of Scotland or the Roman Catholic Church are not public bodies (and see Sch 1: persons excluded from s 6). But where the Church stands in the place of the State (marriage or education) then the Convention rights are relevant to what they do. Courts must pay due regard to the rights guaranteed by Article 9, including, where relevant, the right of a Church to act in accordance with religious belief. Thus a court when considering a dismissal of a teacher at school will have regard to any conduct on his part which is incompatible with the precepts, or with the upholding of the tenets, of the religion or religious denomination in question. Under s 2, the domestic courts will be required to have regard to the jurisprudence of the Convention. Thus Article 12 does not include the right to marry according to a particular ceremony of one's choice or to marry someone of the same biological sex.

Arguably, this section confers an independent jurisdiction on tribunals to comply with the ECHR notwithstanding ss 7(13) and 22(4). It remains to be seen whether this independent jurisdiction conferred on tribunals allows for claims to be based solely on Convention rights in addition to the existing statutory provisions relating to tribunal jurisdiction. The Government has stated that the effect of amendment No 30 is to enable a Minister to confer jurisdiction on a tribunal to determine Convention issues or to grant a remedy where a public authority has acted incompatibly with the Convention rights. The jurisdiction is to be conferred by order. It will be in addition to the existing statutory provisions relating to tribunal jurisdiction: HL Jan 19 Cols 360–362.

4   An appeal before a special adjudicator on asylum issues under s 8 of the Asylum and Immigrations Appeals Act 1993 would allow an adjudicator to consider whether the decision in question would be unlawful under s 6(1) of the Act. Such an appeal might be dismissed on asylum grounds but allowed on the basis that the appellant should not be removed from the UK and be eligible for exceptional leave to remain in the UK on Convention grounds. The same arguments would apply in other tribunals.

Newspapers will not be public bodies and could not be proceeded against directly under the Act. But an Article 8 argument could be raised in proceedings for harassment or a libel action. In such a situation, a judge must consider all the circumstances and find the right balance between Article 8 and Article 10. Courts would normally give precedence to Article 10 in such a case but there is no reason why the courts could not decide, on the facts of the case, that the invasion of privacy outweighs the right to freedom of expression.

5   It is hoped that this provision is construed strictly against the authority relying on it. The burden of establishing such a defence should fall on the authority claiming it.

6   A wide definition of public nature is called for particularly where the decision affects fundamental rights. See note 3 above.

7   Article 9 of the Bill of Rights (1689) states that debates and proceedings in Parliament must not be impeached or questioned in any court or place out of Parliament. This prevents the courts from calling into question the validity of the debates and internal functioning of Parliament.

8   Private acts of organisations are exempt from liability. For example, public utilities developing private property may be exempt. Persons include body corporate or unincorporate: Interpretation Act 1978.

7 Proceedings[1]

(1)   A person who claims that a public authority has acted (or proposes to act) in a way which is made unlawful by section 6(1) may—

> (a) bring proceedings[2] against the authority under this Act in the appropriate court or tribunal, or
>
> (b) rely on the Convention right or rights concerned in any legal proceedings,[3]

but only if he is (or would be) a victim[4] of the unlawful act.[5]

(2)   In subsection (1)(a) 'appropriate court or tribunal' means such court or tribunal as may be determined in accordance with rules; and proceedings against an authority include a counterclaim[5] or similar proceeding.

(3)   If the proceedings are brought on an application for judicial review,[6] the applicant is to be taken to have a sufficient interest in relation to the unlawful act only if he is, or would be, a victim of that act.[7]

(4)   If the proceedings are made by way of a petition for judicial review in Scotland, the applicant shall be taken to have title and interest to sue in relation to the unlawful act only if he is, or would be,[8] a victim of that act.

(5)   Proceedings under subsection (1)(a) must be brought before the end of—

> (a) the period of one year beginning with the date on which the act complained of took place; or
>
> (b) such longer period as the court or tribunal considers equitable having regard to all the circumstances,

but that is subject to any rule imposing a stricter time limit in relation to the procedure in question.[9]

(6)   In subsection (1)(b) 'legal proceedings' includes—

(a) proceedings brought by or at the instigation of a public authority; and
(b) an appeal against the decision of a court or tribunal.

(7)   For the purposes of this section, a person is a victim of an unlawful act only if he would be a victim for the purposes of Article 34[10] of the Convention if proceedings were brought in the European Court of Human Rights in respect of that act.

(8)   Nothing in this Act creates a criminal offence.[11]

(9)   In this section 'rules' means—

(a) in relation to proceedings before a court or tribunal outside Scotland, rules made by the Lord Chancellor or the Secretary of State for the purposes of this section or rules of court,
(b) in relation to proceedings before a court or tribunal in Scotland, rules made by the Secretary of State for those purposes,
(c) in relation to proceedings before a tribunal in Northern Ireland—
    (i)   which deals with transferred matters; and
    (ii) for which no rules made under paragraph (a) are in force,
    rules made by a Northern Ireland department for those purposes,

and includes provision made by order under section 1 of the Courts and Legal Services Act 1990.

(10)   In making rules regard must be had to section 9.

(11)   The Minister who has power to make rules in relation to a particular tribunal may, to the extent he considers it necessary to ensure that the tribunal can provide an appropriate remedy in relation to an act (or proposed act) of a public authority which is (or would be) unlawful as a result of section 6(1), by order add to—

(a) the relief or remedies which the tribunal may grant; or
(b) the grounds on which it may grant any of them.

(12)   An order made under subsection (13) may contain such incidental, supplemental, consequential or transitional provision as the Minister making it considers appropriate.[12]

(13)   'The Minister' includes the Northern Ireland department concerned.

---

1   *General*
    This section provides that a person who claims that a public authority has acted (or proposes to act) in a way which is unlawful, because it is incompatible with the Convention rights, may bring proceedings against that authority under the Act, or may rely on the Convention rights in any legal proceedings. Such a person may bring proceedings or rely on the Convention rights only if he is (or would be) a victim of the unlawful act.
2   For example, judicial review proceedings based solely on the Convention rights expressed in the Schedule to the Act. It is suggested that this section confers on courts and tribunals a distinct free-standing jurisdiction to consider and adjudicate a claim based exclusively on a Convention right or issue. But see s 7(13).
3   Thus one may rely on Article 13 together with the other Convention rights notwithstanding that Article 13 has been omitted from Schedule 1 to the Act. The Government expressed the view (Hansard, 20 May 1998, p 979) that it was inappropriate to include Article 13 in the Act for the following reasons:

    (1) the Act gives effect to Article 13 so there was an issue of duplication,
    (2) s 8 of the Act affords ample protection for individuals' rights under the Convention,
    (3) the inclusion of Article 13 would cause confusion for example by creating remedies beyond those available in s 8.

    The courts would take judicial notice of Article 13 without specifically being bound by it. For example, from time to time the courts will come across problems where they need nevertheless to have regard to Article 13: *Rantzen v Mirror Group Newspapers* [1994] QB 670.

4   To be a 'victim' of a violation, it is sufficient to be directly affected by the alleged breach of the Convention. It is not necessary to show detriment. According to the Strasbourg Courts' well-established case-law, the word 'victim' in Article 25 denotes the person directly affected by the act or omission in issue, the existence of a violation being conceivable even in the absence of detriment; detriment is relevant only in the context of Article 50 (ie just satisfaction = damages): *De Jong, Baljet and Van den Brink v The Netherlands* (1984) 8 EHRR 20, paras 40–41; further, an individual might claim to be the victim of a violation occasioned by the mere existence of such measure without having to allege that they were applied to him, but each must be considered in the light of the right alleged to have been infringed, the secret measures objected to, and the connection between the applicant and those measures; even though he is not able to allege in support of his application that he has been subject to concrete measures of surveillance. The question whether the applicant is actually the victim of any violation of the Convention involves determining whether contested legislation is in itself compatible with the Convention's provisions: *Klass and Others v FRG* (1978) 2 EHRR 214, paras 34 and 38. A person can properly claim to be a 'victim' of an interference with the exercise of his rights under the Convention if he has been directly affected by the matters allegedly constituting the interference. Although the applicant association owned neither the copyright nor the forfeited copy of the film, it was directly affected by the decision on forfeiture: *Otto-Preminger Institute v Austria* (1994) 19 EHRR 34, paras 39–41. In *Sutherland v UK* Application No 25186/94, the Commission held that the applicant (homosexual) who suffered distress in having to choose between engaging in a sexual relationship with a person under the age of 18 and breaking the law was directly affected by the Criminal Justice and Public Order Act 1994 and therefore could claim to be a victim under Article 25 of the Convention.

Victim includes an indirect victim, ie a close relative of a dead victim or one who has a direct and immediate personal interest in complaining about the unlawful act. The intention is that a victim under the Act should be in the same position as a victim in Strasbourg.

In *Times Newspapers Ltd v UK*, the Commission ruled that the newspaper could not claim to be a victim of a breach of free speech under Article 10 in complaining of unpredicitability of jury damages awards in libel cases because it had not shown that its newspapers had been inhibited from imparting information.

The more serious the infringement of fundamental rights at stake the greater will be the willingness of the courts to recognise a complainant as a victim.

The Equal Opportunity Commission or the Commission for Racial Equality may well be victims where the issues raised concern them.

5   The fact that there is no specific legislation for the court to declare incompatibility with the Convention does not affect the ability of the person concerned to obtain a remedy even in cases between private individuals because the court, as a public body, is required to act compatibly with the Convention. The courts in such a case should be prepared to develop the common law to protect the rights of the individual. A person may be able to rely on Convention arguments in any legal proceedings involving a public authority, ie as part of a defence to criminal or civil proceedings, or on seeking judicial review or on appeal. Proceedings against public authorities may be brought on Convention grounds alone independent of any other cause of action and even if no other cause of action exists.

6   Defendants should be aware and willing to raise Convention issues including a claim for damages emanating from a breach of their Convention rights by the authority. Thus, a defendant in criminal proceedings seeking to advance a collateral or defensive challenge that a bye-law or an administrative act undertaken pursuant to it was *ultra vires* and unlawful can raise the question of its substantive or procedural validity against the background of the Convention and such a defendant should not be precluded from raising such a defence in any court including a magistrates' court: *Boddington v British Transport Police* [1998] 2 WLR 639 at 654A. To preclude a defendant challenging the lawfulness of a bye-law or administrative decision on which the prosecution is premised on its validity will contravene Article 6 and Article 13 of the Convention. This means that a defendant may seek to challenge in his criminal trial the validity of an administrative decision on Convention grounds and which he had not challenged by way of earlier judicial review proceedings or on statutory appeal. To deny him this right would contravene the Convention and the criminal court is required to act compatibly with the Convention. It is suggested that the dicta in *R v Wicks* [1988] AC 92 will not prevent a defendant raising Convention grounds in a criminal trial that a local planning authority in issuing an enforcement notice had been motivated by bad faith, bias or other procedural impropriety and that a criminal court is suitably qualified to investigate this matter in the criminal proceedings. In a civil case, when an individual seeks to establish private law rights which cannot be determined without an examination of the validity of a public law decision the court must determine the validity of the public law decision against the background of the Convention and, similarly, when a person seeks to defend himself by questioning the validity of a public law decision. It would not be necessary (but perhaps desirable) to commence judicial review proceedings before instituting private law proceedings in such cases: *Waverley Borough Council v Hilden* [1988] 1 All ER 807 has to be re-examined.

7   Locus standi would depend on the nature of the judicial review proceedings: ordinary common law principles; Convention principles; European Union rights; or a combination of all the above rights.

8   It remains to be seen whether locus standi is limited to personal standing or includes representative standing: *R v Inland Revenue Commissioners, ex parte National Federation of Self-Employed and Small Businesses Ltd* [1982] AC 617; *R v Secretary of State for Foreign and Commonwealth Affairs, ex parte World Development Movement Ltd*

(the Pergau Dam case) [1995] 1 All ER 611; *R v Secretary of State for the Home Department, ex parte Fire Brigades Union* [1995] 2 WLR 464; *R v Inspectorate of Pollution, ex parte Greenpeace Ltd (No 2)* [1994] 4 All ER 329. It is suggested that as far as representative actions are concerned the courts should allow judicial review proceedings to be instituted by a person providing there is a genuine public interest in the decision being challenged and that the applicant before the court is not a mere busybody but is genuinely interested in furthering public interest. Thus, if an applicant is genuinely concerned that the measures adopted by justices in not disclosing the names of sitting magistrates in certain instances for security reasons, this might well affect Article 10 of the Convention (right to receive information) giving the applicant before the court sufficient locus standi to say that he is a 'victim' and that such practice is therefore unlawful: in *R v Felixstowe Justices, ex parte Leight* [1987] QB 582 a journalist was held to have sufficient locus standi to seek a declaration that the policy adopted by the magistrates of not disclosing the names of sitting magistrates in the court on security grounds was unlawful; see also *R v Horsham JJ, ex parte Farquharson* [1982] QB 762.

However, the Lord Chancellor has stated a narrower test will be applied in applications for judicial review in determining whether a person is or is not a 'victim'. The intention is that a victim under the Act should be in the same position as a victim in Strasbourg. Thus, a local authority cannot be a victim under this section because it cannot be a victim in Strasbourg.

Under Article 25 of the Convention, the Commission may receive petitions from any person, non-governmental organisation or group of people claiming to be the victim of a violation of the Convention. Who is a victim in a commercial context will very much depend on the nature of the breach alleged. A complaint under Article 6 of the Convention may be brought by a victim including a limited company, shareholder or director: *Dombo Beheer BV v The Netherlands* (1994) 18 EHRR 213; *Neves Silsva v Portugal* (1989) 13 EHRR 535. Article 1 of the Protocol expressly provides that it applies to both legal and natural persons. In *Agrotexim and Others v Greece* (1996) 21 EHRR 250 the European Court held that Greek limited companies with a combined shareholding of more than 50% in another Greek company lacked the status of victim. The piercing of the 'corporate veil' or the disregarding of a company's separate legal personality will be justified only in exceptional circumstances, in particular where it is established that it is impossible for the company to apply to the Convention institutions through the organs set up under its articles of incorporation or in the event of liquidation through its liquidator.

The Government has expressed the view that this section seeks to mirror the approach taken by the Strasbourg Courts. Reliance on the Convention rights is restricted to victims or potential victims of unlawful acts and the definition of a victim for this purpose is tied to Article 34 of the Convention as amended by the Eleventh Protocol. A 'narrower test' will be applied for bringing applications by judicial review on Convention grounds than an application for judicial review on other grounds. Interest groups will still be able to provide assistance to victims who bring cases under the Act. Interest groups will also be able to bring cases directly where they are victims of an unlawful act. If a group is genuinely acting on behalf of a person, the proceedings can perfectly well be brought in that person's name. The Act does not prevent interest groups from providing assistance to a victim once a case has been brought. The intention

is to permit amicus written briefs from non-governmental organisations taking part, eg Liberty, UNHCR. A third party is not precluded from making written submissions to the court on the issues raised.

8   It is arguable that a person may be a victim of some unlawful act in the near future. How near in the future is a question of fact and degree.

9   The time-limits contained in tribunal rules or regulations and in judicial review proceedings which are stricter than the time-limits stated here therefore apply. But it remains to be seen whether the more generous criteria to extend the time-limits stipulated in s 7(5)(b) will broaden the existing criteria to extend time-limits in different jurisdictions. Proceedings brought on Convention grounds alone fall within s 7(1)(a), in which case the proceedings must be brought within one year beginning with the date on which the act complained of took place, or within such longer period as the court or tribunal considers appropriate. Proceedings brought on Convention grounds together with another cause of action (eg tort or contract) would be governed by the current limitation period: s 7(1)(b). The time-limits in judicial review proceedings will continue to apply. The one-year time-limit under s 7(5)(a) proceedings may be extended where it is appropriate to do so: 314 HC (24 June 1998 at 1094, 1096).

10 For Article 34 see Appendix 6.

11 See Article 7 and the jurisprudence explained in this book. Thus, ill-treatment is contrary to Article 3 of the Convention (prohibition on torture) but this will not be a criminal offence under the Act. However, criminal proceedings under the Offences Against the Person Act 1861 could be brought, but they would be for an alleged breach of the 1861 Act and not for an alleged failure to comply with Article 3. In criminal proceedings, a court will be required not to act incompatibly with the Convention. Thus, it will be unlawful for a Crown Court to give a judgment which is incompatible with the Convention right unless it is required to do so to give effect to a provision of primary legislation or a provision made under it. The fact that in a particular criminal trial a public authority is found to have acted unlawfully will not automatically lead to an acquittal. The nature of the Act and its impact on the trial as a whole will have to be considered. If the effect of the act is such that, for example, a fair trial is impossible, an acquittal would be appropriate (eg evidence acquired by telephone tapping may not be excluded under s 78 of the Police and Criminal Evidence Act 1984).

12　The purpose of this section is to ensure the jurisdiction of all tribunals to deal with Convention right claims. The main purpose of Amendment No 30 was to ensure that the European Court's jurisdiction was applied consistently in asylum and non-asylum appeals. This amendment to confer jurisdiction on tribunals is considered necessary because statutory tribunals possess, according to domestic law, limited jurisdiction. If no relevant rules are made by the relevant Minister then the following points may arise for consideration:

- (i)　can the Minister be compelled by way of judicial review to introduce rules under the usual *Wednesbury* principles; it is one thing to delay bringing the relevant rules into force but quite another to abdicate or relinquish the power altogether: *R v Home Secretary, ex parte Fire Brigade Union* [1995] 2 WLR 464 at 492E. It might be argued that one cannot challenge a failure to legislate under the Act but one may be able to challenge the choice to make legislation which is incompatible with the Convention. An unintentional failure to act by a public authority is to be open to challenge under the Act in the same way as any other failure to act, if that failure is incompatible with Convention rights;
- (ii)　however, the failure to make 'rules' may be immune from challenge under the Act: s 6(6) and ss 7(9) and 21(1);
- (iii)　an applicant before a tribunal may rely directly on s 6(1) despite the absence of rules conferring jurisdiction on the tribunal;
- (iv)　it may be argued before a tribunal that a claim is based solely on a Convention right particularly with regard to the provisions of Article 13 which has been omitted from the Act. The Government has stated that to incorporate Article 13 expressly may lead to the courts fashioning remedies about which we know nothing [Official Report, HL 18 November 1997; Vol 583, c 477]. But the courts should have regard to Article 13.

However, tribunals are capable of providing remedies which are balanced and proportionate and therefore there is no reason why Article 13 cannot be relied upon before a tribunal. Thus, in an asylum context, an appellant who fails to show he is a refugee might succeed in showing that he should not be removed from the UK because to do so would infringe Article 3 or Article 8 of the Convention and that he should be granted exceptional leave to remain in the UK.

The intention of this section according to the Government was to cater for situations where the ground on which proceedings brought before a tribunal are extemely narrowly defined either by statute or by restrictive judicial interpretation of statutory provisions. If no rules are made for such tribunal to deal with Convention rights then judicial review would be the only available course of action.

8　Judicial remedies[1]

(1)　In relation to any act (or proposed act) of a public authority which the court finds is (or would be) unlawful, it may grant such relief or remedy, or make such order, within its powers as it considers just and appropriate.[2]

(2)　But damages[3] may be awarded only by a court which has power to award damages,[4] or to order the payment of compensation, in civil proceedings.[5]

(3)　No award of damages is to be made unless, taking account of all the circumstances of the case,[6] including—

- (a)　any other relief or remedy granted, or order made, in relation to the act in question (by that or any other court),[7] and
- (b)　the consequences of any decision (of that or any other court) in respect of that act,[8]

the court is satisfied that the award is necessary to afford just satisfaction[9] to the person in whose favour it is made.[10]

(4)　In determining—

- (a)　whether to award damages, or
- (b)　the amount of an award,

the court must take into account the principles applied by the European Court of Human Rights in relation to the award of compensation under Article 41 of the Convention.[11]

(5) A public authority against which damages are awarded is to be treated—

  (a) in Scotland, for the purposes of section 3 of the Law Reform (Miscellaneous Provisions) (Scotland) Act 1940 as if the award were made in an action of damages in which the authority has been found liable in respect of loss or damage to the person to whom the award is made;

  (b) for the purposes of the Civil Liability (Contribution) Act 1978[12] as liable in respect of damage suffered by the person to whom the award is made.

(6) In this section—

'court' includes a tribunal;
'damages' means damages for an unlawful act of a public authority;[13] and
'unlawful' means unlawful under section 6(1).

---

1 *General*

  A court or tribunal may grant such relief or remedy, or make such order, within its jurisdiction as it considers appropriate where it finds an authority to have acted unlawfully. It also specifies the circumstances in which an award of damages may be made. The European Court does not award excessive damages. It is anticipated that modest damages will be awarded otherwise the Act would be undermined if damages awards were excessive.

2 The Lord Chancellor has confirmed that the court should consider the principles developed by the European Court and that victims should receive damages equivalent to what they would have obtained in the European Court (582 HL 1232, 3 November 1997). If the domestic court were to hold that an act is unlawful because it violates the Convention, it would not be disabled from giving an effective remedy (583 HL 479, 18 November 1997).

3 It would be harsh if domestic law concepts such as exemplary damages in an appropriate case, which is not a concept that has been developed in European jurisprudence, were to be excluded from application under the Act.

4 A criminal court will not be able to award damages for a Convention breach even if it currently has the power to make a compensation order unless it also has the power to award damages in civil proceedings. A person whose rights have been infringed in the Crown Court will have to pursue compensation in the civil courts.

5 According to the Government debate, this section has the 'widest amplitude' and is wide enough to do the job in that it is capable of providing all the equitable remedies necessary to meet the Convention obligations.

6 The court clearly has to take into account all the circumstances of the case. It is submitted that the principles of Community law (ECJ) should be considered in this context. For example, a victim of loss or injury should be entitled to compensation if there is a breach of a rule of law which is designed to protect him and the breach is sufficiently serious and there is a direct causal link between the breach and the damage sustained by the individual. Thus, any legislation which is clearly discriminatory on the ground of nationality is a manifest breach, albeit taken in good faith, and it was bound to have grave consequences on those affected and therefore, in principle, damages for such a breach were available: *R v Secretary of State for Transport, ex parte Factortame Ltd and Others (No 5)* (1999) *The Times*, 3 November.

7 For example, the court will have a wide discretion to consider not only the harm done to the victim but also whether the remedy given is fair to all those whose rights are violated and its impact on the public purse. The court may award a smaller sum by way of damages or no sum at all if it considers that some other appropriate remedy such as a declaration or injunction or rehearing will suffice. Thus, a breach of a right of hearing under Article 6 may be remedied by a direction for a further rehearing in compliance with this Article. The court must take into account only realistic remedies which are available in the proceedings. Further, the court should not award damages twice, for example damages for breach of the Convention and injury to feelings under the Sex Discrimination Act 1975 or the Race Relations Act 1976. The amount of damages awarded in any particular given area should, where possible, be equivalent to, if not higher than, the amount normally awarded under these Acts or under the common law (eg aggravated damages). The 1998 Act is notably silent as to whether exemplary damages are available. It remains to be seen whether exemplary damages may be awarded for a breach of a Convention right under the 1998 Act because exemplary damages are awarded only in respect of those causes of action for which such damages had not been awarded prior to 1964: *AB and Others v South West Water Services Ltd* [1993] 2 WLR 507. The court may choose not to award damages if it results in the public authorities adopting a more cautious or defensive role in carrying out their duties.

8 This suggests that the courts will have regard to the affect an award of damages may have on the resources of the public authority. For example, the court may be influenced not to award damages if there are several thousand victims which might result in the public authority becoming bankrupt and unable to carry out its duties. On the other hand, the floodgate argument should be adopted with some caution or most public authorities will not be dissuaded from repeating its misdeeds: see *McLoughlin v O'Brian* [1983] 1 AC 410.

Recently, the House of Lords was not dissuaded from stating that Spanish fishermen were entitled to damages (which will no doubt amount to millions of pounds) where the breach of EC law was sufficiently serious: *R v Secretary of State for Transport, ex parte Factortame Ltd and Others (No 5)* (1999) *The Times*, 3 May.

9   Article 50 of the Convention provides:

> 'If the Court finds that a decision or a measure taken by a legal authority or any other authority of a High Contracting Party is completely or partially in conflict with the obligations arising from the present Convention, and if the internal law of the said Party allows only partial reparation to be made for the consequences of this decision or measure, the decision of the Court shall, if necessary, afford just satisfaction to the injured party.'

10 The conduct of the victim is a matter which the court can take into account in reducing damages due. Further, there is no reason why the Civil Liability (Contribution) Act 1978 principles cannot apply when more than one person is liable for the same damage and also there is no reason why the principles in contributory negligence should not apply if appropriate: see *McCann v UK* (1996) 21 EHRR 97.

11 The European Court has applied Article 50 to award compensation to successful candidates in the following situations: (i) damages for pecuniary losses; (ii) non-pecuniary losses. In awarding damages for pecuniary losses the Court has usually awarded damages where there is a proved violation of a substantive Convention right as opposed to a proved violation of a procedural right. Compensation for damage to real property: *Henritch v France* (1995) 21 EHRR 199; *López Ostra v Spain* (1994) 20 EHRR 277. The Court refused to award compensation where a fine was imposed by an administrative body exercising a criminal jurisdiction in contravention of Article 6: *Schmautzer v Austria* (1995) 21 EHRR 511. Compensation for non-pecuniary damages has been awarded to those who have had their liberty denied for excessive periods of detention: *Yagci and Sargin v Turkey* (1995) 20 EHRR 505 (detained awaiting criminal trial); applicant compensated for being assaulted while in police custody: *Ribitsch v Austria* (1996) 21 EHRR 573. *A v UK* Application No 100/1997/884/1096 has been decided by the Strasbourg Court. This case deals with the States' obligation to take measures designed to ensure individuals (and schools for that matter) will not be ill-treated in breach of Article 3 by other individuals and that children are entitled to protection, through effective deterrence, against such treatment. The Court awarded the applicant in this case a sum of £10,000 by way of just satisfaction in respect of non-pecuniary damages (para 33).

12 The 1978 Act provides a right to contribution when more than one person is liable for the same damage. Therefore this provision applies when damages are awarded against a public authority.

13 A claim for pecuniary damage was dismissed because no causal link had been shown between the violation and the pecuniary damage alleged: *Brincat v Italy* (1992) 16 EHRR 591, paras 25–26. This is no different than our domestic ruling on causation: the claimant must show on balance of probabilities that the injury was caused by the breach of conduct or duty of which he complains: *Hotson v Berkshire AHA* [1987] AC 750. Awards tend to range from £5,000 to £15,000 and are not made simply because the Court finds a violation of the Convention (see above).

---

9   Judicial acts[1]

(1)   Proceedings under section 7(1)(a) in respect of a judicial act may be brought only—

   (a) by exercising a right of appeal;
   (b) on an application (in Scotland a petition) for judicial review; or
   (c) in such other forum as may be prescribed by rules.

(2)   That does not affect any rule of law which prevents a court from being the subject of judicial review.[2]

(3)   In proceedings under this Act in respect of a judicial act done in good faith, damages may not be awarded otherwise than to compensate a person to the extent required by Article 5(5) of the Convention.[3]

(4)   An award of damages permitted by subsection (3) is to be made against the Crown; but no award may be made unless the appropriate person, if not a party to the proceedings, is joined.[4]

(5)   In this section—

'appropriate person' means the Minister responsible for the court concerned, or a person or government department nominated by him;
'court' includes a tribunal;

'judge' includes a member of a tribunal, a justice of the peace and a clerk or other officer entitled to exercise the jurisdiction of a court;

'judicial act' means a judicial act of a court and includes an act done on the instructions, or on behalf, of a judge;[5] and

'rules' has the same meaning as in section 7(11).

---

1   *General*

Proceedings against a court or tribunal under s 7 may be brought only by way of appeal or on an application for judicial review and that damages may not be awarded in proceedings under the Act in relation to an act of a court or tribunal.

2   The aim is to preserve the current principle of judicial immunity. Proceeding against a court or tribunal on Convention grounds may be brought only by appeal or by way of judicial review.

3   Where a complaint is made that Article 5 has been breached as a result of a judicial act or omission, it will be necessary first to establish whether the judicial act complained of was unlawful, then to rule on whether the victim is entitled to compensation under Article 5(5) and then to determine the amount of compensation. In determining those questions the court will taken into account the Strasbourg jurisprudence on unlawful detention and on the award of damages as required by ss 2 and 8 of the Act. Previously, under ss 44–45 of the Courts and Legal Services Act 1990, an aggrieved person must prove malice in order to succeed in claiming compensation from the magistrates. European case-law is that a requirement to prove malice as a precondition for compensation does not conform with Article 5(5) of the Convention. This section effectively repeals ss 44–45 of the 1990 Act. Presently, the Home Office is prepared, following a recent case, to consider applications for compensation from those who were wrongly convicted as a result of judicial error: *R v SSHD, ex parte Garner and Others* (1999) *The Times*, 3 May.

4   This provision seems to exclude personal liability and accordingly the principle of vicarious liability does not arise because the appropriate Minister is joined. In practice, the Lord Chancellor will be the appropriate person in many cases concerning judges and magistrates. But there may be cases where the breach of the Article 5 provisions arises from a wholly proper judicial decision required by inconsistent legislation, primary or secondary legislation. In this event, it would be helpful for the Minister responsible for the legislation to be joined.

5   This makes it clear that judicial acts include acts undertaken by court officers performing judicial functions or acting on behalf of the judge or on the instructions of the judge.

Remedial action

10   Power to take remedial action[1]

(1)   This section applies if—

(a)   a provision of legislation has been declared under section 4 to be incompatible with a Convention right and, if an appeal lies—

(i)   all persons who may appeal have stated in writing that they do not intend to do so;

(ii)   the time for bringing an appeal has expired and no appeal has been brought within that time; or

(iii)   an appeal brought within that time has been determined or abandoned; or

(b)   it appears to a Minister of the Crown or Her Majesty in Council that, having regard to a finding of the European Court of Human Rights made after the coming into force of this section in proceedings against the United Kingdom, a provision of legislation is incompatible with an obligation of the United Kingdom arising from the Convention.

(2)   If a Minister of the Crown considers that there are compelling reasons for proceeding under this section, he may by order make such amendments to the legislation as he considers necessary to remove the incompatibility.

(3)   If, in the case of subordinate legislation, a Minister of the Crown considers—

(a)   that it is necessary to amend the primary legislation under which the subordinate legislation in question was made, in order to enable the incompatibility to be removed, and

(b) that there are compelling reasons for proceeding under this section,

he may by order make such amendments to the primary legislation as he considers necessary.

(4) This section also applies where the provision in question is in subordinate legislation and has been quashed, or declared invalid, by reason of incompatibility with a Convention right and the Minister proposes to proceed under paragraph 2(b) of Schedule 2.

(5) If the legislation is an Order in Council, the power conferred by subsection (2) or (3) is exercisable by Her Majesty in Council.[2]

(6) In this section 'legislation' does not include a Measure of the Church Assembly or of the General Synod of the Church of England.[3, 4]

(7) Schedule 2 makes further provision about remedial orders.

---

1 *General*
   This section provides the amendment by order of a provision of legislation which has been declared incompatible with the Convention rights or which, in view of a finding of the European Court, appears to a Minister to be incompatible, so as to remove the incompatibility or possible incompatibility.
2 Subordinate legislation means Orders in Council: s 21(1) of the Interpretation Act 1978.
3 The fast-track system allowing for amendment of the primary legislation by an Order is only applicable where the legislation is declared to be incompatible with the Convention rights and as such is not available to amend unrelated parts of the Act in which the breach is discovered.
4 The Church of England, the Church of Scotland or the Roman Catholic Church as bodies would not be public authorities unless they were standing in the place of the State, in which case Convention rights are relevant to what they do. The two must obvious examples relate to marriages and to the provision of education in Church schools (Hansard 20 May 1998 (Lords) p 1015). Measures are to be treated as primary legislation because, under the Church of England Assembly (Powers) Act 1919, Measures have the force and effect of an Act of Parliament once they receive Royal Assent. If such Measures are declared incompatible by the courts, the Government cannot amend such Measures under the remedial order procedure.

Other rights and proceedings

11 Safeguard for existing human rights

A person's reliance on a Convention right does not restrict—

(a) any other right or freedom conferred on him by or under any law having effect in any part of the United Kingdom; or

(b) his right to make any claim or bring any proceedings which he could make or bring apart from sections 7 to 9.[1]

---

1 For example, a person may claim discrimination under Article 14, under the Race Relations Act 1976 and the Sex Discrimination Act 1975. The courts may in such cases be prepared to interpret Article 14 more widely than would be justified by reference to Strasbourg jurisprudence on Article 14. This section is there to ensure that if a person has existing rights, nothing in the Act shall detract from them in any other way. If the courts are prepared to go further than the Convention jurisprudence in Strasbourg then there is nothing in the Act restricting them. Also there is nothing restricting the common law which goes further than the Convention rights.

---

12 Freedom of expression

(1) This section applies if a court is considering whether to grant any relief which, if granted, might affect the exercise of the Convention right to freedom of expression.[1]

(2) If the person against whom the application for relief is made ('the respondent') is neither present nor represented, no such relief is to be granted unless the court is satisfied—

(a) that the applicant has taken all practicable steps to notify the respondent; or

(b) that there are compelling reasons why the respondent should not be notified.[2]

(3)   No such relief is to be granted so as to restrain publication before trial unless the court is satisfied that the applicant is likely to establish that publication should not be allowed.[3]

(4)   The court must have particular regard to the importance of the Convention right to freedom of expression and, where the proceedings relate to material which the respondent claims, or which appears to the court, to be journalistic, literary or artistic material (or to conduct connected with such material),[4] to—

(a)   the extent to which—
  (i)   the material has, or is about to, become available to the public; or
  (ii)   it is, or would be, in the public interest for the material to be published;
(b)   any relevant privacy code.[5]

(5)   In this section—

'court' includes a tribunal;[6] and
'relief' includes any remedy or order (other than in criminal proceedings).

---

1   This section applies to the press, broadcasters or anyone whose right to freedom of expression might be affected. It is not limited to cases to which a public authority is a party.

2   This provision should be construed restrictively, ie on grounds of national security and during war etc. The Government has stated that it does not anticipate this provision to be used often (Hansard 2 July 1998 p 536). Ex parte injunctions are to be granted only in exceptional circumstances.

3   The Strasbourg jurisprudence on Article 10 reinforces the freedom of expression of the press against, for example, the assertion of rights under Article 8 (news is a perishable commodity and to delay its publication for even a short period may well deprive it of all its value and interest: the 'Spycatcher Case'. The courts should consider the merits of an application when it is made and should not grant an interim injunction simply to preserve the status quo ante between the parties. And no relief is to be granted to restrain publication pending a full trial of the issues unless the court is satisfied that the applicant is likely to succeed at trial.

4   This is intended for cases where journalistic inquiries suggest the presence of a story, but no actual material yet exists.

5   If the court and the parties know that a story will shortly be published in another country or on the Internet then this is an important matter to be taken into account. The privacy code includes the code of practice operated by the Press Complaints Commission, the Broadcasting Standards Commission code, the Independent Television Commission code etc.

6   The criminal courts will be required, like the civil courts, to act in a way that is compatible with Articles 8 and 10.

---

13   Freedom of thought, conscience and religion[1]

(1)   If a court's determination of any question arising under this Act might affect the exercise by a religious organisation[2] (itself or its members collectively) of the Convention right to freedom of thought, conscience and religion, it must have particular regard to the importance of that right.[3]

(2)   In this section 'court' includes a tribunal.

---

1   The new clause is designed to safeguard press freedom. It is open to the court to decide that in some cases the right to privacy outweighs the right to freedom of expression. To restrict a company's freedom of expression by extending a right to privacy to a corporation would be in conflict with Article 10 because a corporation has no right to private life under Article 8: *R v Broadcasting Standards Commission, ex parte British Broadcasting Corporation* (1999) *The Times*, 9 July. In one case, the Court considered that the freedom of expression element of the case was subsidiary to the right to respect for private lives which was principally at issue and the Court found that it was not necessary to examine under Article 10: *Lustig-Prean and Becket v UK* Application No 314117/96, (1999) *The Times*, 11 October. The term 'public interest' has not been defined and it is ultimately for the courts to decide what constitutes public interest.

2   The term 'organisation' is deliberately left undefined so that a wide meaning should be given to it to avoid discriminating between one religion and another. But it is thought such organisations must have religious objectives (Hansard 20 May 1998 p 1021) and may include religious charities.

3   The purpose of this section is not to exempt churches or other religious organisations from the scope of the Act. This section will reassure such organisations that the Act will not be used to intrude upon genuinely held religious practices or beliefs. The intention is to focus the courts' attention in any proceedings on the view generally held by the church in question, and on its interst in protecting the integrity of the common faith of its members against attack, whether by outsiders or by individual dissidents. The Government has stated that this section will not provide absolute protection for churches or other religious organisations as against any claim that might possibly be made against them [Hansard 20 May p 1022]. The important point is that such bodies must be public bodies or bodies performing the functions of a public authority or of a public nature. If it is a public body as defined then all the Convention rights as circumscribed by the Act will apply. Charities are not public bodies per se unless they perform a public function. By way of example, a religous school may wish to appoint a headmaster of the same religious persuasion. In such a case, the school is exercising a public function under its statutory powers but such appointment may not be incompatible with the Convention rights or the Act.

A religious minister has a duty to marry people and in conducting a marriage ceremony he is exercising the powers of the State. If he refuses to marry same-sex couples the court will have regard to s 2, ie the Strasbourg jurisprudence which is clearly to the effect that under Article 12 of the Convention the right to marry does not extend to persons of the same biological sex and does not include the right to marry according to a particular ceremony of one's choice. The right to marry guaranteed by Article 12 refers to the traditional marriage between persons of opposite biological sex and the exercise of that right is to be subject to the national laws of the contracting States: *Sheffield and Horsham v UK* Case No 31-32/1997/815-816/1018-1019 [1998] 2 FLR 928. Further, the court will have to give priority to domestic primary legislation over the Convention rights in the event of a conflict that cannot be reconciled by judicial interpretation. Domestic primary legislation specifically provides that same-sex marriages are void. In taking these factors into account the court will act in accordance with s 13 and give particular attention to the objections of the church or religious minister in this regard. (Note those who are excluded from the definition of public bodies.) But it is not open to a court to give automatic priority in all cases to one Convention right over another (317 HC 1340–1341, 21 October 1998).

Derogations and reservations

14   Derogations[1]

(1)   In this Act, 'designated derogation' means—

  (a)   the United Kingdom's derogation from Article 5(3) of the Convention; and
  (b)   any derogation by the United Kingdom from an Article of the Convention, or of any protocol to the Convention, which is designated for the purposes of this Act in an order made by the Secretary of State.[2]

(2)   The derogation referred to in subsection (1)(a) is set out in Part I of Schedule 3.

(3)   If a designated derogation is amended or replaced it ceases to be a designated derogation.

(4)   But subsection (3) does not prevent the Secretary of State from exercising his power under subsection (1)(b) to make a fresh designation order in respect of the Article concerned.

(5)   The Secretary of State must by order make such amendments to Schedule 3 as he considers appropriate to reflect—

  (a)   any designation order; or
  (b)   the effect of subsection (3).

(6)   A designation order may be made in anticipation of the making by the United Kingdom of a proposed derogation.[3]

1   *General*
    This section makes provision in respect of a 'designated derogation', which it defines as the UK's derogation

from Article 5(3) of the Convention (the text of which is set out in Part I of Schedule 2) and any other derogation from an Article of the Convention or of any protocol to the Convention, which is designated by order. It also provides for the amendment of Schedule 2 to reflect the addition or removal of designated reservations.

2   It is suggested that the courts still have jurisdiction and power to examine whether the derogations are compatible with Article 15 of the Convention in times of war or emergency. Further, it is suggested:

    (i)   that the courts should have regard to the Article 15 jurisprudence in Strasbourg when confronted;

    (ii) that other international jurisprudence on derogations should be taken into account (the Geneva Convention for example);

    (iii) derogations which violate international standards should be declared to be so;

    (iv) courts should examine carefully any interference with non-derogable rights and prevent an interference with these non-derogable rights in times of emergency. It is not clear whether the power to derogate is absolute or whether the derogation relates only to the UK's international obligations (for example, detention of Iraqi nationals during the Gulf crisis).

3   Article 15 of the Convention permits a State, in time of war or other public emergency, threatening the life of the nation to take measures derogating from its obligations to the extent strictly required by the exigencies of the situation, provided that such measures are not inconsistent with its other obligations under international law.

15   Reservations[1]

(1)   In this Act, 'designated reservation' means—

    (a) the United Kingdom's reservation to Article 2 of the First Protocol to the Convention; and

    (b) any other reservation by the United Kingdom to an Article of the Convention, or of any protocol to the Convention, which is designated for the purposes of this Act in an order made by the Secretary of State.

(2)   The text of the reservation referred to in subsection (1)(a) is set out in Part II of Schedule 3.

(3)   If a designated reservation is withdrawn wholly or in part it ceases to be a designated reservation.

(4)   But subsection (3) does not prevent the Secretary of State from exercising his power under subsection (1)(b) to make a fresh designation order in respect of the Article concerned.

(5)   The Secretary of State must by order make such amendments to this Act as he considers appropriate to reflect—

    (a) any designation order; or

    (b) the effect of subsection (3).

1   *General*

    This section makes provision in respect of a 'designated reservation', which it defines as the UK's reservation to Article 2 of the First Protocol to the Convention (the text of which is set out in Part II of Schedule 2), and any other reservations to an Article which is designated by order. It also provides for the amendment of Schedule 2 to reflect the addition or removal of designated reservations.

16   Period for which designated derogations have effect[1]

(1)   If it has not already been withdrawn by the United Kingdom, a designated derogation ceases to have effect for the purposes of this Act—

    (a) in the case of the derogation referred to in section 14(1)(a), at the end of the period of five years beginning with the date on which section 1(2) came into force;

(b) in the case of any other derogation, at the end of the period of five years beginning with the date on which the order designating it was made.

(2) At any time before the period—

(a) fixed by subsection (1)(a) or (b), or
(b) extended by an order under this subsection,

comes to an end, the Secretary of State may by order extend it by a further period of five years.

(3) An order under section 14(1)(b) ceases to have effect at the end of the period for consideration, unless a resolution has been passed by each House approving the order.

(4) Subsection (3) does not affect—

(a) anything done in reliance on the order; or
(b) the power to make a fresh order under section 14(1)(b).

(5) In subsection (3) 'period for consideration' means the period of forty days beginning with the day on which the order was made.

(6) In calculating the period for consideration, no account is to be taken of any time during which—

(a) Parliament is dissolved or prorogued; or
(b) both Houses are adjourned for more than four days.

(7) If a designated derogation is withdrawn by the United Kingdom, the Secretary of State must by order make such amendments to this Act as he considers are required to reflect that withdrawal.

---

1   *General*
     This section provides that a designated derogation will, if not withdrawn before then, cease to have effect for
     the purpose of the Act five years after s 1(2) comes into force unless extended by order for a further five years
     before the end of that period. Such order is to be subject to the affirmative resolution procedure.

---

17   Periodic review of designated reservations[1]

(1) The appropriate Minister must review the designated reservation referred to in section 15(1)(a)—

(a) before the end of the period of five years beginning with the date on which section 1(2) came into force; and
(b) if that designation is still in force, before the end of the period of five years beginning with the date on which the last report relating to it was laid under subsection (3).

(2) The appropriate Minister must review each of the other designated reservations (if any)—

(a) before the end of the period of five years beginning with the date on which the order designating the reservation first came into force; and
(b) if the designation is still in force, before the end of the period of five years beginning with the date on which the last report relating to it was laid under subsection (3).

(3) The Minister conducting a review under this section must prepare a report on the result of the review and lay a copy of it before each House of Parliament.

1   *General*

> This section provides that the appropriate Minister must review the designated reservation to Article 2 of the First Protocol to the Convention within five years of s 1(2) coming into force, and any other reservation within five years of its designation; requires the Minister to lay a copy of the report on the result of any such review before each House of Parliament; and provides for further periodic reviews of the designated reservation while the designation is still in force. Article 64(1) of the Convention allows a State to enter into a reservation when a law in force is not in conformity with a Convention provision. The reservation in this case is that in respect of Article 2 of the First Protocol: (i) no person shall be denied the right to education; (ii) the State shall respect the right of parents to ensure that such education and teaching is in conformity with their own religious and philosophical convictions. The reservation makes it clear that the UK accepts this second principle only so far as it is compatible with the provision of efficient instruction and training, and the avoidance of unreasonable public expenditure.

Judges of the European Court of Human Rights[1]

18   Appointment to European Court of Human Rights

(1)   In this section 'judicial office' means the office of—

    (a)   Lord Justice of Appeal, Justice of the High Court or Circuit judge, in England and Wales;

    (b)   judge of the Court of Session or sheriff, in Scotland;

    (c)   Lord Justice of Appeal, judge of the High Court or county court judge, in Northern Ireland.

(2)   The holder of a judicial office may become a judge of the European Court of Human Rights ('the Court') without being required to relinquish his office.

(3)   But he is not required to perform the duties of his judicial office while he is a judge of the Court.

(4)   In respect of any period during which he is a judge of the Court—

    (a)   a Lord Justice of Appeal or Justice of the High Court is not to count as a judge of the relevant court for the purposes of section 2(1) or 4(1) of the Supreme Court Act 1981 (maximum number of judges) nor as a judge of the Supreme Court for the purposes of section 12(1) to (6) of that Act (salaries etc);

    (b)   a judge of the Court of Session is not to count as a judge of that court for the purposes of section 1(1) of the Court of Session Act 1988 (maximum number of judges) or of section 9(1)(c) of the Administration of Justice Act 1973 ('the 1973 Act') (salaries etc);

    (c)   a Lord Justice of Appeal or a judge of the High Court in Northern Ireland is not to count as a judge of the relevant court for the purposes of section 2(1) or 3(1) of the Judicature (Northern Ireland) Act 1978 (maximum number of judges) nor as a judge of the Supreme Court of Northern Ireland for the purposes of section 9(1)(d) of the 1973 Act (salaries etc);

    (d)   a Circuit judge is not to count as such for the purposes of section 18 of the Courts Act 1971 (salaries etc);

    (e)   a sheriff is not to count as such for the purposes of section 14 of the Sheriff Courts (Scotland) Act 1907 (salaries etc);

    (f)   a county court judge of Northern Ireland is not to count as such for the purposes of section 106 of the County Courts Act (Northern Ireland) 1959 (salaries etc).

(5)   If a sheriff principal is appointed a judge of the Court, section 11(1) of the Sheriff Courts (Scotland) Act 1971 (temporary appointment of sheriff principal) applies, while he holds that appointment, as if his office is vacant.

PART 5
THE ACT

(6)   Schedule 3 makes provision about judicial pensions in relation to the holder of a judicial office who serves as a judge of the Court.

(7)   The Lord Chancellor or the Secretary of State may by order make such transitional provision (including, in particular, provision for a temporary increase in the maximum number of judges) as he considers appropriate in relation to any holder of a judicial office who has completed his service as a judge of the Court.

---

1   *General*

> This section provides that a holder of one of the judicial offices to which the section applies may become a judge of the European Court of Human Rights without being required to relinquish his office, and that he is not required to perform the duties of his judicial office while he is a judge of the Court.

Parliamentary procedure[1]

19   Statements of compatibility

(1)   A Minister of the Crown in charge of a Bill in either House of Parliament must, before Second Reading of the Bill—

    (a) make a statement to the effect that in his view the provisions of the Bill are compatible with the Convention rights ('a statement of compatibility'); or

    (b) make a statement to the effect that although he is unable to make a statement of compatibility the government nevertheless wishes the House to proceed with the Bill.

(2)   The statement must be in writing and be published in such manner as the Minister making it considers appropriate.

---

1   *General*

> The Minister in charge of a Bill in either House of Parliament must make and publish a written statement to the effect either that in his view the provisions of the Bill are compatible with the Convention rights or that, although he is unable to make such statement, the Government nevertheless wishes to proceed with the Bill. It remains to be argued that such a statement made by the Minister does not prevent a court finding that such a Bill which is stated to be compatible with the Convention rights is not indeed compatible. A claimant may rely on Article 13 combined with s 13(1) of the Act. The Lord Chancellor has stated that the Ministerial statements of compatibility will inevitably be a strong spur to the courts to find means of construing statutes compatibly with the Convention (584 HL 1291 19 January 1997).

Supplemental

20   Orders etc under this Act

(1)   Any power of a Minister of the Crown to make an order under this Act is exercisable by statutory instrument.

(2)   The power of the Lord Chancellor or the Secretary of State to make rules (other than rules of court) under section 2(3) or 7(9) is exercisable by statutory instrument.

(3)   Any statutory instrument made under section 14, 15 or 16(7) must be laid before Parliament.

(4)   No order may be made by the Lord Chancellor or the Secretary of State under section 1(4), 7(13) or 16(2) unless a draft of the order has been laid before, and approved by, each House of Parliament.

(5)   Any statutory instrument made under section 18(7) or Schedule 4, or to which subsection (2) applies, shall be subject to annulment in pursuance of a resolution of either House of Parliament.

(6)   The power of a Northern Ireland department to make—

(a) rules under section 2(3)(c) or 7(9)(c), or

(b) an order under section 7(11),

is exercisable by statutory rule for the purposes of the Statutory Rules (Northern Ireland) Order 1979.

(7)   Any rules made under section 2(3)(c) or 7(9)(c) shall be subject to negative resolution; and section 41(6) of the Interpretation Act (Northern Ireland) 1954 (meaning of 'subject to negative resolution') shall apply as if the power to make the rules were conferred by an Act of the Northern Ireland Assembly.

(8)   No order may be made by a Northern Ireland department under section 7(11) unless a draft of the order has been laid before, and approved by, the Northern Ireland Assembly.

21   Interpretation, etc

(1)   In this Act—

'amend' includes repeal and apply (with or without modifications);

'the appropriate Minister' means the Minister of the Crown having charge of the appropriate authorised government department (within the meaning of the Crown Proceedings Act 1947);

'the Commission' means the European Commission of Human Rights;

'the Convention' means the Convention for the Protection of Human Rights and Fundamental Freedoms, agreed by the Council of Europe at Rome on 4th November 1950 as it has effect for the time being in relation to the United Kingdom;

'declaration of incompatibility' means a declaration under section 4;

'Minister of the Crown' has the same meaning as in the Ministers of the Crown Act 1975;

'Northern Ireland Minister' includes the First Minister and the deputy First Minister in Northern Ireland;

'primary legislation' means any—

    (a)   public general Act;

    (b)   local and personal Act;

    (c)   private Act;

    (d)   Measure of the Church Assembly;

    (e)   Measure of the General Synod of the Church of England;

    (f)   Order in Council—

        (i)   made in exercise of Her Majesty's Royal Prerogative;

        (ii)   made under section 38(1)(a) of the Northern Ireland Constitution Act 1973 or the corresponding provision of the Northern Ireland Act 1998; or

        (iii)   amending an Act of a kind mentioned in paragraph (a), (b) or (c);

    and includes an order or other instrument made under primary legislation (otherwise than by the National Assembly for Wales, a member of the Scottish Executive, a Northern Ireland Minister or a Northern Ireland department) to the extent to which it operates to bring one or more provisions of that legislation into force or amends any primary legislation;

'the First Protocol' means the protocol to the Convention agreed at Paris on 20th March 1952;

'the Sixth Protocol' means the protocol to the Convention agreed at Strasbourg on 28th April 1983;

'the Eleventh Protocol' means the protocol to the Convention (restructuring the control machinery established by the Convention) agreed at Strasbourg on 11th May 1994;

'remedial order' means an order under section 10;
'subordinate legislation' means any—

  (a) Order in Council other than one—
      (i) made in exercise of Her Majesty's Royal Prerogative;
     (ii) made under section 38(1)(a) of the Northern Ireland Constitution Act 1973 or the corresponding provision of the Northern Ireland Act 1998; or
    (iii) amending an Act of a kind mentioned in the definition of primary legislation;
  (b) Act of the Scottish Parliament;
  (c) Act of the Parliament of Northern Ireland;
  (d) Measure of the Assembly established under section 1 of the Northern Ireland Assembly Act 1973;
  (e) Act of the Northern Ireland Assembly;
  (f) order, rules, regulations, scheme, warrant, byelaw or other instrument made under primary legislation (except to the extent to which it operates to bring one or more provisions of that legislation into force or amends any primary legislation);
  (g) order, rules, regulations, scheme, warrant, byelaw or other instrument made under legislation mentioned in paragraph (b), (c), (d) or (e) or made under an Order in Council applying only to Northern Ireland;
  (h) order, rules, regulations, scheme, warrant, byelaw or other instrument made by a member of the Scottish Executive, a Northern Ireland Minister or a Northern Ireland department in exercise of prerogative or other executive functions of Her Majesty which are exercisable by such a person on behalf of Her Majesty;

'transferred matters' has the same meaning as in the Northern Ireland Act 1998; and 'tribunal' means any tribunal in which legal proceedings may be brought.

(2)   The references in paragraphs (b) and (c) of section 2(1) to Articles are to Articles of the Convention as they had effect immediately before the coming into force of the Eleventh Protocol.

(3)   The reference in paragraph (d) of section 2(1) to Article 46 includes a reference to Articles 32 and 54 of the Convention as they had effect immediately before the coming into force of the Eleventh Protocol.

(4)   The references in section 2(1) to a report or decision of the Commission or a decision of the Committee of Ministers include references to a report or decision made as provided by paragraphs 3, 4 and 6 of Article 5 of the Eleventh Protocol (transitional provisions).

(5)   Any liability under the Army Act 1955, the Air Force Act 1955 or the Naval Discipline Act 1957 to suffer death for an offence is replaced by a liability to imprisonment for life or any less punishment authorised by those Acts; and those Acts shall accordingly have effect with the necessary modifications.

22   Short title, commencement, application and extent

(1)   This Act may be cited as the Human Rights Act 1998.

(2)   Sections 18 and 20 and this section come into force on the passing of this Act.

(3)   The other provisions of this Act come into force on such day as the Secretary of State may by order appoint; and different days may be appointed for different purposes.

(4)   Paragraph (b) of subsection (1) of section 7 applies to proceedings brought by or at the instigation of a public authority whenever the act in question took place; but

otherwise that subsection does not apply to an act taking place before the coming into force of that section.[1]

(5)   This Act binds the Crown.

(6)   This Act extends to Northern Ireland.

(7)   Section 21(5), so far as it relates to any provision contained in the Army Act 1955, the Air Force Act 1955 or the Naval Discipline Act 1957, extends to any place to which that provision extends.

---

1   Section 22(4) introduces an element of retrospectivity on which victims of acts made unlawful by the Convention may rely under s 7(1)(b): *R v DPP, ex parte Kebilene* [1999] 3 WLR 175 at 185C, (1999) *The Times*, 31 March, CA.

SCHEDULES

SCHEDULE 1

THE ARTICLES

PART I

THE CONVENTION

Rights and Freedoms

Article 2

Right to life

1.   Everyone's right to life shall be protected by law. No one shall be deprived of his life intentionally save in the execution of a sentence of a court following his conviction of a crime for which this penalty is provided by law.

2.   Deprivation of life shall not be regarded as inflicted in contravention of this Article when it results from the use of force which is no more than absolutely necessary:

(a)   in defence of any person from unlawful violence;
(b)   in order to effect a lawful arrest or to prevent the escape of a person lawfully detained;
(c)   in action lawfully taken for the purpose of quelling a riot or insurrection.

Article 3

Prohibition of torture

No one shall be subjected to torture or to inhuman or degrading treatment or punishment.

Article 4

Prohibition of slavery and forced labour

1.   No one shall be held in slavery or servitude.

2.   No one shall be required to perform forced or compulsory labour.

3.   For the purpose of this Article the term 'forced or compulsory labour' shall not include:

(a)   any work required to be done in the ordinary course of detention imposed according to the provisions of Article 5 of this Convention or during conditional release from such detention;

(b)   any service of a military character or, in case of conscientious objectors in countries where they are recognised, service exacted instead of compulsory military service;

(c)   any service exacted in case of an emergency or calamity threatening the life or well-being of the community;

(d)   any work or service which forms part of normal civic obligations.

Article 5

Right to liberty and security

1.   Everyone has the right to liberty and security of person. No one shall be deprived of his liberty save in the following cases and in accordance with a procedure prescribed by law:

(a)   the lawful detention of a person after conviction by a competent court;

(b)   the lawful arrest or detention of a person for non-compliance with the lawful order of a court or in order to secure the fulfilment of any obligation prescribed by law;

(c)   the lawful arrest or detention of a person effected for the purpose of bringing him before the competent legal authority on reasonable suspicion of having committed an offence or when it is reasonably considered necessary to prevent his committing an offence or fleeing after having done so;

(d)   the detention of a minor by lawful order for the purpose of educational supervision or his lawful detention for the purpose of bringing him before the competent legal authority;

(e)   the lawful detention of persons for the prevention of the spreading of infectious diseases, of persons of unsound mind, alcoholics or drug addicts or vagrants;

(f)   the lawful arrest or detention of a person to prevent his effecting an unauthorised entry into the country or of a person against whom action is being taken with a view to deportation or extradition.

2.   Everyone who is arrested shall be informed promptly, in a language which he understands, of the reasons for his arrest and of any charge against him.

3.   Everyone arrested or detained in accordance with the provisions of paragraph 1(c) of this Article shall be brought promptly before a judge or other officer authorised by law to exercise judicial power and shall be entitled to trial within a reasonable time or to release pending trial. Release may be conditioned by guarantees to appear for trial.

4.   Everyone who is deprived of his liberty by arrest or detention shall be entitled to take proceedings by which the lawfulness of his detention shall be decided speedily by a court and his release ordered if the detention is not lawful.

5.   Everyone who has been the victim of arrest or detention in contravention of the provisions of this Article shall have an enforceable right to compensation.

Article 6

Right to a fair trial

1.   In the determination of his civil rights and obligations or of any criminal charge against him, everyone is entitled to a fair and public hearing within a reasonable time by an independent and impartial tribunal established by law. Judgment shall be pronounced publicly but the press and public may be excluded from all or part of the trial in the interest of morals, public order or national security in a democratic society, where the interests of juveniles or the protection of the private life of the parties so require, or to the extent strictly necessary in the opinion of the court in special circumstances where publicity would prejudice the interests of justice.

2.   Everyone charged with a criminal offence shall be presumed innocent until proved guilty according to law.

3.   Everyone charged with a criminal offence has the following minimum rights:

   (a)   to be informed promptly, in a language which he understands and in detail, of the nature and cause of the accusation against him;
   (b)   to have adequate time and facilities for the preparation of his defence;
   (c)   to defend himself in person or through legal assistance of his own choosing or, if he has not sufficient means to pay for legal assistance, to be given it free when the interests of justice so require;
   (d)   to examine or have examined witnesses against him and to obtain the attendance and examination of witnesses on his behalf under the same conditions as witnesses against him;
   (e)   to have the free assistance of an interpreter if he cannot understand or speak the language used in court.

Article 7

No punishment without law

1.   No one shall be held guilty of any criminal offence on account of any act or omission which did not constitute a criminal offence under national or international law at the time when it was committed. Nor shall a heavier penalty be imposed than the one that was applicable at the time the criminal offence was committed.

2.   This Article shall not prejudice the trial and punishment of any person for any act or omission which, at the time when it was committed, was criminal according to the general principles of law recognised by civilised nations.

Article 8

Right to respect for private and family life

1.   Everyone has the right to respect for his private and family life, his home and his correspondence.

2.   There shall be no interference by a public authority with the exercise of this right except such as is in accordance with the law and is necessary in a democratic society in the interests of national security, public safety or the economic well-being of the country, for the prevention of disorder or crime, for the protection of health or morals, or for the protection of the rights and freedoms of others.

Article 9

Freedom of thought, conscience and religion

1.   Everyone has the right to freedom of thought, conscience and religion; this right includes freedom to change his religion or belief and freedom, either alone or in community with others and in public or private, to manifest his religion or belief, in worship, teaching, practice and observance.

2.   Freedom to manifest one's religion or beliefs shall be subject only to such limitations as are prescribed by law and are necessary in a democratic society in the interests of public safety, for the protection of public order, health or morals, or for the protection of the rights and freedoms of others.

Article 10

Freedom of expression

1.   Everyone has the right to freedom of expression. This right shall include freedom to hold opinions and to receive and impart information and ideas without interference by public authority and regardless of frontiers. This Article shall not prevent States from requiring the licensing of broadcasting, television or cinema enterprises.

2.   The exercise of these freedoms, since it carries with it duties and responsibilities, may be subject to such formalities, conditions, restrictions or penalties as are prescribed by law and are necessary in a democratic society, in the interests of national security, territorial integrity or public safety, for the prevention of disorder or crime, for the protection of health or morals, for the protection of the reputation or rights of others, for preventing the disclosure of information received in confidence, or for maintaining the authority and impartiality of the judiciary.

Article 11

Freedom of assembly and association

1.   Everyone has the right to freedom of peaceful assembly and to freedom of association with others, including the right to form and to join trade unions for the protection of his interests.

2.   No restrictions shall be placed on the exercise of these rights other than such as are prescribed by law and are necessary in a democratic society in the interests of national security or public safety, for the prevention of disorder or crime, for the protection of health or morals or for the protection of the rights and freedoms of others. This Article shall not prevent the imposition of lawful restrictions on the exercise of these rights by members of the armed forces, of the police or of the administration of the State.

Article 12

Right to marry

Men and women of marriageable age have the right to marry and to found a family, according to the national laws governing the exercise of this right.

Article 14

Prohibition of discrimination

The enjoyment of the rights and freedoms set forth in this Convention shall be secured without discrimination on any ground such as sex, race, colour, language, religion, political or other opinion, national or social origin, association with a national minority, property, birth or other status.

Article 16

Restrictions on political activity of aliens

Nothing in Articles 10, 11 and 14 shall be regarded as preventing the High Contracting Parties from imposing restrictions on the political activity of aliens.

Article 17

Prohibition of abuse of rights

Nothing in this Convention may be interpreted as implying for any State, group or person any right to engage in any activity or perform any act aimed at the destruction of any of the rights and freedoms set forth herein or at their limitation to a greater extent than is provided for in the Convention.

Article 18

Limitation on use of restrictions on rights

The restrictions permitted under this Convention to the said rights and freedoms shall not be applied for any purpose other than those for which they have been prescribed.

PART II

THE FIRST PROTOCOL

Article 1

Protection of property

Every natural or legal person is entitled to the peaceful enjoyment of his possessions. No one shall be deprived of his possessions except in the public interest and subject to the conditions provided for by law and by the general principles of international law.

The preceding provisions shall not, however, in any way impair the right of a State to enforce such laws as it deems necessary to control the use of property in accordance with the general interest or to secure the payment of taxes or other contributions or penalties.

Article 2

Right to education

No person shall be denied the right to education. In the exercise of any functions which it assumes in relation to education and to teaching, the State shall respect the right of parents to ensure such education and teaching in conformity with their own religious and philosophical convictions.

Article 3

Right to free elections

The High Contracting Parties undertake to hold free elections at reasonable intervals by secret ballot, under conditions which will ensure the free expression of the opinion of the people in the choice of the legislature.

PART III

THE SIXTH PROTOCOL

Article 1

Abolition of the death penalty

The death penalty shall be abolished. No one shall be condemned to such penalty or executed.

Article 2

Death penalty in time of war

A State may make provisions in its law for the death penalty in respect of acts committed in time of war or of imminent threat of war; such penalty shall be applied only in the instances laid down in the law and in accordance with its provisions. The State shall communicate to the Secretary of the Council of Europe the relevant provisions of that law.

SCHEDULE 2

REMEDIAL ORDERS[1]

Orders

1.—(1)   A remedial order may—

(a) contain such incidental, supplemental, consequential or transitional provision as the person making it considers appropriate;

(b) be made so as to have effect from a date earlier than that on which it is made;

(c) make provision for the delegation of specific functions;

(d) make different provision for different cases.

(2)   The power conferred by sub-paragraph (1)(a) includes—

(a) power to amend primary legislation (including primary legislation other than that which contains the incompatible provision); and

(b) power to amend or revoke subordinate legislation (including subordinate legislation other than that which contains the incompatible provision).

(3)   A remedial order may be made so as to have the same extent as the legislation which it affects.

(4)   No person is to be guilty of an offence solely as a result of the retrospective effect of a remedial order.[2]

Procedure[3]

2.   No remedial order may be made unless—

(a) a draft of the order has been approved by a resolution of each House of Parliament made after the end of the period of 60 days beginning with the day on which the draft was laid; or

(b) it is declared in the order that it appears to the person making it that, because of the urgency of the matter, it is necessary to make the order without a draft being so approved.

Orders laid in draft

3.—(1)   No draft may be laid under paragraph 2(a) unless—

(a)   the person proposing to make the order has laid before Parliament a document which contains a draft of the proposed order and the required information; and

(b)   the period of 60 days, beginning with the day on which the document required by this sub-paragraph was laid, has ended.

(2)   If representations have been made during that period, the draft laid under paragraph 2(a) must be accompanied by a statement containing—

(a)   a summary of the representations; and

(b)   if, as a result of the representations, the proposed order has been changed, details of the changes.

Urgent cases

4.—(1)   If a remedial order ('the original order') is made without being approved in draft, the person making it must lay it before Parliament, accompanied by the required information, after it is made.

(2) If representations have been made during the period of 60 days beginning with the day on which the original order was made, the person making it must (after the end of that period) lay before Parliament a statement containing—

(a)   a summary of the representations; and

(b)   if, as a result of the representations, he considers it appropriate to make changes to the original order, details of the changes.

(3)   If sub-paragraph (2)(b) applies, the person making the statement must—

(a)   make a further remedial order replacing the original order; and

(b)   lay the replacement order before Parliament.

(4)   If, at the end of the period of 120 days beginning with the day on which the original order was made, a resolution has not been passed by each House approving the original or replacement order, the order ceases to have effect (but without that affecting anything previously done under either order or the power to make a fresh remedial order).

Definitions

5.   In this Schedule—

'representations' means representations about a remedial order (or proposed remedial order) made to the person making (or proposing to make) it and includes any relevant Parliamentary report or resolution; and
'required information' means—

(a)   an explanation of the incompatibility which the order (or proposed order) seeks to remove, including particulars of the relevant declaration, finding or order; and

(b)   a statement of the reasons for proceeding under section 10 and for making an order in those terms.

Calculating periods

6.   In calculating any period for the purposes of this Schedule, no account is to be taken of any time during which—

(a) Parliament is dissolved or prorogued; or

(b) both Houses are adjourned for more than four days.

---

1   *General*

    This section makes further provision with respect to such a remedial order and also provides that no person shall be guilty of an offence solely as a result of any retrospective effect of such an order. The Government has expressed the view that Parliament would act swiftly to provide a remedial order when the liberty of a subject is in issue (Hansard 24 June 1998 (Lords) p 1138).

2   This is compatible with Article 7 of the Convention rights which prevents criminal sanctions being applied retrospectively.

3   This section provides that a remedial order is to be subject to the affirmative resolution procedure, and that, except in urgent cases, the order must be approved in draft. Where not approved in draft before it is made, it ceases to have effect if not approved by Parliament within 40 sitting days of it having been made.

SCHEDULE 3

DEROGATION AND RESERVATION

PART I

DEROGATION

The 1988 notification

The United Kingdom Permanent Representative to the Council of Europe presents his compliments to the Secretary General of the Council, and has the honour to convey the following information in order to ensure compliance with the obligations of Her Majesty's Government in the United Kingdom under Article 15(3) of the Convention for the Protection of Human Rights and Fundamental Freedoms signed at Rome on 4 November 1950.

There have been in the United Kingdom in recent years campaigns of organised terrorism connected with the affairs of Northern Ireland which have manifested themselves in activities which have included repeated murder, attempted murder, maiming, intimidation and violent civil disturbance and in bombing and fire raising which have resulted in death, injury and widespread destruction of property. As a result, a public emergency within the meaning of Article 15(1) of the Convention exists in the United Kingdom.

The Government found it necessary in 1974 to introduce and since then, in cases concerning persons reasonably suspected of involvement in terrorism connected with the affairs of Northern Ireland, or of certain offences under the legislation, who have been detained for 48 hours, to exercise powers enabling further detention without charge, for periods of up to five days, on the authority of the Secretary of State. These powers are at present to be found in Section 12 of the Prevention of Terrorism (Temporary Provisions) Act 1984, Article 9 of the Prevention of Terrorism (Supplemental Temporary Provisions) Order 1984 and Article 10 of the Prevention of Terrorism (Supplemental Temporary Provisions) (Northern Ireland) Order 1984.

Section 12 of the Prevention of Terrorism (Temporary Provisions) Act 1984 provides for a person whom a constable has arrested on reasonable grounds of suspecting him to be guilty of an offence under Section 1, 9 or 10 of the Act, or to be or to have been involved in terrorism connected with the affairs of Northern Ireland, to be detained in right of the arrest for up to 48 hours and thereafter, where the Secretary of State extends the detention period, for up to a further five days. Section 12 substantially re-enacted Section 12 of the Prevention of Terrorism (Temporary Provisions) Act 1976 which, in turn, substantially re-enacted Section 7 of the Prevention of Terrorism (Temporary Provisions) Act 1974.

Article 10 of the Prevention of Terrorism (Supplemental Temporary Provisions) (Northern Ireland) Order 1984 (SI 1984/417) and Article 9 of the Prevention of Terrorism (Supplemental Temporary Provisions) Order 1984 (SI 1984/418) were both made under Sections 13 and 14 of and Schedule 3 to the 1984 Act and substantially re-enacted powers of detention in Orders made under the 1974 and 1976 Acts. A person who is being examined under Article 4 of either Order on his arrival in, or on seeking to leave, Northern Ireland or Great Britain for the purpose of determining whether he is or has been involved in terrorism connected with the affairs of Northern Ireland, or whether there are grounds for suspecting that he has committed an offence under Section 9 of the 1984 Act, may be detained under Article 4 or 10, as appropriate, pending the conclusion of his examination. The period of this examination may exceed 12 hours if an examining officer has reasonable grounds for suspecting him to be or to have been involved in acts of terrorism connected with the affairs of Northern Ireland.

Where such a person is detained under the said Article 9 or 10 he may be detained for up to 48 hours on the authority of an examining officer and thereafter, where the Secretary of State extends the detention period, for up to a further five days.

In its judgment of 29 November 1988 in the Case of *Brogan and Others*, the European Court of Human Rights held that there had been a violation of Article 5(3) in respect of each of the applicants, all of whom had been detained under Section 12 of the 1984 Act. The Court held that even the shortest of the four periods of detention concerned, namely four days and six hours, fell outside the constraints as to time permitted by the first part of Article 5(3). In addition, the Court held that there had been a violation of Article 5(3) in the case of each applicant.

Following this judgment, the Secretary of State for the Home Department informed Parliament on 6 December 1988 that, against the background of the terrorist campaign, and the over-riding need to bring terrorists to justice, the Government did not believe that the maximum period of detention should be reduced. He informed Parliament that the Government were examining the matter with a view to responding to the judgment. On 22 December 1988, the Secretary of State further informed Parliament that it remained the Government's wish, if it could be achieved, to find a judicial process under which extended detention might be reviewed and where appropriate authorised by a judge or other judicial officer. But a further period of reflection and consultation was necessary before the Government could bring forward a firm and final view.

Since the judgment of 29 November as well as previously, the Government have found it necessary to continue to exercise, in relation to terrorism connected with the affairs of Northern Ireland, the powers described above enabling further detention without charge for periods of up to 5 days, on the authority of the Secretary of State, to the extent strictly required by the exigencies of the situation to enable necessary enquiries and investigations properly to be completed in order to decide whether criminal proceedings should be instituted. To the extent that the exercise of these powers may be inconsistent with the obligations imposed by the Convention the Government has availed itself of the right of derogation conferred by Article 15(1) of the Convention and will continue to do so until further notice.

Dated 23 December 1988.

The 1989 notification

The United Kingdom Permanent Representative to the Council of Europe presents his compliments to the Secretary General of the Council, and has the honour to convey the following information.

PART 5
THE ACT

In his communication to the Secretary General of 23 December 1988, reference was made to the introduction and exercise of certain powers under section 12 of the Prevention of Terrorism (Temporary Provisions) Act 1984, Article 9 of the Prevention of Terrorism (Supplemental Temporary Provisions) Order 1984 and Article 10 of the Prevention of Terrorism (Supplemental Temporary Provisions) (Northern Ireland) Order 1984.

These provisions have been replaced by section 14 of and paragraph 6 of Schedule 5 to the Prevention of Terrorism (Temporary Provisions) Act 1989, which make comparable provision. They came into force on 22 March 1989. A copy of these provisions is enclosed.

The United Kingdom Permanent Representative avails himself of this opportunity to renew to the Secretary General the assurance of his highest consideration.

23 March 1989.

PART II

RESERVATION

At the time of signing the present (First) Protocol, I declare that, in view of certain provisions of the Education Acts in the United Kingdom, the principle affirmed in the second sentence of Article 2 is accepted by the United Kingdom only so far as it is compatible with the provision of efficient instruction and training, and the avoidance of unreasonable public expenditure.

Dated 20 March 1952. Made by the United Kingdom Permanent Representative to the Council of Europe.

SCHEDULE 4

JUDICIAL PENSIONS

Duty to make orders about pensions

1.—(1)　The appropriate Minister must by order make provision with respect to pensions payable to or in respect of any holder of a judicial office who serves as an ECHR judge.

(2)　A pensions order must include such provision as the Minister making it considers is necessary to secure that—

- (a) an ECHR judge who was, immediately before his appointment as an ECHR judge, a member of a judicial pension scheme is entitled to remain as a member of that scheme;
- (b) the terms on which he remains a member of the scheme are those which would have been applicable had he not been appointed as an ECHR judge; and
- (c) entitlement to benefits payable in accordance with the scheme continues to be determined as if, while serving as an ECHR judge, his salary was that which would (but for section 18(4)) have been payable to him in respect of his continuing service as the holder of his judicial office.

Contributions

2.   A pensions order may, in particular, make provision—

(a) for any contributions which are payable by a person who remains a member of a scheme as a result of the order, and which would otherwise be payable by deduction from his salary, to be made otherwise than by deduction from his salary as an ECHR judge; and

(b) for such contributions to be collected in such manner as may be determined by the administrators of the scheme.

Amendments of other enactments

3.   A pensions order may amend any provision of, or made under, a pensions Act in such manner and to such extent as the Minister making the order considers necessary or expedient to ensure the proper administration of any scheme to which it relates.

Definitions

4.   In this Schedule—

'appropriate Minister' means—

(a) in relation to any judicial office whose jurisdiction is exercisable exclusively in relation to Scotland, the Secretary of State; and

(b) otherwise, the Lord Chancellor;

'ECHR judge' means the holder of a judicial office who is serving as a judge of the Court;
'judicial pension scheme' means a scheme established by and in accordance with a pensions Act;
'pensions Act' means—

(a) the County Courts Act (Northern Ireland) 1959;

(b) the Sheriffs' Pensions (Scotland) Act 1961;

(c) the Judicial Pensions Act 1981; or

(d) the Judicial Pensions and Retirement Act 1993; and

'pensions order' means an order made under paragraph 1.

PART 6

APPENDICES

APPENDIX 1

UNIVERSAL DECLARATION OF HUMAN RIGHTS 1948

PREAMBLE

[181]

Whereas recognition of the inherent dignity and of the equal and inalienable rights of all members of the human family is the foundation of freedom, justice and peace in the world,

Whereas disregard and contempt for human rights have resulted in barbarous acts which have outraged the conscience of mankind, and the advent of a world in which human beings shall enjoy freedom of speech and belief and freedom from fear and want has been proclaimed as the highest aspiration of the common people,

Whereas it is essential, if man is not to be compelled to have recourse, as a last resort, to rebellion against tyranny and oppression, that human rights should be protected by the rule of law,

Whereas it is essential to promote the development of friendly relations between nations,

Whereas the peoples of the United Nations have in the Charter reaffirmed their faith in fundamental human rights, in the dignity and worth of the human persons and in the equal rights of men and women and have determined to promote social progess and better standards of life in larger freedom,

Whereas Member States have pledged themselves to achieve, in co-operation with the United Nations, the promotion of universal respect for and observance of human rights and fundamental freedoms,

Whereas a common understanding of these rights and freedoms is one of the greatest importance for the full realisation of this pledge,

Now, therefore, THE GENERAL ASSEMBLY *proclaims*

This Universal Declaration of Human Rights as a common standard of achievement for all peoples and all nations, to the end that every individual and every organ of society, keeping this Declaration constantly in mind, shall strive by teaching and education to promote respect for these rights and freedoms and by progressive measures, national and international; to secure their universal and effective recognition and observance, both among the peoples of Member States themselves and among the peoples of territories under their jurisdiction.

[182]
Article 1
All human beings are born free and equal in dignity and rights. They are endowed with reason and conscience and should act towards one another in a spirit of brotherhood.

[183]
Article 2
Everyone is entitled to all the rights and freedoms set forth in this Declaration, without distinction of any kind, such as race, colour, sex, language, religion, political or other opinion, national or social origin, property, birth or other status.

Furthermore, no distinction shall be made on the basis of the political, jurisdictional or international status of the country or territory to which a person belongs, whether it be independent trust, non self-governing or under any other limitation of sovereignty.

[184]
Article 3
Everyone has the right to life, liberty and the security of person.

[185]
Article 4
No one shall be held in slavery or servitude; slavery and the slave trade shall be prohibited in all their forms.

[186]
Article 5
No one shall be subjected to torture or to cruel, inhuman or degrading treatment or punishment.

[187]
Article 6
Everyone has the right to recognition everywhere as a person before the law.

[188]
Article 7
All are equal before the law and are entitled without any discrimination to equal protection of the law. All are entitled to equal protection against any discrimination in violation of this Declaration and against any incitement to such discrimination.

[189]
Article 8
Everyone has the right to an effective remedy by the competent national tribunals for acts violating the fundamental rights granted him by the constitution or by law.

[190]
Article 9
No one shall be subjected to arbitrary arrest, detention or exile.

[191]
Article 10
Everyone is entitled to full equality to a fair and public hearing by an independent and impartial tribunal, in the determination of his rights and obligations and of any criminal charge against him.

[192]
Article 11
1   Everyone charged with a penal offence has the right to be presumed innocent until proved guilty according to law in a public trial at which he has had all the guarantees necessary for his defence.
2   No one shall be held guilty of any penal offence on account of any act or omission which did not constitute a penal offence, under national or international law, at the time

when it was committed. Nor shall a heavier penalty be imposed than the one that was applicable at the time the penal offence was committed.

[193]
Article 12
No one shall be subject to arbitrary interference with his privacy, family, home or correspondence, nor to attacks upon his honour and reputation. Everyone has the right to the protection of the law against such interference or attacks.

[194]
Article 13
1   Everyone has the right to freedom of movement and residence within the borders of each State.
2   Everyone has the right to leave any country, including his own, and to return to his country.

[195]
Article 14
1   Everyone has the right to seek and to enjoy in other countries asylum from persecution.
2   This right may not be invoked in the case of prosecutions genuinely arising from non-political crimes or from acts contrary to the purposes and principles of the United Nations.

[196]
Article 15
1   Everyone has the right to a nationality.
2   No one shall be arbitrarily deprived of his nationality nor denied the right to change his nationality.

[197]
Article 16
1   Men and women of full age, without any limitation due to race, nationality or religion, have the right to marry and to found a family. They are entitled to equal rights as to marriage, during marriage and at its dissolution.
2   Marriage shall be entered into only with the free and full consent of the intending spouses.
3   The family is the natural and fundamental group unit of society and is entitled to protection by society and the State.

[198]
Article 17
1   Everyone has the right to own property alone as well as in association with others.
2   No one shall be arbitrarily deprived of his property.

[199]
Article 18
Everyone has the right to freedom of thought, conscience and religion; this right includes freedom to change his religion or belief, and freedom, either alone or in community with others and in public or private, to manifest his religion or belief in teaching, practice, worship and observance.

PART 6
APPENDICES

[200]
Article 19
Everyone has the right to freedom of opinion and expression; this right includes freedom to hold opinions without interference and to seek, receive and impart information and ideas through any media and regardless of frontiers.

[201]
Article 20
1   Everyone hs the right to freedom of peaceful assembly and association.
2   No one may be compelled to belong to an association.

[202]
Article 21
1   Everyone has the right to take part in the government of his country, directly or through freely chosen representatives.
2   Everyone has the right of equal access to public service in his country.
3   The will of the people shall be the basis of the authority of government; this will shall be expressed in periodic and genuine elections which shall be by universal and equal suffrage and shall be held by secret vote or by equivalent free voting procedures.

[203]
Article 22
Everyone, as a member of society, has the right to social security and is entitled to realisation, through national effort and international co-operation and in accordance with the organisation and resources of each State, of the economic, social and cultural rights indispensable for his dignity and the free development of his personality.

[204]
Article 23
1   Everyone has the right to work, to free choice of employment, to just and favourable conditions of work and to protection against unemployment.
2   Everyone, without any discrimination, has the right to equal pay for equal work.
3   Everyone who works has the right to just and favourable remuneration ensuring for himself and his family an existence worthy of human dignity, and supplemented, if necessary, by other means of social protection.
4   Everyone has the right to form and to join trade unions for the protection of his interests.

[205]
Article 24
Everyone has the right to rest and leisure, including reasonable limitation of working hours and periodic holidays with pay.

[206]
Article 25
1   Eveyone has the right to a standard of living adequate for the health and well-being of himself and for his family, including food, clothing, housing and medical care and necessary social services, and the right to security in the event of unemployment, sickness, disability, widowhood, old age or other lack of livelihood in circumstances beyond his control.
2   Motherhood and childhood are entitled to special care and assistance. All children, whether born in or out of wedlock, shall enjoy the same social protection.

[207]
Article 26
1   Everyone has the right to education. Education shall be free, at least in the elementary and fundamental stages. Elementary education shall be compulsory. Technical and professional education shall be made generally available and higher education shall be equally accessible to all on the basis of merit.
2   Education shall be directed to the full development of the human personality and to the strengthening of respect for human rights and fundamental freedoms. It shall promote understanding, tolerance and friendship among all nations, racial or religious groups, and shall further the activities of the United Nations for the maintenance of peace.
3   Parents have a prior right to choose the kind of education that shall be given to their children.

[208]
Article 27
1   Everyone has the right freely to participate in the cultural life of the community, to enjoy the arts and to share in scientific advancement and its benefits.
2   Everyone has the right to the protection of the moral and material interests resulting from any scientific, literary or artistic production of which he is the author.

[209]
Article 28
Everyone is entitled to a social and international order in which the rights and freedoms set forth in this Declaration can be fully realised.

[210]
Article 29
1   Everyone has duties to the community in which alone the free and full development of his personality is possible.
2   In the exercise of his rights and freedoms, everyone shall be subject only to such limitations as are determined by law solely for the purpose of securing due recognition and respect for the rights and freedoms of others and of meeting the just requirements of morality, public order and the general welfare in a democratic society.
3   These rights and freedoms may in no case be exercised contrary to the purposes and principles of the United Nations.

[211]–[1000]
Article 30
Nothing in this Declaration may be interpreted as implying for any State, group or person any right to engage in any activity or to perform any act aimed at the destruction of any of the rights and freedoms set forth herein.

PART 6
APPENDICES

APPENDIX 2

INTERNATIONAL COVENANT ON CIVIL AND POLITICAL RIGHTS

16 December 1966
UNTS Vol 999, p 171
Entry into force   23 March 1976

Note   The UK has ratified this Covenant, but not its optional Protocol, which confers on individuals the right to communicate complaints.

PREAMBLE

The states parties to the present Covenant,
Considering that, in accordance with the principles proclaimed in the Charter of the United Nations, recognition of the inherent dignity and of the equal and inalienable rights of all members of the human family is the foundation of freedom, justice and peace in the world,

Recognising that these rights derive from the inherent dignity of the human person,

Recognising that, in accordance with the Universal Declaration of Human Rights, the ideal of free human beings enjoying civil and political freedom and freedom from fear and want can only be achieved if conditions are created whereby everyone may enjoy his civil and political rights, as well as his economic, social and cultural rights,

Considering the obligation of states under the Charter of the United Nations to promote universal respect for, and observance of, human rights and freedoms,

Realising that the individual, having duties to other individuals and to the community to which he belongs, is under a responsibility to strive for the promotion and observance of the rights recognised in the present Covenant,

Agree upon the following articles:

PART I
[1]
Article 1
1   All peoples have the right of self-determination. By virtue of that right they freely determine their political status and freely pursue their economic, social and cultural development.
2   All peoples may, for their own ends, freely dispose of their natural wealth and resources without prejudice to any obligations arising out of international economic co-operation, based upon the principle of mutual benefit, and international law. In no case may a people be deprived of its own means of subsistence.
3   The states parties to the present Covenant, including those having responsiblity for the administration of Non-Self-Governing and Trust Territories, shall promote the realization of the right of self-determination, and shall respect that right, in conformity with the provisions of the Charter of the United Nations.

PART II
[2]
Article 2

1   Each state party to the present Covenant undertakes to respect and to ensure to all individuals within its territory and subject to its jurisdiction the rights recognized in the present Covenant, without distinction of any kind, such as race, colour, sex, language, religion, political or other opinion, national or social origin, property, birth or other status.

2   Where not already provided for by existing legislative or other measures, each state party to the present Covenant undertakes to take the necessary steps, in accordance with its constitutional processes and with the provisions of the present Covenant, to adopt such legislative or other measures as may be necessary to give effect to the rights recognized in the present Covenant.

3   Each state party to the present Covenant undertakes:

(a)   to ensure that any person whose rights or freedoms as herein recognized are violated shall have an effective remedy, notwithstanding that the violation has been committed by persons acting in an official capacity;

(b)   to ensure that any person claiming such a remedy shall have his right thereto determined by competent judicial, administrative or legislative authorities, or by any other competent authority provided for by the legal system of the state, and to develop the possibilities of judicial remedy;

(c)   to ensure that the competent authorities shall enforce such remedies when granted.

[3]
Article 3

The states parties to the present Covenant undertake to ensure the equal right of men and women to the enjoyment of all civil and political rights set forth in the present Covenant.

[4]
Article 4

1   In time of public emergency which threatens the life of the nation and the existence of which is officially proclaimed, the states parties to the present Covenant may take measures derogating from their obligations under the present Covenant to the extent strictly required by the exigencies of the situation, provided that such measures are not inconsistent with their other obligations under international law and do not involve discrimination solely on the ground of race, colour, sex, language, religion or social origin.

2   No derogation from articles 6, 7, 8 (paragraphs 1 and 2), 11, 15, 16 and 18 may be made under this provision.

3   Any state party to the present Covenant availing itself of the right of derogation shall immediately inform the other states parties to the present Covenant, through the intermediary of the Secretary-General of the United Nations, of the provisions from which it has derogated and of the reasons by which it was actuated. A further communication shall be made, through the same intermediary, on the date on which it terminates such derogation.

[5]
Article 5

1   Nothing in the present Covenant may be interpreted as implying for any state, group or person any right to engage in any activity or perform any act aimed at the destruction

of any of the rights and freedoms recognized herein or at their limitation to a greater extent than is provided for in the present Covenant.

2   There shall be no restriction upon or derogation from any of the fundamental human rights recognized or existing in any state party to the present Covenant pursuant to law, conventions, regulations or custom on the pretext that the present Covenant does not recognize such rights or that it recognizes them to a lesser extent.

PART III

[6]

Article 6

1   Every human being has the inherent right to life. This right shall be protected by law. No one shall be arbitrarily deprived of his life.

2   In countries which have not abolished the death penalty, sentence of death may be imposed only for the most serious crimes in accordance with the law in force at the time of the commission of the crime and not contrary to the provisions of the present Covenant and to the Convention on the Prevention and Punishment of the Crime of Genocide. This penalty can only be carried out pursuant to a final judgment rendered by a competent court.

3   When deprivation of life constitutes the crime of genocide, it is understood that nothing in this article shall authorize any state party to the present Covenant to derogate in any way from any obligation assumed under the provisions of the Convention on the Prevention and Punishment of the Crime of Genocide.

4   Anyone sentenced to death shall have the right to seek pardon or commutation of the sentence. Amnesty, pardon or commutation of the sentence of death may be granted in all cases.

5   Sentence of death shall not be imposed for crimes committed by persons below eighteen years of age and shall not be carried out on pregnant women.

6   Nothing in this article shall be invoked to delay or to prevent the abolition of capital punishment by any state party to the present Covenant.

[7]

Article 7

No one shall be subjected to torture or to cruel, inhuman or degrading treatment or punishment. In particular, no one shall be subjected without his free consent to medical or scientific experimentation.

[8]

Article 8

1   No one shall be held in slavery; slavery and the slave-trade in all their forms shall be prohibited.

2   No one shall be held in servitude.

3   (a)   No one shall be required to perform forced or compulsory labour;

    (b)   paragraph 3(a) shall not be held to preclude, in countries where imprisonment with hard labour may be imposed as a punishment for a crime, the performance of hard labour in pursuance of a sentence to such punishment by a competent court;

    (c)   for the purpose of this paragraph the term 'forced or compulsory labour' shall not include:

       (i)   any work or service, not referred to in subparagraph (b), normally required of a person who is under detention in consequence of a lawful order of a court, or of a person during conditional release from such detention;

(ii)   any service of a military character and, in countries where conscientious objection is recognised, any national service required by law of conscientious objectors;

(iii)   any service exacted in cases of emergency or calamity threatening the life or well-being of the community;

(iv)   any work or service which forms part of normal civil obligations.

[9]
Article 9

1   Everyone has the right to liberty and security of person. No one shall be subjectd to arbitrary arrest or detention. No one shall be deprived of his liberty except on such grounds and in accordance with such procedure as are established by law.

2   Anyone who is arrested shall be informed, at the time of arrest, of the reasons for his arrest and shall be promptly informed of any charges against him.

3   Anyone arrested or detained on a criminal charge shall be brought promptly before a judge or other officer authorized by law to exercise judicial power and shall be entitled to trial within a reasonable time or to release. It shall not be the general rule that persons awaiting trial shall be detained in custody, but release may be subject to guarantees to appear for trial, at any other stage of the judicial proceedings, and, should occasion arise, for execution of the judgment.

4   Anyone who is deprived of his liberty by arrest or detention shall be entitled to take proceedings before a court, in order that that court may decide without delay on the lawfulness of his detention and order his release if the detention is not lawful.

5   Anyone who has been the victim of unlawful arrest or detention shall have an enforceable right to compensation.

[10]
Article 10

1   All persons deprived of their liberty shall be treated with humanity and with respect for the inherent dignity of the human person.

2   (a)   Accused persons shall, save in exceptional circumstances, be segregated from convicted persons and shall be subject to separate treatment appropriate to their status as unconvicted persons;

(b)   Accused juvenile persons shall be separated from adults and brought as speedily as possible for adjudication.

3   The penitentiary system shall comprise treatment of prisoners the essential aim of which shall be their reformation and social rehabilitation. Juvenile offenders shall be segregated from adults and be accorded treatment appropriate to their age and legal status.

[11]
Article 11

No one shall be imprisoned merely on the ground of inability to fulfil a contractual obligation.

[12]
Article 12

1   Everyone lawfully within the terrritory of a state shall, within that territory, have the right to liberty of movement and freedom to choose his residence.

2   Everyone shall be free to leave any country, including his own.

3   The above-mentioned rights shall not be subject to any restrictions except those which are provided by law, are necessary to protect national security, public order (*ordre*

public), public health or morals or the rights and freedoms of others, and are consistent with the other rights recognized in the present Covenant.

4   No one shall be arbitrarily deprived of the right to enter his own country.

[13]
Article 13

An alien lawfully in the territory of a state party to the present Covenant may be expelled therefrom only in pursuance of a decision reached in accordance with law and shall, except where compelling reasons of national security otherwise require, be allowed to submit the reasons against his expulsion and to have his case reviewed by, and be represented for the purpose before, the competent authority or a person or persons especially designated by the competent authority.

[14]
Article 14

1   All persons shall be equal before the courts and tribunals. In the determination of any criminal charge against him, or of his rights and obligations in a suit at law, everyone shall be entitled to a fair and public hearing by a competent, independent and impartial tribunal established by law. The Press and the public may be excluded from all or part of a trial for reasons of morals, public order (*ordre public*) or national security in a democratic society, or when the interest of the private lives of the parties so requires, or to the extent strictly necessary in the opinion of the court in special circumstances where publicity would prejudice the interests of justice; but any judgment rendered in a criminal case or in a suit at law shall be made public except where the interest of juvenile persons otherwise requires or the proceedings concern matrimonial disputes or the guardianship of children.

2   Everyone charged with a criminal offence shall have the right to be presumed innocent until proved guilty according to law.

3   In the determination of any criminal charge against him, everyone shall be entitled to the following minimum guarantees, in full equality:

(a)   to be informed promptly and in detail in a language which he understands of the nature and cause of the charge against him;

(b)   to have adequate time and facilities for the preparation of his defence and to communicate with counsel of his own choosing;

(c)   to be tried without undue delay;

(d)   to be tried in his presence, and to defend himself in person or through legal assistance of his own choosing; to be informed, if he does not have legal assistance, of this right; and to have legal assistance assigned to him, in any case where the interests of justice so require, and without payment by him in any such case if he does not have sufficient means to pay for it;

(e)   to examine, or have examined, the witnesses against him and to obtain the attendance and examination of witnesses on his behalf under the same conditions as witnesses against him;

(f)   to have the free assistance of an interpreter if he cannot understand or speak the language used in court;

(g)   not to be compelled to testify against himself or to confess guilt.

4   In the case of juvenile persons, the procedure shall be such as will take account of their age and the desirability of promoting their rehabilitation.

5   Everyone convicted of a crime shall have the right to his conviction and sentence being reviewed by a higher tribunal according to law.

6   When a person has by a final decision been convicted of a criminal offence and when subsequently his conviction has been reversed or he has been pardoned on the ground

that a new or newly discovered fact shows conclusively that there has been a miscarriage of justice, the person who has suffered punishment as a result of such conviction shall be compensated according to law, unless it is proved that the non-disclosure of the unknown fact in time is wholly or partly attributable to him.

7   No one shall be liable to be tried or punished again for an offence for which he has already been finally convicted or acquitted in accordance with the law and penal procedure of each country.

[15]
Article 15
1   No one shall be held guilty of any criminal offence on account of any act or omission which did not costitute a criminal offence, under national or international law, at the time when it was committed. Nor shall a heavier penalty be imposed than the one that was applicable at the time when the criminal offence was committed. If, subsequent to the commission of the offence, provision is made by law for the imposition of a lighter penalty, the offender shall benefit thereby.

2   Nothing in this article shall prejudice the trial and punishment of any person for any act or omission which, at the time when it was committed, was criminal according to the general principles of law recognized by the community of nations.

[16]
Article 16
Everyone shall have the right to recognition everywhere as a person before the law.

[17]
Article 17
1   No one shall be subjected to arbitrary or unlawful interference with his privacy, family, home or correspondence, nor to unlawful attacks on his honour and reputation.

2   Everyone has the right to the protection of the law against such interference or attacks.

[18]
Article 18
1   Everyone shall have the right to freedom of thought, conscience and religion. This right shall include freedom to have or to adopt a religion or belief of his choice, and freedom, either individually or in community with others and in public or private, to manifest his religion or belief in worship, observance, practice and teaching.

2   No one shall be subject to coercion which would impair his freedom to have or adopt a religion or belief of his choice.

3   Freedom to manifest one's religion or beliefs may be subject only to such limitations as are prescribed by law and are necessary to protect public safety, order, health, or morals or the fundamental rights and freedoms of others.

4   The states parties to the present Covenant undertake to have respect for the liberty of parents and, when applicable, legal guardians to ensure the religious and moral education of their children in conformity with their own convictions.

[19]
Article 19
1   Everyone shall have the right to hold opinions without interference.

2   Everyone shall have the right to freedom of expression; this right shall include freedom to seek, receive and impart information and ideas of all kinds, regardless of frontiers, either orally, in writing or in print, in the form of art, or through any other media of his choice.

3   The exercise of the rights provided for in paragraph 2 of this article carries with it special duties and responsibilities. It may therefore be subject to certain restrictions, but these shall only be such as are provided by law and are necessary:

(a)   for respect of the rights or reputations of others;
(b)   for the protection of national security or of public order (*ordre public*), or of public health or morals.

[20]
Article 20
1   Any propaganda for war shall be prohibited by law.
2   Any advocacy of national, racial or religious hatred that constitutes incitement to discrimination, hostility or violence shall be prohibited by law.

[21]
Article 21
The right of peaceful assembly shall be recognized. No restrictions may be placed on the exercise of this right other than those imposed in conformity with the law and which are necessary in a democratic society in the interests of national security or public safety, public order (*ordre public*), the protection of public health or morals or the protection of the rights and freedoms of others.

[22]
Article 22
1   Everyone shall have the right to freedom of association with others, including the right to form and join trade unions for the protection of his interests.
2   No restrictions may be placed on the exercise of his right other than those which are prescribed by law and which are necessary in a democratic society in the interests of national security or public safety, public order (*ordre public*), the protection of public health or morals or the protection of the rights and freedoms of others. This article shall not prevent the imposition of lawful restrictions on members of the armed forces and of the police in their exercise of this right.
3   Nothing in this article shall authorize States Parties to the International Labour Organisation Convention of 1948 concerning Freedom of Association and Protection of the Right to Organise to take legislative measures which would prejudice, or to apply the law in such a manner as to prejudice, the guarantees provided for in that Convention.

[23]
Article 23
1   The family is the natural and fundamental group unit of society and is entitled to protection by society and the state.
2   The right of men and women of marriageable age to marry and to found a family shall be recognized.
3   No marriage shall be entered into without the free and full consent of the intending spouses.
4   States parties to the present Covenant shall take appropriate steps to ensure equality of rights and responsibilities of spouses as to marriage, during marriage and at its dissolution. In the cae of dissolution, provision shall be made for the necessary protection of any children.

[24]
Article 24
1   Every child shall have, without any discrimination as to race, colour, sex, language, religion, national or social origin, property or birth, the right to such measures of

protection as are required by his status as a minor, on the part of his family, society and the state.

2 Every child shall be registered immediately after birth and shall have a name.

3 Every child has the right to acquire a nationality.

[25]
Article 25

Every citizen shall have the right and the opportunity, without any of the distinctions mentioned in article 2 and without unreasonable restrictions:

(a) to take part in the conduct of public affairs, directly or through freely chosen representatives;

(b) to vote and to be elected at genuine periodic elections which shall be by universal and equal suffrage and shall be held by secret ballot, guaranteeing the free expression of the will of the electors;

(c) to have access, on general terms of equality, to public service in his country.

[26]
Article 26

All persons are equal before the law and are entitled without any discrimination to the equal protection of the law. In this respect, the law shall prohibit any discrimination and guarantee to all persons equal and effective protection against discrimination on any ground such as race, colour, sex, language, religion, political or other opinion, national or social origin, property, birth or other status.

[27]
Article 27

In those states in which ethnic, religious or linguistic minorities exist, persons belonging to such minorities shall not be denied the right, in community with the other members of their group, to enjoy their own culture, to profess and practise their own religion, or to use their own language.

PART IV
[28]
Article 28

1 There shall be established a Human Rights Committee (hereafter referred to in the present Covenant as the Committee). It shall consist of eighteen members and shall carry out the functions hereinafter provided.

2 The Committee shall be composed of nationals of the states parties to the present Covenant who shall be persons of high moral character and recognised competence in the field of human rights, consideration being given to the usefulness of the participation of some persons having legal experience.

3 The members of the Committee shall be elected and shall serve in their personal capacity.

[29]
Article 29

1 The members of the Committee shall be elected by secret ballot from a list of persons possessing the qualifications prescribed in article 28 and nominated for the purpose by the states parties to the present Covenant.

2 Each state party to the present Covenant may nominate nor more than two persons. These persons shall be nationals of the nominating state.

3 A person shall be eligible for renomination.

[30]
Article 30
1   The initial election shall be held no later than six months after the date of the entry into force of the present Covenant.
2   At least four months before the date of each election to the Committee, other than an election to fill a vacancy declared in accordance with article 34, the Secretary-General of the United Nations shall address a written invitation to the states parties to the present Covenant to submit their nominations for membership of the Committee within three months.
3   The Secretary-General of the United Nations shall prepare a list in alphabetical order of all the persons thus nominated, with an indication of the states parties which have nominated them, and shall submit it to the states parties to the present Covenant no later than one month before the date of each election.
4   Elections of the members of the Committee shall be held at a meeting of the states parties to the present Covenant convened by the Secretary-General of the United Nations at the Headquarters of the United Nations. At that meeting, for which two thirds of the states parties to the present Covenant shall constitute a quorum, the persons elected to the Committee shall be those nominees who obtain the largest number of votes and an absolute majority of the votes of the representatives of states parties present and voting.

[31]
Article 31
1   The Committee may not include more than one national of the same state.
2   In the election of the Committee, consideration shall be given to equitable geographical distribution of membership and to the representation of the different forms of civilization and of the principal legal systems.

[32]
Article 32
1   The members of the Committee shall be elected for a term of four years. They shall be eligible for re-election if renominated. However, the terms of nine of the members elected at the first election shall expire at the end of two years; immediately after the first election, the names of these nine members shall be chosen by lot by the Chairman of the meeting referred to in article 30, paragraph 4.
2   Elections at the expiry of office shall be held in accordance with the preceding articles of this part of the present Covenant.

[33]
Article 33
1   If, in the unanimous opinion of the other members, a member of the Committee has ceased to carry out his functions for any cause other than absence of a temporary character, the Chairman of the Committee shall notify the Secretary-General of the United Nations, who shall then declare the seat of that member to be vacant.
2   In the event of the death or the resignation of a member of the Committee, the Chairman shall immediately notify the Secretary-General of the United Nations, who shall declare the seat vacant from the date of death or the date on which the resignation takes effect.

[34]
Article 34
1   When a vacancy is declared in accordance with article 33 and if the term of office of the member to be replaced does not expire within six months of the declaration of the

vacancy, the Secretary-General of the United Nations shall notify each of the states parties to the prsent Covenant, which may within two monhs submit nominations in accordance with article 29 for the purpose of filling the vacancy.

2   The Secretary-General of the United Nations shall prepare a list in alphabetical order of the persons thus nominated and shall submit it to the states parties to the present Covenant. The election to fill the vacancy shall then take place in accordance with the relevant provisions of this part of the present Covenant.

3   A member of the Committee elected to fill a vacancy declared in accordance with article 33 shall hold office for the remainder of the term of the member who vacated the seat on the Committee under the provisions of that article.

[35]
Article 35
The members of the Committee shall, with the approval of the General Assembly of the United Nations, receive emoluments from United Nations resources on such terms and conditions as the General Assembly may decide, having regard to the importance of the Committee's responsibilities.

[36]
Article 36
The Secretary-General of the United Nations shall provide the necessary staff and facilities for the effective performance of the functions of the Committee under the present Covenant.

[37]
Article 37
1   The Secretary-General of the United Nations shall covene the initial meeting of the Committee at the Headquarters of the United Nations.

2   After its initial meeting, the Committee shall meet at such times as shall be provided in its rules of procedure.

3   The Committee shall normally meet at the Headquarters of the United Nations or at the United Nations Office at Geneva.

[38]
Article 38
Every member of the Committee shall, before taking up his duties, make a solemn declaration in open committee that he will perform his functions impartially and conscientiously.

[39]
Article 39
1   The Committee shall elect its officers for a term of two years. They may be re-elected.

2   The Committee shall establish its own rules of procedure, but these rules shall provide, *inter alia*, that:

(a)   twelve members shall constitute a quorum;
(b)   decisions of the Committee shall be made by a majority vote of the members present.

[40]
Article 40
1   The states parties to the present Covenant undertake to submit reports on the measures they have adopted which give effect to the rights recognized herein and on the progress made in the enjoyment of those rights:

(a) within one year of the entry into force of the present Covenant for the states parties concerned;

(b) thereafter whenever the Committee so requests.

2   All reports shall be submitted to the Secretary-General of the United Nations, who shall transmit them to the Committee for consideration. Reports shall indicate the factors and difficulties, if any affecting the implementation of the present Covenant.

3   The Secretary-General of the United Nations may, after consultation with the Committee, transmit to the specialized agencies concerned copies of such parts of the reports as may fall within their field of competence.

4   The Committee shall study the reports submitted by the states parties to the present Covenant. It shall transmit its reports, and such general comments as it may consider appropriate, to the states parties. The Committee may also transmit to the Economic and Social Council these comments along with the copies of the reports it has received from states parties to the present Covenant.

5   The states parties to the present Covenant may submit to the Committee observations on any comments that may be made in accordance with paragraph 4 of this article.

[41]
Article 41

1   A state party to the present Covenant may at any time declare under this article that it recognizes the competence of the Committee to receive and consider communications to the effect that a state party claims that another state party is not fulfilling its obligations under the present Covenant. Communications under this article may be received and considered only if submitted by a state party which has made a declaration recognizing in regard to itself the competence of the Committee. No communication shall be received by the Committee if it concerns a state party which has not made such a declaration. Communications received under this article shall be dealt with in accordance with the following procedure:

(a) If a state party to the present Covenant considers that another state party is not giving effect to the provisions of the present Covenant, it may, by written communication, bring the matter to the attention of that state party. Within three months after the receipt of the communication, the receiving state shall afford the state which sent the communication an explanation or any other statement in writing clarifying the matter, which should include, to the extent possible and pertinent, reference to domestic procedures and remedies taken, pending, or available in the matter.

(b) If the matter is not adjusted to the satisfaction of both states parties concerned within six months after the receipt by the receiving state of the initial communication, either state shall have the right to refer the matter to the Committee, by notice given to the Committee and to the other state.

(c) The Committee shall deal with a matter referred to it only after it has ascertained that all available domestic remedis have been invoked and exhausted in the matter, in conformity with the generally recognized principles of international law. This shall not be the rule where the application of the remedies is unreasonably prolonged.

(d) The Committee shall hold closed meetings when examining communications under this article.

(e) Subject to the provisions of subparagraph (c), the Committee shall make available its good offices to the states parties concerned with a view to a friendly solution of the matter on the basis of respect for human rights and fundamental freedoms as recognized in the present Covenant.

(f)   In any matter referred to it, the Committee may call upon the states parties concerned, referred to in subparagraph (b), to supply any relevant information.

(g)   The states parties concerned, referred to in subparagraph (b), shall have the right to be represented when the matter is being considered in the Committee and to make submissions orally and/or in writing,

(h)   The Committee shall, within twelve months after the date of receipt of notice under subparagraph (b), submit a report:

   (i)   if a solution within the terms of subparagraph (e) is reached, the Committee shall confine its report to a brief statement of the facts and of the solution reached;

   (ii)   if a solution within the terms of subparagraph (e) is not reached, the Committee shall confine its report to a brief statement of the facts; the written submissions and record of the oral submissions made by the states parties concerned shall be attached to the report.

In every matter, the report shall be communicated to the states parties concerned.

2   The provisions of this article shall come into force when ten states parties to the present Covenant have made declarations under paragraph 1 of this article. Such declarations shall be deposited by the states parties with the Secretary-General of the United Nations, who shall transmit copies thereof to the other states parties. A declaration may be withdrawn at any time by notification to the Secretary-General. Such a withdrawal shall not prejudice the consideration of any matter which is the subject of a communication already transmitted under this article; no further communication by any state party shall be received after the notification of withdrawal of the declaration has been received by the Secretary-General, unless the state party concerned has made a new declaration.

[42]
Article 42

1   (a)   If a matter referred to the Committee in accordance with article 41 is not resolved to the satisfaction of the states concerned, the Committee may, with the prior consent of the states parties concerned, appoint an *ad hoc* Conciliation Committee (hereinafter referred to as the Commission). The good offices of the Commission shall be made available to the states concerned with a view to an amicable solution of the matter on the basis of respect for the present Covenant;

   (b)   the Commission shall consist of five persons acceptable to the states parties concerned. If the states parties concerned fail to reach agreement within three months on all or part of the composition of the Commission, the members of the Commission concerning whom no agreement has been reached shall be elected by secret ballot by a two-thirds majority vote of the Committee from among its members.

2   The members of the Commission shall serve in their personal capacity. They shall not be nationals of the states parties concerned, or of a state not party to the present Covenant, or of a state party which has not made a declaration under article 41.

3   The Commission shall elect its own Chairman and adopt its own rules of procedure.

4   The meetings of the Commission shall normally be held at the Headquarters of the United Nations or at the United Nations Office at Geneva. However, they may be held at such other convenient places as the Commission may determine in consultation with the Secretary-General of the United Nations and the state parties concerned.

5   The secretariat provided in accordance with article 36 shall also service the commissions appointed under this article.

6   The information received and collated by the Committee shall be made available to the Commission and the Commission may call upon the states parties concerned to supply any other relevant information.

7   When the Commission has fully considered the matter, but in any event not later than twelve months after having been seized of the matter, it shall submit to the Chairman of the Committee a report for communication to the states parties concerned:

(a)   if the Commission is unable to complete its consideration of the matter within twelve months, it shall confine its report to a brief statement of the status of its consideration of the matter;

(b)   if an amicable solution to the matter on the basis of respect for human rights as recognized in the present Covenant is reached, the Commission shall confine its report to a brief statement of the facts and of the solution reached;

(c)   if a solution within the terms of subparagraph (b) is not reached, the Commission's report shall embody its findings on all questions of fact relevant to the issues between the states parties concerned, and its views on the possibilities of an amicable solution of the matter. This report shall also contain the written submissions and a record of the oral submissions made by the states parties concerned;

(d)   if the Commission's report is submitted under subparagraph (c), the states parties concerned shall, within three months of the receipt of the report, notify the Chairman of the Committee whether or not they accept the contents of the report of the Commission.

8   The provisions of this article are without prejudice to the responsibilities of the Committee under article 41.

9   The states parties concerned shall share equally all the expenses of the members of the Commission in accordance with estimates to be provided by the Secretary-General of the United Nations.

10   The Secretary-General of the United Nations shall be empowered to pay the expenses of the members of the Commission, if necessary, before reimbursement by the states parties concerned, in accordance with paragraph 9 of this article.

[43]
Article 43

The members of the Committee, and of the *ad hoc* conciliation commissions which may be appointed under article 42, shall be entitled to the facilities, privileges and immunities of experts on mission for the United Nations as laid down in the relevant sections of the Convention on the Privileges and Immunities of the United Nations.

[44]
Article 44

The provisions for the implementation of the present Covenant shall apply without prejudice to the procedures prescribed in the field of human rights by or under the constituent instruments and the conventions of the United Nations and of the specialised agencies and shall not prevent the states parties to the present Covenant from having recourse to other procedures for settling a dispute in accordance with general or special international agreements in force between them.

[45]
Article 45

The Committee shall submit to the General Assembly of the United Nations, through the Economic and Social Council, an annual report on its activities.

PART V
[46]
Article 46
Nothing in the present Covenant shall be interpreted as impairing the provisions of the Charter of the United Nations and of the constitutions of the specialised agencies which define the respective responsibilities of the various organs of the United Nations and of the specialised agencies in regard to the matters dealt with in the present Covenant.

[47]
Article 47
Nothing in the present Covenant shall be interpreted as impairing the inherent right of all peoples to enjoy and utilise fully and freely their natural wealth and resources.

PART VI
[48]
Article 48
1   The present Covenant is open for signature by any state member of the United Nations or member of any of its specialised agencies, by any state party to the Statute of the International Court of Justice, and by any other state which has been invited by the General Assembly of the United Nations to become a party to the present Covenant.
2   The present Covenant is subject to ratification. Instruments of ratifiation shall be deposited with the Secretary-General of the United Nations.
3   The present Covenant shall be open to accession by any state referred to in paragraph 1 of this article.
4   Accession shall be effected by the deposit of an instrument of accession with the Secretary-General of the United Nations.
5   The Secretary-General of the United Nations shall inform all states which have signed this Covenant or acceded to it of the deposit of each instrument of ratification or accession.

[49]
Article 49
1   The present Covenant shall enter into force three months after the date of the deposit with the Secretary-General of the United Nations of the thirty-fifth instrument of ratification or instrument of accession.
2   For each state ratifiying the present Covenant or acceding to it after the deposit of the thirty-fifth instrument of ratification or instrument of accession, the present Covenant shall enter into force three months after the date of the deposit of its own instrument of ratification or instrument of accession.

[50]
Article 50
The provisions of the present Covenant shall extend to all parts of federal states without any limitations or exceptions.

[51]
Article 51
1   Any state party to the present Covenant may propose an amendment and file it with the Secretary-General of the United Nations. The Secretary-General of the United Nations shall thereupon communicate any proposed amendments to the states parties to the present Covenant with a request that they notify him whether they favour a conference of states parties for the purpose of considering and voting upon the proposals. In the event that at least one third of the states parties favours such a

conference, the Secretary-General shall convene the conference under the auspices of the United Nations. Any amendment adopted by a majority of the states parties present and voting at the conference shall be submitted to the General Assembly of the United Nations for approval.

2   Amendments shall come into force when they have been approved by the General Assembly of the United Nations and accepted by a two-thirds majority of the states parties to the present Covenant in accordance with their respective constitutional processes.

3   When amendments come into force, they shall be binding on those states parties which have accepted them, other states parties still being bound by the provisions of the present Covenant and any earlier amendment which they have accepted.

[52]
Article 52
Irrespective of the notifications made under article 48, paragraph 5, the Secretary-General of the United Nations shall inform all states referred to in paragraph 1 of the same article of the following particulars:

(a)   signatures, ratifications and accessions under article 48;
(b)   the date of the entry into force of the present Covenant under article 49 and the date of the entry into force of any amendments under article 51.

[53]–[70]
Article 53
1   The present Covenant, of which the Chinese, English, French, Russian and Spanish texts are equally authentic, shall be deposited in the archives of the United Nations.

2   The Secretary-General of the United Nations shall transmit certified copies of the present Covenant to all states referred to in article 48.

APPENDIX 3

INTERNATIONAL CONVENTION ON THE ELIMINATION OF ALL FORMS OF RACIAL DISCRIMINATION 1966

The States Parties to this Convention,

Considering that the Charter of the United Nations is based on the principles of the dignity and equality inherent in all human beings, and that all Member States have pledged themselves to take joint and separate action, in co-operation with the Organization, for the achievement of one of the purposes of the United Nations which is to promote and encourage universal respect for and observance of human rights and fundamental freedoms for all, without distinction as to race, sex, language or religion,

Considering that the Universal Declaration of Human Rights proclaims that all human beings are born free and equal in dignity and rights and that everyone is entitled to all the rights and freedoms set out therein, without distinction of any kind, in particular as to race, colour or national origin,

Considering that all human beings are equal before the law and are entitled to equal protection of the law against any discrimination and against any incitement to discrimination,

Considering that the United Nations has condemned colonialism and all practices of segregation and discrimination associated therewith, in whatever form and wherever they exist, and that the Declaration on the Granting of Independence to Colonial Countries and Peoples of 14 December 1960 (General Assembly resolution 1514 (XV)) has affirmed and solemnly proclaimed the necessity of bringing them to a speedy and unconditional end,

Considering that the United Nations Declaration on the Elimination of All Forms of Racial Discrimination of 20 November 1963 (General Assembly resolution 1904 (XVIII)) solemnly affirms the necessity of speedily eliminating racial discrimination throughout the world in all its forms and manifestations and of securing understanding of and respect for the dignity of the human person,

Convinced that any doctrine of superiority based on racial differentiation is scientifically false, morally condemnable, socially unjust and dangerous, and that there is no justification for racial discrimination, in theory or in practice, anywhere,

Reaffirming that discrimination between human beings on the grounds of race, colour or ethnic origin is an obstacle to friendly and peaceful relations among nations and is capable of disturbing peace and security among peoples and the harmony of persons living side by side even within one and the same State,

Convinced that the existence of racial barriers is repugnant to the ideals of any human society,

Alarmed by manifestations of racial discrimination still in evidence in some areas of the world and by governmental policies based on racial superiority or hatred, such as policies of apartheid, segregation or separation,

Resolved to adopt all necessary measures for speedily eliminating racial discrimination in all its forms and manifestations, and to prevent and combat racist doctrines and practices in order to promote understanding between races and to build an inter-national community free from all forms of racial segregation and racial discrimination,

Bearing in mind the Convention concerning Discrimination in respect of Employment and Occupation adopted by the International Labour Organisation in 1958, and the Convention against Discrimination in Education adopted by the United Nations Educational, Scientific and Cultural Organization in 1960,

Desiring to implement the principles embodied in the United Nations Declaration on the Elimination of All Forms of Racial Discrimination and to secure the earliest adoption of practical measures to that end,

Have agreed as follows:

PART I

Article 1

1. In this Convention, the term 'racial discrimination' shall mean any distinction, exclusion, restriction or preference based on race, colour, descent, or national or ethnic origin which has the purpose or effect of nullifying or impairing the recognition, enjoyment or exercise, on an equal footing, of human rights and fundamental freedoms in the political, economic, social, cultural or any other field of public life.

2. This Convention shall not apply to distinctions, exclusions, restrictions or prefer-ences made by a State Party to this Convention between citizens and non-citizens.

3. Nothing in this Convention may be interpreted as affecting in any way the legal provisions of State Parties concerning nationality, citizenship or naturalization, provided that such provisions do not discriminate against any particular nationality.

4. Special measures taken for the sole purpose of securing adequate advancement of certain racial or ethnic groups or individuals requiring such protection as may be necessary in order to ensure such groups or individuals equal enjoyment or exercise of human rights and fundamental freedoms shall not be deemed racial discrimination, provided, however, that such measures do not, as a consequence, lead to the maintenance of separate rights for different racial groups and that they shall not be continued after the objectives for which they were taken have been achieved.

Article 2

1. States Parties condemn racial discrimination and undertake to pursue by all appropriate means and without delay a policy of eliminating racial discrimination in all its forms and promoting understanding among all races, and, to this end:

(a) Each State Party undertakes to engage in no act or practice of racial discrimination against persons, groups of persons or institutions and to ensure that all public authorities and public institutions, national and local, shall act in conformity with this obligation;

(b) Each State Party undertakes not to sponsor, defend or support racial discrimi-nation by any persons or organizations;

(c)   Each State Party shall take effective measures to review governmental, national and local policies, and to amend, rescind or nullify any laws and regulations which have the effect of creating or perpetuating racial discrimination wherever it exists;
(d)   Each State Party shall prohibit and bring to an end, by all appropriate means, including legislation as required by circumstances, racial discrimination by any persons, group or organization;
(e)   Each State Party undertakes to encourage, where appropriate, integrationist multiracial organizations and movements and other means of eliminating barriers between races, and to discourage anything which tends to strengthen racial division.

2. States Parties shall, when the circumstances so warrant, take, in the social, economic, cultural and other fields, special and concrete measures to ensure the adequate development and protection of certain racial groups or individuals belonging to them, for the purpose of guaranteeing them the full and equal enjoyment of human rights and fundamental freedoms. These measures shall in no case entail as a consequence the maintenance of unequal or separate rights for different racial groups after the objectives for which they were taken have been achieved.

Article 3

States Parties particularly condemn racial segregation and apartheid and undertake to prevent, prohibit and eradicate all practices of this nature in territories under their jurisdiction.

Article 4

States Parties condemn all propaganda and all organizations which are based on ideas or theories and superiority of one race or group of persons of one colour or ethnic origin, or which attempt to justify or promote racial hatred and discrimination in any form, and undertake to adopt immediate and positive measures designed to eradicate all incitement to, or acts of, such discrimination and, to this end, with due regard to the principles embodied in the Universal Declaration of Human Rights and the rights expressly set forth in article 5 of this Convention, inter alia:

(a)   Shall declare an offence punishable by law all dissemination of ideas based on racial superiority or hatred, incitement to racial discrimination, as well as all acts of violence or incitement to such acts against any race or group of persons of another colour or ethnic origin, and also the provision of any assistance to racist activities, including the financing thereof;
(b)   Shall declare illegal and prohibit organizations, and also organized and all other propaganda activities, which promote and incite racial discrimination, and shall recognize participation in such organizations or activities as an offence punishable by law;
(c)   Shall not permit public authorities or public institutions, national or local, to promote or incite racial discrimination.

Article 5

In compliance with the fundamental obligations laid down in article 2 of this Convention, States Parties undertake to prohibit and to eliminate racial discrimination in all its forms and to guarantee the right to everyone, without distinction as to race, colour, or national or ethnic origin, to equality before the law, notably in the enjoyment of the following rights:

(a)   The right to equal treatment before the tribunals and all other organs administering justice;

(b)   The right to security of person and protection by the State against violence or bodily harm, whether inflicted by government officials or by any individual group or institution;

(c)   Political rights, in particular the right to participate in elections – to vote and to stand for election – on the basis of universal and equal suffrage, to take part in the Government as well as in the conduct of public affairs at any level and to have equal access to public service;

(c)   Other civil rights, in particular:
   (i)   The right to freedom of movement and residence within the border of the State;
   (ii)   The right to leave any country, including one's own, and to return to one's country;
   (iii)   The right to nationality;
   (iv)   The right to marriage and choice of spouse;
   (v)   The right to own property alone as well as in association with others;
   (vi)   The right to inherit;
   (vii)   The right to freedom of thought, conscience and religion;
   (viii) The right to freedom of opinion and expression;
   (ix)   The right to freedom of peaceful assembly and association;

(e)   Economic, social and cultural rights, in particular:
   (i)   The rights to work, to free choice of employment, to just and favourable conditions of work, to protection against unemployment, to equal pay for equal work, to just and favourable remuneration;
   (ii)   The right to form and join trade unions;
   (iii)   The right to housing;
   (iv)   The right to public health, medical care, social security and social services;
   (v)   The right to education and training;
   (vi)   The right to equal participation in cultural activities;

(f)   The right of access to any place or service intended for use by the general public, such as transport, hotels, restaurants, cafés, theatres and parks.

Article 6

States Parties shall assure to everyone within their jurisdiction effective protection and remedies, through the competent national tribunals and other State institutions, against any acts of racial discrimination which violate his human rights and fundamental freedoms contrary to this Convention, as well as the right to seek from such tribunals just and adequate reparation or satisfaction for any damage suffered as a result of such discrimination.

Article 7

States Parties undertake to adopt immediate and effective measures, particularly in the fields of teaching, education, culture and information, with a view to combating prejudices which lead to racial discrimination and to promoting understanding, tolerance and friendship among nations and racial or ethnical groups, as well as to propagating the purposes and principles of the Charter of the United Nations, the Universal Declaration of Human Rights, the United Nations Declaration on the Elimination of All Forms of Racial Discrimination, and this Convention.

PART II

Article 8

1. There shall be established a Committee on the Elimination of Racial Discrimination (hereinafter referred to as the Committee) consisting of eighteen experts of high moral standing and acknowledged impartiality elected by States Parties from among their nationals, who shall serve in their personal capacity, consideration being given to equitable geographical distribution and to the representation of the different forms of civilization as well as of the principal legal systems.

2. The members of the Committee shall be elected by secret ballot from a list of persons nominated by the States Parties. Each State Party may nominate one person from among its own nationals.

3. The initial election shall be held six months after the date of the entry into force of this Convention. At least three months before the date of each election the Secretary-General of the United Nations shall address a letter to the States Parties inviting them to submit their nominations within two months. The Secretary-General shall prepare a list in alphabetical order of all persons thus nominated, indicating the States Parties which have nominated them, and shall submit it to the States Parties.

4. Elections of the members of the Committee shall be held at a meeting of States Parties convened by the Secretary-General at United Nations Headquarters. At that meeting, for which two thirds of the States Parties shall constitute a quorum, the persons elected to the Committee shall be nominees who obtain the largest number of votes and an absolute majority of the votes of the representatives of States Parties present and voting.

5. (a) The members of the Committee shall be elected for a term of four years. However, the terms of nine of the members elected at the first election shall expire at the end of two years; immediately after the first election the names of these nine members shall be chosen by lot by the Chairman of the Committee;
    (b) For the filling of casual vacancies, the State Party whose expert has ceased to function as a member of the Committee shall appoint another expert from among its nationals, subject to the approval of the Committee.

6. States Parties shall be responsible for the expenses of the members of the Committee while they are in performance of Committee duties.

Article 9

1. States Parties undertake to submit to the Secretary-General of the United Nations, for consideration by the Committee, a report on the legislative, judicial, administrative or other measures which they have adopted and which give effect to the provisions of this Convention:

(a) within one year after the entry into force of the Convention for the State concerned; and
(b) thereafter every two years and whenever the Committee so requests. The Committee may request further information from the States Parties.

2. The Committee shall report annually, through the Secretary-General, to the General Assembly of the United Nations on its activities and may make suggestions and general recommendations based on the examination of the reports and information received from the States Parties. Such suggestions and general recommendations shall be reported to the General Assembly together with comments, if any, from States Parties.

Article 10

1. The Committee shall adopt its own rules of procedure.

2. The Committee shall elect its officers for a term of two years.

3. The secretariat of the Committee shall be provided by the Secretary-General of the United Nations.

4. The meetings of the Committee shall normally be held at United Nations Headquarters.

Article 11

1. If a State Party considers that another State Party is not giving effect to the provisions of this Convention, it may bring the matter to the attention of the Committee. The Committee shall then transmit the communication to the State Party concerned. Within three months, the receiving State shall submit to the Committee written explanations or statements clarifying the matter and the remedy, if any, that may have been taken by that State.

2. If the matter is not adjusted to the satisfaction of both parties, either by bilateral negotiations or by any other procedure open to them, within six months after the receipt by the receiving State of the initial communication, either State shall have the right to refer the matter again to the Committee by notifying the Committee and also the other State.

3. The Committee shall deal with a matter referred to it in accordance with paragraph 2 of this article after it has ascertained that all available domestic remedies have been invoked and exhausted in the case, in conformity with the generally recognized principles of international law. This shall not be the rule where the application of the remedies is unreasonably prolonged.

4. In any matter referred to it, the Committee may call upon the States Parties concerned to supply any other relevant information.

5. When any matter arising out of this article is being considered by the Committee, the States Parties concerned shall be entitled to send a representative to take part in the proceedings of the Committee, without voting rights, while the matter is under consideration.

Article 12

1. (a) After the Committee has obtained and collated all the information it deems necessary, the Chairman shall appoint an ad hoc Conciliation Commission (hereinafter referred to as the Commission) comprising five persons who may or may not be members of the Committee. The members of the Commission shall be appointed with the unanimous consent of the parties to the dispute, and its good offices shall be made available to the States concerned with a view to an amicable solution of the matter on the basis of respect for this Convention.
   (b) If the States Parties to the dispute fail to reach agreement within three months on all or part of the composition of the Commission, the members of the Commission not agreed upon by the States Parties to the dispute shall be elected by secret ballot by a two-thirds majority vote of the Committee from among its own members.

2. The members of the Commission shall serve in their personal capacity. They shall not be nationals of the States parties to the dispute or of a State not Party to this Convention.

3. The Commission shall elect its own Chairman and adopt its own rules of procedure.

4. The meetings of the Commission shall normally be held at United Nations Headquarters or at any other convenient place as determined by the Commission.

5. The secretariat provided in accordance with article 10, paragraph 3, of this Convention shall also service the Commission whenever a dispute among States Parties brings the Commission into being.

6. The States parties to the dispute shall share equally all the expenses of the members of the Commission in accordance with estimates to be provided by the Secretary-General of the United Nations.

7. The Secretary-General shall be empowered to pay the expenses of the members of the Commission, if necessary, before reimbursement by the States Parties to the dispute in accordance with paragraph 6 of this article.

8. The information obtained and collated by the Committee shall be made available to the Commission, and the Commission may call upon the States concerned to supply any other relevant information.

Article 13

1. When the Commission has fully considered the matter, it shall prepare and submit to the Chairman of the Committee a report embodying its findings on all questions of fact relevant to the issue between the parties and containing such recommendations as it may think proper for the amicable solution of the dispute.

2. The Chairman of the Committee shall communicate the report of the Commission to each of the States Parties to the dispute. These States shall, within three months, inform the Chairman of the Committee whether or not they accept the recommendations contained in the report of the Commission.

3. After the period provided for in paragraph 2 of this article, the Chairman of the Committee shall communicate the report of the Commission and the declarations of the States Parties concerned to the other States Parties to this Convention.

Article 14

1. A State Party may at any time declare that it recognizes the competence of the Committee to receive and consider communications from individuals or groups of individuals within its jurisdiction claiming to be victims of a violation by that State Party of any of the rights set forth in this Convention. No communication shall be received by the Committee if it concerns a State Party which has not made such a declaration.

2. Any State Party which makes a declaration as provided for in paragraph 1 of this article may establish or indicate a body within its national legal order which shall be competent to receive and consider petitions from individuals and groups of individuals within its jursdiction who claim to be victims of a violation of any of the rights set forth in this Convention and who have exhausted other available local remedies.

3. A declaration made in accordance with paragraph 1 of this article and the name of any body established or indicated in accordance with paragraph 2 of this article shall be deposited by the State Party concerned with the Secretary-General of the United Nations, who shall transmit copies thereof to the other States Parties. A declaration may be withdrawn at any time by notification to the Secretary-General, but such a withdrawal shall not affect communications pending before the Committee.

PART 6
APPENDICES

4. A register of petitions shall be kept by the body established or indicated in accordance with paragraph 2 of this article, and certified copies of the register shall be filed annually through appropriate channels with the Secretary-General on the understanding that the contents shall not be publicly disclosed.

5. In the event of failure to obtain satisfaction from the body established or indicated in accordance with paragraph 2 of this article, the petitioner shall have the right to communicate the matter to the Committee within six months.

6. (a) The Committee shall confidentially bring any communication referred to it to the attention of the State Party alleged to be violating any provision of this Convention, but the identity of the individual or groups of individuals concerned shall not be revealed without his or their express consent. The Committee shall not receive anonymous communications;

   (b) Within three months, the receiving State shall submit to the Committee written explanations or statements clarifying the matter and the remedy, if any, that may have been taken by that State.

7. (a) The Committee shall consider communications in the light of all information made available to it by the State Party concerned and by the petitioner. The Committee shall not consider any communication from a petitioner unless it has ascertained that the petitioner has exhausted all available domestic remedies. However, this shall not be the rule where the application of the remedies is unreasonably prolonged;

   (b) The Committee shall forward its suggestions and recommendations, if any, to the State Party concerned and to the petitioner.

8. The Committee shall include in its annual report a summary of such communications and, where appropriate, a summary of the explanations and statements of the States Parties concerned and of its own suggestions and recommendations.

9. The Committee shall be competent to exercise the functions provided for in this article only when at least ten States Parties to this Convention are bound by declarations in accordance with paragraph 1 of this article.

Article 15

1. Pending the achievement of the objectives of the Declaration on the Granting of Independence to Colonial Countries and Peoples, contained in General Assembly resolution 1514 (XV) of 14 December 1960, the provisions of this Convention shall in no way limit the right of petition granted to these peoples by other international instruments or by the United Nations and its specialized agencies.

2. (a) The Committee established under article 8, paragraph 1, of this Convention shall receive copies of the petitions from, and submit expressions of opinion and recommendations on their petitions to, the bodies of the United Nations which deal with matters directly related to the priciples and objectives of this Convention in their consideration of petitions from the inhabitants of Trust and Non-Self-Governing Territories and all other territories to which General Assembly resolution 1514 (XV) applies, relating to matters covered by this Convention which are before these bodies;

   (b) The Committee shall receive from the competent bodies of the United Nations copies of the reports concerning the legislative, judicial, administrative or other measures directly related to the principles and objectives of this Convention applied by the administering Powers within the Territories mentioned in subparagraph (a) of this paragraph, and shall express opinions and make recommendations to these bodies.

3. The Committee shall include in its report to the General Assembly a summary of the petitions and reports it has received from United Nations bodies, and the expressions of opinion and recommendations of the Committee relating to the said petitions and reports.

4. The Committee shall request from the Secretary-General of the United Nations all information relevant to the objectives of this Convention and available to him regarding the Territories mentioned in paragraph 2(a) of this article.

Article 16

The provisions of this Convention concerning the settlement of disputes or complaints shall be applied without prejudice to other procedures for settling disputes or complaints in the field of discrimination laid down in the constituent instruments of, or conventions adopted by, the United Nations and its specialized agencies, and shall not prevent the States Parties from having recourse to other procedures for settling a dispute in accordance with general or special international agreements in force between them.

PART III

Article 17

1. This Convention is open for signature by any State Member of the United Nations or member of any of its specialized agencies, by any State Party to the Statute of the International Court of Justice, and by any other State which has been invited by the General Assembly of the United Nations to become a Party to this Convention.

2. This Convention is subject to ratification. Instruments of ratification shall be deposited with the Secretary-General of the United Nations.

Article 18

1. This Convention shall be open to accession by any State referred to in article 17, paragraph 1, of the Convention.

2. Accession shall be effected by the deposit of an instrument of accession with the Secretary-General of the United Nations.

Article 19

1. This Convention shall enter into force on the thirtieth day after the date of the deposit with the Secretary-General of the United Nations of the twenty-seventh instrument of ratification or instrument of accession.

2. For each State ratifying this Convention or acceding to it after the deposit of the twenty-seventh instrument of ratification or instrument of accession, the Convention shall enter into force on the thirtieth day after the date of the deposit of its own instrument of ratification or instrument of accession.

Article 20

1. The Secretary-General of the United Nations shall receive and circulate to all States which are or may become Parties to this Convention reservations made by States at the time of ratification or accession. Any State which objects to the reservation shall, within a period of ninety days from the date of the said communication, notify the Secretary-General that it does not accept it.

2. A reservation incompatible with the object and purpose of this Convention shall not be permitted, nor shall a reservation the effect of which would inhibit the operation of any of the bodies established by this Convention be allowed. A reservation shall be considered incompatible or inhibitive if at least two thirds of the States Parties to this Convention object to it.

3. Reservations may be withdrawn at any time by notification to this effect addressed to the Secretary-General. Such notification shall take effect on the date on which it is received.

Article 21

A State Party may denounce this Convention by written notification to the Secretary-General of the United Nations. Denunciation shall take effect one year after the date of receipt of the notification by the Secretary-General.

Article 22

Any dispute between two or more States Parties with respect to the interpretation or application of this Convention, which is not settled by negotiation or by the procedures expressly provided for in this Convention, shall, at the request of any of the parties to the dispute, be referred to the International Court of Justice for decision, unless the disputants agree to another mode of settlement.

Article 23

1. A request for the revision of this Convention may be made at any time by any State Party by means of a notification in writing addressed to the Secretary-General of the United Nations.

2. The General Assembly of the United Nations shall decide upon the steps, if any, to be taken in respect of such a request.

Article 24

The Secretary-General of the United Nations shall inform all States referred to in article 17, paragraph 1, of this Convention of the following particulars:

(a) Signatures, ratifications and accessions under articles 17 and 18;
(b) The date of entry into force of this Convention under article 19;
(c) Communications and declarations received under articles 14, 20 and 23;
(d) Denunciations under article 21.

Article 25

1. This Convention, of which the Chinese, English, French, Russian and Spanish texts are equally authentic, shall be deposited in the archives of the United Nations.

2. The Secretary-General of the United Nations shall transmit certified copies of this Convention to all States belonging to any of the categories mentioned in article 17, paragraph 1, of the Convention.

APPENDIX 4

FOURTH PROTOCOL TO THE CONVENTION FOR THE PROTECTION OF HUMAN RIGHTS AND FUNDAMENTAL FREEDOMS

PROTOCOL NO 4 TO THE CONVENTION FOR THE PROTECTION OF HUMAN RIGHTS AND FUNDAMENTAL FREEDOMS, SECURING CERTAIN RIGHTS AND FREEDOMS OTHER THAN THOSE ALREADY INCLUDED IN THE CONVENTION AND IN THE FIRST PROTOCOL THERETO, AS AMENDED BY PROTOCOL NO 11

Strasbourg, 16.IX.1963

Headings of articles added and text amended according to the provisions of Protocol No 11 (ETS No 155) as from its entry into force on 1 November 1998.

The governments signatory hereto, being members of the Council of Europe,

Being resolved to take steps to ensure the collective enforcement of certain rights and freedoms other than those already included in Section 1 of the Convention for the Protection of Human Rights and Fundamental Freedoms signed at Rome on 4th November 1950 (hereinafter referred to as the 'Convention') and in Articles 1 to 3 of the First Protocol to the Convention, signed at Paris on 20th March 1952,

Have agreed as follows:

Article 1 – Prohibition of imprisonment for debt

No one shall be deprived of his liberty merely on the ground of inability to fulfil a contractual obligation.

Article 2 – Freedom of movement

1   Everyone lawfully within the territory of a State shall, within that territory, have the right to liberty of movement and freedom to choose his residence.

2   Everyone shall be free to leave any country, including his own.

3   No restrictions shall be placed on the exercise of these rights other than such as are in accordance with law and are necessary in a democratic society in the interests of national security or public safety, for the maintenance of ordre public, for the prevention of crime, for the protection of health or morals, or for the protection of the rights and freedoms of others.

4   The rights set forth in paragraph 1 may also be subject, in particular areas, to restrictions imposed in accordance with law and justified by the public interest in a democratic society.

PART 6
APPENDICES

Article 3 – Prohibition of expulsion of nationals

1   No one shall be expelled, by means either of an individual or of a collective measure, from the territory of the State of which he is a national.

2   No one shall be deprived of the right to enter the territory of the state of which he is a national.

Article 4 – Prohibition of collective expulsion of aliens

Collective expulsion of aliens is prohibited.

Article 5 – Territorial application

1   Any High Contracting Party may, at the time of signature or ratification of this Protocol, or at any time thereafter, communicate to the Secretary General of the Council of Europe a declaration stating the extent to which it undertakes that the provisoins of this Protocol shall apply to such of the territories for the international relations of which it is responsible as are named therein.

2   Any High Contracting Party which has communicated a declaration in virtue of the preceding paragraph may, from time to time, communicate a further declaration modifying the terms of any former declaration or terminating the application of the provisions of this Protocol in respect of any territory.

3[1]   A declaration made in accordance with this article shall be deemed to have been made in accordance with paragraph 1 of Article 56 of the Convention.

4   The territory of any State to which this Protocol applies by virtue of ratification or acceptance by that State, and each territory to which this Protocol is applied by virtue of a declaration by that State under this article, shall be treated as separate territories for the purpose of the references in Articles 2 and 3 to the territory of a State.

5[2]   Any State which has made a declaration in accordance with paragraph 1 or 2 of this Article may at any time thereafter declare on behalf of one or more of the territories to which the declaration relates that it accepts the competence of the Court to receive applications from individuals, non-governmental organisations or groups of individuals as provided in Article 34 of the Convention in respect of all or any of Articles 1 to 4 of this Protocol.

Article 6[1] – Relationship to the Convention

As between the High Contracting Parties the provisions of Articles 1 to 5 of this Protocol shall be regarded as additional Articles to the Convention, and all the provisions of the Convention shall apply accordingly.

Article 7 – Signature and ratification

1   This Protocol shall be open for signature by the members of the Council of Europe who are the signatories of the Convention; it shall be ratified at the same time as or after the ratification of the Convention. It shall enter into force after the deposit of five instruments of ratification. As regards any signatory ratifying subsequently, the Protocol shall enter into force at the date of the deposit of its instrument of ratification.

2   The instruments of ratification shall be deposited with the Secretary of General of the Council of Europe, who will notify all members of the names of those who have ratified.

In witness whereof the undersigned, being duly authorised thereto, have signed this Protocol.

Done at Strasbourg, this 16th day of September 1963, in English and in French, both texts being equally authoritative, in a single copy which shall remain deposited in the archives of the Council of Europe. The Secretary General shall transmit certified copies to each of the signatory states.

Footnotes
1. Text amended according to the provisions of Protocol No 11 (ETS No 155).
2. Text added to the provisions of Protocol No 11 (ETS No 155).

APPENDIX 5

EUROPEAN CONVENTION ON ESTABLISHMENT 1955

The governments signatory hereto, being members of the Council of Europe,

Considering that the aim of the Council of Europe is to safeguard and to realise the ideals and principles which are the common heritage of its members and to facilitate their economic and social progress;

Recognising the special character of the links between the member countries of the Council of Europe as affirmed in conventions and agreements already concluded within the framework of the Council such as the Convention for the Protection of Human Rights and Fundamental Freedoms signed on 4th November 1950, the Protocol to this Convention signed on 20th March 1952, the European Convention on Social and Medical Assistance and the two European Interim Agreements on Social Security signed on 11th December 1953;

Being convinced that, by the conclusion of a regional convention, the establishment of common rules for the treatment accorded to nationals of each member State in the territory of the others may further the achievement of greater unity;

Affirming that the rights and privileges which they grant to each other's nationals are conceded solely by virtue of the close association uniting the member countries of the Council of Europe by means of its Statute;

Noting that the general plan of the Convention fits into the framework of the organisation of the Council of Europe,

Have agreed as follows:

CHAPTER I – ENTRY, RESIDENCE AND EXPULSION

Article 1

Each Contracting Party shall facilitate the entry into its territory by nationals of the other Parties for the purpose of temporary visits and shall permit them to travel freely within its territory except when this would be contrary to *ordre public*, national security, public health or morality.

Article 2

Subject to the conditions set out in Article 1 of this Convention, each Contracting Party shall, to the extent permitted by its economic and social conditions, facilitate the prolonged or permanent residence in its territory of nationals of the other Parties.

PART 6
APPENDICES

Article 3

1. Nationals of any Contracting Party lawfully residing in the territory of another Party may be expelled only if they endanger national security or offend against *ordre public* or morality.

2. Except where imperative considerations of national security otherwise require, a national of any Contracting Party who has been so lawfully residing for more than two years in the territory of any other Party shall not be expelled without first being allowed to submit reasons against his explusion and to appeal to, and be represented for the purpose before, a competent authority or a person or persons specially designated by the competent authority.

3. Nationals of any Contracting Party who have been lawfully residing for more than ten years in the territory of any other Party may only be expelled for reasons of national security or if the other reasons mentioned in paragraph 1 of this article are of a particularly serious nature.

CHAPTER II – EXERCISE OF PRIVATE RIGHTS

Article 4

Nationals of any Contracting Party shall enjoy in the territory of any other Party treatment equal to that enjoyed by nationals of the latter Party in respect of the possession and exercise of private rights whether personal rights or rights relating to property.

Article 5

Notwithstanding Article 4 of this Convention, any Contracting Party may, for reasons of national security or defence, reserve the acquisition, possession or use of any categories of property for its own nationals or subject nationals of other Parties to special conditions applicable to aliens in respect of such property.

Article 6

1. Apart from cases relating to national security or defence,

(a) any Contracting Party which has reserved for its nationals or, in the case of aliens including those who are nationals of other Parties, made subject to regulations the acquisition, possession or use of certain categories of property, or has made the acquisition, possession or use of such property conditional upon reciprocity, shall, at the time of the signature of this Convention, transmit a list of these restrictions to the Secretary General of the Council of Europe indicating which provisions of its municipal law are the basis of such restrictions. The Secretary General shall forward these lists to the other signatories;

(b) after this Convention has entered into force in respect of any Contracting Party, that Contracting Party shall not introduce any further restrictions as to the acquisition, possession or use of any categories of property by nationals of the other Parties, unless it finds itself compelled to do so for imperative reasons of an economic or social character or in order to prevent monopolisation of the vital resources of the country. It shall in this event keep the Secretary General fully informed of the measures taken, the relevant provisions of municipal law and the reasons for such measures. The Secretary General shall communicate this information to the other Parties.

2. Each Contracting Party shall endeavour to reduce its list of restrictions for the benefit of nationals of the other Parties. It shall notify the Secretary General of any such changes and he shall communicate them to the other Parties. Each Party shall also endeavour to grant to nationals of other Parties such exemptions from the general regulations concerning aliens as are provided for in its own legislation.

CHAPTER III – JUDICIAL AND ADMINISTRATIVE GUARANTEES

Article 7

Nationals of any Contracting Party shall enjoy in the territory of any other Party, under the same conditions as nationals of the latter Party, full legal and judicial protection of their persons and property and of their rights and interests. In particular they shall have, in the same manner as the nationals of the latter Party, the right of access to the competent judicial and administrative authorities and the right to obtain the assistance of any person of their choice who is qualified by the laws of the country.

Article 8

1. Nationals of any Contracting Party shall be entitled in the territory of any other Party to obtain free legal assistance under the same conditions as nationals of the latter Party.

2. Indigent nationals of a Contracting Party shall be entitled to have copies of *actes de l'état civil* issued to them free of charge in the territory of another Contracting Party in so far as these are so issued to indigent nationals of the latter Contracting Party.

Article 9

1. No security or deposit of any kind may be required, by reasons of their status as aliens or of lack of domicile or residence in the country, from nationals of any Contracting Party, having their domicile or normal residence in the territory of a Party, who may be plaintiffs or third parties before the Courts of any other Party.

2. The same rule shall apply to the payment which may be required of plaintiffs or third parties to guarantee legal costs.

3. Orders to pay the costs and expenses of a trial imposed upon a plaintiff or third party who is exempted from such security, deposit or payment in pursuance either of the preceding paragraphs of this article or of the law of the country in which the proceedings are taken, shall without charge, upon a request made through the diplomatic channel, be rendered enforceable by the competent authority in the territory of any other Contracting Party.

CHAPTER IV – GAINFUL OCCUPATIONS

Article 10

Each Contracting Party shall authorise nationals of the other Parties to engage in its territory in any gainful occupation on an equal footing with its own nationals, unless the said Contracting Party has cogent economic or social reasons for withholding the authorisation. This provision shall apply, but not be limited, to industrial, commercial, financial and agricultural occupations, skilled crafts and the professions, whether the person concerned is self-employed or is in the service of an employer.

Article 11

Nationals of any Contracting Party who have been allowed by another Party to engage in a gainful occupation for a certain period may not, during that period, be subjected to restrictions not provided for at the time the authorisation was granted to them unless such restrictions are equally applicable to nationals of the latter Party in similar circumstances.

Article 12

1. Nationals of any Contracting Party lawfully residing in the territory of any other Party shall be authorised, without being made subject to the restrictions referred to in Article 10 of this Convention, to engage in any gainful occupation on an equal footing with nationals of the latter Party, provided they comply with one of the following conditions:

(a) they have been lawfully engaged in a gainful occupation in that territory for an uninterrupted period of five years;
(b) they have lawfully resided in that territory for an uninterrupted period of ten years;
(c) they have been admitted to permanent residence.

Any Contracting Party may, at the time of signature or of deposit of its instrument of ratification of this Convention, declare that it does not accept one or two of the conditions mentioned above.

2. Such Party may also, in accordance with the same procedure, increase the period laid down in paragraph 1 (a) of this article to a maximum of ten years, provided that after the first period of five years renewal of an authorisation may in no case be refused in respect of the occupation pursued up to that time nor may such renewal be conditional upon any change in that occupation. It may also declare that it will not in all cases automatically grant the right to change from a wage-earning occupation to an independent occupation.

Article 13

Any Contracting Party may reserve for its own nationals the exercise of public functions or of occupations connected with national security or defence, or make the exercise of these occupations by aliens subject to special conditions.

Article 14

1. Apart from the functions or occupations mentioned in Article 13 of this Convention,

(a) any Contracting Party which has reserved certain occupations for its own nationals or made the exercise of them by aliens, including nationals of the other Parties, subject to regulations or reciprocity, shall at the time of signature of this Convention transmit a list of these restrictions to the Secretary General of the Council of Europe, indicating which provisions of its municipal law are the basis of such restrictions. The Secretary General shall forward these lists to the other signatories;
(b) after this Convention has entered into force in respect of any Contracting Party, that Party shall not introduce any further restrictions as to the exercise of gainful occupations by the nationals of other Parties unless it finds itself compelled to do so for imperative reasons of an economic or social character. It shall in this event keep the Secretary General fully informed of the measures taken, the relevant provisions of municipal law and the reasons for such measures. The Secretary General shall communicate this information to the other Parties.

2. Each Contracting Party shall endeavour for the benefit of nationals of the other Parties:

– to reduce the list of occupations which are reserved for its own nationals or the exercise of which by aliens is subject to regulations or reciprocity; it shall notify the Secretary General of any such changes, and he shall communicate them to the other Parties;

– in so far as its laws permit, to allow individual exemptions from the provisions in force.

Article 15

The exercise by nationals of one Contracting Party in the territory of another Party of an occupation in respect of which nationals of the latter Party are required to possess professional or technical qualifications or to furnish guarantees shall be made subject to the production of the same guarantees or to the possession of the same qualifications or of others recognised as their equivalent by the competent national authority;

Provided that nationals of the Contracting Parties engaged in the lawful pursuit of their profession in the territory of any Party may be called into the territory of any other Party by one of their colleagues for the purpose of lending assistance in a particular case.

Article 16

Commercial travellers who are nationals of a Contracting Party and are employed by an undertaking whose principal place of business is situated in the territory of a Contracting Party shall not need any authorisation in order to exercise their occupation in the territory of any other Party, provided that they do not reside therein for more than two months during any half-year.

Article 17

1. Nationals of any Contracting Party shall, in the territory of another Party, enjoy treatment no less favourable than nationals of the latter Party in respect of any statutory regulation by a public authority concerning wages and working conditions in general.

2. The provisions of this chapter shall not be understood as requiring a Contracting Party to accord in its territory more favourable treatment as regards the exercise of a gainful occupation to the nationals of any other Party than that accorded to its own nationals.

CHAPTER V – INDIVIDUAL RIGHTS

Article 18

No Contracting Party may forbid nationals of another Party who have been lawfully engaged for at least five years in an appropriate occupation in the territory of the former Party from taking part on an equal footing with its own nationals as electors in elections held by bodies or organisations of an economic or professional nature such as Chambers of Commerce or of Agricultural or Trade Associations, subject to the decisions which such bodies or organisations may take in this respect within the limits of their competence.

Article 19

Nationals of any Contracting Party in the territory of any other Party shall be permitted, without any restrictions other than those applicable to nationals of the latter Party, to act as arbitrators in arbitral proceedings in which the choice of arbitrators is left entirely to the parties concerned.

Article 20

In so far as access to education is under State control, nationals of school age of any Contracting Party lawfully residing in the territory of any other Party shall be admitted, on an equal footing with the nationals of the latter Party, to institutions for primary and secondary education and technical and vocational training. The application of this provision to the grant of scholarships shall be left to the discretion of individual Parties. School attendance shall be compulsory for nationals of school age residing in the territory of another Contracting Party if it is compulsory for the nationals of the latter Party.

CHAPTER VI – TAXATION, COMPULSORY CIVILIAN SERVICES, EXPROPRIATION, NATIONALISATION

Article 21

1. Subject to the provisions concerning double taxation contained in agreements already concluded or to be concluded, nationals of any Contracting Party shall not be liable in the territory of any other Party to duties, charges, taxes or contributions, of any description whatsoever, other, higher or more burdensome than those imposed on nationals of the latter Party in similar circumstances; in particular, they shall be entitled to deductions or exemptions from taxes or charges and to all allowances, including allowances for dependants.

2. A Contracting Party shall not impose on nationals of any other Party any residence charge not required of its own nationals. This provision shall not prevent the imposition in appropriate cases of charges connected with administrative formalities such as the issue of permits and authorisations which aliens are required to have, provided that the amount levied is not more than the expenditure incurred by such formalities.

Article 22

Nationals of a Contracting Party may in no case be obliged to perform in the territory of another Party any civilian services, whether of a personal nature or relating to property, other or more burdensome than those required of nationals of the latter Party.

Article 23

Without prejudice to the provisons of Article 1 of the Protocol to the Convention on the Protection of Human Rights and Fundamental Freedoms, nationals of any Contracting Party shall be entitled, in the event of expropriation or nationalisation of their property by any other Party, to be treated at least as favourably as nationals of the latter Party.

CHAPTER VII – STANDING COMMITTEE

Article 24

1. A Standing Committee shall be set up within a year of the entry into force of this Convention. This Committee may formulate proposals designed to improve the practical implementation of the Convention and, if necessary, to amend or supplement its provisions.

2. In the event of differences of opinion arising between the Parties over the interpretation or application of the provisions of Article 6, paragraph 1 (b), and Article

14, paragraph 1(b), of this Convention, the Committee shall at the request of any Party concerned endeavour to settle such differences.

3. The Committee shall arrange for the publication of a periodical report containing all information regarding the laws and regulations in force in the territory of the Parties in respect of matters provided for in this Convention.

4. Each member of the Council of Europe which has ratified this Convention shall appoint a representative to this Committee. Any other member of the Council may be represented by an observer with the right to speak.

5. The Committee shall be convened by the Secretary General of the Council of Europe. Its first session shall take place within three months of the date of its establishment. Subsequent sessions shall be held at least once every two years. The Committee may also be convened whenever the Committee of Ministers of the Council considers it necessary. The period of two years shall run from the date of the end of the last session.

6. Opinions or recommendations of the Standing Committee shall be submitted to the Committee of Ministers.

7. The Standing Committee shall draw up its own Rules of Procedure.

CHAPTER VIII – GENERAL PROVISIONS

Article 25

The provisions of this Convention shall not prejudice the provisions of municipal law, bilateral or multilateral treaties, conventions or agreements which are already in force or may come into force under which more favourable treatment would be accorded to nationals of one or more of the other Contracting Parties.

Article 26

1. Any member of the Council of Europe may, when signing this Convention or when depositing its instrument of ratification, make a reservation in respect of any particular provision of the Convention to the extent that any law then in force in its territory is not in conformity with the said provision. Reservations of a general nature shall not be permitted under this article.

2. Any reservation made under this article shall contain a brief statement of the law concerned.

3. Any member of the Council which makes a reservation under this article shall withdraw the said reservation as soon as circumstances permit. Such withdrawal shall be made by notification addressed to the Secretary General of the Council and shall take effect from the date of the receipt of such notification. The Secretary General shall transmit the text of this notification to all the signatories of the Convention.

Article 27

A Contracting Party which has made a reservation in respect of a particular provision of the Convention in accordance with Article 26 of this Convention may not claim application of the said provision by another Party save in so far as it has itself accepted the provision.

Article 28

1. In time of war or other public emergency threatening the life of the nation, any Contracting Party may take measures derogating from its obligations under this Convention to the extent strictly required by the exigencies of the situation and provided that such measures are not inconsistent with its other obligations under international law.

2. Any Contracting Party availing itself of this right of derogation shall keep the Secretary General of the Council of Europe fully informed of the measures which it has taken and the reasons therefor. It shall also inform the Secretary General of the Council when such measures have ceased to operate and the provisions of the Convention are again being fully executed.

CHAPTER IX – FIELD OF APPLICATION OF THE CONVENTION

Article 29

1. This Convention shall apply to the metropolitan territories of the Contracting Parties.

2. Any member of the Council may, at the time of the signature or ratification of this Convention or at any later date, declare by notice addressed to the Secretary General of the Council of Europe that this Convention shall apply to the territory or territories mentioned in the said declaration and for whose international relations it is responsible.

3. Any declaration made in accordance with the preceding paragraph may, in respect of any territory mentioned in such declaration, be withdrawn according to the procedure laid down in Article 33 of this Convention.

4. The Secretary General shall communicate to the other members of the Council any declaration transmitted to him in accordance with paragraph 2 or paragraph 3 of this article.

Article 30

1. For the purpose of this Convention, 'nationals' means physical persons possessing the nationality of one of the Contracting Parties.

2. No Contracting Party shall be obliged to grant the benefits of this Convention to nationals of another Contracting Party ordinarily resident in a non-metropolitan territory of the latter Party to which the Convention does not apply.

CHAPTER X – SETTLEMENT OF DISPUTES

Article 31

1. Any disputes which may arise between the Contracting Parties concerning the interpretation or the application of this Convention shall be submitted to the International Court of Justice by special agreement or by application by one of the parties to the dispute, unless the parties agree on a different method of peaceful settlement.

2. After the entry into force of the European Convention for the Peaceful Settlement of Disputes, the Parties to that Convention shall apply those of its provisions which are binding upon them to all disputes which may arise between them concerning the present Convention.

3. Any dispute subjected to a procedure referred to in the preceding paragraphs shall be immediately reported by the parties concerned to the Secretary General of the Council of Europe, who shall inform the other Contracting Parties without delay.

4. If one of the parties to a dispute fails to carry out its obligations laid down in a decision of the International Court of Justice or the award of an arbitral tribunal, the other party may appeal to the Committee of Ministers of the Council of Europe. The latter may, if it deems necessary, make recommendations by a majority of two-thirds of the representatives entitled to sit on the Committee with a view to ensuring the execution of the said decision or award.

CHAPTER XI – FINAL PROVISIONS

Article 32

The Protocol attached to this Convention shall form an integral part of it.

Article 33

1. A Contracting Party may denounce this Convention only at the end of five years from the date on which it became a Party to it, having previously given six months' notice by notification addressed to the Secretary General of the Council of Europe, who shall inform the other Parties. A Party which does not so exercise the right of denunciation will remain bound for further successive periods of two years and may denounce this Convention only at the end of any such period, having given notice six months previously.

2. Denunciation shall not have the effect of releasing the Contracting Party concerned from its obligations under this Convention in respect of any act which may have been performed by it before the date upon which the denunciation became effective.

3. Any Contracting Party which ceases to be a member of the Council of Europe shall under the same conditions cease to be a Party to this Convention.

Article 34

1. This Convention shall be open for signature by the members of the Council of Europe. It shall be ratified. Instruments of ratification shall be deposited with the Secretary General of the Council of Europe.

2. This Convention shall come into force on the date of deposit of the fifth instrument of ratification.

3. As regards any signatory ratifying subsequently, the Convention shall come into force on the date of deposit of its instrument of ratification.

4. The Secretary General shall notify all the members of the Council of the entry into force of the Convention, the names of the Contracting Parties which have ratified it, any reservations made and the subsequent deposit of any instruments of ratification.

In witness whereof, the undersigned, being duly authorised thereto, have signed this Convention.

Done at Paris, this 13th day of December 1955, in English and in French, both texts being equally authoritative, in a single copy which shall remain deposited in the archives of the Council of Europe. The Secretary General shall transmit certified true copies to each of the signatories.

Section I – Articles 1, 2, 3, 5, 6, paragraph 1(b), 10, 13 and 14, paragraph 1(b)

(a) Each Contracting Party shall have the right to judge by national criteria:

1. the reaons of '*ordre public*, national security, public health or morality' which may provide grounds for the exclusion from its territory of nationals of other Parties;

2. 'the economic and social conditions' which may prevent the admission of nationals of other Parties to prolonged or permanent residence or the exercise of gainful occupations in its territory;

3. the circumstances which constitute a threat to national security or an offence against *ordre public* or morality;

4. the reasons specified in the Convention for which a Contracting Party may reserve for its own nationals the acquisition, possession or use of any categories of property or the exercise of certain rights and occupations or may make the exercise thereof by nationals of the other Parties subject to special conditions.

(b) Each Contracting Party shall determine whether the reasons for expulsion are of a 'particularly serious nature'. In this connection account shall be taken of the behaviour of the individual concerned during his whole period of residence.

(c) A Contracting Party may only restrict the rights of nationals of other Parties for the reasons set forth in this Convention and to the extent compatible with the obligations assumed by the Parties.

Section II – Articles 1, 2, 3, 10, 11, 12, 13, 14, 15, 16, 17 and 20

(a) Regulations governing the admission, residence and movement of aliens and also their right to engage in gainful occupations shall be unaffected by this Convention in so far as they are not inconsistent with it.

(b) Nationals of a Contracting Party shall be considered as lawfully residing in the territory of another Party if they have conformed to the said regulations.

Section III – Articles 1, 2 and 3

(a) The concept of '*ordre public*' is to be understood in the wide sense generally accepted in continental countries. A Contracting Party may, for instance, exclude a national of another Party for political reasons, or if there are grounds for believing that he is unable to pay the expenses of his stay or that he intends to engage in a gainful occupation without the necessary permits.

(b) The Contracting Parties undertake, in the exercise of their established rights, to pay due regard to family ties.

(c) The right of expulsion may be exercised only in individual cases. The Contracting Parties shall, in exercising their right of expulsion, act with consideration, having regard to the particular relations which exist between the members of the Council of Europe. They shall in particular take due account of family ties and the period of residence in their territory of the person concerned.

Section IV – Articles 8 and 9

Articles 8 and 9 of this Convention in no way affect obligations contracted under The Hague Convention on Civil Procedure.

Section V – Articles 10, 11, 12, 13, 14, 15, 16 and 17

(a) The provisions of Articles 10, 11, 12, 13, 14, 15, 16 and 17 of this Convention shall be subject to the conditions governing entry and residence laid down in Articles 1 and 2.

(b) The husband or wife and dependent children of nationals of any Contracting Party lawfully residing in the territory of another Party who have been authorised to accompany or rejoin them shall as far as possible be allowed to take up employment in that territory in accordance with the conditions laid down in this Convention.

(c) The provisions of Article 12 of this Convention shall not apply to nationals of a Contracting Party residing in the territory of another Party in pursuance of special regulations or engaged in a gainful occupation therein in pursuance of special rules or agreements, including such persons as members, or staff not locally recruited, of diplomatic or consular missions; members of the staff of international organisations; student employees, apprentices, students and persons employed for the purpose of completing their vocational training; crews of ships and aircraft.

(d) For the purpose of Article 16 of this Convention, the Contracting Parties shall not, in their municipal legislation or regulations, treat the occupation of commercial traveller as an itinerant trade or form of hawking.

(e) It is understood that Article 16 applies only to commercial travellers acting under the orders of an undertaking situated outside the receiving country and remunerated solely by such undertaking.

(f) Article 17, paragraph 1, of this Convention shall not apply to the special case of student employees in respect of their remuneration.

Section VI – Articles 2, 11, 12, 13, 14, 15, 16, 17 and 25

(a) It is understood that this Convention shall not apply to industrial, literary and artistic property and new vegetable products, as these subjects are reserved for international conventions or other international agreements relating thereto which are already in force or will come into force.

(b) Those Contracting Parties to this Convention which are now or will be bound by the decisions of the Organisation for European Economic Co-operation governing the employment of nationals of its member countries shall, in their mutual relations and in respect of the exercise of wage-earning occupations, apply the provisions of this Convention or of the said decisions, whichever grant the more favourable treatment to wage-earners. In applying the provisions of Articles 2, 10, 11, 12, 13, 14, 15, 16 and 17 of this Convention and judging the economic or social reasons mentioned in Articles 10 and 14, they shall conform to the spirit and the letter of the said decisions in so far as the latter are more favourable to wage-earners than the provisions of this Convention.

Section VII – Article 26, paragraph 1

The Contracting Parties shall exercise their right to make reservations only in so far as they consider that essential provisions of their municipal law so require.

Section VIII – Article 29, paragraph 1

(a) This Convention shall, in respect of France, also apply to Algeria and the overseas Departments.

(b) The Federal Republic of Germany may extend the application of this Convention to the *Land* Berlin by a declaration addressed to the Secretary General of the Council of Europe who shall notify the other Contracting Parties thereof.

Article 29, paragraph 2

Any member of the Council of Europe which makes a declaration in accordance with Article 29, paragraph 2, of this Convention shall, at the same time and in respect of any territory mentioned in such declaration, transmit to the Secretary General of the Council the lists of restrictions specified in Article 6, paragraph 1, and Article 14, paragraph 1, any declaration made in accordance with Article 12 and any reservation made in accordance with Article 26 of this Convention.

Article 30

The term 'ordinarily resident' shall be defined according to the regulations applicable in the country of which the person concerned is a national.

Section IX – Article 31, paragraph 1

Contracting Parties not party to the Statute of the International Court of Justice shall take the necessary steps to obtain access to the Court.

ANNEX I

Resolution (55) 33 concerning the European Convention on Establishment, adopted by the Committee of Ministers of the Council of Europe, at its 17th Session, in Paris, on 13 December 1955

The Committee of Ministers,

Having approved the text of the draft European Convention on Establishment and having decided to submit this Convention for signature by the governments of the members of the Council;

Considering that the question has arisen whether a signatory Party may, during the interval between the signature and the entry into force of the Convention for that Party, introduce new restrictions in respect of the matters provided for in Articles 6 and 14;

In view of the spirit and fundamental character of this Convention,

Recommends the members of the Council, after the signature of the Convention, to take note of the provisions of paragraph 1(b) of Articles 6 and 14.

ANNEX II

Interpretative text concerning the European Convention on Establishment, approved by the Committee of Ministers of the Council of Europe, at its 17th Session, in Paris, on 13 December 1955

The Committee of Ministers expressed the view that the European Convention on Establishment should not be applicable to foreign currency and exchange regulations.

APPENDIX 6

CONVENTION FOR THE PROTECTION OF HUMAN RIGHTS AND FUNDAMENTAL FREEDOMS

Rome, 4.XI.1950

'The text of the Convention had been amended according to the provisions of Protocol No. 3 (ETS No. 45), which entered into force on 21 September 1970, of Protocol No. 5 (ETS No. 55), which entered into force on 20 December 1971 and of Protocol No. 8 (ETS No. 118), which entered into force 1 January 1990, and comprised also the text of Protocol No. 2 (ETS No. 44) which, in accordance with Article 5, paragraph 3 thereof, had been an integral part of the Convention since its entry into force on 21 September 1970. All provisions which had been amended or added by these Protocols are replaced by Protocol No. 11 (ETS No. 155), as from the date of its entry into force on 1 November 1998. As from that date, Protocol No. 9 (ETS No. 140), which entered into force on 1 October 1994, is repealed and Protocol No. 10 (ETS No. 146), which has not entered into force, has lost its purpose.'

The governments signatory hereto, being members of the Council of Europe,

Considering the Universal Declaration of Human Rights proclaimed by the General Assembly of the United Nations on 10th December 1948;

Considering that this Declaration aims at securing the universal and effective recognition and observance of the Rights therein declared;

Considering that the aim of the Council of Europe is the achievement of greater unity between its members and that one of the methods by which that aim is to be pursued is the maintenance and further realisation of human rights and fundamental freedoms;

Reaffirming their profound belief in those fundamental freedoms which are the foundation of justice and peace in the world and are best maintained on the one hand by an effective political democracy and on the other by a common understanding and observance of the human rights upon which they depend;

Being resolved, as the governments of European countries which are like-minded and have a common heritage of political traditions, ideals, freedom and the rule of law, to take the first steps for the collective enforcement of certain of the rights stated in the Universal Declaration,

Have agreed as follows:

Article 1[1]

Obligation to respect human rights

The High Contracting Parties shall secure to everyone within their jurisdiction the rights and freedoms defined in Section I of this Convention.

PART 6
APPENDICES

SECTION I

RIGHTS AND FREEDOMS

Article 2[1]

Right to life

1. Everyone's right to life shall be protected by law. No one shall be deprived of his life intentionally save in the execution of a sentence of a court following his conviction of a crime for which this penalty is provided by law.

2. Deprivation of life shall not be regarded as inflicted in contravention of this Article when it results from the use of force which is no more than absolutely necessary:

(a)   in defence of any person from unlawful violence;
(b)   in order to effect a lawful arrest or to prevent the escape of a person lawfully detained;
(c)   in action lawfully taken for the purpose of quelling a riot or insurrection.

Article 3[1]

Prohibition of torture

No one shall be subjected to torture or to inhuman or degrading treatment or punishment.

Article 4[1]

Prohibition of slavery and forced labour

1. No one shall be held in slavery or servitude.

2. No one shall be required to perform forced or compulsory labour.

3. For the purpose of this Article the term 'forced or compulsory labour' shall not include:

(a)   any work required to be done in the ordinary course of detention imposed according to the provisions of Article 5 of this Convention or during conditional release from such detention;
(b)   any service of a military character or, in case of conscientious objectors, in countries where they are recognised, service exacted instead of compulsory military service;
(c)   any service exacted in case of an emergency or calamity threatening the life or well-being of the community;
(d)   any work or service which forms part of normal civic obligations.

Article 5[1]

Right to liberty and security

1. Everyone has the right to liberty and security of person. No one shall be deprived of his liberty save in the following cases and in accordance with a procedure prescribed by law:

(a)   the lawful detention of a person after conviction by a competent court;

(b)   the lawful arrest or detention of a person for non-compliance with the lawful order of a court or in order to secure the fulfilment of any obligation prescribed by law;

(c)   the lawful arrest or detention of a person effected for the purpose of bringing him before the competent legal authority on reasonable suspicion of having committed an offence or when it is reasonably considered necessary to prevent his committing an offence or fleeing after having done so;

(d)   the detention of a minor by lawful order for the purpose of educational supervision or his lawful detention for the purpose of bringing him before the competent legal authority;

(e)   the lawful detention of persons for the prevention of the spreading of infectious diseases, of persons of unsound mind, alcoholics or drug addicts or vagrants;

(f)   the lawful arrest or detention of a person to prevent his effecting an unauthorised entry into the country or of a person against whom action is being taken with a view to deportation or extradition.

2. Everyone who is arrested shall be informed promptly, in a language which he understands, of the reasons for his arrest and of any charge against him.

3. Everyone arrested or detained in accordance with the provisions of paragraph l(c) of this Article shall be brought promptly before a judge or other officer authorised by law to exercise judicial power and shall be entitled to trial within a reasonable time or to release pending trial. Release may be conditioned by guarantees to appear for trial.

4. Everyone who is deprived of his liberty by arrest or detention shall be entitled to take proceedings by which the lawfulness of his detention shall be decided speedily by a court and his release ordered if the detention is not lawful.

5. Everyone who has been the victim of arrest or detention in contravention of the provisions of this Article shall have an enforceable right to compensation.

Article 6[1]

Right to a fair trail

1. In the determination of his civil rights and obligations or of any, criminal charge against him, everyone is entitled to a fair and public hearing within a reasonable time by an independent and impartial tribunal established by law. Judgment shall be pronounced publicly but the press and public may be excluded from all or part of the trial in the interests of morals, public order or national security in a democratic society, where the interests of juveniles or the protection of the private life of the parties so require, or to the extent strictly necessary in the opinion of the court in special circumstances where publicity would prejudice the interests of justice.

2. Everyone charged with a criminal offence shall be presumed innocent until proved guilty according to law.

3. Everyone charged with a criminal offence has the following minimum rights:

(a)   to be informed promptly, in a language which he understands and in detail, of the nature and cause of the accusation against him;

(b)   to have adequate time and facilities for the preparation of his defence;

(c)   to defend himself in person or through legal assistance of his own choosing or, if he has not sufficient means to pay for legal assistance, to be given it free when the interests of justice so require;

(d)   to examine or have examined witnesses against him and to obtain the attendance and examination of witnesses on his behalf under the same conditions as witnesses against him;

(e)   to have the free assistance of an interpreter if he cannot understand or speak the language used in court.

Article 7[1]

No punishment without law

1. No one shall be held guilty of any criminal offence on account of any act or omission which did not constitute a criminal offence under national or international law at the time when it was committed. Nor shall a heavier penalty be imposed than the one that was applicable at the time the criminal offence was committed.

2. This Article shall not prejudice the trial and punishment of any person for any act or omission which, at the time when it was committed, was criminal according to the general principles of law recognised by civilised nations.

Article 8[1]

Right to respect for private and family life

1. Everyone has the right to respect for his private and family life, his home and his correspondence.

2. There shall be no interference by a public authority with the exercise of this right except such as is in accordance with the law and is necessary in a democratic society in the interests of national security, public safety or the economic well-being of the country, for the prevention of disorder or crime, for the protection of health or morals, or for the protection of the rights and freedoms of others.

Article 9[1]

Freedom of thought, conscience and religion

1. Everyone has the right to freedom of thought, conscience and religion; this right includes freedom to change his religion or belief and freedom, either alone or in community with others and in public or private, to manifest his religion or belief, in worship, teaching, practice and observance.

2. Freedom to manifest one's religion or beliefs shall be subject only to such limitations as are prescribed by law and are necessary in a democratic society in the interests of public safety, for the protection of public order, health or morals, or for the protection of the rights and freedoms of others.

Article 10[1]

Freedom of expression

1. Everyone has the right to freedom of expression. This right shall include freedom to hold opinions and to receive and impart information and ideas without interference by public authority and regardless of frontiers. This Article shall not prevent States from requiring the licensing of broadcasting, television or cinema enterprises.

2. The exercise of these freedoms, since it carries with it duties and responsibilities, may be subject to such formalities, conditions, restrictions or penalties as are prescribed by law and are necessary in a democratic society, in the interests of national security, territorial integrity or public safety, for the prevention of disorder or crime, for the

protection of health or morals, for the protection of the reputation or rights of others, for preventing the disclosure of information received in confidence, or for maintaining the authority and impartiality of the judiciary.

Article 11[1]

Freedom of assembly and association

1. Everyone has the right to freedom of peaceful assembly and to freedom of association with others, including the right to form and to join trade unions for the protection of his interests.

2. No restrictions shall be placed on the exercise of these rights other than such as are prescribed by law and are necessary in a democratic society in the interests of national security or public safety, for the prevention of disorder or crime, for the protection of health or morals or for the protection of the rights and freedoms of others. This Article shall not prevent the imposition of lawful restrictions on the exercise of these rights by members of the armed forces, of the police or of the administration of the State.

Article 12[1]

Right to marry

Men and women of marriageable age have the right to marry and to found a family, according to the national laws governing the exercise of this right.

Article 13[1]

Right to an effective remedy

Everyone whose rights and freedoms as set forth in this Convention are violated shall have an effective remedy before a national authority notwithstanding that the violation has been committed by persons acting in an official capacity.

Article 14[1]

Prohibition of discrimination

The enjoyment of the rights and freedoms set forth in this Convention shall be secured without discrimination on any ground such as sex, race, colour, language, religion, political or other opinion, national or social origin, association with a national minority, property, birth or other status.

Article 15[1]

Derogation in time of emergency

1. In time of war or other public emergency threatening the life of the nation any High Contracting Party may take measures derogating from its obligations under this Convention to the extent strictly required by the exigencies of the situation, provided that such measures are not inconsistent with its other obligations under international law.

PART 6
APPENDICES

2. No derogation from Article 2, except in respect of deaths resulting from lawful acts of war, or from Articles 3, 4 (paragraph 1) and 7 shall be made under this provision.

3. Any High Contracting Party availing itself of this right of derogation shall keep the Secretary General of the Council of Europe fully informed of the measures which it has taken and the reasons therefor. It shall also inform the Secretary General of the Council of Europe when such measures have ceased to operate and the provisions of the Convention are again being fully executed.

Article 16[1]

Restrictions on political activity of aliens

Nothing in Articles 10, 11 and 14 shall be regarded as preventing the High Contracting Parties from imposing restrictions on the political activity of aliens.

Article 17[1]

Prohibition of abuse of rights

Nothing in this Convention may be interpreted as implying for any State, group or person any right to engage in any activity or perform any act aimed at the destruction of any of the rights and freedoms set forth herein or at their limitation to a greater extent than is provided for in the Convention.

Article 18[1]

Limitation on use of restrictions on rights

The restrictions permitted under this Convention to the said rights and freedoms shall not be applied for any purpose other than those for which they have been prescribed.

SECTION II

EUROPEAN COURT OF HUMAN RIGHTS[2]

Article 19

Establishment of the Court

To ensure the observance of the engagements undertaken by the High Contracting Parties in the Convention and the Protocols thereto, there shall be set up a European Court of Human Rights, hereinafter referred to as 'the Court'. It shall function on a permanent basis.

Article 20

Number of judges

The Court shall consist of a number of judges equal to that of the High Contracting Parties.

Article 21

Criteria for office

1. The judges shall be of high moral character and must either possess the qualifications required for appointment to high judicial office or be jurisconsults of recognised competence.

2. The judges shall sit on the Court in their individual capacity.

3. During their term of office the judges shall not engage in any activity which is incompatible with their independence, impartiality or with the demands of a full-time office; all questions arising from the application of this paragraph shall be decided by the Court.

Article 22

Election of judges

1. The judges shall be elected by the Parliamentary Assembly with respect to each High Contracting Party by a majority of votes cast from a list of three candidates nominated by the High Contracting Party.

2. The same procedure shall be followed to complete the Court in the event of the accession of new High Contracting Parties and in filling casual vacancies.

Article 23

Terms of office

1. The judges shall be elected for a period of six years. They may be re-elected. However, the terms of office of one-half of the judges elected at the first election shall expire at the end of three years.

2. The judges whose terms of office are to expire at the end of the initial period of three years shall be chosen by lot by the Secretary General of the Council of Europe immediately after their election.

3. In order to ensure that, as far as possible, the terms of office of one-half of the judges are renewed every three years, the Parliamentary Assembly may decide, before proceeding to any subsequent election, that the term or terms of office of one or more judges to be elected shall be for a period other than six years but not more than nine and not less than three years.

4. In cases where more than one term of office is involved and where the Parliamentary Assembly applies the preceding paragraph, the allocation of the terms of office shall be effected by a drawing of lots by the Secretary General of the Council of Europe immediately after the election.

5. A judge elected to replace a judge whose term of office has not expired shall hold office for the remainder of his predecessor's term.

6. The terms of office of judges shall expire when they reach the age of 70.

7. The judges shall hold office until replaced. They shall, however, continue to deal with such cases as they already have under consideration.

PART 6
APPENDICES

Article 24

Dismissal

No judge may be dismissed from his office unless the other judges decide by a majority of two-thirds that he has ceased to fulfil the required conditions.

Article 25

Registry and legal secretaries

The Court shall have a registry, the functions and organisation of which shall be laid down in the rules of the Court. The Court shall be assisted by legal secretaries.

Article 26

Plenary Court

The plenary Court shall

(a)   elect its President and one or two Vice-Presidents for a period of three years; they may be re-elected;
(b)   set up Chambers, constituted for a fixed period of time;
(c)   elect the Presidents of the Chambers of the Court; they may be re-elected;
(d)   adopt the rules of the Court, and
(e)   elect the Registrar and one or more Deputy Registrars.

Article 27

Committees, Chambers and Grand Chamber

1. To consider cases brought before it, the Court shall sit in committees of three judges, in Chambers of seven judges and in a Grand Chamber of seventeen judges. The Court's Chambers shall set up committees for a fixed period of time.

2. There shall sit as an *ex officio* member of the Chamber and the Grand Chamber the judge elected in respect of the State Party concerned or, if there is none or if he is unable to sit, a person of its choice who shall sit in the capacity of judge.

3. The Grand Chamber shall also include the President of the Court, the Vice-Presidents, the Presidents of the Chambers and other judges chosen in accordance with the rules of the Court. When a case is referred to the Grand Chamber under Article 43, no judge from the Chamber which rendered the judgment shall sit in the Grand Chamber, with the exception of the President of the Chamber and the judge who sat in respect of the State Party concerned.

Article 28

Declarations of inadmissibility by committees

A committee may, by a unanimous vote, declare inadmissible or strike out of its list of cases an application submitted under Article 34 where such a decision can be taken without further examination. The decision shall be final.

Article 29

Decisions by Chambers on admissibility and merits

1. If no decision is taken under Article 28, a Chamber shall decide on the admissibility and merits of individual applications submitted under Article 34.

2. A Chamber shall decide on the admissibility and merits of inter-State applications submitted under Article 33.

3. The decision on admissibility shall be taken separately unless the Court, in exceptional cases, decides otherwise.

Article 30

Relinquishment of jurisdiction to the Grand Chamber

Where a case pending before a Chamber raises a serious question affecting the interpretation of the Convention or the protocols thereto, or where the resolution of a question before the Chamber might have a result inconsistent with a judgment previously delivered by the Court, the Chamber may, at any time before it has rendered its judgment, relinquish jurisdiction in favour of the Grand Chamber, unless one of the parties to the case objects.

Article 31

Powers of the Grand Chamber

The Grand Chamber shall

(a) determine applications submitted either under Article 33 or Article 34 when a Chamber has relinquished jurisdiction under Article 30 or when the case has been referred to it under Article 43; and

(b) consider requests for advisory opinions submitted under Article 47.

Article 32

Jurisdiction of the Court

1. The jurisdiction of the Court shall extend to all matters concerning the interpretation and application of the Convention and the protocols thereto which are referred to it as provided in Articles 33, 34 and 47.

2. In the event of dispute as to whether the Court has jurisdiction, the Court shall decide.

Article 33

Inter-State cases

Any High Contracting Party may refer to the Court any alleged breach of the provisions of the Convention and the protocols thereto by another High Contracting Party.

Article 34

Individual applications

The Court may receive applications from any person, non-governmental organisation or group of individuals claiming to be the victim of a violation by one of the High Contracting Parties of the rights set forth in the Convention or the protocols thereto. The High Contracting Parties undertake not to hinder in any way the effective exercise of this right.

Article 35

Admissibility criteria

1. The Court may only deal with the matter after all domestic remedies have been exhausted, according to the generally recognised rules of international law, and within a period of six months from the date on which the final decision was taken.

2. The Court shall not deal with any application submitted under Article 34 that

(a)   is anonymous; or
(b)   is substantially the same as a matter that has already been examined by the Court or has already been submitted to another procedure of international investigation or settlement and contains no relevant new information.

3. The Court shall declare inadmissible any individual application submitted under Article 34 which it considers incompatible with the provisions of the Convention or the protocols thereto, manifestly ill-founded, or an abuse of the right of application.

4. The Court shall reject any application which it considers inadmissible under this Article. It may do so at any stage of the proceedings.

Article 36

Third party intervention

1. In all cases before a Chamber of the Grand Chamber, a High Contracting Party one of whose nationals is an applicant shall have the right to submit written comments and to take part in hearings.

2. The President of the Court may, in the interest of the proper administration of justice, invite any High Contracting Party which is not a party to the proceedings or any person concerned who is not the applicant to submit written comments or take part in hearings.

Article 37

Striking out applications

1. The Court may at any stage of the proceedings decide to strike an application out of its list of cases where the circumstances lead to the conclusion that

(a)   the applicant does not intend to pursue his application; or
(b)   the matter has been resolved; or
(c)   for any other reason established by the Court, it is no longer justified to continue the examination of the application.

However, the Court shall continue the examination of the application if respect for human rights as defined in the Convention and the protocols thereto so requires.

2. The Court may decide to restore an application to its list of cases if it considers that the circumstances justify such a course.

Article 38

Examination of the case and friendly settlement proceedings

1. If the Court declares the application admissible, it shall

(a) pursue the examination of the case, together with the representatives of the parties, and if need be, undertake an investigation, for the effective conduct of which the States concerned shall furnish all necessary facilities;
(b) place itself at the disposal of the parties concerned with a view to securing a friendly settlement of the matter on the basis of respect for human rights as defined in the Convention and the protocols thereto.

2. Proceedings conducted under paragraph 1(b) shall be confidential.

Article 39

Finding of a friendly settlement

If a friendly settlement is effected, the Court shall strike the case out of its list by means of a decision which shall be confined to a brief statement of the facts and of the solution reached.

Article 40

Public hearings and access to documents

1. Hearings shall be in public unless the Court in exceptional circumstances decides otherwise.

2. Documents deposited with the Registrar shall be accessible to the public unless the President of the Court decides otherwise.

Article 41

Just satisfaction

If the Court finds that there has been a violation of the Convention or the protocols thereto, and if the internal law of the High Contracting Party concerned allows only partial reparation to be made, the Court shall, if necessary, afford just satisfaction to the injured party.

Article 42

Judgments of Chambers

Judgments of Chambers shall become final in accordance with the provisions of Article 44, paragraph 2.

Article 43

Referral to the Grand Chamber

1. Within a period of three months from the date of the judgment of the Chamber, any party to the case may, in exceptional cases, request that the case be referred to the Grand Chamber.

2. A panel of five judges of the Grand Chamber shall accept the request if the case raises a serious question affecting the interpretation or application of the Convention or the protocols thereto, or a serious issue of general importance.

3. If the panel accepts the request, the Grand Chamber shall decide the case by means of a judgment.

Article 44

Final judgments

1. The judgment of the Grand Chamber shall be final.

2. The judgment of a Chamber shall become final

(a) when the parties declare that they will not request that the case be referred to the Grand Chamber; or

(b) three months after the date of the judgment, if reference of the case to the Grand Chamber has not been requested; or

(c) when the panel of the Grand Chamber rejects the request to refer under Article 43.

3. The final judgment shall be published.

Article 45

Reasons for judgments and decisions

1. Reasons shall be given for judgments as well as for decisions declaring applications admissible or inadmissible.

2. If a judgment does not represent, in whole or in part, the unanimous opinion of the judges, any judge shall be entitled to deliver a separate opinion.

Article 46

Binding force and execution of judgments

1. The High Contracting Parties undertake to abide by the final judgment of the Court in any case to which they are parties.

2. The final judgment of the Court shall be transmitted to the Committee of Ministers, which shall supervise its execution.

Article 47

Advisory opinions

1. The Court may, at the request of the Committee of Ministers, give advisory opinions on legal questions concerning the interpretation of the Convention and the protocols thereto.

2. Such opinions shall not deal with any question relating to the content or scope of the rights or freedoms defined in Section I of the Convention and the protocols thereto, or with any other question which the Court or the Committee of Ministers might have to consider in consequence of any such proceedings as could be instituted in accordance with the Convention.

3. Decisions of the Committee of Ministers to request an advisory opinion of the Court shall require a majority vote of the representatives entitled to sit on the Committee.

Article 48

Advisory jurisdiction of the Court

The Court shall decide whether a request for an advisory opinion submitted by the Committee of Ministers is within its competence as defined in Article 47.

Article 49

Reasons for advisory opinions

1. Reasons shall be given for advisory opinions of the Court.

2. If the advisory opinion does not represent, in whole or in part, the unanimous opinion of the judges, any judge shall be entitled to deliver a separate opinion.

3. Advisory opinions of the Court shall be communicated to the Committee of Ministers.

Article 50

Expenditure on the Court

The expenditure on the Court shall be borne by the Council of Europe.

Article 51

Privileges and immunities of judges

The judges shall be entitled, during the exercise of their functions, to the privileges and immunities provided for in Article 40 of the Statute of the Council of Europe and in the agreements made thereunder.

SECTION III

MISCELLANEOUS PROVISIONS[1, 3]

Article 52[1]

Inquiries by the Secretary General

On receipt of a request from the Secretary General of the Council of Europe any High Contracting Party shall furnish an explanation of the manner in which its internal law ensures the effective implementation of any of the provisions of the Convention.

Article 53[1]

Safeguard for existing human rights

Nothing in this Convention shall be construed as limiting or derogating from any of the human rights and fundamental freedoms which may be ensured under the laws of any High Contracting Party or under any other agreement to which it is a Party.

Article 54[1]

Powers of the Committee of Ministers

Nothing in this Convention shall prejudice the powers conferred on the Committee of Ministers by the Statute of the Council of Europe.

Article 55[1]

Exclusion of other means of dispute settlement

The High Contracting Parties agree that, except by special agreement, they will not avail themselves of treaties, conventions or declarations in force between them for the purpose of submitting, by way of petition, a dispute arising out of the interpretation or application of this Convention to a means of settlement other than those provided for in this Convention.

Article 56[1]

Territorial application

1. [4] Any State may at the time of its ratification or at any time thereafter declare by notification addressed to the Secretary General of the Council of Europe that the present Convention shall, subject to paragraph 4 of this Article, extend to all or any of the territories for whose international relations it is responsible.

2. The Convention shall extend to the territory or territories named in the notification as from the thirtieth day after the receipt of this notification by the Secretary General of the Council of Europe.

3. The provisions of this Convention shall be applied in such territories with due regard, however, to local requirements.

4. [4] Any State which has made a declaration in accordance with paragraph 1 of this Article may at any time thereafter declare on behalf of one or more of the territories to

which the declaration relates that it accepts the competence of the Court to receive applications from individuals, non-governmental organisations or groups of individuals as provided by Article 34 of the Convention.

Article 57[1]

Reservations

1. Any State may, when signing this Convention or when depositing its instrument of ratification, make a reservation in respect of any particular provision of the Convention to the extent that any law then in force in its territory is not in conformity with the provision. Reservations of a general character shall not be permitted under this Article.

2. Any reservation made under this Article shall contain a brief statement of the law concerned.

Article 58[1]

Denunciation

1. A High Contracting Party may denounce the present Convention only after the expiry of five years from the date on which it became a party to it and after six months' notice contained in a notification addressed to the Secretary General of the Council of Europe, who shall inform the other High Contracting Parties.

2. Such a denunciation shall not have the effect of releasing the High Contracting Party concerned from its obligations under this Convention in respect of any act which, being capable of constituting a violation of such obligations, may have been performed by it before the date at which the denunciation became effective.

3. Any High Contracting Party which shall cease to be a member of the Council of Europe shall cease to be a Party to this Convention under the same conditions.

4. [4] The Convention may be denounced in accordance with the provisions of the preceding paragraphs in respect of any territory to which it has been declared to extend under the terms of Article 56.

Article 59[1]

Signature and ratification

1. This Convention shall be open to the signature of the members of the Council of Europe. It shall be ratified. Ratifications shall be deposited with the Secretary General of the Council of Europe.

2. The present Convention shall come into force after the deposit of ten instruments of ratification.

3. As regards any signatory ratifying subsequently, the Convention shall come into force at the date of the deposit of its instrument of ratification.

4. The Secretary General of the Council of Europe shall notify all the members of the Council of Europe of the entry into force of the Convention, the names of the High Contracting Parties who have ratified it, and the deposit of all instruments of ratification which may be effected subsequently.

Done at Rome this 4th day of November 1950, in English and French, both texts being equally authentic, in a single copy which shall remain deposited in the archives of the

PART 6
APPENDICES

Council of Europe. The Secretary General shall transmit certified copies to each of the signatories.

Footnotes

1   Heading added according to the provisions of Protocol No. 11 (ETS No. 155).
2   New Section II according to the provisions of Protocol No. 11 (ETS No. 155).
3   The articles of this Section are renumbered according to the provisions of Protocol No. 11 (ETS No. 155).
4   Text amended according to the provisions of Protocol No. 11 (ETS No. 155).

INDEX

References are to paragraph numbers.